The Crucible of Revolutionary and Napoleonic Warfare and European Transitions to Modern Economic Growth

Library of Economic History

General Editors

Peer Vries (*International Institute of Social History, Amsterdam*)
Jeroen Touwen (*Leiden University*)

VOLUME 15

The titles published in this series are listed at *brill.com/lehi*

The Crucible of Revolutionary and Napoleonic Warfare and European Transitions to Modern Economic Growth

Edited by

Patrick Karl O'Brien

BRILL

LEIDEN | BOSTON

Cover illustration: Napoleon and his staff are returning from Soissons after the battle of Laon, Jean-Louis-Ernest Meissonier, 1864, Paris, Musée d'Orsay, Public Domain.

Library of Congress Cataloging-in-Publication Data

Names: O'Brien, Patrick Karl, editor.
Title: The crucible of Revolutionary and Napoleonic warfare and European transitions to modern economic growth / edited by Patrick Karl O'Brien.
Description: Leiden ; Boston : Brill, [2022] | Series: Library of economic history, 1877-3206 ; volume 15 | Includes bibliographical references and index. | Summary: "Historiographically, this book rests on the fact that European transitions to modern economic growth were obstructed and promoted by the Revolution in France and 15 years of geopolitical conflict sustained by Napoleon in order to establish French Hegemony over the states and economies of Britain, France, Germany, the Netherlands, Italy, Spain, Portugal, and overseas commerce. The chapters reveal that the nature and significance of connections between geopolitical and economic forces lend coherence to a collaborative endeavour utilising comparative methods to address a mega question: What might be plausibly concluded about the economic costs and the benefits of this protracted conjuncture of Revolutionary and Napoleonic Warfare?"– Provided by publisher.
Identifiers: LCCN 2021043530 (print) | LCCN 2021043531 (ebook) | ISBN 9789004472730 (hardback ; alk. paper) | ISBN 9789004472754 (ebook)
Subjects: LCSH: War–Economic aspects–Europe–History. | Europe–Economic conditions–1789-1900. | Napoleonic Wars, 1800–1815–Economic aspects. | France–History–Revolution, 1789–1799–Economic aspects.
Classification: LCC HC240.9.D4 C78 2022 (print) | LCC HC240.9.D4 (ebook) | DDC 330.94–dc23
LC record available at https://lccn.loc.gov/2021043530
LC ebook record available at https://lccn.loc.gov/2021043531

Typeface for the Latin, Greek, and Cyrillic scripts: "Brill". See and download: brill.com/brill-typeface.

ISSN 1877-3206
ISBN 978-90-04-47273-0 (hardback)
ISBN 978-90-04-47275-4 (e-book)

In memoriam to Cassy O'Brien 1936-1921

Contents

List of Maps, Figures and Tables IX
Notes on Contributors XIII
Preface XVII

1 Exploring Connections between the Revolutionary and Napoleonic Wars, State Formation and the Growth of European Economies 1
Patrick Karl O'Brien

2 Britain's Wars with France 1793–1815 and Their Contribution to the Consolidation of Its Industrial Revolution 22
Patrick Karl O'Brien

3 In the Epicentre of the Storm?: The Effects of the Revolution and Warfare on the French Economy, 1789–1815 50
Loïc Charles, Guillaume Daudin and Silvia Marzagalli

4 War, State Growth, and Germany's Transition to Post-Malthusian Growth 82
Ulrich Pfister

5 Revolutionary Wars and Economic Change in the New State of the Netherlands, 1795–1815 114
Marjolein 't Hart and Johan Joor

6 Napoleon in Italy: A Legacy of Institutional Reform? 141
Mark Dincecco and Giovanni Federico

7 The Napoleonic Wars: A Watershed in Spanish History 169
Leandro Prados de la Escosura and Carlos Santiago-Caballero

8 Portugal's French Wars: Cost, Loss, Missed Opportunities? 1793–1850 203
Cristina Moreira, Jaime Reis and Rita Martins de Sousa

9 The Long-Term Effects of the French and Napoleonic Wars on the Global Economy 250
Peter M. Solar

Index 281

Maps, Figures and Tables

Maps

3.1 French external trade, 1787–1789. Sources: *Archives Nationales*, Paris (hereinafter AN) F12 251, authors' computations. 63
3.2 French external trade, 1818–1820. Sources: AN F12 251, authors' computations. 64

Figures

3.1 Total length of post roads in km within current French borders, 1708–1833. Source: Verdier & Bretagnolle (2007). 54
3.2 French state income, 1650–1913. Source: Dincecco 1991, authors' computations. 57
3.3 The growth of ministerial personnel, 1770–1850. Source: Church 1981, 73. 58
3.4 Sectoral shares of French exports. Sources: AN F12 251, TOFLIT18, authors' computations. 66
3.5 Sectoral share of French imports. Sources: AN F12 251, TOFLIT18 data, authors' computations. 66
3.6 External market dependence rate of some French industries, 1787–89 and 1818–20. Sources: Trade: Toflit18 data. Value- added: Toutain (1961a, 212); Toutain (1961b, 6); Markovitch (1966, table 3). 67
3.7 Sectoral contributions to trade balance, 1787–89 and 1818–20. Sources: AN F12 251, authors' computations. 68
3.8 French population growth, 1740–1840 74
4.1 Nominal and real wages of unskilled urban construction workers, 1760–1850. Source: Pfister (2017, online appendix s3). 90
4.2 Nominal and real fixed-term leases on five estates in Westphalia, 1760–1850. Source: Bracht and Pfister (2020, 168, 231); data series in GESIS ZA8703. 90
4.3 Output of principal food crops in Saxony, 1743–1849 (millions of grain equivalents). Source: Pfister and Kopsidis (2015, 295). 91
5.1 Gross tonnage of Dutch shipping, thousand tons, 1800–1850. Source: Dutch National Accounts, https://nationalaccounts.niwi.knaw.nl/table/expend11.htm. 126
6.1 Per capita GDP in the center-north of Italy, 1700–1860. Sources: Malanima (2010) for Center-North of Italy; Broadberry et al. (2015) for England (including Wales). 144

6.2 Per capita GDP in the center-north of Italy under French Rule. Source: Malanima (2010). 145
6.3 Changes in price dispersion of wheat, 1700–1860. Source: Federico et al. (2018). 150–151
6.4 Per capita tax revenue in Piedmont, 1750–1860 152
6.5 Per capita tax revenue in Lombardy-Veneto, 1750–1860 153
6.6 Per capita tax revenue in the South, 1750–1860 155
7.1 Monthly mortality in the cities of Albacete and Ávila, 1807–1816 (Jan-Dec 1807= 100). Source: Own estimates from the records of the parish of San Juan Bautista (Albacete) and the parishes of San Juan Bautista, Santiago and San Pedro (Ávila) retrieved from familysearch.com. 171
7.2 Marriages in the cities of Albacete and Ávila, 1801–19 (5-year moving average 1801=100). Source: Same as Figure 7.1. 172
7.3 Population conjectures: Spain, 1780–1820 (million). Source: Prados de la Escosura et al. (2020). 172
7.4 Mortality in Spanish regions, 1800–1815 (1800–1815=100). Source: Canales (2018). 173
7.5 Real agricultural output per head, 1780–1815 [1790/99=100). Source: Prados de la Escosura et al. (2020). 174
7.6 Agricultural output and precipitation anomalies 1500–1860 Sources: Agricultural output, Álvarez-Nogal et al. (2016); Precipitation, Rodrigo et al. (1999). 175
7.7 Real land rent and wage rates, 1780–1820 (1790/99=100). Source: Álvarez-Nogal and Prados de la Escosura (2013). 176
7.8 Inequality trends: Real land rent/wage rate ratio, 1780–1820 (1790/99=100). Source: Álvarez-Nogal and Prados de la Escosura (2013). 177
7.9 Inputs bought by Erasmo de Gómina's cotton textile company (1802–04=100). Source: Sánchez (2010). 177
7.10 Spanish net imports from the rest of the world (excl. Spanish America), 1778–1820: with and without smuggling (000 1808 Reales). Source: Prados de la Escosura (1993). 179
7.11 Market integration: average wheat price differentials (%). Source: Llopis Agelán (2010). 179
7.12a Real domestic exports, net imports, and re-exports, 1778–1820 (1808 reales). Sources: Prados de la Escosura (1993). 180
7.12b Trade shares: Domestic exports, net imports, and re-exports, 1778–1820 (% GDP). Sources: Trade, Prados de la Escosura (1993); GDP, Prados de la Escosura et al. (2020). 181
7.13 The evolution of public revenues, 1778–1820 [million reales, 1808 prices). Source: Prados de la Escosura (1993). 183

7.14 Real GDP per head, 1780–1820 (1790/99=100). Source: Prados de la Escosura et al. (2020). 184
7.15 Population, 1530–1857. Sources: Prados de la Escosura et al. (2020). 188
7.16 Adjusted urbanization rates (less population living on agriculture) 1530–1857 (%). Sources: Prados de la Escosura et al. (2020). 188
7.17 Real consumption per head in agriculture, 1815–1850 (1850/9=100). Sources: Álvarez-Nogal and Prados de la Escosura (2013). 189
7.18 Total factor productivity in agriculture, 1760–1860 (1790/9=100). Sources: Álvarez-Nogal and Prados de la Escosura (2007). 190
7.19 Investment in Catalan cotton textiles, 1760–1840 (1760–1771=100). Source: Sánchez (2000). 191
7.20 Terms of trade between Spain and Britain, 1784–1857 (1854=100). Sources: Prados de la Escosura (1994). 192
7.21 Real GDP per head and population, 1815–1850 [1850/59=100). Source: Prados de la Escosura et al. (2020). 193
7.22 Real land rent and wages, 1815–1850 (1790/99=100). Source: Álvarez-Nogal and Prados de la Escosura (2013). 193
7.23 Inequality trends: Real land rent/wage rate ratio, 1815–1845 (1790/99=100). Source: Álvarez-Nogal and Prados de la Escosura (2013). 194
8.1 Total state expenditure and revenue, and military expenditure, 1790–1815 (at 1800 prices) (in *contos*). Source: Livros da Receita e da Despesa Corrente do Tesoureiro Mor do Erário Régio, *Arquivo Histórico do Tribunal de Contas*. For the price deflator, see Palma and Reis (2019). 210
8.2 Consolidated public debt (1796–1851) (in *contos*, nominal values). Sources and methods: see Appendix table 8.4. 215
8.3 Yearly population losses (number of persons), 1808–1815. Sources: Palma et al. (2020); and text. 219
8.4 Real gross agricultural output per capita (1750 =100) (1750–1850). Source: Reis (2017). 222
8.5 Annual agricultural losses as percentage of output (1808–1815). Source: Reis (2017). 223
8.6 Coefficient of variation of wheat prices (1750–1850). Sources: Wheat prices from PWR-Portugal data base: http://pwr-portugal.ics.ul.pt/?page_id=31. 228
8.7 Portuguese real GDP per capita (1750=100) (1750–1815). Source: Palma and Reis (2019). 233
8.8 Annual losses from war as a percentage of GDP (1808–1815). Source: Palma and Reis (2019). 233
8.9 Portugal's real GDP per capita, 1800–1850: Actual and projected (in GK dollars). Sources: Palma and Reis (2019). 238

9.1 Sugar production, 1770-1845 (tons) Source: estimates, sometime guestimates, are based on the figures in Noël Deerr, The History of Sugar (2 vols, London: Chapman & Hall, 1949). 263
9.2 Tea exports from Canton (piculs). Source: Hosea Ballou Morse, *The Chronicles of the East India Company, Trading to China, 1635-1834* (5 vols, Oxford: Clarendon Press, 1926-1929), vols. 4, 5. 264
9.3 Transatlantic slave trade (slaves per annum). Source: Slave Voyages. 272

Tables

3.1 French geography of trade, excluding precious metals, trade with the colonies and trade in plantation foodstuffs, 1787–1789 and 1818–1820 65
3.2 French population, 1740–1840 72
3.3 Growth of the French population, 1740–1840 73
3.4 Growth of the French population, 1780–1800 73
5.1 Trends in Dutch-European shipping overseas from the late eighteenth century up to the early decades of the 1800s, by tonnage and by trade region 122
5.2 Public loans contracted in the Netherlands annually 1780–1810, in millions of guilders 128
5.3 Amount of debt and debt charges in millions of guilders, and nominal debt as percentage of Dutch national income (1795–1850) 132
6.1 Tax revenue in Italy, 1750–1860 148
6.2 Years of Napoleonic-era reforms in Italy 158
7.1 Structural breaks in main economic variables, 1750–1850 195
7.2 Main economic variables: Post-war counterfactual and actual levels 196
8.1 Portugal's French invasions, 1807–1811 205
8.2 Full and national costs of the Anglo-Portuguese war against the French in *contos* (1800 prices) 213
8.3 Factories in Portugal and their condition in 1811–13 225
8.4 Portuguese consolidated public debt (nominal values) (in *contos*) 242
9.1 Naval strength of Western Powers (sailing fleets only; 1000 tons) 255
9.2 Merchant shipping fleets 257
9.3 U.K. imports by origin (£m; current prices) 258
9.4 U.K. Intercontinental trade by commodity (£ m, current prices) 261
9.5 Intercontinental trade: Major commodity imports to U.K. 262
9.6 Tea exports from Canton by shipper (1000 piculs) 265
9.7 U.K. Re-exports 269
9.8 Ratios of European to Asian prices 271
9.9 Intercontinental labour movements (1000s per year) 273

Notes on Contributors

Patrick Karl O'Brien
spent his career at the London School of Economics, the University of Oxford and as Director of the Institute of Historical Research, London University. He has published and edited, with editorial essays, twenty books. He has also published over 100 essays in edited volumes and academic journals.

Loïc Charles
is Professor in Economics at the University of Paris 8 Saint-Denis and fellow-researcher at the Institut National d'études démographiques. His research area is economic history and history of economics knowledge. His latest research encompasses such themes as the history of 18th century French external trade, the physiocratic school and more generally the history of French 18th century political economy as well as the history of visualisation in social science (1900–1945).

Guillaume Daudin
(https://gdaudin.github.io) has been Professor of Economics at the University of Paris-Dauphine (LEDa-DIAL) since 2012. He is a specialist in early modern economic history and commercial globalization. His most recent work focuses on the eighteenth century Balance of Trade Bureau, the effect of internal migration on nineteenth-century fertility trends in France, current value-added trade and the structure of trade costs. Together with Loïc Charles, he has co-directed the ANR project "TOFLIT18" on what foreign trade teaches us about France in the eighteenth century (https://toflit18.hypotheses.org and http://toflit18.medialab.sciences-po.fr). He was President of the Association Française d'Histoire Économique from 2016 to 2019.

Mark Dincecco
is Associate Professor of Political Science at the University of Michigan. He specializes in historical political economy and the political economy of development. He is the author of *Political Transformations and Public Finances: Europe, 1650–1913* (Cambridge 2011) and *State Capacity and Economic Development: Present and Past* (Cambridge 2017). His most recent book is *From Warfare to Wealth: The Military Origins of Urban Prosperity in Europe*, coauthored with Massimiliano Onorato (Cambridge 2017). This book won the 2018 William H. Riker Best Book Award.

Giovanni Federico
is currently professor of Economic History at New York University Abu Dhabi. He has been professor of Economic History at the European University Institute and at the University of Pisa. He has published *An Economic History of the Silk Industry, 1800–1938* (Cambridge 1997), *The Economic Development of Italy*, with Jon Cohen (Cambridge 2000), *Feeding the World: An Economic History of World Agriculture* (Princeton 2005), edited the *Handbook of Historical Economics*, with Alberto Bisin (Elsevier 2021), and has written extensively on world trade, globalization, and European market integration, as well as on many issues in Italian economic history.

Johan Joor
studied Economic and Social History (University of Amsterdam). He is a widely known specialist on the Napoleonic period in Holland. He is an independent researcher, was fellow at the International Institute of Social History and worked, until recently, at the Huygens Institute for the History of the Netherlands on a project on the consequences of the Continental System for Rotterdam. His PhD-thesis De Adelaar en het Lam ('The Eagle and the Lamb') (2000) dealt with the anti-regime protests during these years. With Katherine Aaslestad he edited Revisiting Napoleon's Continental System: Local, Regional and European Experiences (2015).

Rita Martins de Sousa
has a B.A. in Economics and a PhD in Economic and Social History. She is a Senior Associate Professor at ISEG – Lisbon School of Economics and Management, University of Lisbon, and a researcher member of the Office of Economic and Social History (GHES).
She has participated in several projects in Economic History and has published mainly in the domain of Monetary History.

Silvia Marzagalli
graduated at the European University Institute with a dissertation on port cities in the Napoleonic era, and was consequently recruited at the University of Bordeaux. She is presently full professor of Early Modern History at the University Côte d'Azur and honorary member of the Institut Universitaire de France. Her main research interests concern eighteenth-century maritime trade and shipping in the Atlantic and Mediterranean worlds, notably the reorganization of commercial and merchant networks in wartime. She is currently PI of Portic, a digital humanities program aiming at criss-crossing

French shipping data with the French balance of trade, and offering interactive visualization tools.

Cristina Moreira

has a PhD in Economics and is a member of the Department of Economics, School of Economics and Management and of the Interdisciplinary Centre of Social Sciences of Minho University.
She is an assistant professor of Economics and specializes in History of the Portuguese trade and the impacts of war. She is the main researcher in several projects on economic history.
She has supervised several masters' and doctorates' thesis and has several papers indexed in ISI and Scopus. Her publications, both nationally and internationally, have focused particularly on the Revolutionary and Napoleonic Wars.

Ulrich Pfister

received his PhD at the University of Zürich, Switzerland, in 1984 and has been professor of social and economic history at the University of Münster, Germany, since 1996. He has published on regional proto-industries, demographic history, history of religion, and agrarian history. His recent work focuses on the long-run development of the German economy from the sixteenth to the nineteenth centuries.

Leandro Prados-de-la-Escosura

D. Phil. Modern History (Oxford) and Ph.D. Economics (Complutense, Madrid), is Professor of Economic History (Universidad Carlos III). He has taught at Georgetown University (Prince of Asturias Professor) and UCSD. He has been Honorary Maddison Chair (Groningen) Leverhulme Professorial Fellow at the LSE, and Visiting Fellow, All Souls College, Oxford. He has published on long-run growth in Spain, Latin American since independence, economic freedom, and human development in the world. His latest book is *Spanish Economic Growth, 1850–2015* (Palgrave-Macmillan, 2017). His new book *Human Development in the Modern World* will be published by Cambridge University Press in 2022.

Jaime Reis

has a B.A. and a D. Phil. from Oxford University and an M.A. from the Fletcher School of Law and Diplomacy. He has taught at Vanderbilt, Leicester and Glasgow Universities, the European University Institute, and NOVA SBE (Lisbon). He retired as Research Professor from the Instituto de Ciências Sociais of the University of Lisbon.

He has published extensively in various fields of Economic History. He was a founder of the European Historical Economic Society and an editor of the European Review of Economic History and of the Economic History Review. He belongs to the Academy of Sciences of Lisbon.

Carlos Santiago-Caballero
D. Phil Economic History (LSE), is Associate Professor of Economic History (Universidad Carlos III). His research interests have focused on preindustrial economic inequality, agrarian history, anthropometry, and long run economic growth. His work has been published in academic outlets like Explorations in Economic History, European Review of Economic History, Revista de Historia Económica, Cliometrica, Cambridge University Press or Routledge. His most recent work focuses on brain drainage in the age of mass migrations, the effects of modernisation in social mobility, and the rise of capitalism in Spain.

Peter M. Solar
is Professor Emeritus of Economics at the Vrije Universiteit Brussel and is currently affiliated with CEREC at the Université Saint-Louis – Bruxelles and the Faculty of History at the University of Oxford. His research deals mainly with the economic history of Ireland and Britain during the eighteenth and nineteenth centuries. Recently, he has written on the 1799–1801 subsistence crisis in Ireland, the improvement of cotton spinning machinery and several aspects of British maritime history.

Marjolein 't Hart
is Senior Researcher at the Huygens Institute for the History of the Netherlands, Amsterdam, and Professor of the History of State Formation in Global Perspective at VU University Amsterdam. She held positions at various universities and in various disciplines (history, sociology, political sciences). Her current research interests focus on the social and economic aspects of warfare, revolution and state formation. She is the author of, among others, The Dutch Wars of Independence. War and commerce in the Netherlands 1570–1680 (2014) and, with others, of A Financial History of the Netherlands (1997).

Preface

The historiographical case for this book of essays, located in European economic history, emanates from a recognition by scholars in the field that the histories of Europe's national economies are both punctuated and, positively as well as negatively, correlated with their states' engagement in warfare. The wars investigated here began with the French Revolution and continued for some 15 years of military conflict attributable to Napoleon's drive to establish imperial hegemony over the states and societies of Western Europe. These "French Wars" conditioned the diverse outcomes observed for the economic development of Europe's national economies in ways that persisted for decades after the Treaty of Vienna restored peace to the continent in 1815.

To explore connections between this major geopolitical conjuncture in European History and its range of impacts on the growth of national economies, the editor recruited a team of senior economic historians to write chapters on Britain, France, Germany, The Netherlands, Italy, Spain, Portugal, and the international economy. Regrettably, but unavoidably, the book is not comprehensive enough to include chapters on major polities such as Belgium, Scandinavia, Russia and the United States as well as the Ottoman and European empires overseas. Their rates, patterns and potential for economic growth were clearly, and in some economies significantly, affected by the warfare unleashed by the Revolution in France and propagated by Napoleon. Fortunately, our Network was able to invite Alejandra Irigoin and Bishnu Gupta to present papers on South America and India. We also invited a range of academics and graduate students with relevant expertise and/ or interests in connections between mercantilist warfare and economic growth to participate in our conferences. We are particularly grateful for the contributions made by Steven Broadberry, Joel Felix, William Godsey, Reka Juhaz, Nuno Palma, Hamish Scott, Chistopher Storrs, Peer Vries, and Patrick Winton to this collaborative endeavour.

The logistical and administrative tasks involved in these programmes are complex and time consuming. The formulation of a mission statement to obtain generous funding from the Leverhulme Trust for this venture could not have succeeded without efficient help from Loraine Long. The travail involved in publication could not have proceeded in a time of Covid without the daily support and intellectual enthusiasm of my wife, Cassy. Wendel Scholma has acted with patience and understanding to ensure that the manuscript was delivered on time and properly formatted for Brill. The commitment of

Priscilla Frost to the tasks involved in dealing with multiple authors and their drafts has exceeded anything that any academic could expect and hope for. As ever the mistakes are my own.

Patrick O'Brien
March 2021

CHAPTER 1

Exploring Connections between the Revolutionary and Napoleonic Wars, State Formation and the Growth of European Economies

Patrick Karl O'Brien

My introduction will be an editor's attempt to synthesize the specification of questions, the evidence presented, the inferences drawn, and conclusions reached from a collaborative exercise in the comparative economic history of Western Europe. It is located within a historiography concerned with the Revolutionary and Napoleonic Wars 1792–1815 and is focussed on an analysis of immediate and longer-term economic outcomes that flowed from this protracted and costly conjuncture for the long-term growth of Western Europe's national economies (Aerts and Crouzet 1996; Bell 2007; Blanning 2008).[1]

Economic historians have traced the positive, as well as the more obvious negative, outcomes from the transition to modern economic growth that appeared during these wars, outcomes that were barely discussed at the Congress of Vienna in 1815. Such historians have agreed with their colleagues in European history that the emergence of stronger, centralized, and more liberal states, as well as the maintenance, under British naval hegemony, of a superior system of international relations among Europe's warring states, that endured for a century of relative peace and stability down to 1914, can be represented as a reaction to twenty-three years of costly warfare (Schroeder 1994; Thompson 2000; O'Brien and Clesse 2002; Grotke and Prutch 2014; Jarrett 2014; Vick 2014; Evans 2016). During that century the territorial frontiers, constitutions, property rights, institutions and cultures surrounding the national and regional economies of Western Europe progressed from this violent political and geopolitical conjuncture[2] in ways that, in retrospect, many historians

1 The modern European state was rooted in war, or more precisely, the costs of war whose weight grew heavier from the late sixteenth century (Bien, David. 2014. *Interpreting the Ancien Regime*: Oxford: Voltaire Foundation)The authors of the chapters analysing the experiences of France, Germany, The Netherlands, Italy, Spain and Portugal will not necessarily agree with the interpretations that have been informed by my reading of the literature in geopolitical history and debates at the conferences.

2 The term 'conjuncture' is used here to refer to a cluster of interconnected exogeneous events that alter the rate and patterns of long-term economic growth. Historiographically,

 | DOI:10.1163/9789004472754_002

have plausibly represented as a discontinuity for Europe's ancient political regimes and their economies (McKay and Scott 1983; Broers 1996; Blanning 2008; Broers 2015). Thus, the mission established for our collaborate intellectual endeavour here is designed to ascertain what a team of modern economic historians might add to the limited concern that their discipline has displayed towards the longer-term impact that this famous conjuncture may have had on transitions to modern economic growth, as experienced by the diverse range of Western European economies that they study (Dincecco 2009). As part of this we wish to include a final chapter that analyses the changes to the international economic order in which such nations traded with each other and the rest of the world between 1789 and 1914 (Holsti 1991; O'Brien and Clesse 2002; Paquette 2019).

The costs and benefits of the immediate, short and longer term economic effects that attended the mobilization of fiscal, financial and real resources for purposes of virtually unavoidable armed conflicts with rival powers, as well as the relatively peaceful coexistence and commerce that followed from the experience (and "memories") of a protracted conjuncture of warfare and treaties concluded at Vienna, are the meta questions pursued by the authors of the chapters below (Blanning 2002; Forrest 2009; Hageman 2016).[3] The chapters marshal historical evidence, and where possible the statistical data, to analyse how, and to what degree, the economic trajectories for a sample of Western European economies were directly affected by more or less active participation in the armed conflicts of this conjuncture and/or were influenced by violent disruptions to normal commercial relations with each other and with their colonies overseas (Contamine 2000; Findlay and O'Rourke 2007; Backhaus 2016).

The Revolutionary and Napoleonic Wars became an armed conflict to defend the sovereignty and resources of the Republican state of France that emerged in 1792, and extended its territory through military victories. For almost a decade under Napoleon that state aspired to become an empire by pursuing a strategy for the exercise of French power and influence over the territories, colonies, institutions, natural resources, capital and populations of European rivals (Blanning 1986; Ellis 1991; Bell 2007; Esdaile 2007; Andress 2012).

Historiographically, the primary concerns of economic historians have been to ascertain to what extent the costs and benefits of participation in interstate warfare by France – supported by its allies, clients and satellites – with its

this conjuncture is located in an age or era of revolutions from 1760–1840 (Armitage and Subruhmanyam 2010).

3 My understanding of the significance of social memory has been informed by Blanning 2002; Forrest 2009 and Hagemann 2016.

enemies (principally Britain, Austria, Prussia and Russia) could be represented as significant for their long-term transitions to modern economic growth? (Aerts and Crouzet 1996; Torres-Sánchez 2007; Alvarez-Nogal and Prados de la Escosura 2013).

Economic historians appreciate, however, that the theoretical and statistical problems of defining and measuring the costs and benefits of diverting resources from peace time conditions for production, in order to engage or indeed to avoid active engagement in warfare, is complex (Gonzalez-Enciso 2016). For, this protracted interlude of intense geopolitical and mercantilist warfare, that led to fundamental changes in the contexts in which Europe's economies had operated for centuries, exercises, in cost benefit analysis, not only lack data that is virtually impossible to locate and calibrate, but could well fail to capture significant and enduring connections that emerged during the years 1792–1815 (Dincecco 2011; Karaman and Pamuk 2013; Meagher 2017). Nevertheless, the geopolitical element is being restored, as chapters in metanarratives that are written by economic historians endeavouring to explain the "wealth and poverty of nations" as well as "divergence" in standards of living between countries and entire continents over eras of time (O'Brien 2011, 2014 and 2021). For this period, dominated by bouts of violent warfare and its aftermath, they offer nothing that is superior for "ways of knowing" than those recommended to historians generations ago by Marc Bloch and Max Weber: namely, reciprocal comparisons. They include whatever statistical evidence that happens to be available for well-specified contrasts in the trajectories pursued by Europe's national economies before and after their states had mobilized resources to engage in more or less intensified and protracted geopolitical challengers to their external security and sovereignty (Findlay 2006; Gat 2006; Torres-Sanchez 2015).

Between 1792 and 1815, engagements in warfare varied country by country from: large scale mobilization of resources for aggression, defence and resistance; to coping both politically and economically with defeat, occupation and predation by Napoleon's armies. Analogous costs also include those incurred by states to comply with French conditions for their international, political and commercial neutrality (Black 2008; Blanning 2008; Broers 2015).

Throughout this period the origins and source of seriously intensified challenges to the geopolitical status quo *ante bellum* that confronted all the states, polities and economies of Western Europe, emanated from the armed forces – mobilized initially for defence, but maturing into aggression – from a single great power: Republican and Napoleonic France (Grab 2003; Scott 2006; Bell 2007). The challenge to the security and autonomy of the states and economies of *ancien regime* Europe that originated with the French Revolution, varied from year to year. It promoted a range of responses that formed, and became an omnipresent part of, the international, political and economic order, within which Europe's mercantilist states and their economies had and continued to operate historically both before, and for decades after, the final defeat in 1815 of the aspirations of Napoleonic France to regulate that order (Forrest 2009; Broers et al 2012; Vick 2014).

Thereafter, and following from, and congruent with, the agreements reached among European powers at Vienna in 1815 to restore, reconstruct, and confer legitimacy upon, the sovereignties and frontiers of states that had been disrupted, destabilized and, in some cases, partitioned by the military drive for hegemony by Napoleonic France, the economies of Western Europe began to operate within a reformed international, political and economic order. This has often been reductively, but simplistically, analysed as the legacy of the French Revolution and Napoleon (Grotke and Prutch 2014; Broers 2015; Graaf 2019).

The political maps of Western Europe that emerged from negotiations at the Congress of Vienna reveal that several states had extended, centralized and intensified control beyond the territories, resources and populations that they had ruled over before the outbreak of warfare with Revolutionary France in 1792 (O'Brien 1999; Scott 1990; Blanning 2008). First and foremost among the victors that emerged with widely envied gains in 1815, was the United Kingdom (Andress 2012; Knight 2014). In the absence of competition from rivals, who were more intensely engaged in warfare on the mainland of Europe, British power continued to bring territory, populations, assets and fiscal capacity nominally under the sovereignty of the Mughal empire in South Asia, into the control of a privately owned and corporately governed British East India Company, pursuing commercial interests throughout the Orient (Bayly 1985; Marshall 1998; Roy 2013). In the wake of a serious rebellion against English rule in Ireland in 1798, the Westminster government removed all semblance of autonomy and authority from the Irish Parliament. The union in 1801 consolidated its formal powers to legislate for all the realm's Celtic provinces and their economies (Ehrman 1996; Hilton 2006).

Politically and legally both the domestic and imperial markets of a newly United Kingdom became more integrated than they had been before the outbreak of wars with France (Hilton 1977). Furthermore, and although the Liverpool administration followed the advice of Castlereagh and returned Dutch colonies in the East Indies to an enlarged Kingdom of the Netherlands, Britain's post-war government, strengthened by the Royal Navy's command of the oceans, retained the islands and maritime bases of Malta, Mauritius, Cape Town, Ceylon, the Ionian Isles, Trinidad, Tobago, St Lucia, Demerara, Essequibo, Berbice and Heligoland (Marshall 1998; Rodger 2004; Black 2007).

Furthermore, and as the state that had invested more resources than any other European power in the naval and military force required to defeat the Imperial ambitions of Napoleonic France, for more than a century the United Kingdom retained a paramount degree of influence over intra-European international economic relations. At the same time, British naval hegemony secured and maintained the kingdom's status as Europe's leading maritime economy with proven fiscal and sea power to protect its own external security and imperial interests, while continuing to play a dominant role in maintaining a favourable balance of power on the mainland of Europe (Backhouse 2008; Simms 2013). Thus, after the defeat of Napoleonic pretensions to hegemony, Britain's long-established strategies for the defence of an island economy and protection of its assets and access to markets overseas, provided its industry with an unrivalled, unmeasurable, but possibly significant addition to its natural and comparative advantages in international trade in commodities, services and investment overseas (O'Brien and Clesse 2002; Morris 2004; Findlay and O'Rourke 2007; O'Brien 2014; Clark et al 2014;).

Despite the costs associated with a succession of military defeats, invasions, conquests, predations, annexations and geopolitical coercion from Revolutionary and Napoleonic armies, the only other economic history that could plausibly represent that conjuncture, as a clear and potentially significant base period for a trajectory leading to accelerated economic progress, was that of the German-speaking polities, regions and cities of Western and Central Europe (Breuilly 1996; Becker et al 2018). Although a balance sheet of costs and benefits attributable to their relations with Revolutionary and Napoleonic France will remain impossible to construct, the consensus among historians of Germany that they can be represented as significant for the formation of an integrated German economy, continues to be plausible (Pierkemper and Tilly 2004; Wolf 2017; Tilly and Kopsididis 2020).

On the eve of the French Revolution, with the exception of the residents of some notable cities outside the Habsburg lands and Brandenburg-Prussia, the majority of Western and Central Europe's German-speaking populations lived and worked within no less than 388 political units. Since the Peace of Westphalia in 1648, external security for these polities had been largely maintained by the voluntary participation of their hereditary and ecclesiastical rulers in a confederation. That confederation, the Holy German Roman Empire, operated under constitutional arrangements with antecedents that can be traced back beyond Charlemagne. They included formal legal and diplomatic procedures for the political settlement of territorial and dynastic disputes among the polities of the empire, as well as for internal conflicts between nobles and their monarch (Wilson 2016). Its constitution also embodied procedures for the funding, conscription and mobilization of armed forces to protect Christian Europe against threats from an expansionist Islamic Ottoman Empire and possible takeovers by states with large standing armies, such as Bourbon France and Prussia. Within the empire the Habsburg dynasty maintained a relatively large standing army, fiscal capacity and geopolitical power, and occupied a hegemonic position. From 1440 onwards, the head of the dynasty, ruling over extensive territories and multi-ethnic populations, was usually elected as Emperor of the confederation. After the horrific and destructive Thirty Years War, the united geopolitical, judicial and diplomatic functions of this so-called Empire, contributed to the maintenance of stability, internal order and external security for the multiplicity of complex polities claiming autonomy and sovereignty over the German speaking populations and territories of Western and Central Europe (Sheehan 1989; Wilson 2006 and 2016). In theory, the Holy German Roman Empire provided the security required to allow the hereditary and ecclesiastical elites, ruling over this extraordinary number and diverse array of German polities, the autonomy and sovereignty required to establish institutions and enforce rules for internal order and property rights for the conduct of economic activity within their defined and respective jurisdictions (Whaley 2012).

Provided commerce and factor mobility are not obstructed by political authorities and tariffs, decentralization is not necessarily inimical to economic growth in a European international economic order riven by dynastic warfare and mercantilist competition. Nevertheless, it left the polities and economies of Germanic Europe vulnerable to threats and predation. Furthermore, the limited size of domestic markets and low fiscal capacities led to inefficient fiscal systems and high degrees of rent-seeking by political elites, as well as a sub-optimal provision of the public goods, institutions and infrastructures required to promote transitions to modern economic growth (Breuilly 1992; Ogilvie 1996; Schroeder 1994; Findlay 2006; Cardoso and Lains 2010; Yun-Casalilla and O'Brien 2012). By the end of the long wars with France, Germanic Europe had changed radically (Sheehan 1989; Blanning 2008). Invasions, occupations, annexations, amalgamations and the abolition of ancient clerical and aristocratic regimes by French armies, had redrawn frontiers and formed new states dominated by non-noble and secular elites that, for several years between 1792–1815, had been subjected to the power, if not the direct control and coercive diplomacy, of the French state (Schroeder 1994; Bell 2007; Blanning 2008; Broers 2015). Historians of German State formation between 1789 and 1815 have outlined a constitutional process whereby, in stages, the power of Revolutionary and Napoleonic France reduced the sovereignties and privileges of monarchs and their clerical and aristocratic elites for more than 300 German polities, by consolidating and enlarging their territories, resources and populations into thirty-seven political units, plus the free cities of Hamburg, Frankfurt, Bremen and Lubeck (Boehme 1978; Sheehan 1989; Wilson 2016). In that process, tariffs and other obstructions to cross border trade declined and extended markets for German producers (Tilly and Kopsidis 2020).

By 1815, several middling Germanic states (including Bavaria, Baden, Wüttenberg and Hanover) had extended their sovereignties over the natural resources, and the human and physical capital acquired during this interlude of warfare. Others, such as Saxony and the Napoleonic creation of Westphalia (whose rulers had allied their states with Napoleon's strategic ambitions for a French empire) lost control over resources and territory to the Hohenzollern monarchy. Along with Habsburg Austria, Prussia had, however, paid a very heavy economic price in tribute for serious costly resistance to Napoleon's ambitions for French political and economic hegemony over Europe. Ultimately, four polities emerged as the major victors over France at the Congress of Vienna. Excluding Russia, which has, alas, not been discussed in this book, only three, Britain, Prussia and Habsburg Austria, emerged with their original political potential for modern economic growth enhanced or, in the Austrian case, weakened but intact (Zamoyski 2007; Black 2008; Broers 2015; Godsey 2016; Becker 2018). After Napoleon's conclusive defeat at Waterloo, first and foremost among the victors was the United Kingdom, and, at the Congress of Vienna, Prussia also emerged as a major power (Chapman 1998; Scott 2006). The Hohenzollern Kingdom retained undisputed control of its earlier conquests over Silesia as well as Posen, plus other parts of Poland, most of Saxony and the eastern hinterland of the Rhineland. Through alliances with Russia and Britain, and understandings with its erstwhile Germanic rival Austria, the Prussian state secured promises of protection against French revanchism, which might otherwise have threatened its future development into the leading military and industrial power on the mainland of Western Europe (Clark 2006). Fatally for Napoleon's imperial ambitions, the naval defeat at Trafalgar in 1805, and his unenforceable strategy of excluding British exports from European markets, provoked his disastrous invasion of Russia, the defeat in the Battle of the Nations (Leipzig 1813), and the downfall at Waterloo two years later (Crouzet 1989; Parsons 2012; Broers 2015). With hindsight (and a teleology that has become acceptable in their discipline), economic historians might now accept as a plausible a geoeconomic view that the defeats of Prussia by French Revolutionary armies in the 1790s, and more destructively by Napoleonic forces in 1806, created pressures and conditions for political, military and institutional reforms to an autocratic *ancien regime* that reinforced its determination to join coalitions to defeat Napoleon. This outcome and cumulatively over time led to Prussia's acquisition of nearly half of the Saxon economy, responsibility for defence of the Rhineland, and a leading role in the formation of a customs union. Within a half-century of Waterloo and Vienna, it had become integrated into a large market that formed the basis for the development of the modern national market economy of Germany (Ogilvie 1996; Wolf 2014; Hagemann 2016; Backhaus 2016).

At, and after, the Congress of Vienna, Prussia's rival for power and prosperity over the Germanic populations of central Europe, Habsburg Austria, persisted in an ultimately futile strategy. This was to form a centralized state without the fiscal, financial and bureaucratic capacities required to rule over a multi-ethnic empire that had been seriously weakened, but not reformed, in the wake of protracted warfare with France (Judson 2018). The Austrian Chancellor, Metternich, pressed for the restoration of the Bourbon monarchy to rule France and, with more success, the containment of French power within the kingdom's frontiers of 1790. With strong support from Britain and Russia, he also persuaded the Congress to allow for the restoration of a United Netherlands and, as some recompense for the empire's costs and role in resisting and defeating France, the Habsburg dynasty acquired sovereignty over Napoleonic conquests in Northern Italy (Lombardy, Venice and the Veneto) (Godsey 2016; Scott 2016; Wolf 2017). Fifteen years after the Congress, the Netherlands split up and ceased to act as a buffer state against potential French expansion northward and eastward into the Low Countries and the Germanic polities of central Europe. By default, their defence became the responsibility of the State of Prussia whose territory, prestige and geopolitical power had been significantly augmented by the role its army had played in the final stages of the struggle with French imperialism. Prussia's status as a great power was confirmed by the Congress of Vienna (Dwyer 2019). Ironically, in less than half a century after the Congress, Habsburg rule over Lombardy and the Veneto was superseded, with French help, by the House of Savoy, Prussia's ally in Southern Europe. Also, just five years after losing all semblance of power in a unified Italy, Austrian forces were decisively defeated by the Prussian army at Königgratz in 1866. Thereafter, the Prussian State continued to exercise its indisputable lead in promoting the transformation of a unified Germany into Europe's premier industrial economy (Breuilly 1996; Hagemann 2016; Backhaus 2016).

In brief, the case of Germany supports the view that the geopolitical outcomes that evolved from the Revolution in France and Napoleon's imperial strategy, set in motion a process of state formation and geopolitical transformation that became significant as contexts for the diverse roles and patterns of structural development pursued by the sub-continent's national economies over the long nineteenth century (Breuilly 1992; Black 2007; Scott and Simms,

2007; Broers 2012). No example supports the case more for representing this famous geopolitical interlude as a complex conjuncture in the political economy of Western Europe, than the economic transformation of *ancien regime* France. The French economy experienced Europe's most profound constitutional and institutional revolution to its framework of laws and codes surrounding property rights for production and trade, as well as radical reforms to its fiscal and financial systems. Thus, the modern economic as well as the political changes, and history of France, should be associated with its Revolution as well as twenty-three years of warfare on land and sea against a succession of European alliances (Crouzet 1989 and 1996). Two centuries later it has, however, become intellectually contentious to represent the economic outcomes that flowed from these geopolitically momentous events as necessary prerequisites for liberal reforms to the political regime and the institutions of culture surrounding the economy of Republican and Napoleonic France. Yet, in 1781, the Bourbon government had organized a coalition of powers that successfully restrained Britain's strategy to maximize the gains from colonizing territories and monopolizing returns from trade and servicing commerce with the Americas.

In the 1780s, the Bourbon regime continued to maintain a military and commercial presence within the Mughal empire in India. French merchants and investors were receiving increasing returns from its trade in sugar and other tropical groceries from colonial plantations in the Caribbean. Over the same decade, the state also became seriously engaged in bilateral negotiations to liberalize trade with Britain (Ehrman 1962). There seems to be insufficient historical evidence to support neo-liberal, Eurocentric and Marxist arguments that, in the absence of a revolutionary transformation to the institutions of an *ancien regime* (that were already being reformed), the French economy would counterfactually have failed to adopt and adapt to the innovations that were in the process of modernizing the states and economies of Britain, and other European economies, in those critical years that came in the wake of the American rebellion against the Hanoverian kingdom (Milward and Saul 1973; O'Brien and Keyder 1978; Crouzet 2001 and 2008).

Both Britain and France emerged from the War for American Independence burdened with debt and afflicted with diminishing returns from inflexible bases for fiscal extraction (Page 2015). Nevertheless, the British economy enjoyed relative advantages over its traditional rival, that included superior endowments of accessible coal and mineral ores, more elastic supplies of skilled labour, large fleets of war and merchant ships, an ostensibly more efficient framework of institutions for the exploitation of its agricultural land, and a more advanced fiscal and financial system (O'Brien and Keyder 1978; Crouzet

2008; Baugh 2011; O'Brien 2021). Nevertheless, it remains difficult to demonstrate that in 1789 (when the growth of Britain's population was attracting Malthusian predictions) a destructive Revolution, let alone protracted years of engagement and investment in imperialism on the mainland of Europe, can be represented as a precondition for a reasonably rapid rate of convergence towards British levels of productivity and real incomes *per capita* (Venturi 1984; Blanning 1986; Bien 2014, but see Acemoglu et al 2011).

At that early and particular stage in the long transition to modern economic growth, neither the institutional nor technological contrasts between the two economies embodied the potential for the degree and extent of differentials in labour productivities that subsequently emerged during the long Victorian boom. Although the Revolution can be credited with laudable measures for the redistribution of wealth and income, the entire corpus of "reforms" to the framework of laws and institutions surrounding the operations of the Republic's economy are no longer regarded as necessary, let alone sufficient for the long-term economic growth of France (Crouzet 1989 and 2001). French society was not devoid of entrepreneurs, creative artisans, enlightened aristocrats or gains from expenditures funded by owners of ecclesiastical property rights (Furet 1992; Venturi 1984; Scott 1990; Poussou 2000). Although these points cannot be supported with hard data, the historiographical consensus that has been outlined in the chapter on France suggests that the groups that benefitted most from the political, fiscal and institutional reforms that accompanied the Revolution were the peasantry, and apparently the denizens of smaller towns. Their augmented demands for goods and services and weak propensities to migrate internally to cities or overseas, shaped the rate and pattern of French macro-economic growth once Napoleonic Imperialism came to its inevitable, but sorry, end in 1812–1815 (O'Brien and Keyder 1978; Ellis 1991; but *vide* the contrasting views of Acemoglu et al 2011 and Lafrance 2019).

Meanwhile, the economic effects of a highly destructive civil war that accompanied the Revolution, can be described in detail, but cannot be calibrated into accounts by historians that might conceivably quantify the real costs of the endlessly analysed events and stages that led the French republican state and its domestic economy to a position of external security and internal stability (Furet 1992). Perhaps the diminution of the gross domestic product of France, attributable to those years of potentially avoidable internal conflict and violent change, may have exceeded the economic gains that accrued over time from the fiscal reforms and redistribution of property rights. Some economists still classify these changes as significant dynamic benefits that can be regarded as virtually inconceivable without a revolution and engagement in intensified and protracted interstate warfare (Acemoglu et al 2011).

Despite the redistribution of wealth and income, years of glory, and ruthless predation that left France with a relatively small sovereign debt after 1815, it remains difficult for economic historians to clarify what Napoleonic conquests and warfare contributed to long-term growth of the French economy and the welfare of its population (Furet 1992; Crouzet 1989, 1996 and 2008; Poussou 2000; Furet and Ozouf 2007; Blanning 2008). Napoleon's blockade against British manufactured exports generated some positive, infant industry effects (Davis and Engerman 2006). For a short while, his armies opened European markets to French manufactures and diffused the secular ideals and institutions associated with the Revolution (Joor and Aaslestad 2016). The years of mass mobilization for warfare might, moreover, be included among the variables explaining the precocious fall in the marital fertility rate and the virtual disappearance of those all too predictable Malthusian crises from the demographic history of France (Perrin 2021). On the debit side stands the failure of a blockade designed to undermine Britain's fiscal and financial capacity to wage war, which led to Napoleon's ill-fated decision to invade Russia and the loss of potential gains that could counterfactually have been derived from a more prolonged period of French geopolitical hegemony (Crouzet 1986; Parker 1990; Parsons 2012).

For the rest of mainland Western Europe, the years of Napoleonic imperialism have been represented as an interlude in economic history and marked, in no small degree by the ruthless and ultimately counter-productive exploitation of fiscal, financial, social and human resources of European states who joined alliances and coalitions both for, and against, French aggression (Ellis 1991; Bell 2007; Esdaile 2007; Andress 2012). In retrospect, no perception seems to make any sense of the unimpressive post-war economic performances of The Netherlands and Italy, and likewise for Spain and Portugal as well (Thompson 1998; Torres-Sánchez 2007).[4] Arguments that the political and economic institutions conditioning the progress of Europe's pre-industrial economies could only have been reformed along lines associated with the French Revolution and Napoleonic power, will continue to be contested by national historians as ideologically *charged* and Francophile (Scott and Simms 2007; Broers et al 2012). Recent historiography does, however, recognize that one significant economic gain emerged from the upheavals associated with the Revolutionary and Napoleonic Wars, one that has become compelling enough for economic and other historians to take it seriously when constructing narratives of Europe's

4 The authors of chapters 7 and 8 below may not agree. For more recent cliometrically based analysis, see the chapter on Spain in this volume and the cliometric analysis of Alvarez-Nogal and Prados de la Escosura 2013.

economic progress from 1815 to 1914 (O'Brien and Clesse 2002). Compared to the twentieth and earlier centuries, this period maintained geopolitical conditions that were favourable to stable diplomatic relations.

Before the Great War, states avoided the frequency and intensity of mercantilist warfare exemplified by the violence and instability of the years from 1792–1815 (Thompson 2000). Both the ideological and frontal military attacks by Napoleonic France on the propertied classes, and the constitutions and institutions of Europe's *ancien regimes*, left memories of costly violence and political instability that disposed the restored monarchs, aristocracies and wealthy elites to favour stronger, more centralized states with the fiscal, financial and bureaucratic capacities to resist outside aggression, maintain internal order and to manage acceptable rates of political, social and economic change (Blanning 2002; Forrest et al 2009; Cardoso and Lains 2010; Broers et al 2012; Grotke and Prutch 2014).

From a bicentennial perspective, founded on historical research into the complex conditions and factors surrounding the diverse trajectories for economic development pursued by western polities and societies, the contribution of peace and internal stability that accompanied the economic progress of the West between 1815–1914, can only be regarded as positive (Thompson 2000; Jarrett 2014; Vick 2014). Nevertheless, Dutch historians will remind us that this positive outcome was hardly sufficient to compensate the economy of The Netherlands for losses incurred from years of French dominion and the decision of the Congress of Vienna to unite the North and South of the Netherlands into a single kingdom in order to contain French monarchism. Yet, historians of Italy and Iberia will point out that their post-war rates of growth and structural changes could hardly have been augmented by the presence of French, British or Austrian military power within their national borders. Furthermore, Iberian merchants and investors surely lost opportunities to exploit potential material benefits and returns from centuries of prior investment in South America (Maxwell 2004; Grafe and Irigoin 2006; Grafe 2012; Paquette 2013). Six years of intensive and costly military warfare in the Iberian Peninsula appears, moreover, to have been more costly for all the protagonists involved, especially Spain, than any offsetting benefits for the post-1815 development of their national economies, attributable to political and institutional reforms connected to the occupation, invasions and predations of both French and British armies between 1808–14 (Tortella 2000; Cardoso and Lains 2010; Alvarez-Nogal and Prados de la Escosura 2013).

Britain's continental commitment to engage in a highly destructive war with French armies in Iberia, and to seize the opportunity provided by that engagement by promoting successful movements for colonial independence in Spanish America and Portuguese Brazil, can be read as an additional obstruction to any transition to a modern market economy by Spain and Portugal and their colonies in South America (Hampson 1988; Grafe and Irigoin 2006; Torres-Sánchez 2015). However, and for this unsettled and ongoing debate (which endeavours to deal with the costs and benefits of French imperialism for Europe's possessions overseas), these connections look difficult enough to specify, and impossible to quantify (Adelman 2010; Palma and Reis 2019). Thus, and for the commercially advanced economies of the Low Countries and Italy, it remains difficult to represent the history of their relations with Revolutionary and Napoleonic France in any way but negative terms. Between 1792 and 1815 their economies were afflicted by heavy French predation on the wealth and resources of their citizens. This occurred on a scale that *prima facie* was hardly counter-balanced by the political and institutional reforms that accompanied their interludes of contact and connections with French ideology and power (Cohen and Federico 2001; Dincecco et al 2011; Grotke and Prutch 2014, La France 2019).

To conclude, although accounts of costs and benefits can be recommended and envisaged as heuristic for historical debates and narratives, they are rarely measured. Economic historians looking backward and forward at the meagre evidence for the construction of the macro-economic indices required to assess outcomes connected to the Revolution in France and Napoleonic imperialism over a conjuncture in European history (spanning the years from 1783–1848), seem to agree that only two of Europe's national economies (Britain and ultimately Prussia) clearly emerged from these geographically momentous years with clearly enhanced capacities for long-term growth (Clark 2006; Hagemann 2016; Broers 2015; Dwyer 2019).

The conjuncture in Europe's geopolitical history from 1789 to 1815, which began with a social revolution in France and the overthrow of its *ancien regime*, promoted a transition to a highly effective military state operating within a mercantilist international economic order in which predation, fiscal extraction and the accumulation of sovereign debt for purposes of defence, aggression and geopolitical power had long been omnipresent (Findlay et al 2006; Philp 2007; Mathan 2017). Revolution and civil war in France led, for some twelve years, to the consolidation of a more centralized, efficient mercantilist and military French state that, under Napoleon, engaged the rest of Europe in a predictably protracted, costly and geographically extensive period of conquest, armed conflict and diplomatic coercion. That occurred at a time when technological, commercial and institutional reforms were beginning to create greater possibilities for economic growth, structural change, technological innovation and accelerated productivity than ever before (Milward and Saul 1973; Goodman and Honeyman 1988; Crouzet 1989, 1996 and 2001).

During that period, the opportunity costs of allocating resources for participation in warfare rose everywhere, but in different degrees. Worthy of further debate and research are the hypotheses and meta questions formulated and configured at three conferences and elaborated in nine chapters in this volume. Apart from the case of Spain (which elicited an heuristic and sophisticated response based upon cliometric methods), in general the consensus among economic historians is that, in retrospect, the economies of France, The Netherlands, Portugal, perhaps Italy and possibly Spain, were all, in diverse ways and in different degrees, denuded of some unmeasurable potential, for more rapid and probably more humane transitions into modern economies, by the French Revolution, the subsequent warfare and Napoleonic Imperialism (Noel 1990; Blanning 2008; Dincecco 2009). Over the century to 1914, the power of historical memory associated with this protracted conjuncture of European geopolitical violence did, however, maintain a diplomatic system of international economic relations more favourable to liberal commerce and trade than the mercantilist economic order that took twenty-three years of warfare to bring to a close. Furthermore, the investments by governments in naval power embodied positive externalities for the accelerated diffusion of innovations in shipbuilding, as well as the radical reductions in the costs of shipping freight by sea that came on stream in the post-war years (O'Rourke 2006; Solar 2013).

Nevertheless, this book conveys a nuanced impression that only two of today's Western European states and their economies seem to have emerged from this interlude of violence and inter-state warfare to occupy geopolitical positions that consolidated and enhanced their prospects and potential for accelerated transitions to modern economic growth. Arguments that this was transparently the case for the United Kingdom (clear to British and European statesmen and economists of the day, but neglected by modern economic historians) is elaborated in Chapter 2. A moment's reflexion on the historically plausible counterfactual, namely a successful invasion of the realm by French armies led by Napoleon, might convince social scientists (who no longer read international history) that this view is virtually unavoidable. From a political rather than an economic perspective, the notion of an economic *Sonderweg* remains in place, that is a trajectory for modern economic growth for Germany led by Prussia, that can be traced back to the political and geopolitical conflicts of 1792–1815. Thomas Nipperdey's classical study on the history of modern Germany begins with the sentence: "in the beginning was Napoleon." Indeed, no other German state emerged from this conflict with the fiscal, financial, organizational and military capacities required to check future invasions into Germanic territories by France (Nipperdey 2014; Dwyer 2019). The unification of Germany and its subsequent economic *Sonderweg* could conceivably have occurred under Habsburg leadership. Nevertheless, there is an extensive volume of evidence and analyses now in print that suggests that large scale multi-ethnic empires of early modern times were incapable of providing either the fiscal and financial bases, or the efficient degrees of governance, for the provision of the public goods required for the transition to modern economic growth (Storrs 2009; Parsons 2012; Yun-Casililla and O'Brien 2012 and 2021).

Finally, the view that favourable conditions for international and transcontinental commerce flowed, albeit gradually, and in some reductionist but unmeasurable extent, from this conjuncture and its aftermath, has become acceptable (Findlay and O'Rourke 2007). Gains from trade and specialization have been plausibly correlated to the consolidation of the United Kingdom's indisputable "command of the oceans" between 1805 and 1941 (Morris 2017). Twenty-three years of violent conflict among European powers at sea facilitated the rise of a fiscal state and the growth of a merchant marine in the United States (Edling 2015). It also led to the recently measured long-term reductions in the risks and costs of shipping commodities and labour by sea by the British, American, Dutch and other merchant navies (Kelly 2019).

To that suggestion can be added the collapse of mercantilist restrictions on waterborne trade that followed from transitions to independence by the empires of Spain, Portugal and France in Southern America and the Caribbean, as well as the opening of the Mughal, Qing and Dutch empires in Asia to transcontinental trade (Bayly 1985; Roy 2013).[5] Slowly but surely, the Royal Navy consolidated British power into hegemony over global commerce during the wars with France, and the political barriers to international specialization diminished (Cipolla 2006; O'Brien and Clesse 2002; Rodger 2004; Herman 2005; O'Brien 2014; Backhaus 2008 and 2016). Furthermore, the case that the evolution of global trade away from mercantilism towards liberal diplomacy occurred as a reaction by the aristocratic and wealthy elites of Western Europe to the violent attempt by Napoleonic France to exercise hegemony over the pre-modern international economic order, looks like a secure view for historians to hold (Findlay et al 2006 parts IV and V; Findlay and O'Rourke 2007).

5 For more recent cliometrically based analysis read the chapter on Spain in this volume and the cliometric analysis of Alvarez-Nogal and Prados de la Escosura 2013.[this is a partial repetition of the previous footnote].

References

Acemoglu, Daron et al. (2011). (eds). "The Consequences of Radical Reform: The French Revolution." *American Economic Review*, 101 (7): 3286–3307.

Adelman, Jeremy. 2010. "Iberian Passages, Continuity and Change in the South Atlantic." Armitage, David and Subrahmanyam, Sanjay. 2010 (4): 59–83.

Aerts, Erik and Crouzet, François. 1996. (eds). *Economic Effects of the French Revolutionary and Napoleonic Wars*. Leuven: Leuven University Press.

Alvarez-Nogal, Carlos and Prados de la Escosura, Leandro. 2013. "The Rise and Fall of Spain 1270–1850." *Economic History Review* 66 (1): 1–37.

Andress, David. 2012. *The Savage Storm*. London: Little Brown.

Armitage, David and Subrahmanyam, Sanjay. 2010. *The Age of Revolutions in Global Context c1760–1840*. Basingstoke: Palgrave.

Backhaus, Jurgen. 2012. (ed). *Navies and State Formation*. Berlin: Verlag.

Backhaus, Jurgen et al. 2016. *The Congress of Vienna in Contemporary Economic and Political Literature and Historiography*. Marburg: Verlag.

Baugh, Daniel. 2011. *The Global Seven Years War*. London: Routledge.

Bayly, Christopher. 1985. "State and Economy in India over Seven Hundred Years," *Economic History Review* 38 (4): 583–96.

Becker, Steven et al. 2018. "Wars, Local Institutions and Fiscal Capacity. Evidence from Six Centuries of German History." *Warwick Economics Research Papers* 1182.

Bell, David. 2007. *The First Total War. Napoleon's Europe and the Birth of Modern Warfare*. London: Bloomsbury.

Bien, David. 2014. *Interpreting the Ancien Regime*. Oxford: Voltaire Foundation.

Black, Jeremy. 2007. *Trade, Empire and British Foreign Policy 1689–1815*. London: Routledge.

Black, Jeremy. 2008. *Great Powers and the Quest for Hegemony: the World Order Since 1500*. New York: Routledge.

Blanning, Timothy. 1986. *The Origins of the French Revolutionary Wars*. London: Routledge.

Blanning, Timothy. 2002. *The Culture of Power and the Power of Culture. Old Regime Europe 1660–1789*. Oxford: Oxford University Press.

Blanning, Timothy. 2008. *The Pursuit of Glory. The Five Revolutions that Made Modern Europe 1648–1815*. London: Penguin Books.

Boehme, Hans. 1978. *Introduction to the Social and Economic History of Germany. Politics and Economic Change in the Nineteenth Century*. Oxford. Oxford University Press.

Breuilly, John. 1992. *The National Idea in the Making of a Modern State*. Basingstoke: Palgrave Macmillan.

Breuilly, John. 1996. *The Formation of the First German Nation State 1800–1871*. Basingstoke. Palgrave Macmillan.

Broers, Michael. 1996. *Europe After Napoleon 1814–48.* Manchester: Manchester University Press.

Broers, Michael. 2012 (ed). *The Napoleonic Empire and the New European Political Culture.* Basingstoke. Palgrave Macmillan.

Broers, Michael. 2015. *Europe Under Napoleon.* London: Tauris.

Cardoso, Jose and Lains, Pedro. 2010. (eds). *Paying for the Liberal State. The Rise of Public Finance in Nineteenth Century Europe.* Cambridge: Cambridge University Press.

Chapman, Timothy. 1998. *The Congress of Vienna. Origins, Process Results.* London: Routledge.

Cipolla, Carlo. 2006. *The Economic Decline of Empires.* London: Routledge.

Clark, Christopher. 2006. *Iron Kingdom: The Rise and Downfall of Prussia 1600–1947.* London: Allen Lane.

Clark, Gregory et al. 2014. "The Growing Dependence of Britain on Trade During the Industrial Revolution." *Scandinavian Economic History Review* 62 (2): 109–36.

Cohen, John and Giovanni, Federico. 2001. *The Economic Development of Italy.* Cambridge: Cambridge University Press.

Contamine, Philippe. 2000. (ed). *War and Competition Between States.* Oxford: Oxford University Press.

Crouzet, François. 1986. *L'Economie britannique et le blocus continentale, 1806–13.* Paris: Presses Universitaires de France.

Crouzet, François. 1989. "Les consequences economique de la Revolution Française." *Revue economique* 40 (6): 1189–1203.

Crouzet, François. 1996. "The Second Hundred Years War. Some Reflection." *French History* 10 (4): 432–50.

Crouzet, François. 2001. *A History of the European Economy 1000–2000.* London: University Press of Virginia.

Crouzet, François. 2008. *La guerre economique Franco-anglaise au XVIII siècle.* Paris: Fayard.

Davis, Lance and Engerman, Stanley. 2006. *Naval Blockades in Peace and War. An Economic History.* Cambridge: Cambridge University Press.

Dincecco, Mark et al. 2009. "Warfare, Taxation and Political Change: Evidence from the Italian Risorgimento." *Journal of Economic History* 71 (2): 887–914.

Dincecco, Mark. 2011. *Political Transformations and Public Finances in Europe.* Cambridge. Cambridge University Press.

Dwyer, Philip. 2019. *Modern Prussian History.* London: Longman.

Edling, Max. 2015. *A Hercules in the Cradle. War, Money and the American State.* Chicago: Chicago University Press.

Ehrman, John. 1962. *The British Government and Commercial Negotiations with Europe.* Cambridge: Cambridge University Press.

Ehrman, John. 1996. *The Younger Pitt. The Consuming Struggle.* London: Constable.

Ellis, Geoffrey. 1991. *The Napoleonic Empire*. London: Macmillan.

Esdaile, Charles. 2007. *Napoleon's Wars: An International History 1803–15*. London: Allen Lane.

Evans, Richard. 2016. *The Pursuit of Power. Europe 1815–1914*. London: Allen Lane.

Findlay, Ronald et al. 2006. (eds). *Eli Heckshe. International Trade and Economic Growth.* Cambridge Mass. MIT Press.

Findlay, Ronald and O'Rourke, Kevin. 2007. *Power and Plenty. Trade War and the World Economy.* Princeton: Princeton University Press.

Forrest, Alan. 2009. *The Legacy of the French Revolutionary Wars: The Nation in Arms in Republican Memory.* Cambridge: Cambridge University Press.

Forrest, Alan. 2009. *Soldiers, Citizens and Civilians. Experiences and Perceptions of the Revolutionary and Napoleonic Wars 1790–1820.* Basingstoke: Palgrave Macmillan.

Furet, François. 1992. *Revolutionary France 1770–1880*. Oxford: Blackwell.

Furet, François and Ozouf, Mona. 2007. *Dictionnaire de la révolution Française.* Paris: Flammarion.

Gat, Azar: 2006. *War in Human Civilization*. Oxford: Oxford University Press.

Godsey, William. 2016. *The Sinews of Habsburg Power. Austria as a Fiscal Military State 1648–1815*. Oxford: Oxford University Press.

Gonzalez-Encisco, Augustin. 2016. *War and the Economy. Mercantilism and State Formation in the Eighteenth Century.* London: Routledge.

Goodman, Jordan and Honeyman, Katrina. 1988. *Gainful Pursuits. The Making of Industrial Europe 1600–1914*. London. Arnold.

Graaf, Beatrice de. 2019. (ed). *Securing Europe after Napoleon and the New European Security Culture*. Cambridge: Cambridge University Press.

Grab, Alexander. 2003. *Napoleon and the Transformation of Europe.* New York: Palgrave Macmillan.

Grafe, Regina. 2012. *Distant Tyranny, Marketing Power and Backwardness in Spain.* Princeton: Princeton University Press.

Grafe, Regina and Irigoin, Alejandra. 2006. "The Spanish Empire and its Legacy." *Journal of Global History* 1 (2): 241–67.

Grotke, Karen and Prutch, Martin. 2014. *Monarchical Constitutionalism in Post Napoleonic Europe. Concept and Practice.* Oxford: Oxford University Press.

Hagemann, Karen. 2016. *Revisiting Prussia's Wars Against Napoleon. History, Culture and Memory.* Cambridge: Cambridge University Press.

Hampson, Norman. 1988. *The Perfidy of Albion*. London: Longmans.

Herman, Arthur. 2005. *To Rule the Waves. How the British Navy Shaped the Modern World.* London: Hodder.

Hilton, Boyd. 1977. *Corn, Cash and Commerce 1815–30*. Oxford: Oxford University Press.

Hilton, Boyd. 2006. *A Mad, Bad and Dangerous People. England 1753–1846*. Oxford: Oxford University Press.

Holsti, Kalevi. 1991. *Peace and War. Conflicts and the International Order.* Cambridge: Cambridge University Press.

Jarrett, Mark. 2014. *The Congress of Vienna and its Legacy.* London: Tauris.

Joor, Johan and Aaslestad, Katherine. 2016. *Revisiting Napoleon's Continental System.* Basingstoke: Palgrave Macmillan.

Judson, Philip. 2018. *The Habsburg Empire. A New History.* Cambridge: Cambridge University Press.

Karaman, Kivanç and Pamuk, Şevket. 2013. *Different Paths to the Modern State in Europe: The Interaction Between Warfare, Economic Structure, and Political Regime.* Cambridge: Cambridge University Press.

Kelly, Morgan et al. 2019. "Safety at Sea During the Industrial Revolution." *Dublin Centre for Research Working Paper* 19: 1–47.

Knight, Roger. 2014. *Britain Against Napoleon. The Organization of Victory 1793–1815.* London: Allen Lane.

Lafrance, Xavier. 2019. *The Making of Capitalism in France: Class Structure, Economic Development, the State and the Formation of the French Working Class 1750–1914.* Leiden: Brill.

Marshall, Peter. 1998. (ed). *The Oxford History of the British Empire. Vols 1 and 2.* Oxford: Oxford University Press.

Mathan, Anne de et al. 2017. (eds). *La Mer, la guerre et les affaires.* Rennes: Presses Universitaire de Rennes.

Maxwell, Kenneth. 2004. *Conflicts and Conspiracies. Brazil and Portugal. 1750–1808.* London: Routledge.

McKay, Derek and Scott, Hamish. 1983. *The Rise of the Great Powers 1648–1815.* London: Longman.

Meagher, Thomas. 2017. *Financing Armed Conflict.* Basingstoke: Palgrave.

Milward, Alan and Saul, Berrick. 1973. *The Economic Development of Continental Europe.* London: Allen and Unwin.

Morris, Roger. 2004. *Naval Power and British Culture 1760–1850. Public Trust and Government Ideology.* Aldershot: Ashgate.

Morris, Roger. 2017 *Naval Power ....* (Alter date from 2004 top 2017).

Nipperdey, Thomas. 2014. *Germany From Napoleon to Bismarck 1800–1866.* Princeton: Princeton University Press.

Noel, Charles. 1990. "Charles III of Spain." Scott, Hamish (ed). *Enlightened Absolutism, Reform and Reformers in Later Eighteenth Century Europe.* Basingstoke: Macmillan: 119–45.

O'Brien, Patrick. 1999. (ed). *Philips Atlas of the World History*, London: Philips.

O'Brien, Patrick. 2014 "The Formation of States and Transitions to Modern Economies: England, Europe and Asia Compared." Neal, Larry and Williamson,

Jeffrey. (eds). *The Cambridge History of Capitalism*, Vol. 1. Cambridge: Cambridge University Press.

O'Brien, Patrick. 2021. *The Economies of Imperial China and Western Europe. Debating the Great Divergence*. Basingstoke Palgrave Macmillan.

O'Brien, Patrick and Clesse, Armand. 2002. (eds). *Two Hegemonies: Britain 1846–1914 and the United States 1941–2001*. Aldershot: Ashgate.

O'Brien, Patrick and Keyder, Caglar. 1978. *Economic Growth in Britain and France 1780–1914*, London: Allen and Unwin.

Ogillvie, Sheilagh. 1996. (ed). *Germany. A New Social and Economic History* 1450–1630. Vol. 1. London: Arnold.

O'Rourke, Kevin. 2006. "The Worldwide Economic Impact of the French Revolutionary and Napoleonic Wars 1793–1815." *Journal of Global History* 1 (1): 123–49.

Page, Antony. 2015. *Britain and the Seventy Years War 1744–1815*. Basingstoke. Palgrave.

Palma, Nuno and Jaime Reis. 2019. "From Convergence to Divergence: Portuguese Economic Growth 1527–1850." *Journal of Economic History* 79 (2): 1–30.

Paquette, Gabriel. 2013. *Imperial Portugal in the Age of Atlantic Revolution*. Cambridge: Cambridge University Press.

Paquette, Gabriel. 2019. *European Seaborne Empires from the Thirty Years War to the Age of Revolutions*. New Haven: Yale University Press.

Parker, Harold. 1990. "Why Did Napoleon Invade Russia?" *Journal of Military History* 54 (2): 131–46.

Parsons, Timothy. 2012. *The Rule of Empires. Those Who Built Them. Those Who Endured Them and Why They Always Fall.* Oxford: Oxford University Press.

Perrin, Faustine. 2021. "On the Origins of the Demographic Transition." *Bureau d'Economie Theorique et Applique Working Paper*, 2021–22.

Philp, Mark. 2007. *Resisting Napoleon*. Aldershot: Ashgate.

Pierenkemer, Toni and Tilly, Richard. 2004. *The German Economy During the Nineteenth Century*. Oxford; Berghahn Books.

Poussou, Jean-Pierre. 2000. *L'Economie française du XVIII*e *au XX*e *siècle.* Paris: Presses du Université de Paris.

Rodger, Nicholas. 2004. *Command of the Oceans. A Naval History of Britain. Vol. 2.* London: Allen Lane.

Roy, Tirthankar. 2013. *An Economic History of Early Modern India*. London: Routledge.

Schroeder, Paul. 1994. *The Transformation of European Politics 1763–1848.* Oxford: Clarendon Press.

Scott, Hamish. 1990. *Enlightened Absolutism, Reform and Reformers in Later Eighteenth Century Europe.* Basingstoke; Macmillan.

Scott, Hamish. 2006. *The Birth of the Great Power System 1740–1815.* Harlow: Pearson-Longman.

Scott, Hamish. 2016. "The Habsburg Fiscal Military State in International Perspective." Unpublished paper.

Scott, Hamish and Simms, Brendan. 2007. (eds) *Cultures of Power in Europe During the Long Eighteenth Century.* Cambridge: Cambridge University Press.

Sheehan, James. 1989. *German History 1770–1866.* Oxford: Clarendon Press.

Simms, Brendan. 2013. *Europe. The Struggle for Supremacy*. London. Allen Lane.

Solar, Peter. 2013. "Opening to the East. Shipping Between Europe and Asia, 1770–1830." *Journal of Economic History* 703 (3): 625–61.

Storrs, Christopher. 2009. *The Fiscal Military State in Eighteenth Century Europe.* Farnham: Ashgate.

Thompson, James. 1998. *Decline in History. The European Experience.* Cambridge: Cambridge University Press.

Thompson, William. 2000. *The Emergence of Global Political Economy.* London: Routledge.

Tilly, Richard and Kopsidis, Michael. 2020. *From Old Regime to Industrial State. A History of German Industrialization from the Eighteenth Century to World War I.* Chicago: Chicago University Press.

Torres-Sánchez, Rafael. 2007. *War, State and Development. Fiscal Military States in the Eighteenth Century.* Pamplona: Navara Universidad.

Torres-Sánchez, Rafael. 2015. *Constructing a Fiscal-Military State in Eighteenth Century Spain.* Basingstoke. Palgrave Macmillan.

Tortella, Gabriel. 2000. *The Development of Modern Spain. An Economic History of the Nineteenth and Twentieth Centuries.* Cambridge: Cambridge University Press.

Venturi, France. 1984. *The End of the Old Regime in Europe 1776–89. Vols. 1 and 2.* Princeton: Princeton University Press.

Vick, Brian. 2014. *The Congress of Vienna. Power and Politics after Napoleon.* Cambridge Mass: Harvard University Press.

Whaley, Joachim. 2012. *Germany and the Holy Roman Empire.* Oxford: Oxford University Press.

Wilson, Peter. 2006. "Still a Monstrosity. Some Reflections on Early Modern German Statehood." *Historical Journal* 49 (2): 565–76.

Wilson, Peter. 2016. *The Heart of Europe. The Holy Roman Empire.* Cambridge: Cambridge University Press.

Wolf, Nikolaus et al 2014. "Do Trade Agreements Increase Trade? Evidence from the Zollverein." *Journal of Economic History* 74 (2): 1168–1204.

Wolf, Nikolaus. 2017. *How England Unified Germany. Geography and the Rise of Prussia.* CEPR Discussion Paper 3634.

Yun-Casililla, Bartolome and O'Brien, Patrick. 2012. *The Rise of Fiscal States: A Global History 1500–1914.* Cambridge: Cambridge University Press.

Zamoyski, Adam. 2007. *Rites of Peace. The Fall of Napoleon and the Congress of Vienna.* New York: Harper Collins.

CHAPTER 2

Britain's Wars with France 1793–1815 and Their Contribution to the Consolidation of Its Industrial Revolution

Patrick Karl O'Brien

> There is no mortal to whom Great Britain has greater obligation than this blackguard, for it is the events that he has brought about which have raised England's greatness, security and wealth so high. They are Lords of the sea and neither in this dominion nor in the world trade have they any rivals left to fear. [1]

1 Mercantilist Warfare and the Rise of the British Economy

No doubt the insurmountable theoretical and empirical difficulties involved explains why the modern bibliographies for British economic history do not include a historiography that has engaged seriously enough with debates on the economic outcomes that flowed from the state's sequence of geopolitical conflicts between 1651 and 1846 (Ashton 1959; Brewer 1989; Hudson 1995; Daunton 1998; Allen 2009; Mokyr 2009). International, imperial and military histories have accorded more attention to the problems and effects flowing from the taxes, loans and monetary policies implemented to mobilize resources for warfare (Fynn-Paul 2014). Nevertheless, their primary concerns have been with the origins and processes involved in engagements in warfare, supplemented by accounts of the gains and losses that accrued from peace treaties concluded at the end of persistent interludes of armed conflict (Brewer 1989; Jones 1989; Stone 1994; Bowen 1998; Marshal 1998; Black 1999; Conway 2000 and 2006; Baugh 2011; Knight 2013; Page 2014).

1 A Prussian General's reference to Napoleon at the Congress of Vienna in 1815, cited by Rodger, 2004, p. 574.

 | DOI:10.1163/9789004472754_003

Economic historians prefer structuralist approaches that analyse and compare examples of mobilization for warfare by several European polities. They also endeavour to quantify the significance of institutions established and maintained to service geopolitical strategies. These, over time, augmented the comparative advantages that particular national economies derived from the formation of more centralized and efficient states that emerged from their engagements in warfare (Prados de la Escosura 2004; Torres-Sánchez 2007; Chang 2007; Dincecco 2011; O'Brien 2014, 357–402). For example, the institutions established by England's Republican regime during and, in the wake of the Civil War. This included an enlarged standing navy, excise duties, and reformed navigation acts, all of which embodied long-term externalities for private capital formation and innovation in domestic agriculture and industry linked to the Island's trade, shipping, commercial services, and to colonization overseas.

Following from this interregnum of violent disruption to internal order, the political consensus that emerged among England's aristocratic and mercantile elites became effective enough to maintain centralized monarchical control over foreign, strategic and fiscal policy for an expanding kingdom and its empire overseas. The political regime that evolved in the wake of Britain's destructive civil war provided investors and businessmen with internal stability and external security, plus a rigorous enforcement of property rights. At the same time, the kingdom's bellicose foreign policy supported an ideology of xenophobia, and deference to hierarchy. It also went together with relatively high levels of compliance with taxation imposed by monarchical and aristocratic governments to fund naval and military power along with imperial expansion overseas (Graham and Walsh 2016).

As their access to tax revenues rose, Britain's monarchs and aristocratic elites became more confident that "their" state could accumulate and service ever-increasing levels of debt and credit to fund more aggressive geopolitical, imperial and mercantilist policies against the country's main economic rivals, including the Netherlands, Scandinavia, Russia, Spain and, above all, France. (Ashworth 2017; O'Brien, 2007, 177–98; 2011, 427–48 and 2014, 357–402). Although this provoked a tax rebellion among thirteen colonies in North America, which developed into an open conflict with other European powers, commercial relations with an independent United States resumed soon after the Peace of Paris in 1783 when the King, his ministers and their subservient Parliaments simply gave up on pretensions to tax and regulate the economic affairs of "subjects" living 3000 miles away (Liss 1983; Koehn 1994; Conway 2000; Page 2015; Hopkins 2018).

Between the wars with America and France, Pitt the Younger and his able advisers then set about reforming the kingdom's fiscal and financial system in order to regain the realm's geopolitical and economic position over rivals from the mainland (Ehrman 1969). The economy appears to have been on track when Great Britain's undemocratic system of "royal parliaments" and its propertied elites were confronted by the most sustained and expensive challenge to the political security and prosperity of the Isles since attacks by the Spanish armadas in the late 16th century (Dickinson 1989; Harvey 1992; Uglow 2014).

2 Fiscal and Financial Costs of the Revolutionary and Napoleonic Wars

Revenues (taxes plus loans) raised for armed conflict between 1793 and 1815 exceeded by a long way anything previously witnessed to prosecute warfare against the kingdom's enemies (Conway and Torres Sánchez 2011). By the close of the war, expenditures on the naval and military forces of the Crown had risen five times in real terms and from around 6% to 22% of national income. Tax "burdens" per capita had multiplied by a factor of seven compared to amounts appropriated under William III to fund the Dutch coup d'état of 1688, which enabled him to acquire the fiscal and financial base necessary to support the kingdom's re-engagement in European power politics in a conflict aptly called King William's war, 1689–97 (Hopitt 2000). By any historical or comparative standards the taxation carried by British society and the economy to service the debt and fund the resources allocated to defeat Revolutionary and Napoleonic France, looks like an extraordinarily significant impediment to the growth of the economy.[2]

Furthermore, and contrary to claims by some historians, Britain's Industrial Revolution only helped the kingdom's already developed fiscal and financial systems to appropriate extra taxes and borrow more money than ever before to a marginal degree. Less than 10% of the incremental taxation levied on the economy emanated from additions to the volumes of goods and services already taxed before the outbreak of war in 1793. Taxes introduced in wartime (particularly the income tax) provided a further 35%, leaving a residual 55% imputable increase in the rates of taxation on commodities, services and real property already established as components of a fiscal system that had evolved

2 Data cited or deployed for this chapter is elaborated, calibrated and referenced in a working paper by O'Brien 2017.

historically since the interregnum of the mid-17th century (Cookson 1983, 37–60; O'Brien 1988, 1–32 and Storrs 2009).

Over the 22 years of warfare between 1793–1815, expenditures by the state increased at an annual average rate of 5%, while current estimates for the growth of GDP suggest deceleration to around 1.5%. Unless the elasticity of tax revenues with respect to changes in national income amounted to an implausible coefficient of 3.3, the logical inference must be that, *ceteris paribus*, the protracted engagement in warfare with Revolutionary and Napoleonic France imposed serious constraints on Britain's transition to an industrial economy (Emsley 1979; Cookson 1985, 44–88).

My chapter will, however, argue that such a theoretically plausible, but pessimistic inference - derived from data displaying steep upswings in the revenues and expenditures of the central government - could well be anachronistic. Furthermore, and in retrospect, the French wars from 1793–1815 can be represented as marking the beginning of the end of Europe's mercantilist, geopolitical and economic order. During that order and between 1651 and 1793, the British state had been more consistently, persistently, and successfully engaged in mercantilist competition and warfare for the defence of the realm and the gains from trade and colonization, than any of its rivals on the mainland of Europe (Horn 1967; Jones 1980; McKay and Scott 1983; Stone 1994; Marshal 1998; Black 2007 and O'Brien 2014, 357–402).

From the vantage point of 1793, it would have been futile to argue that the geopolitical strategies and imperial policies pursued by successive British governments (operating since the Republican Interregnum within a mercantilist economic order) had not made an unmeasurable but significant contribution to the progress of a small island economy. (Ashworth 2017) To Pitt and other statesmen of that year, Britain's external security, internal stability and continued progression and prosperity appeared to be menaced by forces unleashed by the Revolution in France. Clearly that perception was shared by the majority of "Britons" (Dickson 1989; MaCleod 1992 and Colley 1992 and Uglow 2014). Continued victories by the French army on the mainland suggests that an invasion by troops led by Napoleon could conceivably have set back the Industrial Revolution for decades.

Thus, any analysis of connections between warfare and Britain's economic growth is realistically conducted by specifying and, where possible, marshalling evidence to answer two counterfactual questions. Firstly, why did 22 years of warfare fail to depress the growth of GDP even further below levels that might have been predicted on the basis of trends in investment, structural change and technological innovation discernible during the decade of recovery that succeeded the Treaty of Paris in 1783? Secondly, what might be plausibly claimed as positive legacies and spin-offs for this particular protracted and costly "conjuncture" of warfare, that witnessed the development of an economy on a course leading to the long Victorian boom and Britain's interlude of hegemony as the commercial hub and industrial workshop of the world? (Allen 2009; Mokyr 2009).

Although fiscal and financial accounts provide the most accessible and impressionable bodies of data for historians who attempt to analyse the costs inflicted on economies from engagements in warfare, they may obscure the real or opportunity costs of resources mobilized for that unavoidable purpose. They might also divert attention away from consideration of the long-term material gains that might flow from money spent effectively by states waging war in the context of a mercantilist international economic order (Zielinsky 2016). Apart from these benefits, imputable to victory rather than defeat, engagements in warfare carried in train some positive outcomes. These can retrospectively be represented as fostering the accumulation of human, social and physical capital; the diffusion of technologies; the enhancement of competitive advantages for commerce overseas; and, above all, for the formation of more efficient systems for central governance for the consolidation of institutions promoting Britain's precocious transition to modern economic growth (Ashworth 2017).

3 Labour 1793–1815

Perhaps the most significant of the factors for production reallocated from employment in the private economy - either to serve in or, indirectly, to provide goods and services for the forces of the Crown - was manpower. By the latter years of the Napoleonic War, Parliament voted to pay and feed military, naval and ordnance forces in excess of a half a million men, compared with 75,000 in 1788–92. The numbers under arms, funded by the British state, included Irishmen, foreigners and Indians in the pay of the East India Company. Parliamentary votes for annual budgets can be transformed into rough estimates that suggest that the incremental share of the "British" workforce (including Irishmen) recruited to serve in the armed forces comes to around 6% of the country's labour force and 11% of its males in their prime years (Clode 1869; Fortescue 1910; Chart 1911, 102–32; Glover 1963). No records are available that record the numbers of civilian workers who were redeployed to produce the incremental amounts of food, clothing, shelter, ships, weapons, munitions, transport, commercial services, etc., consumed by the forces of the Crown. My crude estimate for their numbers has been derived from figures of additions to the funds voted by Parliament to enlarge the total size of the armed forces between 1793–1815. My conjecture is that less than 20% of all British males between the ages of 15–40 might have been either directly or indirectly involved in the "war effort". Parliament did not, moreover, pay market wages to troops and sailors, and that ratio could understate the opportunity costs incurred to redeploy labour.

Yet, histories of the mobilization of manpower for this war are marked by a consensus that both the army and the navy relied in no small degree on duplicity and coercion to bring regiments of troops and crews of warships up to the required strength. The state operated with a system of "informal conscription" and obtained a high proportion of manpower but recruited it from the lower ends of pay and skill categories (Clode 1869; Fortescue 1910; McGuffie 1956; Ward 1953; Lewis 1960; Emsley 1979; Cookson 1997; Lloyd 1968; Rodger 2004; Morriss 2011; Knight 2013). Any reading of the primary sources pertaining to the elasticity of supply for unskilled labour (including data for: population growth, movements in nominal and real wage rates, the recorded occupations of recruits for the army and navy, expenditures on poor law relief, and the successful repression of collective bargaining) will be left with an unquantifiable impression that Britain's armed forces recruited/conscripted manpower that included a considerable share of under-employed, unskilled labour (McGuffie 1956; Emsley 1979; Williams 1981; Feinstein 1998). This impression has, however, and will doubtless continue, to be debated (Hueckel 1973, 309–29; Mokyr and Savin 1976, 198–259; Anderson 1972 and 1974, 610–18).

Furthermore, the historical evidence for conditions in the British labour market during the war and over several post-war years of depression and unemployment, lend support to a perception that some form of military Keynesianism operated over this period, and mitigated potentially malign economic effects that would otherwise accompany manpower shortages for the private economy. (Armstrong 1981; Uglow 2014, Feinstein 1998, 625–58). The socio-economic characteristics of most men recruited to serve in the army and navy also implies that the loss to the economy from the unfortunate victims of this prolonged interlude of interstate violence was lower than records of numbers of casualties might suggest (Greenwood 1942, 4–7; Hodge 1855, 208–12 and 1956, 264–66). Economically, the losses of "human capital" could, moreover, have been, to some degree, offset by the inculcation of skills, positive attitudes to hierarchical disciplined work and bodily health that supposedly flows from service aboard warships and/or in the colours (White 1963; Colley 1992; Cookson 1997; Charters 2006). Contemporaries and historians have also observed that the response to French aggression by an aristocratic officer class generated an upsurge in loyalty and deference among the population at large that helped to maintain the stability of Britain's *ancien regime* (Chalmers 1812; Lowe 1822; Emsley 1979, Dickinson 1989; Russell 1995; Price 1999; Gee 2003; Uglow 2014).

In short, service in the forces contributed positively to sustain the good order that infused the culture, and carried the British economy through difficult years of transition to an industrial society (Ackworth 1925; Gordon 1976 and 1979; Hilton 1977; James 2001; Burns and Innes 2003).

4 Capital Formation 1793–1815

Stocks of fixed and circulating capital may have increased by 27% (a rate of around 1% per annum) between 1792 and 1816. How rapidly capital might have accumulated in the absence of the French Wars remains virtually impossible to measure (Feinstein 1978, 28–94 and 1981, Crafts and Mills, 2016). Loans and credits extended to the state to sustain a larger army in the field and a huge navy at sea, may, to some unmeasurable degree, have crowded out private investment and borrowing potentially undertaken for more productive purposes. The question by how much is interesting to contemplate, and has been extensively debated. Theoretically plausible models can be rigorously specified to span possibilities from crowding out on a one-to-one basis to crowding in on the same basis (Friedman 1984; Boskin 1987; Barro 1987; Williamson 1987; Edelstein 1990; Temin and Voth 2012; Ventura and Voth 2015, 1–19).

For several reasons there seems, however, to be no point in toying with hypotheses that the elasticity of substitution between borrowing by the government and investment by the private sector might counterfactually have been close to unity, even though the "nominal level amounts" of Britain's sovereign debt rose from £292 million before the war to reach £862 million in 1817. (Wilkinson 1987; McDonald 2003; Caselli 2008, Temin and Voth 2012). First and foremost, this is because historians will regard the argument as malposed and anachronistic, because the funds raised by deficit finance were utilized to "crowd out" a potential takeover of the state by French armies. Historically it seems more heuristic to analyse why private investment continued at a "high" rate throughout the years of warfare marked by an extraordinary accumulation of sovereign debt. Private savings and capital formation continued at surprisingly high levels partly because Pitt and his successors at the Treasury departed radically from the kingdom's traditional strategy, and began to fund far higher proportions of the resources required to engage in conflict with Revolutionary and Napoleonic France by substituting taxes for loans. By the time Napoleon had been defeated at Waterloo, 58% of the money raised to secure victory had emanated from taxation, that included the introduction of the country's first but regressive income tax. This can be compared with a ratio of 21% for four previous wars (O'Brien 2008, 179–209).

Furthermore, the Treasury persisted with the policy again initiated by Pitt before the war, when he imposed extra taxation in order to accumulate a Sinking Fund designated to redeem debt once the traditional wartime policy of deficit finance had reverted to the established peacetime convention of balanced budgets (Hargreaves 1930; Ehrman 1969; O'Brien 2007; Caselli 2008). Pitt's controversial policy of borrowing in wartime to sustain a commitment to convert Britain's sovereign debt (denominated in irredeemable bonds and short-term bills) into a debt composed largely of fixed nominal rates of interest on long term bonds and short term bills, incurred criticism at the time, which matured thereafter into an unquestioned critique (Ackworth 1925; Viner 1955; Ehrman 1969; Gordon 1976 and 1979; Hilton 1977; Crouzet 1987; Williamson 1987; Aerts and Crouzet 1996). Combined with, and complemented by, the suspension of the convertibility of the paper currency and deposits issued by the Bank of England into specie, this strategy successfully maintained the confidence of both domestic and foreign investors in both bills discounted and long-term bonds, sold by the state on the London capital market (O'Brien 2017; Gant 2015). Rates of interest remained surprisingly low over a protracted period of warfare when the "nominal" value of Britain's outstanding sovereign debt rose to reach 2.5 times current estimates of GDP for 1819. The policy has, however, been convincingly defended in two unpublished theses (O'Brien and Palma forthcoming 2022; and Gant 2015; vide: Heim and Mirowski 1987; Wright 1996; Caselli 2008; Broadberry et al 2015).

The fiscal, financial and monetary policies pursued by Pitt and his successors to prosecute the most expensive war in British history, secured the funds required to achieve a final victory over France and her allies, but with difficulty and moments of crisis. Nevertheless, they worked without breakdowns in any of the systems and institutions managed by the pre-modern British state operating in the mercantilist, geopolitical and economic international economic order, an order that *afflicted* all European economies for centuries before the Royal Navy achieved indisputable command over the oceans and sea lanes of the world (Cookson 1983, 37–60 and 1985, 44–88; Rodger 2004).

The fiscal, financial and monetary policies formulated and pursued to wage warfare against an implacable foe, succeeded not merely in defending the realm and its economy, but left both the Hanoverian state and the private sector with an extended and more efficient set of institutions for the governance and development of an economy on the move to becoming the workshop and commercial hub of an expanding empire and world economy (O'Brien and Palma 2019, 1–37).

Fiscally, the state had demonstrated its prowess to fund a protracted and expensive period of warfare and to service a sovereign debt accumulating to levels way beyond the capacities of any of its rivals on the mainland of Europe (Storrs, 2009). Financially, and in close cooperation with the Bank of England, the state had also conducted a successful and enduring experiment with fiat paper money that served to extend and improve Britain's system of financial intermediation to service demands from both domestic commerce and international trade and investment (Wood 1939; Aston and Sayers 1953; Pressnell 1956; Collins 1992; O'Brien and Palma forthcoming 2021).

International markets for credit and longer-term loans had been integrating for several decades before the French Revolution, and became a serious threat to all forms of *ancien regime* wealth and property. Revolutionary and Napoleonic armies disrupted the operations of markets for capital, credit and tradeable commodities in Antwerp, Amsterdam, Venice, Frankfurt, Hamburg and other mainland cities. London became Europe's safe haven for mobile capital and for the mercantile and financial skills of migrants from the mainland (Neal 1990 and 1991; Aerts and Crouzet 1990; Chapman 1992; McCusker and Morgan 1943 and Gauci 2006).

At the same time, unintended but positive consequences flowed from the unavoidable decision to release Britain's monetary system from constraints associated with its 18th century version of the gold standard. Assisted by the flexibility introduced into supplies of paper money and credit, financial intermediaries (merchants, metropolitan and country banks and insurance companies) extended their services for the economy to include significant numbers of hitherto riskier clients. In effect, the suspension of cash payments monetized a wider range of assets, cushioned at the safer end of portfolios by Government bonds and bills bearing higher rates of interest, that were predicted to appreciate once peace was restored (Silberling 1924, 214–33; Cannan 1925; Cameron 1967; Bordo and Capie 1994; O'Brien and Palma 2019, 1–37 and 2021).

The hopes of Napoleon, and the dire predictions of bullionists, that the British monetary system would collapse, never came to pass (Fetter 1959; Crouzet 1987; Aerts and Crouzet 1996). By 1815, London had clearly emerged as the world's leading financial, commercial, shipping, distribution and insurance centre for imported, as well as domestic commodities. Furthermore, the command of stocks of durable naval and military capital and knowledge that had accumulated during the long conflict with France, allowed Great Britain's victorious, well-armed and more centralized state to protect the economy's access to foreign, as well as to its extended imperial, markets overseas (Prados de la Escosura 2004; O'Brien 2017).

With external security and open access to markets overseas, and investments in colonies overseas, guaranteed by the Royal Navy's indisputable command of the oceans, the state could concentrate the surplus (amounting to some 40% of tax revenues) at its disposal. This was after servicing a huge debt on the relatively small professional army required to maintain political stability and social order for a national economy becoming more rapidly urbanized and industrialized (Crouzet 1990; Russell 1995; Gambles 1996; Cookson 1997; Black 1999; James 2001; Findlay 2006; Hilton 2006; Findlay and O'Rourke 2007).

In short, for Britain's commerce overseas and industry, the upswing in expenditure and investment by the state on warfare against Revolutionary and Napoleonic France helped to create favourable long-term political and geopolitical conditions and prospects for an expansion of the export of services and commodities overseas. The funding of these expenditures with loans and credits served to extend, integrate and improve markets for capital invested at home and abroad. Finally, a forthcoming article adds a suggestion that Napoleon's impressions that the French wartime blockade of European markets could bring about the collapse of Britain's fiscal and financial system, led to his fatal decision to invade Russia (O'Brien and Palma 2021).

5 Agricultural Expansion before, during and after the Wars: 1793–1846

Between 1793 and 1815 the expansion of British and Irish agricultures, already underway before the wars, can be represented as a long cycle of accelerated, but largely extensive, growth that continued down to the sector's so-called golden age in the middle decades of the 19th century (Allen 1994, 96–123 and 2004, 96–117). During the years of conflict, the United Kingdom's agricultural sector played a significant role in providing forces for the crown with manpower, food, fibres, horses and timber, as well as high proportions of the incremental taxation levied upon landed incomes, foodstuffs and organic materials. Fortunately, for ministers seeking to secure compliance with their demands for higher taxes and requests for loans from an affluent class of aristocratic landowners and tenant farmers, the realm's agrarian sector contained both a sufficient area of under-utilized land and elastic supplies of underemployed labour available to respond to rising demands for manpower, food and raw materials. At one and the same time, agriculture supported accelerated population growth, migration to towns and purchases by the state for provisions, fibres, horses, timber, etc.

A generation of agrarian historians have described how effectively and how well British and Irish landowners and farmers responded to incentives to profit from population growth augmented by state demands for its armed forces (Allen 1990; Overton 1996; Allen 2004, 96–117). Once peace had been restored the sector confronted the challenge of adjustment to falling prices for primary products, the resumption of imports, rising demands for poor relief, the integration of Ireland, and the persistence of high levels of indirect taxes, to service an extraordinary level of sovereign debt. [3]

Attempts to quantify a rich tradition of the realm's dense agrarian history with relevant statistical indicators continues, but remains an area of dispute over data and estimates marking turning points for output, investment, profits, rents, yields and factor productivities, that continue to display unsettled diversity (Broadberry et al 2015). Nevertheless, most authors suggest acceleration during the wars, a continuation of trends during the decades of "post-war depression" down to the golden age of 1846–73 (Hueckel, 1973, 365–96 and 1976, 401–14; Crafts 1985; Jackson 1985, 333–51; Clark 1990, 445–60; Allen 1990, 209–35; 1992, 1994, 96–123 and 2004, 96–117; Overton, 1996; Meredith and Oxley, 2014, 163–214).

Contemporary perceptions, as well as the voluminous rich bibliography in agrarian history, are consistent with a range of conjectural estimates that suggests upswings in rates of growth, investment and productivity growth proceeding for three long cycles of rising and falling prices of primary products before (1783–93), during, and after the wars, down to the repeal of the Corn Laws in 1846. The wartime cycle witnessed a positive response to rising prices, and produced a shift in the inter-sectoral terms of trade promoted by flexible access to credit, lagging agricultural wages, extensions to the margins of cultivation, and the diffusion of known techniques of cultivation, to feed the realm's growing and urbanizing population, as well as its armed forces. Landowners, farmers and cheap agricultural labour pushed the margin for cultivation outwards onto waste and scrub land and up the hillsides of northern England. They consolidated estates in more efficient managerial units with larger scale farms, drained, marled and limed soils, and diffused well publicized and proven techniques for the growth of crops and the rearing of farm animals (Gayer et al 1953; O'Brien 1985, 773–99; Overton 1996; Broadberry et al 2015).

3 The bibliography of books, articles and Parliamentary Papers is too extensive to cite here, but is accessible in my Working Paper Department of Economic History, LSE No. 259/2017).

Over the second cycle, marked by declining prices and an elevation of burdens in the form of higher taxation and poor relief, Parliaments of aristocratic landowners sought relief by repealing the income tax and diversifying their portfolios of wealth into minerals, transportation and urban property. There is no evidence that the areas of arable land and pasture extended in wartime reverted to pre-war levels. Thus, a price and rent cycle coinciding with 22 years of warfare may be represented as a fortuitous geopolitical interlude, which helped an industrializing economy circumvent the tendency of agriculture to run into diminishing returns (Clark 2002; Kelly et al 2014, 363–89).

After the French wars, an *ancien regime* of less than progressive landowners and tenant farmers entered a cage that maintained imperatives to invest and innovate on their estates and farms in order to preserve their wealth, status, local responsibilities and political power in the wake of a social revolution in France that had overturned a similar ruling elite across the Channel (Allen 2009). Britain's famous controversy over the Corn Laws never plunged society into any prolonged, politically destabilizing and unprofitable conflict between agrarians and industrializers of the kind that hindered structural change on the mainland (More 1847; Dickinson 1989; Gambles 1996; Hilton 2006).

6 Industrial Production and Technological Innovation before, during and after the Wars: 1763–1846

A serious critic of the estimates currently in print purporting to measure rates of growth for industrial production over a long period that concluded twenty-two years of warfare, concluded that after a prolonged debate "we have long reached the stage of analysing the same body of data over and over again" (Cuenca-Esterban 1994, 105). There is no consensus in sight, but for present purposes we note that on none of the several rival indices now in print did the wars of 1793–1815 precipitate fundamental discontinuities, negative or positive, in the pace and pattern of industrialization (Dickinson 1989; Crafts and Harley 1992, 703–30; Cuenca-Esterban 1994, 66–105; Mokyr 2009; Broadberry et al 2015; Crafts and Mills 2016). Nobody at the time claimed they did. Mercantilists reassured their fellow Britons that their state possessed capacities to defeat France and extolled "the wealth, power and resources of the British Empire" (Cookson 1983, 59–60; Colley 1992; Magnusson 1994; McCleod 1998).

On that most frequently posited of connections between warfare and industrial growth, namely, technological invention, the bibliography exposes a limited range of examples that could be significant for the longer-term growth of the economy or the effectiveness of its armed forces. There are references to experiments with methods for the preservation of food, to steam pumps operating to fill tanks aboard warships with fresh water, for Brunel's blocks and pulleys for the rigging of their sails, and a machine for the manufacture of boots for the army (O'Connell 1989; Van Creveld 1989; Hoffman 2015; Morris 2020). Recent and unpublished research utilizing patent data classified with reference to the prior and longer-term significance of registered patents does, however, reveal that "high value patenting coincides with the French wars", and suggests that the "wars permanently accelerated British patenting and presumably inventive behaviour" (Billington 2018).

Nevertheless, connections seem stronger for innovation than invention. In general they can be plausibly read as an elaboration and more rapid diffusion for sequences of improvements associated with the spread of the more efficient coordination in arms production, the take-up of steam power, and above all the construction and maintenance of warships, which embodied potential spill-overs for post-war longer term development of ship-building, shipping, metallurgy and engineering (Winter 1975; Morriss 2011 and 2020; Bottomley 2014; Hoffman 2015; Ashworth 2017; Satia 2018).

Obviously the monetary, fiscal, financial and commercial policies pursued by the state to raise revenues for war had diverse impacts upon the growth of each and every British industry. Wartime policies certainly reinforced established precepts of fiscal mercantilism that had operated to promote exports and maintain lower rates of taxation on imported inputs utilized by domestic industry (Kennedy 1913; Dome 2004). In a desperate search for tax revenues, the state revised tariffs on almost all commodities manufactured and sold within the kingdom. Tariff rates rose to become virtually prohibitive (Beckett and Turner 1990; O'Brien 2008 and 2011; Storrs 2009; He 2013). Perhaps the Napoleonic blockade of Britain's export markets on mainland Europe reinforced their protective potential for innovation in order to extend and integrate home markets? (Juhasz 2018).

The elevation of tariffs, together with the rise in the risks and costs of shipping timber and bar iron from the Baltic, almost certainly contributed to the pronounced accelerated rates of growth of outputs experienced by both the iron and coal industries between 1788–92 and 1821, when the latter's transition from charcoal to coke smelting was completed and the latter's level of output had doubled (Ashton 1924; Riden 1977; Hyde 1977; Flinn 1984). Over the second half of the 18th century, coal fields beyond those established in north-eastern England opened up. Mines began to utilize improved Newcomen and eventually Watt engines for drainage and haulage, as well as railed ways to connected an extended network of inland waterways (Galloway 1893; Ashton and Sykes 1929; Flinn 1984). Factor productivity may not have gone up though (Clark and Jacks 2007). Nevertheless, the exploitation of coal as a cheaper source of energy and fuel for heat-intensive industries, such as iron, copper, glass, salt, brewing and sugar, promoted fixed investment and maintained a trajectory for the heavy industries of the First Industrial Revolution, both during the war and thereafter (Flinn 1984; Feinstein and Pollard 1988; Allen 2004; Malamina 2016). Coal's contribution to England's precocious industrialization, and to feeding the nation in wartime, cannot be understated (Wrigley 2015).

To sum up: all the indices show that after these wars industry rebounded, and displays what cliometricians would be pleased to calibrate as a "structural break" (Broadberry et al 2015; Crafts and Mills 2016). Major industries including iron, coal, cotton and armaments improved upon capacities built up in the hothouse conditions of a wartime economy (Uglow 2014). They held onto the advantages of entry and access to foreign markets, secured, retained and expanded for the economy thanks to the Royal Navy and the Island's expanded mercantile marine. Victory represented the culmination of the Island's successful maritime strategy for security, naval hegemony and economic progress (Wilkinson 2004; Herman 2005; O'Brien 2007 and 2014).

7 Geopolitical and Economic Outcomes from the Revolutionary and Napoleonic Wars

Looking back from the Treaty of Vienna, historians of geopolitics have appreciated that Britain emerged from the wars with Revolutionary France in pole position in an emerging and potentially more open and liberal international economic order. It had a vastly extended territorial empire, naval bases in ports throughout the world, and a greatly enlarged maritime sector linked to technologically advanced industries, poised to sell higher shares of their outputs overseas (O'Brien 2006).

That situation had emerged after a quarter of a century of coordinated and complementary investment by the state and the private sector for the construction of ships and the training of seamen, together with the expansion and reorganization of the commercial and financial institutions in London and other port cities to fund, insure and transport merchandise and passengers by sea to every part of an integrating world economy. Competition with rivals for the gains from trade had provided space and opportunities for the Island's maritime sector since the times of Cromwell. Global markets had been helping the economy to reach a plateau of opportunities from where a sustainable transition to an urban industrialized economy would no longer be contained by the relatively small size of the United Kingdom's home market.

Furthermore, the risks of specialization arising from shortages of food and raw materials to support the urbanization of a growing share of a national labour force generating increasing returns by way of agglomerating economic activities in towns and workforces in factories, were also alleviated by the engagement in commerce with the rest of the world. Perceptions of such close connections between seaborne commerce, warfare and the Industrial Revolution would not, moreover, have surprised mercantilists, who hardly hesitated to extoll links between power and profit (Schmoller 1896; Lane 1979; Holsti 1991; Cookson 1997; Findlay and O'Rourke 2007: O'Brien 2007 and 2014; Magnusson 2009; Reinert 2011; Vries 2015).

Nevertheless, it remains impossible to validate educated perceptions of the day, as noted, summarized, and analysed by historians, without reference to a fully articulated balance of payments and accounts, going back to the Republic (Imlah,1958; Davis 1973). The data available for commerce with the rest of the world is largely for commodities alone, and has been utilized patriotically to obscure plausible exogeneous connections to the development of the international economy. This may have accorded undue attention to economic theories of connections between trade and growth and the calibration of weights, that purport to measure the significance of overseas trade for Britain's transition through an industrial revolution (Crouzet 1980; Rashid 1980; Schaefer 1981; Magnusson 1994; Cuenca 1997).

Fortunately, that debate has now hopefully been settled in favour of "strong" significance, by way of a seminal article aptly entitled 'Britain's Growing Dependence of Trade During the Industrial Revolution' and the exposure of neo-liberal biases against all forms of mercantilism by Reinert and his associates from "the other cannon" (Clark 2014; Reinert 2011).

What will remain contentious, however, despite the impressive endeavours by Brezis, Nash and Cuenca-Esterban to produce reliable figures, are estimates of net returns from the sales of shipping, insurance, banking and other services that are now recorded as invisibles on the kingdom's balance of payments accounts (Brezis 1995, 506–21 and 1997, 129–32; Nash 1997, 110–25; Cuenca-Esterban 2001, 54–86).

There is, however, an extensive bibliography of contemporary and historical literature that includes official statistics recording the movements of ships in and out of British ports before, during, between, and after two major wars from 1776–83 and 1793–1815. That literature, which is summarized and referenced in a long working paper to accompany this chapter, includes a substantial and unequivocal library of historical publications that supports some plausible conclusions (O'Brien 2017).

First, that Britain's prospects for dominating global commerce in manufactured commodities and services for an expanding world economy had been damaged by defeat in the American War of Independence (Conway, 2000 and 2006; Page, 2014). Recovery began during an interlude of peace and naval rearmament between 1783 and 1793 (Ehrman 1962). Full recovery, followed by an acceleration to a position of hegemony, occurred before 1800. This can be represented as perhaps the major and enduring outcome of the wars against France from 1793–1815. A year after the battle of Trafalgar in 1805, Britain's foreign secretary could convincingly proclaim: "the sea is ours and we must maintain the doctrine that no nation, no fleet, no cock-boat shall sail upon it without our permission" (Harvey 1992, 81).

His claim has been analysed and validated by an outstanding body of historical scholarship produced by British naval historians (Parkinson 1977; Ehrman 1962 and 1969; Lavery 1987; Baugh 1988 and 2011; Glete 1993, Morris 2011; Rodger 2004; Wilkinson 2004; Black 2007; Knight and Wilcox 2010; Robson 2014). Their scholarship is, moreover, congruent with a set of carefully constructed and unchallenged estimates by Cuenca-Esterban. They provide quantified conjectures for the kingdom's net position on the income account of its balance of payments from 1772–1820. This was a period that includes cycles of decline and expansion in international trade in commodities and services during two major wars and a decade of peace after 1783 (Prados de la Escosura 2004; Sims 2007; Findlay and O'Rourke 2007; O'Brien, 2017).

Once the long conflict with Revolutionary and Napoleonic France was over, and the advantages of naval protection and predation upon foreign (and neutral shipping) and other extortions associated with mercantilist warfare came to an end, European and American competitors recovered some of the international commerce they had lost in wartime from financing and transhipping commodities by sea around the world. Nevertheless, Britain's top position had been secured. A liberal international economic order gradually emerged under the benign hegemony of the Royal Navy. During the Pax Britannia the Island economy retained and built upon the extraordinary shares of the profits (acquired and seized during an age of mercantilism) from building and supplying ships, shipping, marine insurance, banking, commercial, and entrepôt services for the rest of the world economy (including the polity's own extended empire overseas) (O'Brien 2007, 177–98 and 2014, 357–402).

Geopolitical conjunctures in economic history, when the long run growth of national economies might well have been thrown off course in developing comparative advantages that depended upon the maintenance of external security and the retention of naval supremacy over rival powers competing for gains from trade and specialization (linked to technological change), are complex to model (Backhaus 2012; Billington 2018). Early modern international history is not an ontologically convenient arena for economic theories, however, rigorously designed to test connections between trade and growth, except by resorting to unreal counterfactuals of peace with free trade, derived from Adam Smith's premature advocacy of a more enlightened international economic order. If, however, we take account of the insights of "Gentlemanly Capitalism" we might well reflect upon the shares of imports retained, consumed and utilized by the economy of the United Kingdom from 1815 to 1941 that were funded by net receipts from the sale of services to the empire and the rest of the world. This was supplemented in ever increasing proportions over time from inflows of dividends and interest from investments overseas (Cain and Hopkins 1993; Hopkins 2018).

Historians cannot avoid the question of how, when, and why that pattern of specialization (with externalities) connected to long run growth of an industrial economy, came to pass and was sustained for so long (Black 2007; Clark 2010). From today's post hoc perspective, is it anachronistic to underestimate the kingdom's pursuit of a mercantilist strategy for development, or to ignore the massive expenditures incurred to defeat Revolutionary and Napoleonic France? (Bannerman 2008; Ashworth 2017)

National versions of mercantilism were supported by the mainstream of European economic thought between 1651 and 1846, and were accepted as a sensible foundation for geopolitical policy by all British Parliaments and governments of the day (Jomo and Reinert, 2005; Ormrod 2020). Smithian views continued to be as deviant and premature as universal suffrage, religious toleration, rights for women, sexual freedom and other demands for "enlightenment" until well into the 19th century (Reinert 2011). An Industrial Enlightenment succeeded rather than preceded Britain's precocious transition to a modern industrial market economy (Holsti 1991; Hont 2005; Israel 2010; but *vide* Mokyr 2009).

After Trafalgar and Waterloo, the economic ramifications and significance of Britain's victory over Revolutionary and Napoleonic France were widely recognized by European statesmen, intellectuals and historians as a conjuncture in European and global history that marked the beginning of the end of a malign international economic order (Jarrett 2013). Economic historians have no need or warrant to underplay the significance of states or geopolitics when they construct historical narratives to explain the First Industrial Revolution (Bates 2017).

References

Ackworth, Angus.1925. *Financial Reconstruction in England, 1815–22*: London: King.

Aerts, Erik and Crouzet, François (eds.). 1996. *Economic Effects of the French Revolutionary and Napoleonic Wars*: Leuven: Leuven University Press.

Allen, Robert. 1990. "Tracking the Agricultural Revolution in England?" In *Economic History Review*, 52, (1).

Allen, Robert. 1992. *Enclosure and the Yeoman. The Agricultural Development of the South Midlands*: Oxford: Oxford University Press.

Allen, Robert. 1994. "Agriculture During the Industrial Revolution," In Floud, Roderick and McCloskey, Donald (eds,). *The Economic History of Britain Since 1700*, Vol. I: Cambridge University Press.

Allen, Robert. 2004. "Agriculture During the Industrial Revolution" In Floud, Roderick and Johnson, Paul (eds.) *Cambridge Economic History of Modern Britain Since 1700*, Vol. II: Cambridge: Cambridge University Press.

Allen, Robert. 2009. *The British Industrial Revolution in Global Perspective*: Cambridge: Cambridge University Press.

Anderson, John. 1972. "Aspects of the Effect on the British Economy of the Wars Against France." *Australian Economic History Review*, 12, (1).

Anderson, John. 1974. "A Measure of the Effect of British Public Finance, 1713–1815." *Economic History Review*, 27, (4).

Armstrong, William. 1981. "The Influence of Demographic Factors on the Position of Agricultural Labour in England and Wales c. 1750–1914." *Agricultural History Review*, 29, (2).

Ashton, Robert. 1961. "The Crown and the Money Market, 1603–1640." *The Economic Journal*, 71 (284).

Ashton, Thomas. 1924. *Iron and Steel in the Industrial Revolution*: Manchester: Manchester University Press.

Ashton, Thomas and Sykes, John. 1929. *The Coal Industry of the Eighteenth Century*: Manchester: Manchester University Press.

Ashton, Thomas and Sayers, Richard. 1953. *Papers in English Monetary History*: Oxford: Oxford University Press.

Ashton, Thomas. 1959. *Economic Fluctuations in England 1700–1800*: Oxford: Oxford University Press.

Ashworth, William. 2017. *The Industrial Revolution: The State, Knowledge and Global Trade*. London: Bloomsbury.

Backhaus, Jurgen. 2012. *Navies and State Formation*: Berlin: Verlag.

Bannerman, Gordon. 2008. *Merchants and the Military in Eighteenth century Britain, 1739–63*: London: Pickering.

Barro, Robert. 1987. "Government Spending, Interest Rates, Prices and Budget Deficits in the United Kingdom, 1701–1918." *Journal of Monetary Economics*, 20, (2).

Bates, Robert. 2017. *The Development Dilemma: Security, Prosperity and a Return to History*. Princeton: Princeton University Press.

Baugh, Daniel. 1988. "Britain's Blue Water Policy, 1689–1815." *International History Review*, 10, (1).

Baugh, Daniel. 2011. *The Global Seven Years War, 1756–63*: London: Routledge.

Beckett, John, and Turner, Michael. 1990. "Taxation and Economic Growth in Eighteenth Century England." *Economic History Review*, 43, (3).

Billington, Stephen. 2018. "War, What Is It Good For?": *Queen's University Centre for Economic History Working Paper*, No. 1, 8–12.

Black, Jeremy. (ed.). 1999. *European Warfare 1453–1815*: Basingstoke: Palgrave.

Black, Jeremy. 2007. *Trade, Empire and British Foreign Policy, 1689–1815*: London: Routledge.

Black, Jeremy. 2007. *Great Powers and the Quest for Hegemony: The World Order Since 1500*: New York: Routledge.

Bordo, Michael and Capie, Forrest (eds). 1994. *Monetary Regime in Transition*: Cambridge: Cambridge University Press.

Boskin, Michael et al (eds). 1987. *Private Savings and Public Debt*: Oxford: Oxford University Press.

Bottomley, Sean. 2014. *The British Patent System During the Industrial Revolution*: Cambridge: Cambridge University Press.

Bowen, Huw. 1998. *British Society, 1688–1815*: Cambridge: Cambridge University Press.

Brewer, John. 1989. *The Sinews of Power, War, Money and the English State, 1683–1783*: Cambridge, Mass: Harvard University Press.

Brezis, Elise. 1995. "Foreign Capital Flows in the Century of Britain's Industrial Revolution. New Estimates Controlled Conjectures." *Economic History Review*, 48, (2).

Brezis, Elise. 1997. "Did Foreign Capital Flows Finance the Industrial Revolution? A Reply." *Economic History Review*, 50, (1).

Broadberry, Stephen. et al. 2015. *British Economic Growth 1270–1870*: Cambridge: Cambridge University Press.

Burns, Arthur, and Innes, Jo (eds.). 2003. *Rethinking the Age of Reform*: Oxford: Oxford University Press.

Cain, Peter and Hopkins, Antony. 1993. *British Imperialism, Innovation and Expansion, 1688–1914*: London: Routledge.

Cameron, Rondo et al (eds.). 1967. *Banking in the Early Stages of Industrialization*: Oxford: Oxford University Press.

Cannan, Edwin. 1925. *The Paper Pound 1797–1921*: London: Routledge.

Caselli, Fausto. 2008. *Government Debts and Financial Markets in Europe*: London: Pickering & Chatto.

Chalmers, George. 1812. *Historical View of the Domestic Economy of Britain and Ireland*: London: Goldsmith's Collection.

Chang,Ha-Joon.2007.*InstitutionalChangeandEconomicDevelopment*:NewYork:United Nations University Press.

Chapman, Sidney. 1992. *Merchant Enterprise in Britain from the Industrial Revolution to World War I*: Cambridge: Cambridge University Press.

Chart, David. 1911. "Irish Levies." *English Historical Review,* 26, (101).

Charters, Erica. 2006. *Disease, War and the Imperial State*: Chicago: Chicago University Press.

Clark, Gregory. 1990. "Yields per Acre in English Agriculture 1250–1860. Evidence from Labour Inputs." *Economic History Review,* 44, (3).

Clark, Gregory. 2002. "Land rental values and the Agrarian Economy of England and Wales." *European Review of Economic History*, 6, (3).

Clark, Gregory. 2010. "The Macro-Economic Aggregates for England, 1209–2008." *Research in Economic History*, 27, (March).

Clark, Gregory et al. 2014. "The Growing Dependence of Britain on Trade during the Industrial Revolution." *Scandinavian Economic History Review* ,62, (2).

Clark, Gregory and Jacks, David. 2007. "Coal and the Industrial Revolution 1700–1869" In *European Review of Economic History,* 11, (1).

Clode, Charles. 1869. *Military Forces of the Crown,* 2 vols: London: Murray.

Colley, Linda. 1992. *Briton's Forging the Nation 1707–1837*: New Haven: Yale University Press.

Collins, Michael. 1992. *Money and Banking in the United Kingdom*: London: Routledge.

Conway, Steven. 2000. *The British Isles and the War of American Independence*: Oxford: Oxford University Press.

Conway, Steven. 2006. *War, State and Society in mid-Eighteenth Century England and Ireland*: Oxford: Oxford University Press.

Conway, Steven and Torres-Sanchez, Raphael. 2011. *The Spending of States. Military Expenditure During the Long Eighteenth Century.* Germany: Saarbruken VDM : Verlag.

Cookson, John. 1983. "Political Arithmetic and War in Britain" In *War and Society*, 1, (2).

Cookson, John. 1985. "British Society and the French Wars 1793–1815." *Australian Journal of Politics and Society* 31, (2).

Cookson, John. 1997. *The British Armed Nation 1793–1815*: Oxford: Oxford University Press.

Crafts, Nicholas. 1985. *British Economic Growth 1700–1850*: Cambridge: Cambridge University Press.

Crafts, Nicholas and Harley, Knick. 1992. "Output, Growth and the British Industrial Revolution. A Restatement of the Crafts-Harley View." *Economic History Review* 45, (4).

Crafts, Nicholas and Mills, Terrence. 2016. "Six Centuries of British Economic Growth" Working Paper 297, Warwick University.

Crouzet, François. 1980. "Towards an Export Economy: British Exports During the Industrial Revolution." *Explorations in Economic History* 17, (1).

Crouzet, François. 1987. *L'Economie Britannique et le Blocus Continental*: Paris: Presse Universitaire De France.

Crouzet, François. 1990. *Britain Ascendant: Comparative Studies in Franco-British History*: Cambridge: Cambridge University Press.

Crouzet, François. 1996. "The Second Hundred Years War. Some Reflections." *French History* 10, (4).

Crouzet, François. 2008. *La guerre economique Franco-Anglaise au XVIIIe Siecle*: Paris: Fayard.

Cuenca-Esterban, Javier. 1994. "British Textile Prices, 1770–1831. Are British Growth Rates Worth Revision Again?" *Economic History Review* 47, (1).

Cuenca-Esterban, Javier. 1997. "The Rising Share of Industrial Exports in Industrial Output, 1700–1851." *Journal of Economic History*, 57, (4).

Cuenca-Esterban, Javier. 2001. "The British Balance of Payments, 1772–1820: Indian Transfers and War Finance." *Economic History Review* 54, (1).

Cuenca-Esterban, Javier. 2007. "India's Contribution to the British Balance of Payments, 1757–1812." *Explorations in Economic History* 454, (2).

Daunton, Martin. 1998. *Progress and Poverty. An Economic and Social History of Britain 1700–1850*: Oxford: Oxford University Press.

Davis, Ralph. 1962. *The Rise of the English Shipping Industry*: London: Macmillan.

Davis, Ralph. 1973. *The Rise of Atlantic Economies*: Ithaca: Cornell University Press.

Davis, Ralph. 1979. *The Industrial Revolution and British Overseas Trade*: Leicester: Leicester University Press.

Dickinson, Harold (ed.). 1989. *Britain and the French Revolution*: Basingstoke: Palgrave.

Dickson, Peter. 2016. *The Financial Revolution in England. A Study in the Development of Public Credit 1688–1756:* London: Routledge.

Dincecco, Mark. 2011. *Political Transformation and Public Finances in Europe*: Cambridge: Cambridge University Press.

Dome, Takuo. 2004. *The Political Economy of Public Finance in Britain*: London: Routledge.

Edelstein, Michael. 1990. "What Price Cold War? Military Spending and Private Investment in the US, 1946–1979." *Cambridge Journal of Economics* 48 (2).

Ehrman, John. 1962. *The British Government and Commercial Negotiations with Europe, 1783–1793:* Cambridge: Cambridge University Press.

Ehrman, John. 1969. *The Younger Pitt. The Years of Acclaim*: London: Constable.

Emsley, Clive. 1979. *British Society and the French Wars*: London: Macmillan.

Feinstein, Charles. 1978. "Capital Formation in Great Britain." Mathias, Peter and Poston, Munia (eds.). *Cambridge Economic History of Europe*, 7. Cambridge: Cambridge University Press.

Feinstein, Charles. 1981. "Capital Accumulation in the Industrial Revolution" Floud, Roderick and McCloskey, Donald (eds.). *The Economic History of Britain Since 1700*, 1: Cambridge: Cambridge University Press.

Feinstein, Charles and Pollard, Sydney (eds.). 1988. *Studies in Capital Formation in the United Kingdom*: Oxford: Oxford University Press.

Feinstein, Charles. 1998. "Pessimism Perpetuated: Real Wages and the Standard of Living in Britain During and After the Industrial Revolution." *Journal of Economic History* 58, (3).

Fetter, Frank. 1959. "The Politics of the Bullion Report." *Economica* 26/102.

Fetter, Frank. 1965. *The Development of British Monetary Orthodoxy*: Cambridge, Mass: Harvard University Press.

Findlay, Ronald et al (eds.). 2006. *Hecksher, International Trade and Economic History*: Cambridge, Mass: MIT Press.

Findlay, Ronald and O'Rourke, Kevin. 2007. *Power and Plenty. Trade, War and the World Economy in the Second Millennium*: Princeton: Princeton University Press.

Flinn, Michael. 1984. *History of the British Coal Industry*, 2 vols: Oxford: Oxford University Press.

Fortescue, John. 1910. *A History of the British Army*: London: Macmillan.

Friedman, Benjamin. 1984. "The Effects of Large Government Deficits on Interest Rates and Equity Returns." *Oxford Review of Economic Policy*, 1, (2).

Fynn-Paul, Jeff. 2014. (ed.). *War Entrepreneurs and the State in Europe and the Mediterranean 1300–1800*. Leiden: Brill.

Galloway, Robert. 1893. *Annals of Coal Mining*: London: Colliery Guardian.

Gambles, Anna. 1996. *The Boundaries of Political Economy. Tory Economic Arguments 1809–47*: Oxford: Unpublished thesis.

Gant, John. 2015. *The Sustainability of Britain's Public Debt in the Period 1765–1850*. Unpublished Master's Thesis, Department of Economic History, London School of Economics.

Gauci, Paul. 2006. *Expansion of the World. The Merchants of London, 1660–1800*: Oxford: Oxford University Press.

Gayer, Arthur et al. 1953. *Growth and Fluctuations in the British Economy*, 2 vols: Oxford: Oxford University Press.

Gee, Austin. 2003. *The British Volunteer Movement, 1794–1814*: Oxford: Oxford University Press.

Glete, Jan. 1993. *Navies and Nations. Warships, Navies and State Building*: Stockholm: Almquist.

Glover, Richard. 1963. *Britain at Bay*: London: Allen and Unwin.

Gordon, Barry. 1976. *Political Economy in Parliament 1819–23*: London: Macmillan.

Gordon, Barry. 1979. *Economic Doctrine and Tory Liberalism, 1824–30*: London, Macmillan.

Graham, Aaron and Walsh, Patrick. 2016. *The British Fiscal Military State, 1660–1783*: Farnham: Ashgate.

Greenwood, James. 1942. "British Loss of Life in the Wars, 1793–1815 and 1914–18." *Journal of the Royal Statistical Society* 105, (1).

Hargreaves, Eric. 1930. *The National Debt*. London: Arnold.

Harvey, Arnold. 1978. *Britain in the Early Nineteenth Century*: London: Batsford.

Harvey, Arnold. 1992. *Collision of Empires. Britain in Three World Wars, 1793–1815*: London: Hambledon.

He, Wenkai. 2013. *Paths Towards the Modern Fiscal State. England, Japan and China*: Cambridge, Mass: Harvard University Press.

Heim, Carol and Mirowski, Philip. 1987. "Interest Rates and Crowding Out During Britain's Industrial Revolution." *Journal of Economic History*, 47 (1).

Herman, Arthur. 2005. *To Rule the Waves: How the British Navy Shaped the Modern World*: London: Hodder & Stoughton.

Hilton, Boyd. 1977. *Corn, Cash and Commerce*: Oxford: Oxford University Press.

Hilton, Boyd. 2006. *A Mad, Bad and Dangerous People. England 1783–1846*: Oxford: Oxford University Press.

Hodge, Brian. 1855 and 1856. "On the Mortality from Naval Operations" and "On the Mortality Arising from Military Operations." *Journals of the Royal Statistical Society* 18, (3) and 19, (3).

Hoffman, Philip. 2015. *Why Did Europe Conquer the World?*: Princeton: Princeton University Press.

Holsti, Kalevi. 1991. *Peace and War. Conflicts and the International Order, 1648–1989*: Cambridge: Cambridge University Press.

Hont, Istavan. 2005. *The Jealousy of Trade and the Nation State in Historical Perspective*: Cambridge: Cambridge University Press.

Hopitt, Julian. 2000. *A Land of Liberty, 1689–1727*. Oxford: Clarendon Press.

Hopkins, Antony. 2018. *The American Empire*: Princeton: Princeton University Press.

Horn, David. 1967. *Great Britain and Europe in the Eighteenth Century*: Oxford: Oxford University Press.

Horn, Jeffrey et al (eds). 2010. *Reconceptualizing the Industrial Revolution:* Cambridge, Mass: Harvard University Press.

Hudson, Patricia. 1995. *The Industrial Revolution*: London: Edward Arnold.

Hueckel, Glenn. 1973. "War and the British Economy, 1793–1815: A General Equilibrium Analysis." *Explorations in Economic History* 10, (4).

Hueckel, Glenn. 1973. "The Napoleonic Wars and their Impact on Factory Returns and Output Growth in England 1793–1815." *Journal of Economic History* 33, (1).

Hueckel, Glenn. 1976. "Relative Prices and Supply Response in English Agriculture During the Napoleonic Wars." *Economic History Review* 29, (3).

Hyde, Charles. 1977. *The British Iron Industry*: Princeton: Princeton University Press.

Imlah, Albert. 1958. *Economic Elements in the Pax Britannica*: Cambridge, Mass: Harvard University Press.

Israel, Jonathan. 2010. *Enlightenment Contested: Philosophy, Modernity and Emancipation of Man, 1670–1750*: Oxford: Oxford University Press.

Jackson, Robert. 1985. "Growth and Deceleration in English Agriculture." *Economic History Review* 38, (3).

James, Lawrence. 2001. *Warrior Race. History of the British at War:* London: St Martin's.

Jarrett. Mark. 2013. *The Congress of Vienna and its Legacy*: London: Tauris.

Jomo, Jamil and Reinert, Erik (eds). 2005. *Development Economics. How Schools of Economic Thought Have Addressed Development*: London: Zed.

Jones, David. 1989. *War and Economy in the Age of William III and Marlborough.* Oxford: Blackwell.

Jones, John. 1980. *Britain and the World 1649–1815*. Brighton: Harvester Press.

Juhász, Réka, 2018. "Temporary Protection and Technology Adoption: Evidence from the Napoleonic Blockade." *American Economic Review*, 108:11; 3339–3376.

Kelly, Morgan et al. 2014. "Precocious Albion: A New Interpretation of the Industrial Revolution." *Annual Reviews of Economics* (6).

Kennedy, William. 1913. *English Taxation 1646–1799*: London: Bell.

Knight, Roger. 2013. *Britain Against Napoleon. The Organization of Victory 1793–1815:* London: Allen-Lane.

Knight, Roger and Wilcox, Richard. 2010. *Sustaining the Fleet 1793–1815*: Woodbridge: Boydell Press.

Koehn, Nancy. 1994. *The Power of Commerce and Governance in the First British Empire*: Ithaca: Cornell University Press.

Lane, Frederick. 1979. *Profits from Power. Readings in Protection and Violence*: Albany: State University of New York.

Lavery, Brian. 1987. *The Arming and Fitting of English Ships of War*: London: Conway Maritime Press.

Lewis, Michael. 1960. *A Social History of the Navy*: London: Allen and Unwin.

Liss, Peggy. *Atlantic Empires. The Network of Trade and Revolution, 1713–1826.* Baltimore: Johns Hopkins University Press.

Lloyd, Christopher. 1968. *The British Seaman, 1200–1860*: London: Collins.

Lowe, Joseph. 1822. *The Present State of England*: London: Goldsmiths Collection.

MaCleod, Emma. 1998. Wars of Ideas. *British Attitudes to Wars Against Revolutionary France, 1792–1802*: Aldershot: Ashgate.

Magnusson, Lars. 1994. *Mercantilism: The Shaping of an Economic Language*: London: Routledge.

Magnusson, Lars. 2009. *Nation, State and the Industrial Revolution*: London: Routledge.

Malamina, Paulo. 2016 "Energy Consumption in England and Italy" In *Economic History Review* 69, (1).

Marshall, Peter (ed). 1998. *The Oxford History of the British Empire* vols 1–3: Oxford: Oxford University Press.
McCusker, John and Morgan, Kenneth (eds.). 2001. *The Early Modern Atlantic Economy*. Cambridge: Cambridge University Press.
McDonald, James. 2003: *A Free Nation Deep in Debt*: Princeton: Princeton University Press.
McGuffie, Thomas. 1956. "Recruiting for the Ranks of the Regular British Army." *Journal of the Society for Army Historical Research* 34, (1).
McKay, Derek and Scott. Hamish. 1983. *The Rise of the Great Powers, 1648–1815*: London: Longman.
Meredith, David and Oxley, Deborah. 2014. "Food and Fodders. Feeding Britain 1700–1900." *Past and Present* 222, (1).
Mokyr, Joel. 2009. *The Enlightened Economy. An Economic History of Britain*: New Haven: Yale University Press.
Mokyr, Joel and Savin, Norman. 1976. "Stagnation in Historical Perspective – the Napoleonic Wars Revisited." Uselding, Paul (ed.). *Research in Economic History* 1.
More, William. 1847. *The Commercial Policies of Pitt and Peel*: London: Murray.
Morgan, Victor. 1943. *The Theory and Practice of Central Banking, 1797–1913:* Cambridge: Cambridge University Press.
Morriss, Roger. 2011. *The Foundations of British Maritime Ascendency. Logistics and the State*: Cambridge: Cambridge University Press.
Morriss, Roger. 2020. *Science, Utility and British Naval Technology. Samuel Bentham and the Royal Dockyards*: London: Routledge.
Nash, R. 1997. "The Balance of Payments and Foreign Capital Flows in Eighteenth Century England." *Economic History Review*, 50, (1).
Neal, Larry. 1990. *The Rise of Financial Capitalism*: Cambridge: Cambridge University Press.
Neal, Larry. 1991. "A Tale of Two Revolutions. International Capital Flows 1789–1819" In *Bulletin of Economic Research* 43, (1).
O'Brien, Patrick. 1967. "Government Revenue 1793–1815: A Study in Fiscal and Financial Policy in the Wars Against France." D.Phil. University of Oxford.
O'Brien, Patrick. 1985. "Agriculture and the Home Market for English Industry 1660–1820." *English Historical Review* 397 (100).
O'Brien, Patrick. 1988. "The Political Economy of British Taxation, 1660–1815." *Economic History Review* 41, (1).
O'Brien, Patrick. 2006. "The Hanoverian State and the Defeat of the Continental System." Findlay, Ronald et al (eds.). *Heckscher, Eli, International Trade and Economic History*: Cambridge, Mass: MIT Press.

O'Brien, Patrick. 2007. "State Formation and the Construction of Institutions for the First Industrial Revolution." Chang, Ha-Joon (ed.). *Institutional Change and Economic Development*: New York: United Nations University Press.

O'Brien, Patrick. 2008. "Mercantilist Institutions for the Pursuit of Power with Profit. The Management of Britain's National Debt, 1756–1815." Caselli, Fausto (ed.). *Government Debts and Financial Markets in Europe*: London: Chatto.

O'Brien, Patrick. 2009. "Taxation for the Wars Against Revolutionary and Napoleonic France." Storrs, Christopher *The Fiscal Military State in Eighteenth Century Europe*: Farnham: Ashgate.

O'Brien, Patrick. 2011. "The Nature and Evolution of an Exceptional Fiscal State and its Possible Significance for the Precocious Commercialization and Industrialization of the British Economy from Cromwell to Nelson." *Economic History Review* 64, (2).

O'Brien, Patrick. 2014. "The Formation of States and Transitions to Modern Economies." Neal, Larry and Williams, Jeffrey (eds.) *The Cambridge History of Capitalism* 1, (12): Cambridge University Press.

O'Brien, Patrick. 2017. "The Contribution of Warfare with Revolutionary and Napoleonic Force to the Consolidation and Progress of the British Industrial Revolution." *Department of Economic History, L.S.E. Working Paper 259/2017*.

O'Brien, Patrick and Hunt, Philip. 1999. "England" In Bonney, Richard (ed.). *The Rise of the Fiscal State in Europe c. 1200–1815*: Oxford: Oxford University Press.

O'Brien, Patrick and Palma, Nuno. 2019. "Danger to the Old Lady of Threadneedle Street. The Bank Restriction Act and the Regime Shift to Paper Money 1797–1821." *European Review of Economic History*, 10 (22).

O'Brien, Patrick and Palma, Nuno. 2021. "Not An Ordinary Bank But A Great Engine of State. The Bank of England and the British Economy 1694–1844." *CEPR Discussion Paper* 15400.

O'Connell, Robert. 1989. *Of Arms and Men. A History of War, Weapons and Aggression*: New York: Oxford University Press.

Ormrod, David and Rommelse, Gijs. 2020. *War, Trade and the State*: London: Boydell.

O'Rourke, Kevin. 2006. "The Worldwide Impact of the French Revolutionary and Napoleonic Wars 1793–1815." *Journal of Global History* 1, (1).

Overton, Mark. 1996. *Agricultural Revolution in England. The Transformation of the Agrarian Economy, 1500–1800*: Cambridge: Cambridge University Press.

Page, Anthony. 2015. *Britain and the Seventy Years War 1744–1815*: Basingstoke: Palgrave.

Parkinson, Cyril. 1977. *Britannia Rules. The Classic Age of Naval History 1793–1815:* London: Weidenfeld and Nicolson.

Presnell, Leslie. 1956. *Country Banking in the Industrial Revolution*: Oxford: Oxford University Press.

Price, Richard. 1999. *British Society 1680–1980*: Cambridge: Cambridge University Press.

Prados De La Escosura, Leandro, 2004. *Exceptionalism and Industrialization. Britain and its European Rivals, 1688–1815*: Cambridge: Cambridge University Press.

Rashid, Shahidur. 1980. "Economists, Economic Historians and Mercantilism." *Scandinavian Economic History Review* 28, (1).

Reinert, Sophus. 2011. *Translating Empire. Emulation and the Origins of Political Economy*: Cambridge, Mass: Harvard University Press.

Riden, Philip. 1977. "The Output of the British Iron Industry before 1870." *Economic History Review* 30, (3).

Robson, Martin. 2014. *A History of the Royal Navy. The Napoleonic Wars*: London: Bloomsbury.

Rodger, Nicholas. 2004. *The Command of the Ocean. A Naval History of Britain, 1649–1815*: London: Allen-Lane.

Russell, Gillian. 1995. *The Theatres of War. Politics, Performance, Society*: Oxford: Oxford University Press.

Satia, Priya. 2018. *Empire of Guns. The Violent Making of the Industrial Revolution*: New York: Penguin.

Schaefer, Ronald. 1981. "The Entelechies of Mercantilism." *Scandinavian Economic History Review* 29, (1).

Schmoller, Gustav. 1896. *The Mercantile System and its Global Significance*: New York: Macmillan.

Silberling, Norman. 1924. "Financial and Monetary Policy in the Wars Against France." *Quarterly Journal of Economics* 38, (2).

Simms, Brendan. 2007. *Three Victories and a Defeat. The Rise and Fall of the First British Empire*: New York: Basic Books.

Stone, Lawrence (ed). 1994. *An Imperial State at War, 1689–1815*: London: Routledge.

Storrs, Christopher (ed). 2009. *The Fiscal Military State in Eighteenth Century Europe. Essays in Honour of P.M.G. Dickson*: Farnham: Ashgate.

Temin, Peter and Voth, Joachim. 2012. *Prometheus Reshackled. Goldsmiths, Banks and England's Financial Revolution after 1700:* Oxford: Oxford University Press.

Torres-Sánchez, Rafael. 2007. *War, State and Development. Fiscal Military States in the Eighteenth Century*: Pamplona: EUNSA.

Uglow, Jennifer. 2014. *In These Times. Living in Britain Through Napoleon's Wars, 1793–1815*: London: Faber and Faber.

Van Creveld, Martin. 1989. *Technology and War from 2000BC to the Present*: London: Touchstone.

Ventura, Jurgen and Voth, Joachim. 2015. "Debt with Growth. How Sovereign Debt Accelerated the First Industrial Revolution." *National Bureau of Economic Research Working Paper* 21280.

Viner, Jacob. 1955. *Studies in the Theory of International Trade*: London: Allen and Unwin.

Vries, Peer. 2015. *State, Economy and the Great Divergence. Great Britain and China 1680s-1850s*: London: Bloomsbury.

Ward, John. 1953. *The English Land Tax in the Eighteenth Century*: Oxford: Oxford University Press.

White, Archie. 1963. *The Story of Army Education 1643–1963*: London: Harrap.

Wilkinson, Clive. 2004. *The British Navy and the State in the Eighteenth Century*: London: Boydell Press.

Williams, Kevin. 1981. *From Pauperism to Poverty*: London: Routledge.

Williamson, Jeffrey. 1984. "Why Was British Growth So Slow during the Industrial Revolution?" *Journal of Economic History* 44, (3).

Williamson, Jeffrey. 1987. "Debating the British Industrial Revolution." Explorations in *Economic History* 24, (3).

Winter, Jay (ed). 1975. *War and Economic Development*: Cambridge: Cambridge University Press.

Wright, John. 1996. "Government Borrowing and the Interest Rates 1750–1815" (Unpublished paper, Trinity College, Oxford).

Wrigley, Antony. 2015. *The Path to Sustained Growth*: Cambridge: Cambridge University Press.

Zielinsky, Rosella. 2016. *How States Pay For Wars*: Ithaca: Cornell University Press.

CHAPTER 3

In the Epicentre of the Storm?: The Effects of the Revolution and Warfare on the French Economy, 1789–1815

Loïc Charles, Guillaume Daudin and Silvia Marzagalli

For more than two decades, France was the main protagonist in a period of almost continuous European warfare, beginning with the declaration of war voted by the National Assembly against the King of Bohemia and Hungary in April 1792. The Revolutionary and Napoleonic wars (1792/93–1815) were the consequence of a process set in motion by the Estates General's decision in June 1789 to transform France into a constitutional monarchy. The difficulties of stabilizing the new political foundations were exacerbated by the King's attempt to flee from France in June 1791, after which many of the competing parties hoped a war would help to advance their cause – be it the restoration of the Old Regime, or the permanent establishment of a new political constitution. By the end of 1792, France was fighting against a large coalition, reinforced by Great Britain and the Netherlands the following year. This conflict shaped the course of the revolutionary process. The successes of the French Revolutionary armies changed its nature from a defensive to an offensive war. By seizing power through a *coup d'état* in 1799, Bonaparte sought to use military conquest both as a source of legitimacy and as a mean to externalise France's financial burdens. Thus, war was one of the pillars of the Napoleonic empire.

It is very difficult to disentangle the consequences of war on the French economy from those linked to political decisions in Revolutionary and Napoleonic France. Would, for instance, the 1789 nationalisation of Church real estate have produced the same results for the structure of ownership if the French revolutionaries had not been compelled to indiscriminately increase the issues of paper money (*assignats*), which were originally secured on nationalised ecclesiastical property, to wage the conflict? And would the slave revolt in Saint-Domingue, which started in August 1791, have resulted in the 1794 abolition of slavery and in Haitian independence in 1804, if France had not been at war, and therefore unable to dispatch military forces across the Atlantic?

 | DOI:10.1163/9789004472754_004

An additional difficulty in assessing the evolution of the French economy during this period stems from the fact that the historiographical debate on these issues has long been deeply affected by scholars' ideological positions on the Revolution.[1] Historians have focused on the Revolution as such, rather than on warfare, as the key force driving the economic changes that occurred in France. French historians have acrimoniously debated the consequences of the Revolution upon the economy. Whereas Marxist historiography presented it as a fundamental momentum in the transition toward a capitalist economy – best illustrated by the end of the seigneurial system, the establishment of a modern system of property rights, and the dissolutions of guilds – others stressed its disruptive effects on France''s economic growth, and more particularly on its trade and urbanisation.[2]

Because the major political changes that occurred in France during the Revolutionary and Napoleonic era cannot be separated from warfare, nor disentangled from intrinsic ideological biases, we have decided to proceed by comparing the French economy before and after the Revolution. We propose to discuss the evolution of the French economy during the period that opened with the fall of the Bastille and closed with the final collapse of the French Empire in 1815, by prioritising a long-term view. We believe it is only by adopting this perspective that historians might provide a convincing analysis of the economic consequences of the 1789–1815 conjuncture.[3] This study therefore compares the situation and dynamics of the French economy in the decades preceding the Revolution and those following the Restoration.

The first section discusses the institutional transformations that took place between 1789 and 1815. They reinforced the authority of the central state, the rural world and small cities. The second section adopts a disaggregated approach in order to establish that the French economy was structurally different after 1815. Finally, the last section presents the macroeconomic trends for the French economy from c.1715 to c.1848. Institutional and geographical changes during this period contributed to the opposition between 'Paris and the French desert'. (Gravier 1947; Fox 1971) Along with major social upheavals,

1 For a general bibliography and a comprehensive assessment of this debate, see the special issue of the *Revue économique* on this subject in 1989.

2 However, the recent Marxist historiography tend to lessen the impact of the French revolution and Napoleon's Empire on the French economy and argued that it was only through the agency of the French state that France finally became a capitalist and industrialised country (Lafrance 2019).

3 This methodological stance should not be taken as a sign that we believe that political and military events did not affect the French economy.

these changes shaped the rural, small-city France of the nineteenth century, that took an original path into the twentieth century. (O'Brien & Keyder 2012) This was detrimental to Atlantic France, big cities (especially ports) and, almost certainly, to France's overall macroeconomic dynamism.

1 Institutions

This section looks at long-term institutional changes introduced during the Revolutionary and Napoleonic era that impacted the evolution of the French economy. The Revolution initiated a profound reorganisation of French society and its foundations. It did away with privilege as the fundamental principle of political, social and economic structure. It simplified property rights through the generalisation of *propriété libre* (freehold), abolishing feudal and ecclesiastical institutions as well as marginalizing local rights. More generally, a strong centralised state came into being transforming permanently the general institutional framework of the French economy and society. Historians argue that these reforms contributed to the modernisation of the French economy in the nineteenth century, and through their diffusion into polities under French military occupation during the Napoleon Empire was also a decisive factor in European modernization. (Acemoglu *et al.* 2011; Dincecco 2011; Yun-Casalilla & O'Brien 2012; Dincecco & Katz 2014; Lafrance 2019)

1.1 *Disappointing Reforms?*

The First Republic introduced a set of institutional reforms that were later confirmed and deepened by the Napoleonic administration. They transformed the social and cultural environments in which the economy was embedded, but their aggregate effects are difficult to measure.

The abolition of all internal barriers and tariffs and the liberalisation of the labour market were among the first political decisions made by the French National Assembly. Although the state allowed the reintroduction of certain tolls, like the Parisian *octroi*, to sustain municipal budgets and to pay for the maintenance of roads, the new system was much lighter than the old one. (Conchon 2002) The unification of weights and measures, the introduction of a decimal system, and the 1807 *Code du Commerce* promoted the circulation of goods and complemented Colbert's ordinance of 1673, which had already unified commercial law.

The low speed and high-cost overland transportation system of France had long been recognised as a major impediment to internal trade and economic efficiency. (Daudin 2010) The eighteenth-century state had already improved the road network (Arbellot 1973; Blond 2014): according to a nineteenth-century survey, the mean speed (including stops) of the *Messageries* was 2.2 kph in the seventeenth century, 3.4 kph in the late eighteenth century, and 4.3 kph in 1814. (Foville 1880) Whereas it took two weeks to travel between Paris and Bordeaux in 1740, that time had already dropped to 6 days in 1780 and to 4–5 days by 1795. Warfare stimulated at least one major technological invention that speeded up the transmission of information, Chappe's telegraph, but it was restricted to a military use and not available to private businesses before the 1830s. Faster communication went along with a consistent decrease in transport prices, and nominal road transport costs declined by 51% between 1800 and 1820. (Chabert 1945)

Nevertheless, the overall transport network only improved slightly (see Figure 3.1). In the 1780s, there were approximately 25.000 km of 'royal roads.' During the Revolutionary and early Imperial period, the transport infrastructure was not a priority and deteriorated. Despite a significant effort to build new roads and canals to mitigate the effects of the British blockade, the total length of 'national roads' was only 27.000 km and that of canals only 1.271 km by 1814. (Chabert 1949, 304–306; Abellot, Lepetit & Bertrand 1987, 14) The evolution of the network of post roads (whether royal or national) confirms both the regression of the Revolutionary years and the recovery that followed. Nevertheless, this recovery was not rapid enough to catch up on Old Regime trends.

The impact of transport improvements on internal trade during the period remains debatable because data on most goods traded internally do not exist. (Daudin 2010) It is, however, possible to compare the situation in the grain market before 1789 and after 1815.[4] Measuring grain market integration based on the evolution of wheat price dispersion in France, suggests that, after some progress between 1750–1788, the 1793–1815 period was, at first approximation, one of strong market integration. However, this period is best represented as an exceptional phase of disintegration in 1793–1794, followed by a period of integration in 1812–1813. Outside of these dates, market integration did not make any significant progress. Over the long run, the trends before 1789 and after 1815 are similar. (Chevet & Saint-Amour 1992, 153; Saint-Amour & Chevet 1991, 93–119) The Old Regime trend towards greater market integration from 1700 to 1790 was thus interrupted by the

4 The Old Regime French economy was increasingly, but incompletely, integrated – the price of wheat on local markets could vary by 300%: Weir (1991), 926. In 1781–1787, a hectolitre of wheat cost 7.93 *livres tournois* in Douai (Nord) and 23.37 *livres tournois* in Aix (Bouches-du-Rhône).

FIGURE 3.1 Total length of post roads in km within current French borders, 1708–1833
SOURCE: VERDIER & BRETAGNOLLE (2007)

Revolution and warfare. While some market integration occurred during the French Empire, it was not statistically significant. (Federico 2012, 470–497)

New inheritance laws introduced by the Convention granted equal rights to all children. They aimed at fostering equality as the basis for a democratic regime. This was another important reform to a traditional system of property rights.[5] Tocqueville considered that this political decision multiplied the number of small properties – and thereby contributed to French agriculture's low propensity to innovate.[6] However, by 1846, the number of units of land ownership had in fact increased by a mere 5.9%, and this increase chiefly affected the largest parcels. (Steiner 2008, 84)[7] Thus, it is not clear that this reform did much to foster equality.

5 Napoleon's 1804 *Code civil* allowed people to favour, only very moderately, one child over the others.

6 Negative judgments on smaller holdings can be traced back to physiocratic ideas. Lemarchand (2008), 234–235 offers a more nuanced picture and stresses how the persistence of small property mitigated the social tragedies of rapid industrialisation.

7 Industrial capital found an effective means of avoiding too much division through inheritance, mainly through inbred marriage: Hirsch (1991), 291–312.

The educational system was largely taken over by the state after 1789. After a short-lived attempt to offer free education for all children in 1793, the Revolutionaries opted for a more limited policy by focusing on the formation of a new elite. This led for example to the creation of the *lycées* (secondary education institutions for boys aged 10 and over). Over a third of their positions were reserved for the sons of civil servants and military officers. A nationwide selective examination was introduced for the recruitment of teachers, it still exists today. The foundation of the *Grandes Écoles* had begun in mid-eighteenth century, with the *École des ponts et chaussées* in 1747 followed by the *École des mines* in 1783. In 1794, the Revolutionaries established the *École polytechnique*, the *Conservatoire national des arts et métiers* and the *École Normale.* The Restoration introduced the *École Normale supérieure de commerce* (1819), among other institutions. The effect on the general population was minimal. Literacy continued to improve during the period, but the trend witnesses no radical change. Men and North-eastern France continued to be considerably more literate than the rest of the French population.

The example of education suggests the outcomes of the institutional reforms of the Revolution on the population at large should not be overestimated. However, these reforms did change the composition of the elites. Social background remained as the fundamental element in determining access to education, but birth alone no longer guaranteed access to positions of wealth and power. Upward mobility was promoted, but the main beneficiary of these institutional reforms was the central state.

1.2 *The Central State*

On the eve of the French Revolution, half of state income was transferred as interest on the public debt. This large debt was the result of the persistent structural imbalance between state revenues and expenditures. (Guery 1978, 216–239; Morineau 1980, 269–336) This abysmal deficit and debt were exacerbated by the absence of institutions to assist the state to fund extraordinary needs in times of war. French Kings were obliged to contract loans on disadvantageous terms. Repeated attempts to reform the fiscal system proved fatal to the absolute monarchy, leading to the convocation of the Estates General in 1789 and an awakening of hopes for a profound reform to relations between the monarchy and the country's economic elites. (Bosher 1964; Bonney 2004, 191–215; White 1995, 227–255) Fiscal reforms – including the rationalisation of the administration in charge of the treasury and tax collection – were promoted by the Revolutionaries to manage a sovereign debt that had led to the collapse of the Old Regime. In parallel, the creation of the *Banque de France* in 1800 provided a solution to the issue of public credit.

During the Revolutionary and Napoleonic period, profits from the nationalisation and sale of Church property were allocated to repay the sovereign debt, while the cost of warfare was carried in large part by conquered economies. From 1805 to 1814, Napoleonic expenditures amounted to 8,347 million francs, including 5,610 on the armed forces. French taxation covered all civil expenditures, and 49% of war expenditures. The remainder was largely financed through the extraction of resources from plunder, requisitions, indemnities and war subsidies. (Branda 2007, 358)

By 1815, the total French debt amounted to 695 million Francs, compared to more than 3 billion in 1789. (Branda 2007, 496) Although Revolutionary governments recognised the debts of the Old Regime, the sale of ecclesiastical estates, the inflation of the *assignats*, and the 1797 repudiation of two-thirds of the nominal value of the French debt, more or less abolished it. This reduction is all the more impressive given that France was almost continuously at war for 22 years. State expenditure rose from 550 million in 1801 to 975 million in 1813, when war costs absorbed between 74% of the total. (Branda 2007, 358) By that time, half of the cost of warfare was funded by forced contributions from allies and defeated enemies. Military victories extended the French fiscal base and the number of tax-payers. Napoleon did not borrow to pay for the cost of war, but he increasingly resorted to war indemnities – a strategy that lasted until 1811. Indemnities effectively levied on Austria, Prussia, the Italian peninsula and Portugal during the Napoleonic wars amounted to at least 400 million francs (Gabillard 1953, 359–60), and trade statistics record total imports of 631 million francs' worth of precious metal between 1797 and 1814. (TOFLIT18 data) A large but unquantifiable portion of war-related costs, however, was not recorded in the French budget, as requisitions were directly spent abroad by the army.

Warfare was also financed by national tax payers. Their compliance was facilitated by the suppression of feudal and ecclesiastical dues and by the rationalisation of the fiscal administration during the turmoil of the Revolution. The move from a system of tax farming to a system of direct collection ensured that a larger share of collected taxes made their way into the state's coffers. (White 2004, 636–663; Johnson 2006, 963–991) The abolition of venality in the legal and fiscal administration of France and the introduction of recruitment on the basis of merit for state employees, had net positive effects on tax revenues. (Doyle 1996) Figure 3.2 contrasts the actual growth of per capita state income after 1788 with its projected evolution based on the 1740–1788 geometric trend. Central state income increased strongly after 1815 (Dincecco 2011, 137–147), but because of the disorganisation of the 1790s, France went through some years of very low taxation. As a result, the extra taxation from 1792 to 1815 was only

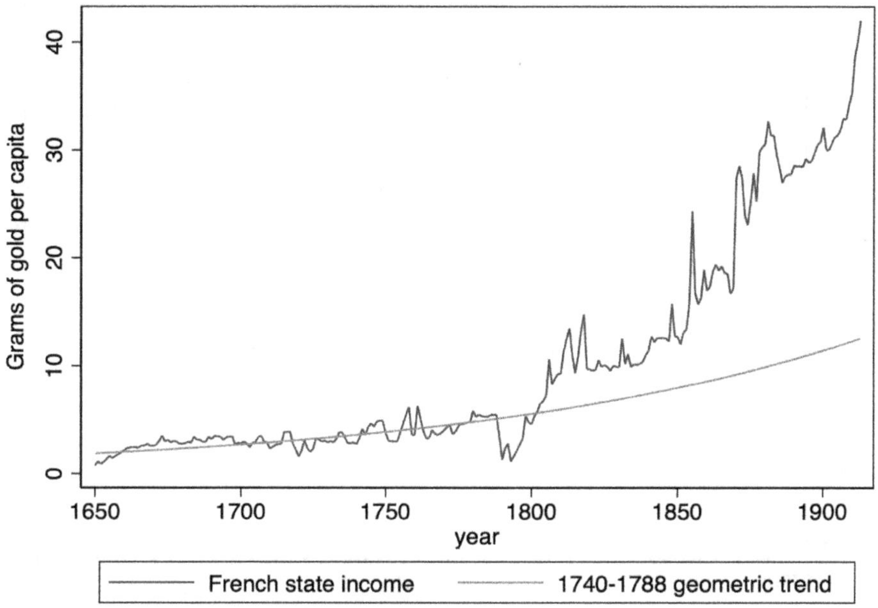

FIGURE 3.2 French state income, 1650–1913
SOURCE: DINCECCO 1991, AUTHORS' COMPUTATIONS

20% higher than the 1740–1788 geometric trend, while from 1804 to 1815 it rose to 65% above the geometric trend.

The evolution of the number of central state personnel is another sign of the improvement of the central state's capacity (see Figure 3.3). Some of these trends were visible before 1789, but the political and military situation that developed between 1792 and 1815 had a deep and lasting impact. The first peak of 1793–1795 corresponds to the intense mobilisation of the French state's resources to fight the counter-revolution on both internal and external fronts. This episode was followed by a period of consolidation during the Directory, when the disparate range of new functions was progressively standardised and rationalised across the central administration. This continued after the advent of Napoleon. If a viable system of formal career paths was not enforced at that time, some steps were taken in this direction. They initiated a tendency towards the rationalisation of the state bureaucracy that culminated in the reforms of 1944–1946. After 1818 (1819–1850), the number of public servants witnessed a slight growth, comparable to the pre-1793 period. There were, however, five times more civil servants employed in French ministries in 1820 compared to 1790.

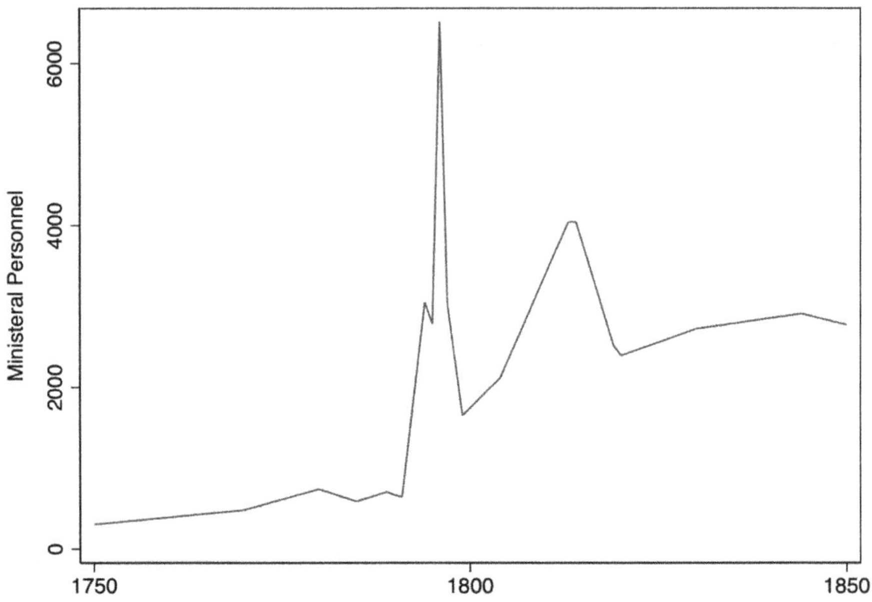

FIGURE 3.3 The growth of ministerial personnel, 1770–1850
SOURCE: CHURCH 1981, 73

This period also witnessed a deep change in the nature of the civil service. Before 1792, it was a collection of individuals who were dependent on office holders for their posts. Thereafter it evolved into a bureaucracy in the Weberian sense with a set of positions organised into a formal hierarchy, and a salariat of civil servants with foreseeable career prospects recruited, at least in principle if not in fact, on seniority and merit.

1.3 *The Rise of Rural France*

The central state was not the sole beneficiary of the institutional reforms initiated during the period, rural and small-city France also gained significantly. Under the Old Regime, French peasants who leased farmland experienced an increase in rents between 1726–1750 and 1781–1787. Rent rose faster than agricultural wages, but slower than wheat prices. (Weir 1991, 934–935) Landowners and, perhaps even more so, owners of seigneurial privileges were thus the main beneficiaries of agricultural growth.[8] Most rent was transferred to a small

8 For a thorough discussion of the differences between rents linked to landowning, and owning of seigneurial privileges and their evolution in the eighteenth century, see O'Brien and Heath (1994), 23–62.

elite. The Church owned 6.5% of French soil, the nobility slightly less than a third, and members of urban bourgeoisie approximately a quarter – with enormous differences across provinces – while the remainder (1/3) was owned by peasants. (Sée 1925) As state taxation fell on peasants rather than on landowners, the state did not benefit from the enrichment of the latter. Peasants were caught between the royal state, eager to increase taxation to meet its growing financial needs, and the rising rents imposed by landlords.

The nationalisation of Church estates was driven by fiscal urgency, due to the financial collapse of the monarchy. The nationalisation of ecclesiastical real estate in 1789 – followed by that of the property of the *émigrés* in 1792 – galvanised the market, and approximately 10% of the French farmland changed ownership. This shattered the social structure of the Old Regime beyond repair. The Church lost almost all its real estate and the share of land held by the nobility declined dramatically. At a micro level, the effects of the sale of nationalised estates were extremely diverse, and depended on the number and size of estates and on the varying ways (in time and space) in which they were sold. In some instances, transfers of land benefitted the urban bourgeois who received rents – a change that did not encourage innovation. At the same time, these changes benefitted manufacturers who needed space and real estate for their workshops, as well as peasants and farmers who worked the land they had bought. (Béaur, Minard & Laclau 1997, 48–49; Bodinier & Teyssier 2000) These effects were compounded by the hyperinflation episode of the *assignats* (1791–1795), which redistributed wealth from creditors to debtors. For the agricultural sector, historians consider that inflation had a redistributive impact comparable in magnitude to that of the nationalisation of ecclesiastical estates. (Béaur *et al.* 1997, 58)

The transformation of the taxation system also favoured the peasantry.[9] The reform of the tax system was understandably one of the first priorities of the French National Assembly. A set of small, but key universal taxes were introduced. The new fiscal system made landowners liable for direct taxes. And the new land tax was assessed on the basis of cadastral surveys, which were not completed until the 1840s. Other direct taxes were based on visible signs of wealth as well as on productive and commercial activities. This new system (which lasted with minor changes until World War I) significantly altered the distribution of wealth. Schnerb computed that the land tax amounted on average to 15% of gross agricultural output in 1791, but to less than 10% in 1821.

9 For a very good synthesis of the fiscal situation in the 1780s, and its evolution during the Revolution and the Empire, see White (1995), 227–255.

Furthermore, rates were equalised across the different parts of France.[10] The abolition of seigneurial dues contributed to a geographical equalisation of land tax. During the Old Regime, taxation differed greatly between French provinces. Taxes deprived peasants of approximately 15% of their income in the Toulouse region, but were consistently heavier in Bourgogne or Brittany. In these regions, before peasants paid taxes to the state and set aside seeds for the next sowing – which might require 20 to 25% of the wheat harvest – they delivered up to a quarter of their crops to the Church and local *seigneur.* (Gallet 1999) The suppression of both seigneurial dues and tithes not only improved fiscal uniformity across France, but it also alleviated burdens on peasants. In addition, in the interval between the abolition of non-state taxes collected by the Church and nobility and the reorganisation of taxation by the state, families enjoyed a few years of very low taxation in the early 1790s. (see Figure 3.2) In the long run, the purchasing power of the French peasantry as a whole increased. Furthermore, more clearly defined and stable property rights provided stronger incentives to improve the land. Although the effects of this radical change in taxation were delayed by war-related fiscal burdens, it certainly contributed to the dynamism of French agriculture after 1815. (Rosenthal 1992)

The creation of *départements* in 1790 also had a significant qualitative impact on the organisation of the French political economic space. *Départements* were smaller administrative units than Old Regime provinces. The reforms created new '*chefs-lieux*', or small administrative towns in the interior. They contrasted with the large cities that had played a central role in the Old Regime economy. *Chefs-lieux* provided a favourable institutional framework for the construction of new roads (and later railways), efficient public services, and a more geographically uniform allocation of state expenditures. Their populations grew at a faster pace than those of the largest cities, which also benefitted their agricultural hinterlands. (Margadant 1992; Lepetit 1988, 238–322) In contrast with the Old Regime, the consumption levels in rural areas and small cities grew significantly after 1815.

2 Structural Change

After the French Wars, the trajectory of the French economy became qualitatively different from that of the Old Regime, and the long-term impact of the

10 In 1791, the *département* burdened with the highest rates of taxation contributed seven times more revenue than *départements* with the lowest rates, but the ratio dropped to one to three by 1821: Schnerb (1972), 97.

institutional reforms associated with the Revolution and warfare will be clarified below by analysing the sectors of agriculture, foreign trade and industry.

2.1 *Agriculture*

Recent evaluations of the general trend in agricultural production are fairly convergent. (Postel-Vinay 1989, 1015–1046; Toutain 1992–1993; Toutain 1997; Daudin 2005, 31) Per capita output increased moderately throughout the eighteenth century, which among other things resulted in the disappearance of nationwide famines after 1709. Given that the population grew at a rate of 0.3% per annum, a plausible conjecture would be a 0.4% increase in the total production. Toutain's figures have been heavily criticised by historians who tend to focus on wheat production, which grew more slowly. (Le Roy Ladurie 1968, 1086–1102; Morineau 1971) Agreed, there was no major technical or institutional breakthrough in French agriculture before the Revolution, but this does not imply that the sector was stuck in a low level productivity trap. In fact, the proportion of wheat to other food crops decreased over the eighteenth century. Substitutes, such as rice, vegetables, and particularly maize and potatoes, gained ground in France over wheat, both in production and in consumption (especially among the lower classes). In addition, marketable outputs including wine, animal products, and raw materials for industry, acquired more importance. The consumption of additional non-starch substitutes for traditional foods and drinks, such as sugar, coffee, cocoa and tobacco, grew very fast. (Béaur 2000)

After 1815, French agriculture grew at an accelerated pace of around 1% per annum throughout the 1815–1850 period. To some extent, this faster growth reflected population trends (see section 3 below), but it was also due to the relative increase in agricultural prices that took place during and after the war period. (Verley 1997, 349–353) Although the trend had begun in the second half of the eighteenth century, agricultural prices rose steadily in the 1815–1850 period. The shares of substitutes for wheat (such as potatoes, maize and vegetables) continued to rise, and cash crops, such as wine, meat and beetroots, grew much faster than cereal production. The salaries of agricultural workers rose slightly more rapidly than those in the other sectors. Combined with very slow urbanisation, this implies that agriculture represented a large share of national income in the first half of the nineteenth century – more than 40% in the 1830s, and 37–38% in the 1850s and 1870s. The share of the population that depended on agriculture had been 66% in 1789 and 57% in 1846, which implies that there was a slight increase in agricultural production per worker. (Verley 1997, 356; Molinier 1977, 80) Institutional changes during this period favoured the French peasantry, but they also slowed down the economy's structural change.[11]

2.2 *International Trade*

External (including colonial) trade had been a dynamic sector across eighteenth century Europe. For France, the sum of imports and exports increased from 5.5% of GDP c.1720 to 20% of GDP in 1789 – the fastest increase in Europe. (O'Rourke, Prados de la Escosura and Daudin 2010, 106) The loss of Saint-Domingue in the Revolutionary turmoil, that of Mauritius in 1815, and the other effects of war reduced this ratio to 10% in 1820.[12] Steady growth barely resumed before the 1840s, and the ratio of openness achieved by the French economy in 1789 (20%) was not recovered until the 1860s. In absolute values (excluding the trade of precious metals), the mean annual value of imports and exports declined from 1 billion francs in 1787/1789 to 0.83 billion francs in 1818/1820; 30% of total exports in 1789 consisted of colonial re-exports: sugar, coffee, indigo, etc. By 1820, these trades had disappeared. Although it is difficult to assess the connections between re-exports and the long-term growth and structural change of the French economy, they were an important source of trading and shipping income for merchant capitalists, and their disappearance severely affected French Atlantic ports. Even if we exclude colonial re-exports from the analysis, trade was reduced by a quarter (instead of one half) in proportion to the GDP. The French share of the expanding global economy of the nineteenth century was much smaller than it could have been without the losses linked to the long-term effect of the English blockade and the shrinking of the French overseas possessions. Indeed, the net loss for the French port cities, maritime economy and merchant capitalism is sizeable. Here, Maps 3.1 and 3.2 illustrate the evolution and geographical transformation of French external trade.

The geography of trade changed, even if we exclude colonial trade and re-exports of colonial commodities (Table 3.1). The collapse of colonial trade was partly compensated for by the rise of trade with the United States. Other

---

11 Hoffman (1996), 194–198 argues that the French Revolution had on the whole a deleterious impact on agricultural productivity through a combination of devastations linked to warfare and troop movements, the destruction of the sources of agricultural capital, and the disruption of trade.

12 To some extent, the decline of the first French colonial empire began even before its peak with the loss of Newfoundland in 1713 and that of Canada in 1763. However, the losses associated with the 1792–1815 period were much more significant for external trade. They included the loss of markets in India and other places that were incorporated into the British Empire.

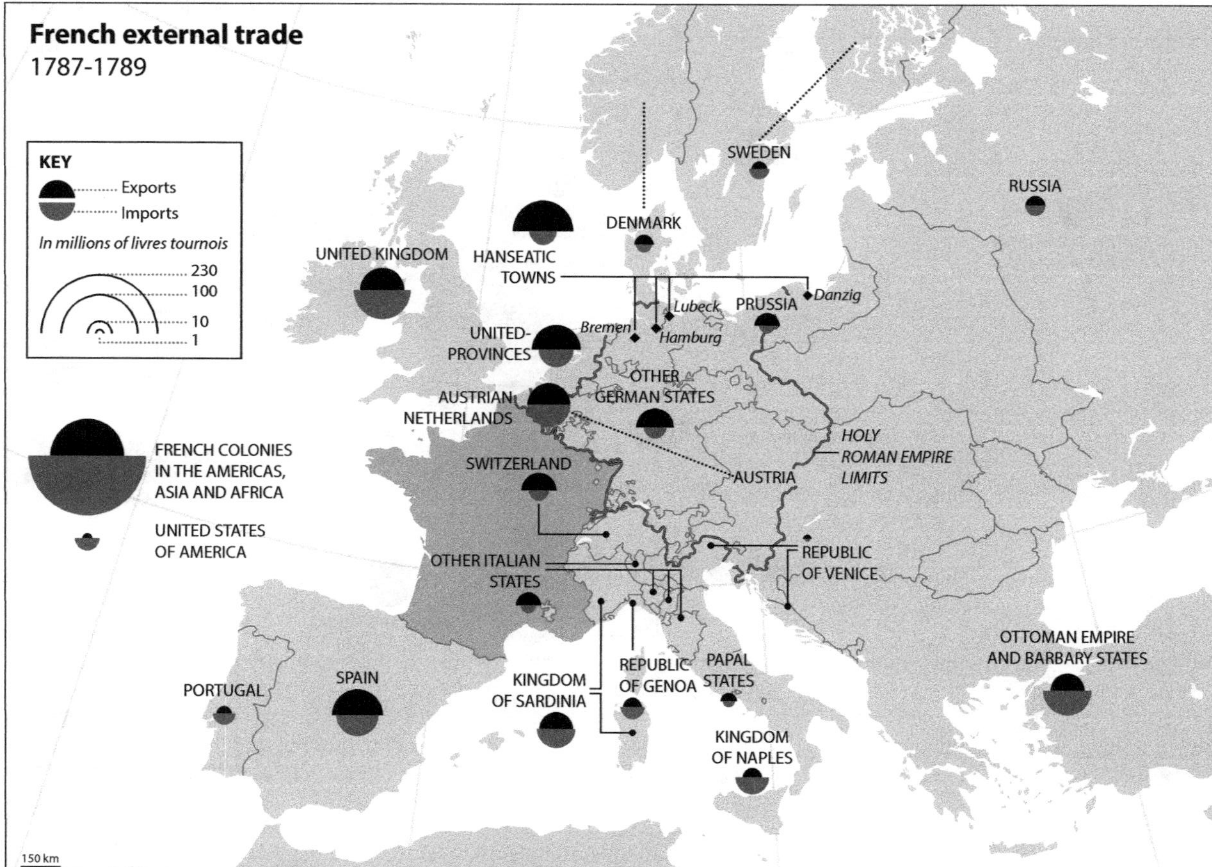

MAP 3.1 French external trade, 1787–1789

SOURCES: *ARCHIVES NATIONALES*, PARIS (HEREINAFTER AN) F12 251, AUTHORS' COMPUTATIONS

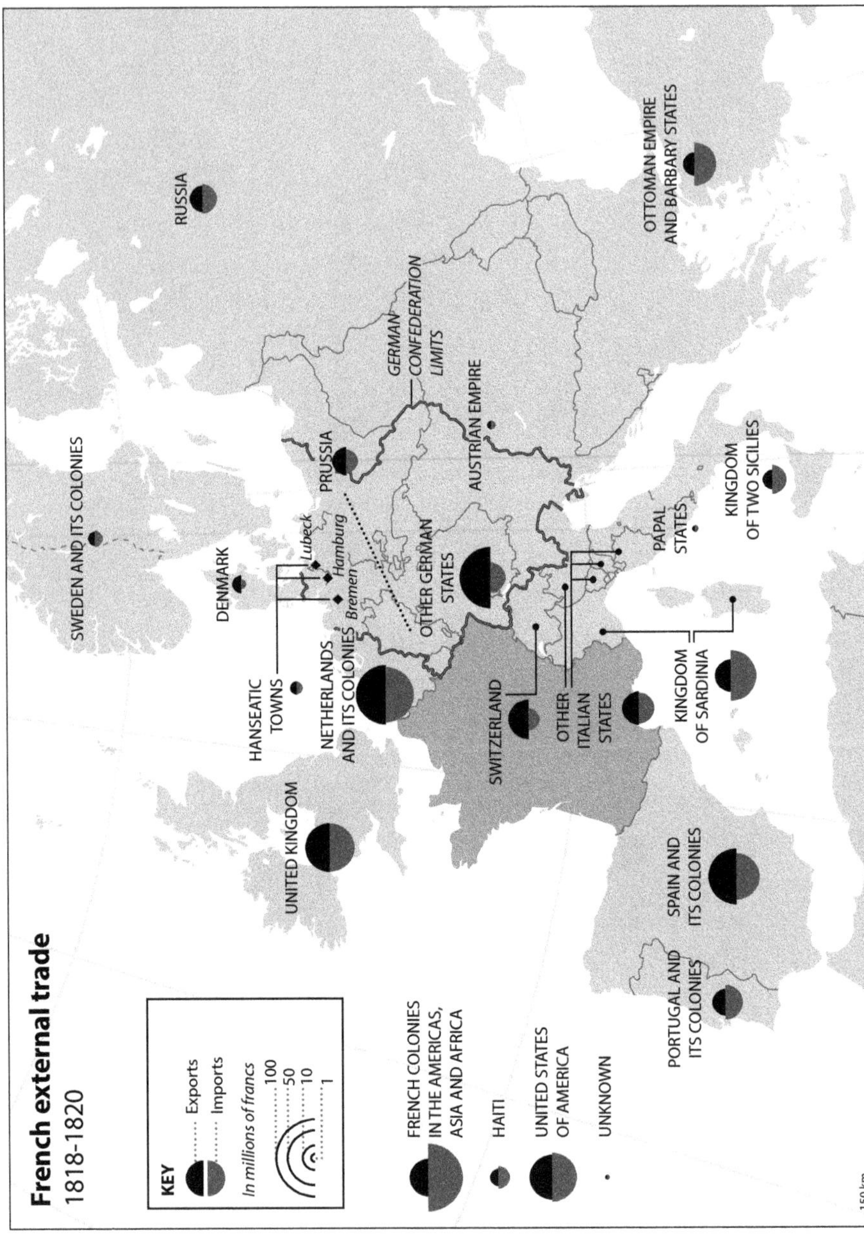

MAP 3.2 French external trade, 1818–1820
SOURCES: AN F12 251, AUTHORS' COMPUTATIONS

TABLE 3.1 French geography of trade, excluding precious metals, trade with the colonies and trade in plantation foodstuffs, 1787–1789 and 1818–1820

	1787–1789	1818–1820
'Italy'	18%	16%
United Kingdom	17%	11%
Holland (including Belgium)	16%	16%
Spain	13%	12%
Baltic, Scandinavia and Russia	11%	9%
Ottoman Empire and Barbary States	10%	6%
Land trade with Germany	6%	11%
Switzerland	4%	5%
United States of America	2%	10%
Portugal	2%	4%

SOURCES: AN F12 250, F12 1835 AND AUTHORS' COMPUTATIONS (SEE TOFLIT18 DATA HTTP://TOFLIT18.HYPOTHESES.ORG/). THE CORRELATION IS 0.65.

maritime trades declined (United Kingdom, North Africa and the Near East), whereas short-distance land trade (e.g. with 'Germany'), which had been encouraged by the Continental system, increased.

To some extent, the trade data enables us to identify structural changes in French trade between 1787/1789 and 1818/1820. The re-export trade of plantation foodstuffs virtually disappeared, even though colonial imports for domestic consumption remained significant. A few aspects remained unchanged, such as the importance of wine and industrial exports, and that of raw material imports.

On the eve of the French Revolution, industrial products accounted for some 53% of French domestic exports (TOFLIT18 data). This percentage was consistently lower than the ratio for Great Britain, which has led some historians to conclude that French trade did little to foster industrialization. (Meignen 1973, 583–614; Léon 1974, 407–432) This is confirmed by the dependency rate of most French industries on external markets, which can be computed by using the value-added estimates from the ISMEA team (see Figure 3.6). This rate was relatively small and declined further during the wars, which reinforces the argument about the rising importance of internal demand.

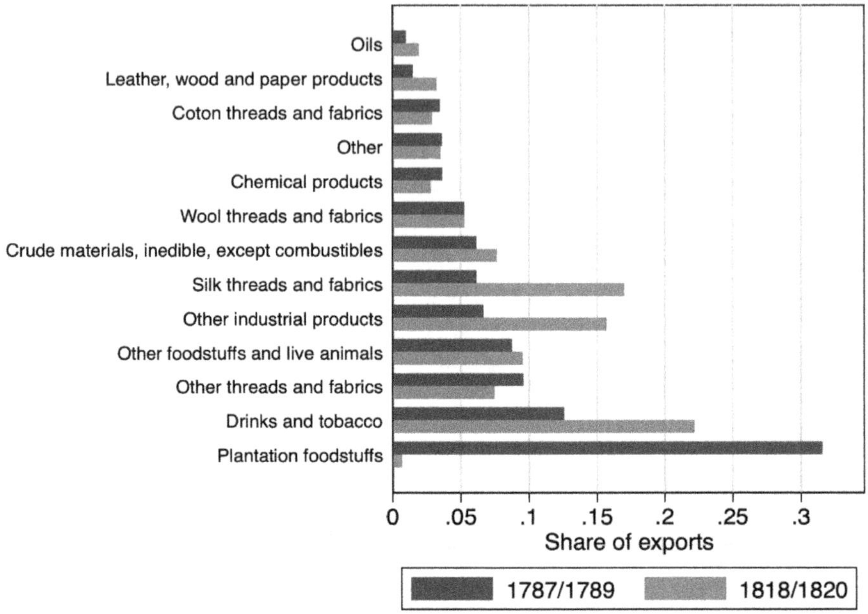

FIGURE 3.4 Sectoral shares of French exports
SOURCES: AN F12 251, TOFLIT18, AUTHORS' COMPUTATIONS

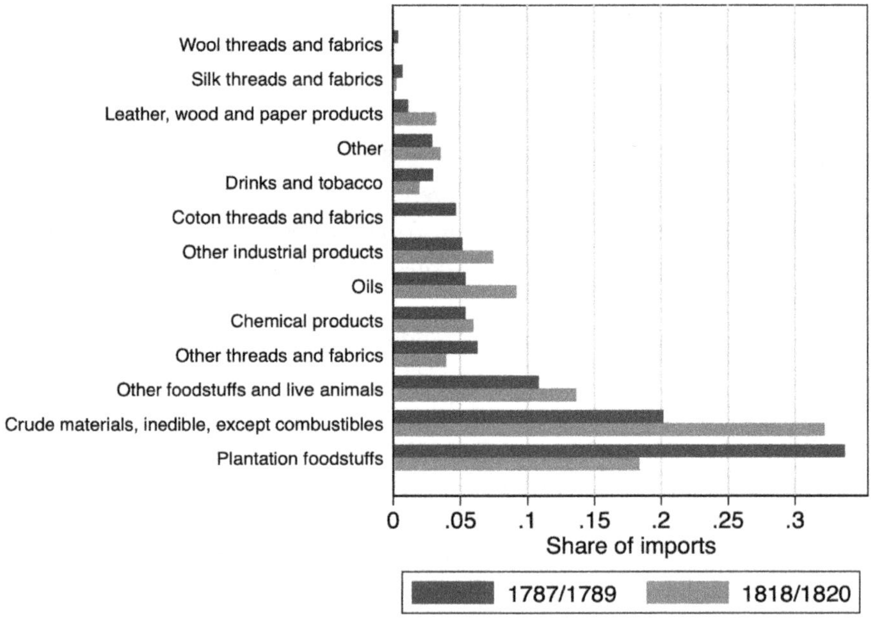

FIGURE 3.5 Sectoral share of French imports
SOURCES: AN F12 251, TOFLIT18 DATA, AUTHORS' COMPUTATIONS

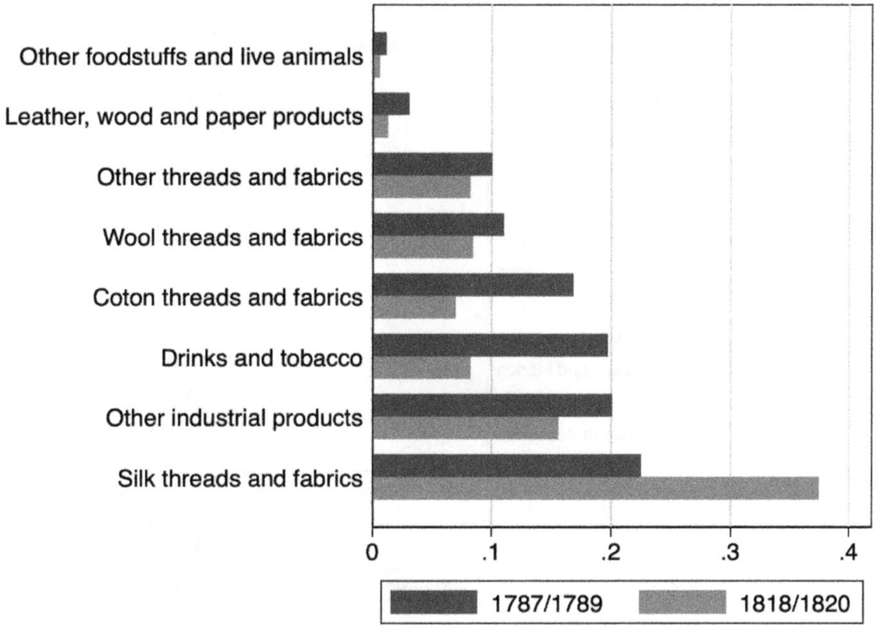

FIGURE 3.6 External market dependence rate of some French industries, 1787–89 and 1818–20
Note: External market dependence rate as measured by exports divided by value-added (including clothing for textile sectors).
SOURCES: TRADE: TOFLIT18 DATA. VALUE-ADDED: TOUTAIN (1961A, 212); TOUTAIN (1961B, 6); MARKOVITCH (1966, TABLE 3)

The industrial transformations induced by the events of 1792–1815 can be measured by identifying the evolution of the comparative advantage of the French economy revealed through the computation of 'Contributions to the Trade Balance' (CTB), as formulated by Lafay in 1992.[13] These figures measure the trade balance of each sector corrected for the overall trade balance, so that the sum of CTBs is equal to zero. The formula is:

$$CTB_k = \frac{100}{X+M} \bullet \left[(X_k - M_k) - (X - M) \bullet \left(\frac{X_k + M_k}{X+M} \right) \right]$$

13 We prefer this measure to the more usual Balassa indicator because of the prevalence of intra-industrial trade; in most sectors, France was both an importer and an exporter: Lafay (1992), 209–234.

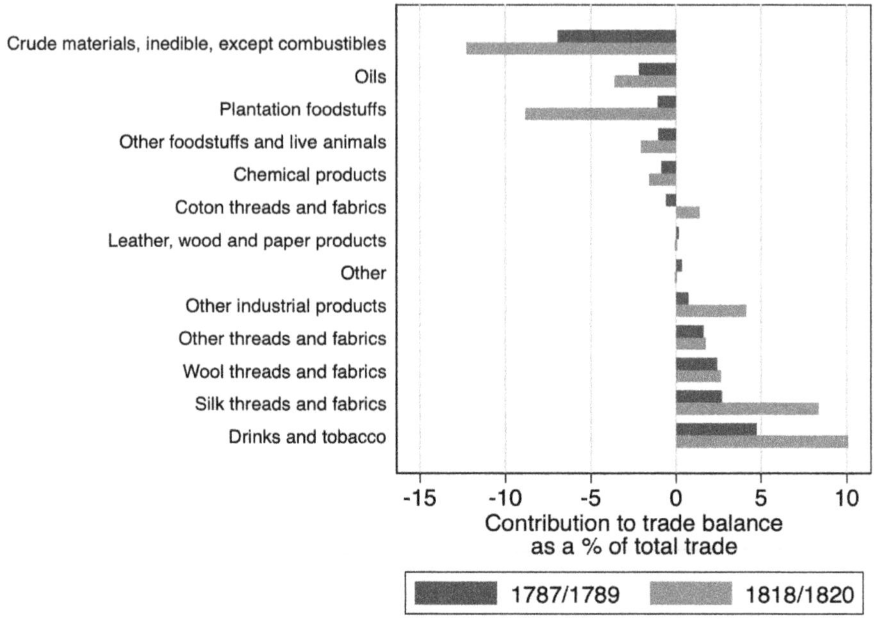

FIGURE 3.7 Sectoral contributions to trade balance, 1787–89 and 1818–20
SOURCES: AN F12 251, AUTHORS' COMPUTATIONS

where X and M are total exports and imports and X_k and M_k are sectoral exports and imports.

Figure 3.7 shows a strong continuity in France's comparative advantages. Except for the 'drinks and tobacco' sector (mostly wine), all surplus sectors weres industrial, both before 1789 after 1815. The largest deficit sector was raw materials. This is consistent with the trading profile of an industrial country. This argument is reinforced by the fact that cotton threads and fabrics moved from a deficit to a surplus sector. The Continental blockade had a positive and lasting impact on the French cotton industry. (Juhász 2018)

The variance of the CTB also increased during this period. This was partly due to the evolution of the total value of trade, and with the vanishing of colonial re-export trade, total trade was reduced. Thus, the CTB, expressed in percentage of total trade, increased. But even a 30% reduction in trade cannot account for the doubling of the CTB. Somewhat paradoxically, despite its lesser integration into world trade, France's specialisation deepened after 1815, suggesting that France was then more able to exploit its comparative advantages. This might have been due to a deeper international division of labour encouraged by the blockade and enforced by the Continental system,[14] which systematically encouraged French industrial exports and raw material imports. (Chabert 1949, 303) Alternatively, it might be correlated to the fact that the more 'superfluous' intra-industrial trade, reliant on the consumers' taste for diversity, was the first victim of decreasing trade volumes.

To summarise, the analysis of French foreign trade points to the disruptive effects of warfare, most notably on Atlantic trade, causing a collapse that affected the trajectory of French economic growth. The increase of non-maritime trade suggests that the wars probably encouraged the unification of Continental European markets, which benefitted Revolutionary and Napoleonic France. This might have partly compensated for the loss of the first French colonial empire. Furthermore, the institutional construction of a unified home market, combined with the proactive role of the Revolutionary and Napoleonic state, significantly increased the role of domestic demand for the French economy. Therefore, besides the mostly short-term negative macroeconomic effects that warfare had on the French economy, and in particular on foreign trade, these wars also triggered a deep geographical reorientation of French trade toward domestic – and to a lesser extent continental – markets.

Colonial markets lost their importance for French industrial products, and the rise of continental markets only partially compensated for this loss. Domestically, the redistribution of spending power from declining urban centres to the countryside, shifted demand away from semi-luxury industries and towards more basic goods. Since the demand for French luxury products did not decline, a dualism emerged in French industry. The Revolution and warfare thus witnessed a change in the structure and dynamism of the French economy. This process certainly had detrimental consequences on specific regions (Brittany and the South-West) that were previously dependent on colonial and overseas trade. On the other hand, new industries (chemicals, cotton, iron) in other regions benefited from this discontinuity.

2.3 *Industry*

Throughout the eighteenth century, the growth of French industry had been to a large extent driven by external trade. In such traditional textile sectors as

14 While the Continental Blockade aimed to shut out British trade and manufactured goods from the continent, the Continental System – a system of power relations within the continent – imposed trade treaties and duties upon vassal states and allies that aimed to secure the economic pre-eminence and international protection of French interests. On the conceptual differences, see Dufraisse (1966), 518–534. The impacts on different parts of Europe have recently been discussed in Joor and Aaslestad (2014).

cloth and linens, the rise was steady, if limited (about 1% per year), and faster before 1750 than after. The cotton, silk and iron industries were much more dynamic. The production of calicoes imitated from Asian products took off spectacularly after the removal of the ban in 1759. This link between industrial output and foreign markets was severed during the wars. Many industries suffered from the demise of the first French colonial empire and the continued difficulties of maritime trade.

The volume of French industrial output stagnated during the 1789–1815 period; the early 1790s were extremely disruptive for French industry. From 1793 onwards, the maritime war, combined with the effects of the revolt in Saint-Domingue, hit export industries severely. Furthermore, the chaotic situation in Vendée, and the violent repression of the Federalist movement during the Terror, generated negative shocks for French industrial production, for example for the woollen industry. (Chassagne 1978) The situation improved, and in the years before the crisis that spelled the end of the Napoleonic regime (1812–1815), French industry as a whole recovered. In the short term, protection from British competition was decisive, particularly for the cotton industry in Alsace and Northern France. (Juhász 2018) Since the data is either incomplete or unreliable, it would be difficult to provide a comparison of the total French industrial output before 1789 and after 1815. Most economic historians posit either very moderate growth, or stagnation.

The composition of industrial output was rather different in 1815 compared to 1789. At least two sectors – cotton and iron – experienced impressive growth as well as technological innovations. In cotton, from 1789 to 1814, the total number of mechanical mills in use in France rose from 6 to 272. This progression was not linear. From 1789 to 1799, there were few changes, but the industry changed rapidly from 1800 to 1806, although growth was negligible during the last years of the Empire. For example, the Languedoc textile industry shows that, in most cases, war-related demand sustained production, but often at a lower level compared to the 1780s. In the iron industry, total production increased from 600,000 tons in the late 1780s to 900,000 tons at the end of the Empire. The chemical industry also developed, but it remained a small sector. Traditional sectors, such as linen and hemp textiles, were on the wane, while woollens did slightly better. Silk, however, fared much better, as did most luxury industries.[15]

---

15 Figures for the cotton mills and iron industry come from Woronoff (1994), 193–194. For the Languedoc, see Johnson (1995).

The geographical location of industries over French territory changed considerably. The West of France (e.g. Brittany) began to de-industrialise. Northern and eastern France benefitted from the proximity of coal deposits and continental markets, while Paris gained from the increased centralisation of economic and political power and the revival of demand for its luxury industries. (Juhász 2018; Chassagne 1978; Bergeron 1978)

Without the Revolution and substantial warfare, extra-European markets would have been kept open to French industry, thereby benefitting sectors such as linen production in Western France. If the 1786 free trade Eden-Rayneval Treaty with Great Britain had been upheld, it is, however, unclear whether France could have developed an internationally competitive cotton industry or not. This context would have perhaps been more favourable to merchants than to industrialists.

3 Macroeconomic Trends

The decline of external, and the rise of rural, demand together with the consolidation of links with continental Europe, contributed to a wide sectoral and geographical rebalancing of the French economy. This rebalancing had an effect on long-term development as some sources of growth were thwarted. This section seeks to provide a better understanding of the nature of the impact that the 1789–1815 years had on the French economy by considering a period that runs from the death of Louis XIV in 1715 to the end of the July Monarchy in 1848.

For premodern economies such as France, population was one of the main, if not the main, macroeconomic variable. In comparison with other economic variables, the evolution of the French population over the long term is well documented. Within its 1789 frontiers, France grew from 24 million inhabitants in 1740, to 34 million in 1840. [16] (Table 3.2) Table 3.3 shows that the 1790–1815 period altered a century-long trend towards an accelerated population growth (despite a slight decrease in the natality rate from 1740). Table 3.4 shows that the most significant part of the loss occurred in the first five years. From 1792–97, wars against the European coalition as well as civil strife in Western France, had dire consequences for both birth and mortality rates. Moreover, there was significant emigration (around 200,000) due to the demise of the monarchy.

16 It should be noted that the 1815 frontiers were almost identical to those of 1789 but differed significantly from those after 1871.

TABLE 3.2 French population, 1740–1840

Year	1740	1765	1790	1815	1840
Population (millions)	24.108	25.578	28.028	29.694	34.202

SOURCE: SEE NOTE 17

The direct loss of French population due to the wars has been estimated at between 1.3 and 1.4 million from 1797 to 1815. (Henry and Blayo 1975) As a result, the actual rate of population increase was only 0.23% per annum compared to what it would predictably have been without the political turmoil – namely a natural rate of increase that could be crudely estimated at 0.44%.[17] This is indeed a notable short-term consequence that could be attributed to warfare.

However, recovery was quick. From 1795, when order was restored, the population grew again despite continuing external conflict, and it did so at a faster pace than before the Revolution despite the well-known, if unexplained decline of the natality rate.[18] During the Restoration, the losses were fully made up, and the annual growth rate for the 1790–1840 period was similar to that for 1740–1790.

When one goes into factors conditioning population growth, a pattern emerges. The mortality rate began to drop after the two major demographic crises: the 1709 famine and the 1720 plague (in Marseille and Provence) that followed the '*années de misère*'. Most of the gains resulted from the drop of infant mortality rates. At least until the end of the eighteenth century they were linked first and foremost to the disappearance of the mortality peaks

17 We obtained this figure by roughly adding up the various losses (civil and military deaths and emigration) to our total for 1815. The total population would then have been around 31.5 million instead of 29.694 million.

We calculated the data from the following sources: Dupâquier (1988); Henry and Blayo (1975). The evaluation of losses due to emigration is from Dupâquier (1988), 76; and that of those due to military losses is from Henry and Blayo (1975), 104–107. The various estimations of civil losses for the 1790–1795 period, especially in the Western part of France, are messy at best, since the records are unreliable in this period of quasi-civil war. Reasonable estimates go from 200,000 to 400,000 casualties (including disease outbreaks).

18 Conscription, introduced in 1798, increased the marriage rate (as married men were not called to serve in the army), and thus natality rates. For a detailed case study, see Jean-Pierre Bois (1976), 467–493.

TABLE 3.3 Growth of the French population, 1740–1840

Year	1740–1765	1765–1790	1790–1815	1815–1840
Annual rate of growth (%)	0.4	0.37	0.23 (0.44)	0.57

SOURCE: SEE NOTE 17

TABLE 3.4 Growth of the French population, 1780–1800

Year	1780–1790	1790–1795	1795–1800	1790–1800	1800–1815
Variation in population (thousands)	1,029	-400	890	490	1176
Annual rate of growth (%)	0.37	-0.28	0.63	0.17	0.26

SOURCE: SEE NOTE 17

associated with poor harvests.[19] This trend continued throughout the whole period, and were not significantly altered in the long term by the short-term mortality crises caused by revolutionary turmoil and the Napoleonic wars. Finally, the natality rate moved more slowly but began to drop in the 1740s, much earlier than anywhere else in Europe. This decline accelerated from the 1790s onward and ultimately accounted for the progressive slackening of the growth of the French population from 1840 onwards. All in all, the analysis of the long-term evolution of the French population suggests that warfare had a sizeable short-term impact, but a much smaller effect in the long term.

French population growth was significantly lower over the whole period than in other European countries, particularly England. The difference was limited during the first part of the eighteenth century, when only England and

19 From the last quarter of the eighteenth-century, inoculation campaigns also positively affected mortality rates.

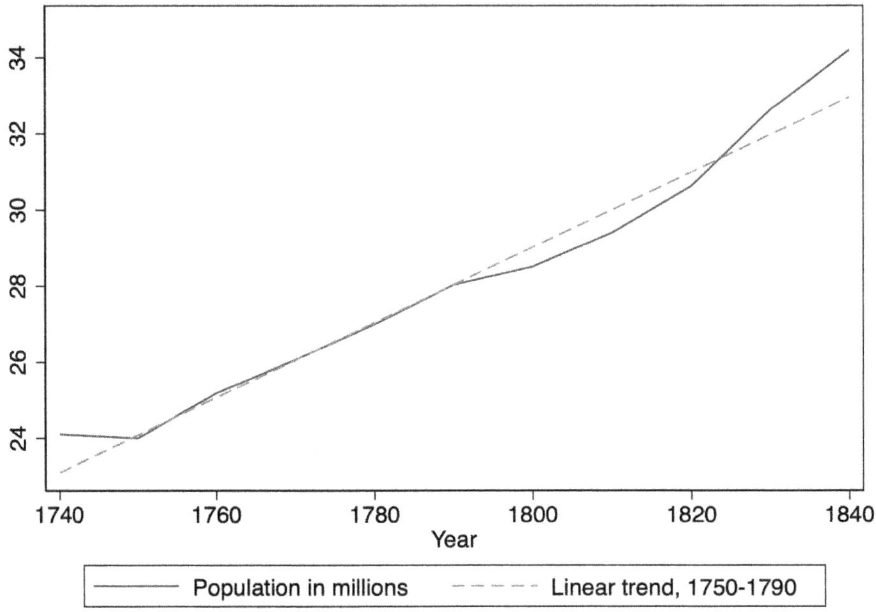

FIGURE 3.8 French population growth, 1740–1840
SOURCE: SEE NOTE 17

Russia significantly outperformed France. The 1789–1815 period represented a turning point, when the growth rate of the English population doubled (from 0.65% to 1.3%) and remained more or less at that level throughout the nineteenth century. By 1815, the population of the German states also began to grow at a much faster pace than the French population. (Bardet & Dupâquier 1998, 291 (England) and 406–407 (France)) These discrepancies had major implications in terms of economic growth, since they resulted in a relative slackening of French internal demand compared to the other North and West European regions, although France still remained the most populous country in Europe (excluding Russia). Counterfactually, if France had not experienced the Revolution and warfare, we have little evidence to suggest that the evolution of the total population would have been different. Yet, diminished reliance on the domestic market implies that the consequences for French industry would have been milder.

The strong impact of the French Revolution on the urbanisation of the French population also contributed to the relative weakness of French internal demand. Again, it seems that the crucial period comes before 1806, and that the Napoleonic wars had a weaker impact than the political turmoil caused by the Terror and the civil war that plagued large parts of French territory from

1793 to 1796. From 1780 to 1806, the combined population of the 10 biggest French cities stalled (1.256 million compared to 1.215 million in 1780). Growth started again in the 1800s, but as a whole the proportion of the population living in cities decreased slightly from 1789 to 1815 and only grew very slowly after 1815. The French rate of urbanisation (i.e., the share of the population living in cities of over 2,000 inhabitants) can be estimated at 18% in 1740, 20.5% in 1790, 19% in 1806 and 21.5% in 1836. (Lepetit 1988, 399) Major Atlantic port cities such as Bordeaux and Nantes, which enjoyed a rapid growth during the eighteenth century, never recovered their dynamism in the nineteenth century. (Lepetit 1988, Appendix 2) Demographic and urbanisation factors are important because all the countries or regions (including France) that underwent a slower demographic and urban growth during this period (including the Netherlands, Spain, Portugal and Italy) experienced significant declines in urbanization and lower economic growth rates compared to more dynamic regions (England, Switzerland, Belgium and even the German states) from agglomeration.

There is no consensus on the evolution of French gross domestic product. Data for the pre-1789 period was published by the ISEA in the early 1960s and revised in the 1990s. This data was based on contemporary estimates. (Molinier 1957, 875–897; Marczewski 1961, 369–86) Evidence is weak, but Morrisson and Daudin have published plausible conjectures for the growth of GDP for the 1715–1789 period: 0.6% (Daudin 2005) and 0.4% (Morrisson 2007, 153–165) The lower bound estimate assumes that it was equal to the rate of population growth, or 0.3% per annum.[20] Although Leonardo Ridolfi recently argued in his Ph.D. thesis that the French GDP per capita stagnated during the eighteenth century, his argument goes against the grain of both quantitative and qualitative evidence. (Ridolfi 2016 and Ridolfi 2019) The only reliable macroeconomic variable is based on data for external trade; this grew at a fast pace both in absolute terms (2.25% per annum) and per capita terms (1.95%) from 1715 to 1789. Moreover, it has been established that the end of famine-related mortality crises after 1709 was an acceptable proxy for increases in the French standard of living. (Daudin 2005, 218–220; Braudel & Labrousse 1993, 693–708)[21]

The consensus among economic historians is, however, that growth decelerated from 1789 to 1815. This was not because of material losses. Despite the seizure of ships, and the loss of private property in Haiti, war was not as destructive as it became in the twentieth century. Most of the military action occurred

20 Daudin (2005) selects 0.24%, but he uses population totals from Henry and Blayo (1975). This article uses re-evaluated figures from Dupâquier (1988).

21 See above for detail on external trade and agriculture production.

outside France. For part of the Napoleonic period (1803–1812), Toutain's estimates refer to an annual GDP growth of 0.41%, which is barely more than the demographic growth rate. The evidence, such as it is, seems to indicate that, at best, the same GDP per capita growth rate prevailed for the Revolutionary years, when the state's statistical apparatus was disrupted and hyperinflation renders a precise evaluation impossible. According to Toutain, this trend continued for some time during the Restoration period, which implies that GDP growth per capita for the decade 1815–1824 was a mere 0.11% per annum. (Toutain 1997, 18–19) This rate accelerated again in the subsequent decade and stayed at a high level until the political and economic crises of 1848. The overall trend seems to be congruent with trends in the evolution of the French population. The period provoked an important deviation from the French economy's long-term trend, but the divergence was only temporary. Compared to Britain, the important point to emphasize is that French growth did not accelerate. The differential in income per head that increased from 1789 to 1815 persisted until the early twentieth century. French GDP per capita was 75% of the British one around 1789 and only reached the same level around 1900. (Bolt *et al.* 2018)

4 Conclusion

The Revolution and Napoleonic Imperialism altered French economic development in very profound ways. Whereas before the Revolution, the French economy was relatively open to external trade, by 1815 the picture had changed dramatically. External trade had been shattered by more than two decades of war and blockades, and most of the dynamism of the French economy had been transferred from coastal ports and regions to the interior, making way for what the historian Edward Fox has labelled the 'Other France.' (Fox 1971; Crouzet 1964, 567–588) Warfare comes at a cost, and growth remained slow between 1789 to 1815. Furthermore, the redistribution of land and the transformation of the fiscal system changed the foundations for the growth of the French economy. In eighteenth-century France, demand for manufactured commodities was driven by foreign trade and increasingly by the expenditures of rich and urban elites, both noble and non-noble – a pattern with strong similarities to England. After 1815, the incomes and consumption of peasants was the main source of demand for French industrial products. In essence, the growth of the French economy throughout the nineteenth century was sustained by internal demand, which stemmed basically from the rural population rather than the urban bourgeoisie. This made the slow demographic growth of France more of a handicap that it could have been without the 1789–1815 political upheavals and their consequences on French trade. Due to the slow growth of the French population and the slow rate of urbanisation, growth was also less dynamic than in other European countries, such as Belgium, England, Switzerland and Germany. France represents a case of too much structural change rather than too little.

That said, we have found it difficult to devise a counterfactual. The Revolution and the Empire shaped France, and it is difficult to imagine the country without these events. More fundamentally, devising a counterfactual requires passing judgement on the political, social and economic sustainability of the Old Regime, which was based on internal privileges and on slavery in the colonies. Although the history of nineteenth century Central and Eastern Europe and that of the Southern United States show that its quick demise was not inevitable, it is doubtful that such a system was compatible with modern economic growth in the long run. Still, the geographical and structural break introduced by the Revolution and the Empire and its associated costs were not necessary for the transformation of France into a modern economy. We can only imagine a more gradual process that might not have engulfed Europe in a protracted period of warfare.

References

Acemoglu, Daron, Davide Cantoni, Simon Johnson, and James A. Robinson. 2011. "The Consequences of Radical Reform: The French Revolution." *American Economic Review* 101, 7: 1–30.

Arbellot, Guy. 1973. "La grande mutation des routes en France au XVIIIe siècle". *Annales. Économies, Sociétés, Civilisations* 28, 3: 765–791.

Abellot, Guy, Bernard Lepetit, and Jacques Bertrand. 1987. *Atlas de la Révolution Française : 1. Routes et Communications*. Paris: Éditions de l'EHESS.

Bardet, Jean-Pierre, and Jacques Dupâquier. 1998. *Histoire des populations de l'Europe*, vol. 2, *La Révolution démographiques*. Paris: Fayard.

Béaur, Gérard, Philippe Minard, and Alexandra Laclau. 1997. *Atlas de la Révolution Française. Économie*. Paris: EHESS.

Béaur, Gérard. 2000. *Histoire agraire de la France au XVIIIe siècle*. Paris: Sedes.

Bergeron, Louis. 1978. *Banquiers, négociants et manufacturiers parisiens du Directoire à l'Empire*. Paris-The Hague-New York: Mouton.

Blond, Stéphane. 2014. *L'Atlas de Trudaine. Pouvoirs, cartes et savoirs techniques au siècle des Lumières*. Paris: CTHS.

Bodinier, Bernard, and Éric Teyssier. 2000. *L'événement le plus important de la Révolution. La vente des biens nationaux*. Paris: CTHS.

Bois, Jean-Pierre. 1976. "Conscrits du Maine-et-Loire sous l'Empire. Le poids de la conscription, 1806–1814". *Annales de Bretagne et des pays de l'Ouest,* 83 :3, 467–493. doi : 10.3406/abpo.1976.2826.

Bolt, Jutta, Robert Inklaar, Herman de Jong, and Jan Luiten van Zanden. 2018. "Rebasing 'Maddison': new income comparisons and the shape of long-run economic development". Maddison Project Working paper 10.

Bonney, Richard. 2004. "Towards the comparative fiscal history of Britain and France during the 'long' eighteenth century". *Exceptionalism and Industrialisation. Britain and Its European Rivals (1688–1815),* edited by Leandro Prados de la Escosura, 191–215. Cambridge: Cambridge University Press.

Bordo, Michael D. and Eugene N. White. 1991. "A Tale of Two Currencies: British and French Finance During the Napoleonic Wars". *Journal of Economic History* 51: 303–316.

Bosher, John F. 1964. *The Single Duty Project. A Study of the Movement for a French Customs Union in the Eighteenth Century.* London: University of London.

Branda, Pierre. 2007. *Le Prix de la Gloire. Napoléon et l'Argent.* Paris: Fayard.

Braudel, Fernand, and Ernest Labrousse (eds.). 1993. *Histoire économique de la France. II.1660–1789.* Paris: PUF-Quadridge.

Chabert, Alexandre. 1945. *Essai sur les mouvements des prix et des revenus en France de 1789 à 1820.* Paris: Librairie de Médicis.

Chabert, Alexandre. 1949. *Essai sur les mouvements des revenus et de l'activité économique en France de 1789 à 1820.* Paris: Librairie de Médicis.

Chassagne, Serge. 1978. "L'industrie lainière en France à l'époque révolutionnaire et impériale (1790–1810)". *Voies Nouvelles pour l'histoire de la Révolution Française.* Paris: Bibliothèque Nationale: 143–167.

Chevet, Jean-Michel, and Pascal Saint-Amour. 1992. "L'intégration des marches du blé en France aux XVIIIe et XIXe siècles". *Cahiers d'économie et de sociologie rurale* 22, 152–175.

Church, Clive H. 1981. *Revolution and Red Tape. The French Ministerial Bureaucracy 1770–1850.* Oxford: Clarendon Press.

Conchon, Anne. 2002. *Le péage en France au XVIIIe siècle: Les privilèges à l'épreuve de la réforme.* Paris: CHEF.

Crouzet, François. 1964. "Wars, Blockade and Economic Change in Europe, 1792–1815". *Journal of Economic History* XXIV: 567–588.

Daudin, Guillaume. 2005. *Commerce et prospérité. La France au XVIIIe siècle.* 2nd ed. Creative commons.

Daudin, Guillaume. 2010. "Domestic Trade and Market Size in Late-Eighteenth-Century France". *Journal of Economic History,* 70, n°3: 716–743.

De Foville, Alfred. 1880. *La Transformation des moyens de transport et ses conséquences économiques et sociales.* Paris : Guillaumin et Cie.

Dincecco, Mark. 2011. *Political Transformations and Public Finances: Europe, 1650–1913*. Cambridge: Cambridge University Press.

Dincecco, Mark, and Gabriel Katz. 2014. "State Capacity and Long-Run Economic Performance." *The Economic Journal* 126, n° 590: 189–218.

Doyle, William. 1996. *Venality: The Sale of Offices in Eighteenth-Century France*. Oxford: Oxford University Press.

Dufraisse, Roger. 1966. "Régime douanier, blocus, système continental: essai de mise au point", *Revue d'histoire économique et sociale* 44: 518–534.

Dupâquier, Jacques. 1988. *Histoire de la population française*, vol. 3 : *de 1789 à 1914*. Paris: PUF, coll. Quadrige.

Federico, Giovanni. 2012. "How Much Do We Know about Market Integration in Europe?", *The Economic History Review* 65, n° 2: 470–497. doi:10.1111/j.1468-0289.2011.00608.x.

Fox, Edward Whiting. 1971. *History in Geographic Perspective. The Other France*. New York: Norton.

Gabillard, Jean. 1953. "Le financement des guerres napoléoniennes et la conjoncture du Premier Empire". *Revue économique* 4, n°4: 359–360.

Gallet, Jean. 1999. *Seigneurs et paysans en France*, 1600–1793. Rennes: Ouest-France.

Gravier, Jean-François. 1947. *Paris et le désert français*. Paris: Portulan.

Guery, Alain. 1978. "Les finances de la monarchie française sous l'Ancien Régime", *Annales Économies, Société, Civilisation* 33, n°2: 216–239.

Henry, Louis, and Yves Blayo. 1975. "La population de la France de 1740 à 1860". *Population*, 30:1: 71–122.

Hirsch, Jean-Pierre. 1991. *Les deux rêves du commerce. Entreprise et institution dans la région lilloise* (1780–1860). Paris: EHEES.

Hoffman, Phillip T. 1996. *Growth in a Traditional Society. The French Countryside, 1450–1815*. Princeton: Princeton University Press.

Johnson, Christopher H. 1995. *The Life and Death of Industrial Languedoc 1700–1920*. Oxford: Oxford University Press.

Johnson, Noel D. 2006. "Banking on the king: The evolution of the royal revenue farms in Old Regime France". *The Journal of Economic History* 66, n°4: 963–991.

Joor, Johan and Katherine Aaslestad (eds.). 2014. *Revisiting Napoleon's Continental System: Local, Regional, and European Experiences*. Basingstoke: Palgrave.

Juhász, Réka. 2018. "Temporary Protection and Technology Adoption: Evidence from the Napoleonic Blockade". *American Economic Review*, 108:11, 3339–3376.

Lafay, Gérard. 1992. "The measurement of revealed comparative advantages." *International trade modelling*, edited by M.G. Dagenais and P.-A. Muet. London: Chapman & Hall, 209–234.

Lafrance, Xavier. 2019. *The Making of Capitalism in France*. Leiden and Boston: Brill.

Lemarchand, Guy. 2008. *L'économie en France de 1770 à 1830. De la crise de l'Ancien Régime à la révolution industrielle*. Paris: Armand Colin.

Léon, Pierre. 1974. "Structure du commerce extérieur et évolution industrielle de la France à la fin du XVIIIe siècle". *Conjoncture économique, structures sociales. Hommages à Ernest Labrousse.* Edited by Fernand Braudel *et al.* Paris-The Hague: Mouton, 407–432.

Lepetit, Bernard. 1988. *Les villes dans la France moderne (1740–1840)*. Paris: Albin Michel.

Le Roy Ladurie, Emmanuel. 1968. "Les comptes fantastiques de Gregory King", *Annales Économies, Sociétés, Civilisations* XXII, 5: 1086–1102.

Marczewski, Jean. 1961. "Some Aspects of the Economic Growth of France, 1660–1958". *Economic Development and Cultural Change* 9:3, 369–386.

Margadant, Ted W.. 1992. *Urban rivalries in the French Revolution.* Princeton: Princeton University Press.

Markovitch, Tihomir J. 1966. "L'industrie française de 1789 à 1964 – Analyse des faits (suite)". *Économies et sociétés, série AF*, n°6.

Meignen, Louis. 1973. "Le commerce extérieur de la France à la fin de l'Ancien Régime", *Revue historique du droit français et étranger* 56, 4: 583–614.

Molinier, Jean. 1957. "Les calculs d'agrégats en France antérieurement à 1850". *Revue d'économie politique* 67: 875–897.

Molinier, Jean. 1977. "L'évolution de la population agricole du XVIIIe siècle à nos jours". *Économie et statistiques* 91: 79–84.

Morineau, Michel. 1971. *Les faux-semblants d'un démarrage économique: agriculture et démographie en France au XVIIIe siècle.* Paris: Armand Colin.

Morineau, Michel. 1980. "Budgets de l'état et gestion des finances royales en France au dix-huitième siècle", *Revue historique* CCLXIV, n°2: 269–336.

Morrisson, Christian. 2007. "La production française au XVIIIe siècle: stagnation ou croissance?". *Revue européenne des sciences sociales* XLV-137: 153–165.

O'Brien, Patrick K., and Daniel Heath. 1994. "English and French Landowners 1688–1789". *Landowners, Capitalists, and Entrepreneurs. Essays for Sir John Habakkuk*, edited by F.M.L. Thompson, 23–62. Oxford: Clarendon Press.

O'Brien, Patrick, and Çağlar Keyder. 2012. *Economic Growth in Britain and France 1780–1914: Two Paths to the Twentieth Century.* London: Routledge.

O'Rourke, Kevin H., Leandro Prados de la Escosura, and Guillaume Daudin. 2010. "Trade and Empire". *The Cambridge Economic History of Modern Europe, vol. 1, 1700–1870*, directed by Stephen Broadberry and Kevin O'Rourke, 96–121. Cambridge: Cambridge University Press.

Postel-Vinay, Gilles. 1989. "A la recherche de la révolution économique dans les campagnes (1789–1815)", *Revue économique* 40, 6: 1015–1046.

Ridolfi, Leonardo. 2016. *The French economy in the longue durée. A study on real wages, working days and economic performance from Louis IX to the Revolution (1250–1789)*, Unpublished Ph.D. thesis, Lucca.

Ridolfi, Leonardo. 2019. "Six Centuries of Real Wages in France from Louis IX to Napoleon III: 1250–1860". *The Journal of Economic History* 79, 3: 589–627.

Rosenthal, Jean-Laurent. 1992. *The Fruits of Revolution: Property Rights, Litigation, and French Agriculture. 1700–1860*. Cambridge: Cambridge University Press.

Saint-Amour, Pascal, and Jean-Michel Chevet. 1991. "L'intégration des marches du blé en France au XIXe siècle", *Histoire & Mesure* 6, n°1: 93–119. doi:10.3406/hism.1991.1386.

Schnerb, Robert. 1972. *Deux siècles de fiscalité en France XIXe-XXe siècles*. Paris: Mouton.

Sée, Henry. 1925. *La France économique et sociale au XVIIIe siècle*. Paris: Armand Colin.

Steiner, Philippe. 2008. "L'héritage au XIXe siècle en France. Loi, intérêt de sentiment et intérêt économiques". *Revue économique* 59, n°1 : 75–98.

TOFLIT18. 2018. *Transformations of the French Economy through the Lens of International Trade. 1716–1821*. Paris : Sciences Po. http://toflit18.medialab.sciences-po.fr/ and http://toflit18.hypotheses.org/).

Toutain, Jean-Claude. 1961a. "Le produit de l'agriculture française de 1700 à 1958: I.-Estimation du produit au XVIIIe siècle". *Économies et sociétés, série AF*, n°1.

Toutain, Jean-Claude. 1961b. "Le produit de l'agriculture française de 1700 à 1958: II.-La Croissance". *Économies et sociétés, série AF*, n°2.

Toutain, Jean-Claude. 1992–1993. "La production agricole de la France de 1810 à 1990: départements et régions." *Économies et Sociétés, série* AF, 17, 3 vols.

Toutain, Jean-Claude. 1997. "La Croissance française, 1789–1990: nouvelles estimations", *Cahiers de l'ISMEA, série HEQ* 1: 5–136.

Verdier, Nicolas, and Anne Bretagnolle. 2007. "L'extension du réseau des routes de poste en France, de 1708 à 1833". *Histoire des reseaux postaux en Europe du XVIIIe au XXIe siècle*, edited by Muriel Le Roux, 155–193. Paris: Comité pour l'histoire de la Poste.

Verley, Patrick. 1997. *L'échelle du monde. Essai sur l'industrialisation de l'Occident*. Paris: Gallimard.

Weir, David. 1991. "Les crises économiques et les origines de la révolution française." *Annales* 4 (July-August): 917–947.

White, Eugene N. 1995. "The French Revolution and the Politics of Government Finance, 1770–1815". *The Journal of Economic History* 55, n°2 (June): 227–255.

White, Eugene N. 2004. "From privatized to government-administered tax collection: tax farming in eighteenth-century France". *The Economic History Review* 57, n°4: 636–663.

Woronoff, Denis. 1994. *Histoire de l'industrie en France*. Paris: Editions du Seuil.

Yun-Casalilla, Bartolomé, and Patrick O'Brien. 2012. *The rise of fiscal states: A global History, 1500–1914*. Cambridge: Cambridge University Press.

CHAPTER 4

War, State Growth, and Germany's Transition to Post-Malthusian Growth

Ulrich Pfister

1 Introduction

No other part of mainland Europe was as affected by the Revolutionary and Napoleonic Wars as the lands that would become Germany in the course of the nineteenth century. The dismantling of the Holy Roman Empire implied the disappearance of clerical principalities, autonomous cities as well as small dominions, and led to the creation of relatively large territorial states. From about 150 major polities and hundreds of tiny dominions in the 1790s, the number of political units shrank to about 35 in 1815.[1] 60 per cent of the German population became citizens of one of the two largest states, Prussia and Bavaria. In economic respects, the early nineteenth century constitutes a major historical watershed. By the late 1810s, the German economy had clearly exited the Malthusian era and embarked on growth path corresponding to a post-Malthusian regime. Thus, whereas the wars brought hardship and serious dislocation in the short term, the concomitant political shocks may have had positive effects on economic development in the long run.

This chapter begins with an overview of the principal phases of the war period, including the main consequences of the Vienna settlement for Germany. The next two sections provide short surveys of the character and magnitude of the war effort of German states and of the short-term economic effects of war, respectively. The final part explores potential links between war-related events and the subsequent transition to a post-Malthusian regime of economic growth.

1 The German Federation (*Deutscher Bund*), formed in 1815 and including Austria and Luxemburg as member states, had 38 members. In 1792, the Holy Roman Empire included 153 estates, but several princes possessed more than one vote; cf. von Lancizolle (1830, 1–6, 134–35).

 | DOI:10.1163/9789004472754_005

2 War and Political Change in the German Lands, 1792–1815

The first coalition against revolutionary France was formed around the Habsburg Empire and Prussia. From 1793 it included all members of the Empire, Great Britain and other European powers. War began in 1792 and formally ended in 1797 with the Peace of Campo Formio. From late 1792 the Upper Rhine region became a theatre of war, and hostilities ceased in 1796. The main results of the War of the First Coalition were the annexation of the Habsburg Netherlands (from 1830 Belgium) and the left bank of the Rhine by France (for syntheses of the history of the German lands during the Revolutionary and Napoleonic Wars, see Fehrenbach 2001; Fiedler 1988; Nipperdey 1998, 11–101; Rothenberg 2006; Wehler 1987, 347–546).

Since the Habsburg monarchy was the only power in Central Europe that continued to oppose France after 1797, Germany was little involved in the Wars of the Second and the Third Coalitions (1799–1801/02 and 1805). Important exceptions include a campaign from the Rhine to Southern Bavaria in 1800 and hostilities in Eastern Swabia (mostly near Ulm) in 1805, which ended in the defeat of Austria. This phase of the war saw two major political changes:

First, compensation of German princes who had experienced territorial losses on the left bank of the Rhine in the wake of the War of the First Coalition led to the so-called *Reichsdeputationshauptschluss* in 1803. This decree secularized clerical principalities, that is, it dissolved polities governed by bishops. They had constituted an important element of the political landscape of the old Empire and often ruled over sizeable territories. Furthermore, most self-governing cities that had been subordinate to the Emperor (so-called Imperial cities or *Reichsstädte*) and principalities of the lesser nobility were absorbed by larger dominions. The main beneficiaries of the *Reichsdeputationshauptschluss* were Bavaria, Prussia, Baden and Württemberg; they all increased their territories significantly.

A second major change flowed from the Treaty of Pressburg (Bratislava, 1805). In late 1806 Franz of Austria, the ruler of the Habsburg lands, resigned from his office as Emperor, which effectively dissolved the old Empire. The Habsburg monarch's move was a reaction to the accession of Bavaria and Württemberg to full sovereignty in the wake of the Treaty of Pressburg (Bratislava, 1805) and the formation of the Rhine Federation (*Rheinbund*, 1806–1813). Its members had formally left the Empire in summer 1806 to join an alliance under the personal protectorate of Napoleonic France. By the early 1810s the Rhine Federation included nearly all Germanic territory aside from the Habsburg lands, Prussia and territories that had become part of France. Planned by the French as an instrument of political change and social progress, the Rhine Federation in effect operated as a military alliance between France and the majority of German states. Members of the Federation were quite heterogeneous: The southern states—Bavaria, Württemberg, Baden and Hessen-Darmstadt—were largely independent allies of Napoleon pursuing their own specific policies of administrative, social and economic reform. Other territories were satellite states ruled by relatives of Napoleon. They included the Grand Duchy of Berg, the Kingdom of *Westphalen* and the Grand Duchy of Frankfurt.[2] A third group adhered to the federation primarily for military reasons and the reforms pursued in core member states had little impact upon them. The most important case in this group was Saxony.

The salient feature of the War of the Fourth Coalition (1806/07) was that Prussia actively entered the camp of Napoleon's adversaries. Hostilities centring on Thuringia culminated in the defeat of Prussia in the battles of Jena and Auerstedt in autumn 1806, which came to be seen as a nadir of Germany's fate by later nationalist historiography. Subsequent events led to the occupation of many parts of Prussia, including Berlin, by French troops. In the treaty of Tilsit (1807) Prussia temporarily lost about half of its territory, endured French occupation, which ended only in 1808, and paid a large indemnity. As a reaction to defeat, Prussian authorities initiated a series of far-flung reforms that provided the basis for the emergence of Prussia as the leading German state during the first half of the nineteenth century.

In the War of 1809 Bavaria became the battleground of the fight between France and the Habsburg monarchy. The French victory can be represented as the beginning of a short period of Napoleon's undisputed hegemony over the European continent. This was marked by the incorporation of the north-western coast of Germany and its hinterland into France in 1810/11 following the annexation of the Batavian republic.

The French invasion of Russia and the ensuing wars of liberation (as they are called in German historiography) marked the final phase of the Napoleonic Wars (1812–1814). Hostilities connected with the Russian campaign took place outside Germany, but German states were heavily involved in the French war effort through the provision of military personnel and supplies. Napoleon's defeat in Russia gave a boost to Prussian nationalism and to the creation of volunteer corps that eventually led Prussia into the camp of Napoleon's adversaries. In 1813 Saxony and the adjoining areas of Prussia became a major theatre

---

2 The contemporary spelling of *Westphalen* is chosen because the territorial boundaries of this state were little related both to pre-modern Westphalia and the later Prussian province bearing this name. The kingdom stretched over a large area that notably included Hessen-Kassel, southern lower Saxony, western Sachsen-Anhalt and eastern Westphalia.

of war. French defeat in the battle of Leipzig in October of that year marks the collapse of the Napoleonic system. With a participation of about 600,000 soldiers and an estimated 80 to 110 thousand killed, this encounter was the largest battle in Europe prior to World War I.

Two outcomes of the Vienna settlement of 1815, which concluded the Revolutionary and Napoleonic Wars, should be stressed: First, it consolidated the political landscape of Germany that had emerged over the wars as consisting of Prussia plus a cluster of small to medium sized sovereign territorial states. Some independent cities and minor principalities remained in existence, but their political relevance had become marginal. Second, the potentially negative economic effects of continued political fragmentation were mitigated by the creation of the first international governmental organization (IGO) in history, namely, the Central Commission for Navigation on the Rhine. The Commission acted as an international court and in 1831 drafted a convention that established a unified institutional framework for river transport on the Rhine (Klemann 2013; Thiemeyer and Tölle 2011). In the aftermath of the Congress of Vienna, similar organizations were created for other major rivers, notably the Elbe.

3 The Economic Dimension of the War Effort

Economic resources were mobilized for war through three channels: The first consisted of levies exacted by military units, the requisition of supplies and shelter, and marauding by troops. The second involved the recruitment of military personnel, and the third operated through state expenditures. The first channel constituted the most direct involvement of the population at large with the war (Esser 2020, 100–03; Planert 2007, 159–263). By its nature, the magnitude of this component of the war effort is impossible to quantify. That it constituted a systemic element of resource mobilization, however, testifies to the fact that on the European mainland most states had to conduct large-scale warfare in a context of poorly monetized economies and weekly developed fiscal states, whereas the British were able to mobilize resources mainly via taxes and loans (North 2012, 159–160).

The number of military personnel involved constitutes a rough quantitative indicator of the scale of mobilization for warfare (Fiedler 1988, 105, 115, 149, 158, 162). From 1806 the member states of the Rhine Federation had to provide troops for the French army. Starting at 63 thousand the quota rose to 130 thousand on the eve of the invasion of Russia in 1812. This number equalled less than one per cent of a total population of 14.6 million in 1808 (Wehler 1987, 369). If we assume that about a quarter of the population consisted of males capable of work, the share of military personnel in the adult male work-force was about 3.5 per cent.[3] In the War of the Fourth Coalition (1806/07) Prussia's army comprised about 63 thousand men. With a population of roughly 10 million in 1815 this implies a share of military personnel in the adult male population at an order of magnitude of 2.5 per cent. As a result of military reforms and the creation of popular militias Prussia's armed forces became much larger during the early 1810s. From 80,000 in 1811 the armed forces rose to 300 thousand in 1813. Assuming a much reduced population of about 5 million, these figures imply a rapid rise in of the ratio of military personnel to the adult male work-force from 6 to 24 per percent.

The fiscal component of the war effort consisted mainly of expenditure for troops and military campaigns as well as transfers to French authorities and military forces. The magnitude of war-related expenditure is impossible to quantify since public accounts lacked a consistent standard and records fell into disorder during wartime. The small and inflexible resource base of most states meant that their capacity to engage in military conflict was limited, at least during the initial phases of the war. Thus, Prussia withdrew from the anti-French coalition in 1795 mainly for fiscal reasons. Public debt at that time amounted to around 48 million *Taler*, about double the amount of regular state revenues. With a population of some ten million, this corresponds to about five *Taler* per head, which in turn is roughly equivalent to the amount of money that an unskilled urban day labourer earned in seventeen days (the day wage was about a third *Taler*). The cautious foreign policy that Prussian authorities pursued over the next ten years contributed to moderate fiscal consolidation, but the campaign in 1806, which led to the disaster of Jena and Auerstedt, again raised the kingdom's liabilities to 48 million *Taler* (Klein 1974, 60–63; Ullmann 2005, 22–24).[4]

The situation for public finance seems to have worsened after 1806. In Prussia alone, the treaty of Tilsit required the kingdom to pay France an indemnity of more than 30 million *Taler*. Estimates suggest that between 1806 and

3 According to Pfister and Fertig (2010, 37), the share of individuals aged 15–65 in total population was 0.63 at the beginning of the nineteenth century. The assumption that a quarter of the population consisted of males capable of work presupposes that about one fifth of all males aged 15–65 were irrelevant in terms of the recruitment base of military personnel.

4 A Prussian *Taler* weighed 16.7 grams of silver, the *Konventionstaler* used in most other parts of Germany contained 17.5 grams of silver. The nominal day wage of unskilled urban construction workers in 1803/07 and 1808/12 amounted to 5.0 grams of silver on average; cf. Figure 4.1 below.

1808 French authorities obtained an additional 200 million *Taler* in the form of direct transfers to troops and from the confiscation of state property and state revenues. At the same time, mostly due to the territorial losses annual state revenues dwindled from 27 million *Taler* in 1805/6 to ten to twelve million *Taler* during the following years. All this plus the costs of subsequent military campaigns in 1813 (29 million *Taler*) and 1815 (the campaign of Waterloo cost the Prussian state 20 million *Taler*) led to an inflation of both state debt and the debt service burden. French reparations after 1815 contributed little to the fiscal stabilization of Prussia. Despite the fact that in 1816–1819 state revenues rose to a range between 40 and 56 million *Taler*, expenditures still exceeded revenues by the large margin of 25 per cent. Consequently, in 1820 Prussian state debt amounted to 232 million *Taler*, about 21 *Taler* per head. Other German states found themselves in a rather worse situation: Public debt in 1820 reached 31 million *Taler* in Baden and 102 million *Taler* in Bavaria, equal to 29 and 28 *Taler* per capita, respectively (Klein 1974, 103–13; Ullmann 2005, 22–24; the population figures from Fertig et al. 2018). These figures are equivalent to 60–100 times the daily wage of unskilled workers, which indicates that state debt was rather less than national income. Debt burdens of German states were thus considerably lower than those of Great Britain and the Netherlands.

Public authorities used a variety of expedients to close the gap between rising state expenditures and unresponsive revenues. As the 1790s progressed foreign capital markets dried up, and both British subsidies and domestic capital markets, notably in Frankfurt, provided only limited funds. In this situation, the authorities resorted to forced loans, the issuing of notes and to increasing seigniorage by minting debased coin. This contributed to inflation. By 1803–1817 consumer prices were on average 66 per cent higher than in 1788–1792. Finally, some states such as Prussia and the Kingdom of *Westphalen* temporarily defaulted wholly or partly on their obligations in 1808 and 1812, repseectively (Klein 1974, 104–11; Ullmann 2005, 22–24). The contrast between the modest size of armies during most of the war period and the fiscal nightmare that resulted from financing them highlights the difficulties of staging large-scale military operations in an economy characterized by poor levels of monetization and financial development (on levels of monetization from the 1830s, see Tilly 1966, 19–45, 77–79).

The strains that the wars put on public finances forced most states to modernize their fiscal systems during the 1800s and 1810s. Important measures included the centralization of authority with a ministry of finance, state control of revenue collection as well as a rationalization of tax systems and public debt administrations (Klein 1965, ch. 1, 1974, 104–11; Ullmann 1982, 1986, 2005, 25–30; von Witzleben 1985). These measures were insufficient to balance state budgets even after peace had returned in 1815. In Prussia, for example, debt service consumed about 20 per cent of public expenditure in 1820, which contemporary observers considered unsustainable. Hence, public authorities inaugurated a second round of reforms around 1820. To the extent that reforms were not accompanied by a transition to parliamentary control of government their effect on the extractive capacity of the state was modest. In Prussia, nominal tax revenues per capita in the 1840s were not higher than a century earlier (Dincecco 2009, 53, 58, 67, 2011, 21–31, 60–63, 99–107; Klein 1974, 112–19; Siegert 2001; Spoerer 2004, 2010; Ullmann 2005, 31–37).

4 Economic Consequences of War in the Short Run

War shifted demand from consumer goods to weaponry and other goods for military use, and disrupted trade. This should have benefitted armament and import-competing industries, and harmed all other sectors. Moreover, war had four potentially negative effects: First, recruitment of soldiers diverted labour from peacetime activities, most notably in agriculture. Battle casualties and deaths caused by diseases, whose spread was facilitated by war-related geographical mobility and by sieges, augmented the loss in human resources. Second, horses and cattle, by serving as draught animals, by providing manure and by constituting sources of protein-rich food, had long been essential capital goods in agriculture. Their use in the war economy reduced the capital-land and possibly capital-labour ratios in agriculture. Third, war-related disruption of international trade depressed income in regions that relied heavily on industrial exports (O'Rourke 2006). Fourth, the use of non-market related mechanisms to mobilize resources for war, such as coercion, forced loans and inflations tax, may have had compounded the adverse economic effects of the other three factors.

The disruption of international trade went together with losses of cargos at sea and recurrent financial crises. As a result, many merchant houses fell bankrupt during the war period. The disruption of trade routes and the slump of the service sector reduced demand for exports. Linen dominated German exports in the eighteenth century, and quantities exported by Lusatia, a major centre of linen manufacture, declined by half between 1792 and 1814/15, and the financial crises of 1793 and 1799 were associated with a strong decline of linen exports (Banken 2019, Schäfer 2016, 136–44; Schulte Beerbühl 2018).

The potentially beneficial effect of the disruption of international trade on import-competing industries will be discussed below in section 5.2. Since Germany enjoyed a comparative advantage in metallurgy and the production of metal goods, demand for weapons could have given a boost to mining and metal processing industries. There is only scarce evidence on this point, and it is ambiguous. Given the importance of lead in the manufacture of ammunition of guns, the mining of this metal in the eastern Harz experienced a boom in the early 1800s, which ended in a serious recession after the war (1817). By contrast, the important iron manufacturing activities in the Rhineland and Westphalia did not apparently experience expansion. An attempt to galvanize gun manufacturing in Essen by introducing experienced entrepreneurs and skilled labourers from Liège failed before the war had ended. Other iron processing industries in the region show no sign of significant expansion during the war period. Pig iron output of one blast furnace situated in southern Westphalia stagnated from c. 1780 to 1812 and rose rapidly after 1817. War-related demand for armaments appears to have had little effect on Germany's economy (Bartels 1992, 399–409; Hinz 1977, 249–50, Kermann 1972, 520–604).

The evolution of aggregate income during the war period can be selectively documented using day wages of unskilled labourers in urban construction (Figure 4.1) and land rent from fixed lease contracts on five estates in Westphalia (Figure 4.2). Nominal wages measured in grams of silver experienced a massive upward shift from 1794 to 1806 and remained roughly stable until the 1830s when another slow rise set in. The massive increase around 1800 did not compensate for inflation, however. Real wages had been in decline from the 1730s. This trend continued without apparent change over the first phase of the war until 1807. The low values for 1807, 1813 and 1817 mark a long-term minimum level of labour income during the modern era. Since they merely constitute the endpoint of a development that set in much earlier, they should probably not be related to the war. By 1815, real wages were only marginally below the level prevailing in 1792.

Nominal lease rents on five estates in Westphalia are the only other available information concerning income from land that spans the late eighteenth and early nineteenth centuries. After a long period of stagnation that also began in the 1730s, nominal rents in terms of grams of silver per hectare rose vigorously from the early 1780s to 1810, fell back slightly until the late 1820s and rose again thereafter. Real rents are not easy to track in a meaningful way because contracts were renewed at intervals of six years or longer. Thus, price fluctuations led to movements in real rents that did not reflect market outcomes. For this reason, interpretation of Figure 4.2 should focus on the smoothed series of real lease rents. In contrast to wage rates, nominal lease rents more than kept up with wartime inflation during the early 1800s, but this merely compensated for the downturn of real rents in the 1790s that probably emanated from the serious harvest failure in 1794. Around 1815 real land rents were roughly at the

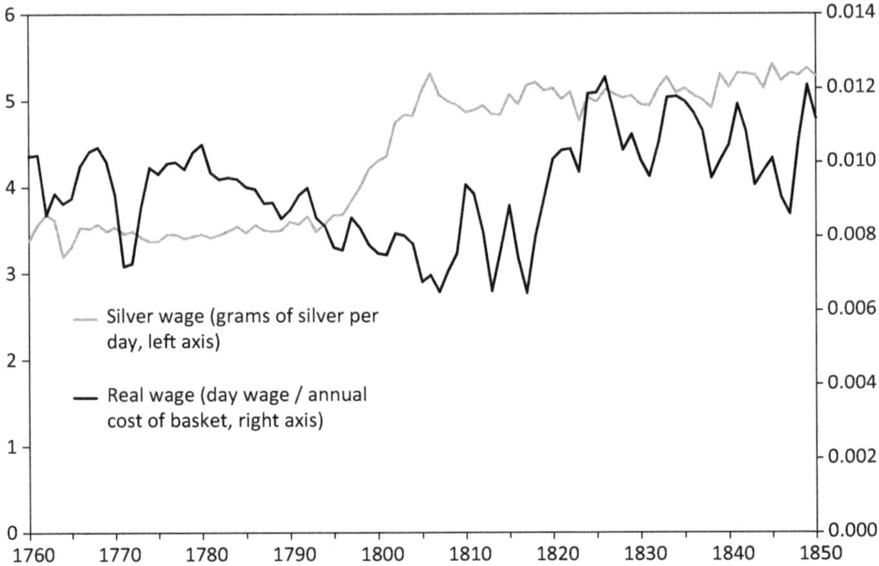

FIGURE 4.1 Nominal and real wages of unskilled urban construction workers, 1760–1850. Nominal wage is in grams of silver per day; real wage is nominal wage divided by the annual cost of a consumption basket of eleven goods with fixed quantities (also in grams of silver).
SOURCE: PFISTER (2017, ONLINE APPENDIX S3)

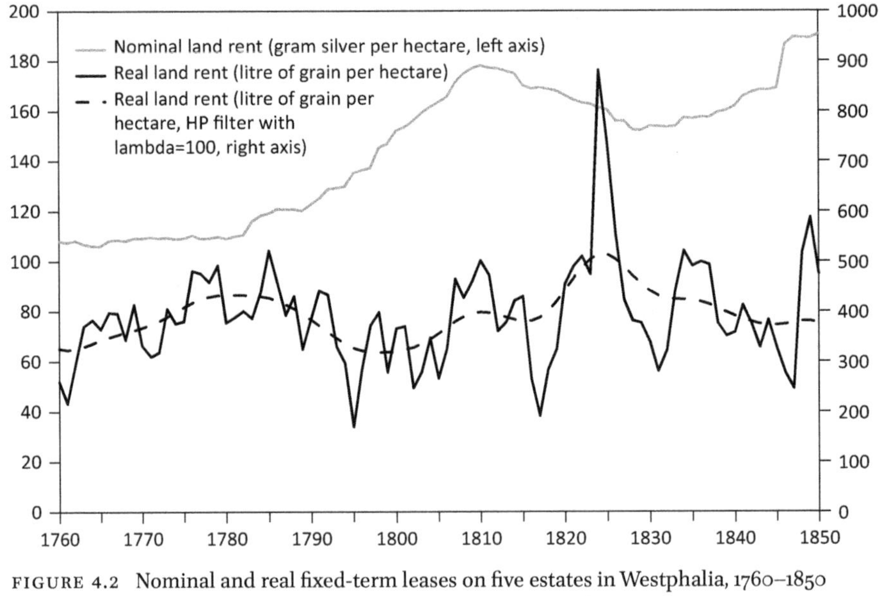

FIGURE 4.2 Nominal and real fixed-term leases on five estates in Westphalia, 1760–1850
SOURCE: BRACHT AND PFISTER (2020, 168, 231); DATA SERIES IN GESIS ZA8703

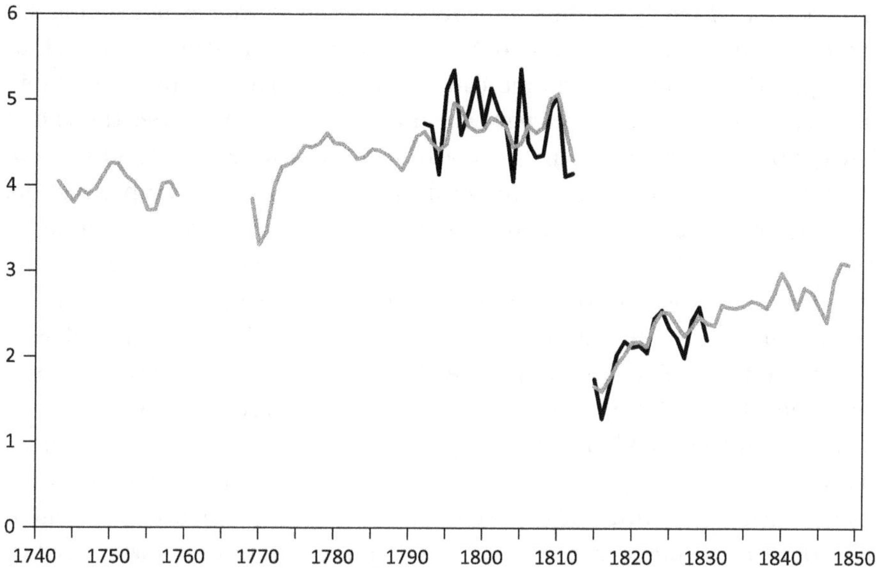

FIGURE 4.3 Output of principal food crops in Saxony, 1743–1849 (millions of grain equivalents) Principal food crops include rye, wheat, and potatoes. Black line: observed values; grey line: values estimated from wages and prices using a consumption function. The massive decline in level from 1812 to 1815 is due to the fact that Saxony lost about 60 per cent of her territory in the wake of the Congress of Vienna.
SOURCE: PFISTER AND KOPSIDIS (2015, 295)

same level as during the early 1790s. In sum, there is no evidence that the war negatively affected factor incomes in the short run.

The behaviour of output in agriculture, the most important sector at that time, can be studied in some detail for Saxony (Figure 4.3). During the first phase of the war until 1805 vegetable output in the Electorate of Saxony increased at an annual rate of 0.4 per cent, which is slightly below population growth. From 1805 to 1812, when records end, output fell at an annual rate of -2.2 per cent, so that output in 1810/12 was 11 per cent lower than in 1803/05. As population fell by less than one per cent over this time interval there was a clear reduction in the availability of locally produced food per capita.

At the same time, the structure of output changed in that output of rye and wheat fell over the entire war period, whereas production of oats and potatoes expanded until 1805 and contracted only slightly thereafter. Thus, there occurred a shift to crops demanding fewer inputs of manure and draught animals than dominant winter grains. Declining productivity as indicated by the output to seed ratio was the most important proximate cause of the poor output performance. This and the shift towards more robust crops such as oats and rye may be partly attributed to climatic factors in that average temperature declined during the 1790s and 1800s. It is highly significant, however, that seed quantities, which are an indicator of land and labour input, expanded at an annual rate of only 0.2 per cent up to 1805 and stagnated thereafter. Already before Saxony became involved in the war in 1806 expanding population and worsening climate reduced the growth rate of food production. This suggests a role for demand in that it was probably not worthwhile to grow more food. Saxony depended heavily on manufactured exports, and the collapse of long-distance trade after 1791 may have reduced the income of outworkers and, consequently, food demand. After 1805, the stagnation of seed inputs and the decline of output to seed ratios tentatively suggest that negative effects flowed from the diversion of labour and farm animals to the war economy (Kopsidis and Pfister 2013, 17–21, 25–26, 31, 34; on climate, see Glaser and Riemann 2009, 442; data from Luterbacher et al. 2004). In combination, recessions in agriculture and export industries, together with the involvement in warfare, contributed to a tangible loss of human resources as witnessed by a negative deviation of population from its long-term trend by about 5 per cent in 1815.[5]

Scattered evidence from other parts of Germany suggests considerable regional variation in the performance of the agricultural sector. In Bavaria, which was heavily affected by the initial phases of the war, output may have declined by an annual rate of -0.6% during the 1800s. By contrast, sharecropping returns in the small dominion of Anholt in the lower Rhine area indicates that output in 1804–1813 exceeded the level prevailing before and after the war. This region, which did not really participate in the war effort and was little affected by military action, may have benefitted from supply bottlenecks arising from the shift of resources to the war effort elsewhere (Böhm 1995, 386; Kopsidis et al. 2017, 35–36).

In sum, it is not easy to demonstrate positive effects attributable to the Revolutionary and Napoleonic Wars on armaments and related industries and negative effects on the aggregate economy. This suggests that the last major war of the preindustrial era was still a relatively marginal phenomenon in economic terms, reflecting the small magnitude of the war effort as documented above. Regional experiences, however, must have differed considerably. A region like Saxony, which was a major theatre of war and depended heavily

5 In the Electorate of Saxony population in 1815 was 5.1 per cent below the figure predicted by the exponential trend in 1763–1792 (0.5 per cent p. a., R^2=0.90); source for population figures is Schirmer (1996, 57–58).

upon exports, experienced a significant decline of activity also in agriculture and suffered a non-negligible loss in human resources. Finally, frequent harvest failures (possibly aggravated by the disruption of markets during the war-period), led to repeated spikes in food prices (Albers et al. 2018, 93). For Britain Baten et al. (2014) have shown that food shortages during the Revolutionary and Napoleonic Wars have had negative effects on the cognitive ability of children, which adversely affected human capital accumulation over the long run. A similar effect may have prevailed in Germany as well.

5 Long-Term Consequences

5.1 *Overview*

In the 1810s Germany transited into a post-Malthusian regime of economic growth: The harvest failures of 1816/17 did not lead to an excess of deaths over births, and the short-term Malthusian positive check virtually disappeared after 1815. During the eighteenth century, the German population had remained highly vulnerable to short-term food crises. Whereas the annual rate of population growth doubled from 0.4 percent in 1730–1799 to 0.8 percent in 1815–1870 the real wage stayed roughly constant between the late 1810s and the 1870s. The negative association between population and labour productivity, which characterizes Malthusian economies and which also prevailed in early modern Germany, was clearly broken. Aggregate labour demand experienced a dramatic rise during the late 1810s and continued to shift outwards subsequently (Fertig et al. 2018; Pfister et al. 2012, 15, 21–2; Pfister and Fertig 2020; Tilly and Kopsidis 2020, ch. 1). The evolution of agricultural production in Saxony confirms the existence of a post-war boom: Output of principal food crops expanded by 46 per cent from 1815 to 1824 and continued to grow at a rate of about 1 per cent a year during the next quarter century (Figure 4.3).

The most plausible interpretation of the positive economic shock of the late 1810s is one that links it to the political transformations that took place during the Revolutionary and Napoleonic Wars and builds on the work of Mancur Olson. Olson argued that social and political stability creates a potential for interest groups to press for policies that increase their rents but create exclusive institutions that preclude open access to markets. The slow economic growth that prevailed in much of eighteenth-century Europe, resulted from institutional rigidities and rent-seeking by elite groups and merchant and craft guilds. The social dislocation that occur during major wars removes or weakens special interest groups and distributional coalitions. This undermines institutional rigidities and opens the way for reforms that improve the universal protection of individual property rights and create inclusive markets. World War II and the Revolutionary and Napoleonic Wars were both events that may have produced such effects (Olson 1982, chs. 3 and 4; see also Acemoglu and Robinson 2012; North et al. 2009).

My argument will explore two variants of the Olsonian hypothesis and offer a third view, which emphasises the effects that the wars had on state formation. Nevertheless, it would not be appropriate to assess the significance of war-related social and political dislocation without considering other potential explanations for the positive outcomes that came on stream after the war. An important economic element of the wartime regime was the Napoleonic Continental Blockade, which disrupted trade with Great Britain from 1806–13. Protection from British competition created a potential for catch-up growth for continental industries, particularly for cotton textile firms that attained the scale necessary for sustained development after the war. Factors unconnected to the war as such may also, however, have influenced the magnitude of economic growth around 1820, namely, post-war reconstruction and climatic factors. Thus, the following review of the long-run consequences of the Revolutionary and Napoleonic Wars on the German economy begins with post-war reconstruction and climate (section 5.2). It continues by assessing the effects of the Continental Blockade on the cotton industry (section 5.3). The final part reviews the evidence concerning the three hypotheses concerning institutional change and state formation in sections 5.4–6.

5.2 *Post-War Reconstruction and Climate*

There is a widely held consensus that the golden age of economic growth in Europe during the third quarter of the twentieth century was at least partly due to reconstruction after World War II. According to cross-country growth regressions, the reconstruction effect had a tangible impact on economic growth for some ten years after the war and disappeared in the second half of the 1950s (Vonyó 2008, 230–35; Wolf 1995, 226–28, 248). This history provides a benchmark for assessing the possible relevance of post-war reconstruction after the Napoleonic Wars.

According to the Solow growth model, post-war reconstruction is the transition from a disequilibrium to a steady state capital-output ratio. War-time destruction and diversion of capital to the war economy imply that at the end of wars the stock of useful capital per unit of labour had fallen below its long-term equilibrium. Capital accumulation combined with a high marginal product of capital then leads to rapid growth and a return to the equilibrium capital-labour ratio. In the early nineteenth century production was certainly much less capital-intensive than in the middle of the twentieth century. Farm animals probably constituted the most important component of the capital stock that was negatively affected by war. Herds could be restored rapidly at low cost. We might expect that post-war reconstruction after the Napoleonic Wars occurred rather more rapidly than after World War II. Furthermore, as the short-term negative effects of war were moderate (cf. section 4), the potential for growth based upon reconstruction was modest.

Available evidence indeed suggests that post-war reconstruction was completed by the early 1820s. Since economic growth during the decades prior the onset of war was small or non-existent (see the evolution of the real wage and the real land rent from the 1760s to the early 1790s in Figures 4.1 and 4.2) values in 1792 can be considered as a benchmark of peace-time economic activity. Aggregate labour demand reached the level of 1792 in 1821 and continued to shift outwards over the following years (Pfister et al. 2012, 15). In 1823 food crop production (rye, wheat and potatoes) in the *Erzgebirge* district (the only major administrative district of Saxony that was not affected by the boundary changes of 1815) equalled output in 1791/92. In the much smaller *Vogtländer Kreis* pre-war levels of food crop production were surpassed in 1819 and again in 1822 (data from Kopsidis and Pfister 2013). This evidence suggests that the potential for reconstruction growth had been fully exploited by the early 1820s. Thus, the persistence of economic growth beyond the early 1820s cannot be attributed to post-war reconstruction.

The long cycle from c. 1790 to 1830 in consumer prices that underlie the real wage series in Figure 4.1 and in Saxon agricultural output data is paralleled by a similar swing in annual temperatures (Glaser and Riemann 2009, 442; data from Luterbacher et al. 2004). Average temperature fell during the 1790s and 1800s, and the period 1812–16 was marked by a series of relatively cold years. Thereafter, temperature increased; the early 1820s presented exceptionally favourable conditions for arable farming, which depressed grain prices. From the mid-1820s average temperature fell again, to levels of the mid-1810s by c. 1840. The unfavourable climate prevailing around 1815 produced a strong base effect on the evolution of the post-year economy, and part of the positive shock occurring in the late 1810s and early 1820s could well be attributed to increases in annual temperatures. At the same time, however, the wedge that opened up after the mid-1820s between falling temperature and a roughly stable real wage corroborates the impression of a sustained increase in labour demand beyond post-war reconstruction.

5.3 *The Continental Blockade (1806–1813) and the Infant Industry Argument*

Between the Declaration of Berlin late in 1806 and the early 1810s trade between Britain and the mainland regions controlled by France became progressively more and more restricted. The volume of trade between Germany and Britain for 1807–1812 dropped to about a third of the level recorded for 1800–06. The reduction of commercial activity and privateering seems to have damaged the trades of port cities and moved locational advantages to internal trade for decades thereafter. The Blockade also shifted relative prices in favour of import-competing industries, particularly cotton textiles. To the extent that the emerging cotton industry was characterized by externalities from learning by doing it displayed increasing returns, which created entrance barriers for newcomers. Thus, the Continental Blockade may have been vital in offering infant industry protection to the nascent cotton textile industry (Denzel 2015; Dufraisse 1992, 245–94; Kutz 1974, 42–43, 59–69, 94; Marzagalli 1999; O'Rourke 2006, 143–46; Saalfeld, 1987; Spaulding 2015).

For some manufacturing regions of Germany, the era of the Continental Blockade became a boom period during which many new businesses were created (Fehrenbach 2001, 95–108). In cotton manufacture the number of mechanical spindles rose from 22,000 in 1800 to 69,000 in 1806, 140,000 in 1810 and 360,000 in 1815. Rapid growth took place without significant technological and organizational development. Firms created during the era of high import protection were small and used primitive technology. The Continental Blockade simply prolonged the period during which it was profitable to employ simple spinning machinery that was way behind the technological frontier of the day. The end of the Continental Blockade was followed by a severe slump that only gave way to recovery in the 1820s. The regional pattern of growth in Germany differed from France, where cotton manufacturing districts located near the coast, whose markets increased as a result of the Blockade, experienced faster growth during subsequent decades than inland districts (Juhász 2018). In Germany, the growth in the number of mechanical spindles that took place during the era of the Continental Blockade was concentrated on Saxony, which accounted for 62 percent of the production capacity of the *Zollverein* as late as 1838. Cotton districts located closer to Britain, which enjoyed greater relative protection as a result of the Blockade, such as the lower Rhineland, experienced only a modest expansion in the number of cotton spindles in 1807–1812 (Fischer 1962, 194–280; Kermann 1972, 194–99; Kirchhain 1977, 39–42; Schäfer 2016, 83–136, 453–54). In contrast to the experience of France, the available evidence suggests that the Continental Blockade did not promote catch-up growth of cotton manufacturing in the German lands. It cannot explain this country's transition to the post-Malthusian era.

5.4 *The Olsonian View in the Narrow Sense: Welfare Effects of French Rule*

Territories that became part of the French empire during the 1790s and in 1810/11 (see above, section 2) experienced drastic changes in their institutional frameworks. To a weaker extent, this was also true for satellite states established from 1806, since they also adopted French legislation (Fehrenbach 2001, 82–94, 213–27; Berding 1973; Dethlefs et al. 2008). In an Olsonian perspective we should expect that outside intervention by French rule overcame institutional rigidities that protected rent-seeking by individuals and corporate groups and imposed an institutional framework providing for inclusive markets and universal protection for individual property rights.

Direct and indirect French rule affected two broad sets of economic institutions, namely, rural property rights and markets for non-agricultural products, including services. Comprehensive land reform abolished serfdom, terminated feudal obligations and established individual property rights over land. In regions with a vibrant commercial sector, the parallel secularization of church property led to the creation of an active market in land and large buildings that could serve as factories. The compound effect of agrarian reform on rural institutions must have been small, however. In the lower Rhine region, the most developed region under French rule, manorial institutions had already given way to leasehold arrangements during the pre-modern period, and these were not affected by French legislation. Furthermore, the dissolution of common lands, which was pivotal for the transition to techniques involving more intensive land use, was only tackled later under Prussian rule (Dufraisse 1989, 149–50; Engels 1957; Esser 2020; Kopsidis et al. 2017).

Institutions governing the non-agricultural sectors were transformed along two lines: First, access to factor and commodity markets was eased by abolishing guilds and by enforcing freedom of trade. Individuals were allowed to pursue any economic activity independent from their backgrounds. In particular, this allowed non-burghers and immigrants to participate in local markets. Microstudies on local elites and regional export industries indeed show an expansion of opportunities for newcomers and outsiders (Diefendorf 1980, 159–84, 203–09; Fehrenbach 2001, 224–25; Kisch 1989, 197–206, 211–13; Kriedte 2007, 339–40, 382–407). Second, the introduction of French commercial law and the establishment of commercial courts potentially reduced transaction costs for trade. In the early modern period, commercial law had evolved independently in large cities that were centres of trade and finance. In 1806 there existed 55 separate regulations for bills of exchange in Germany. With the French *Code de commerce* of 1807, which was also adopted by some territories located to the east of the Rhine (such as Baden and parts of Berg), market transactions began to operate within a unified legal framework and within larger political territories (Amend-Traut 2009, 124–30, 413–16). French commercial law also created a framework for the creation of joint stock companies, which may partly explain why roughly half of these enterprises founded in Prussia during the first half of the nineteenth century were domiciled in the Rhine province (Reckendrees 2012).

There are some econometric tests of the economic consequences of French rule using the duration of French presence as proxy for the strength of French influence. Acemoglu et al. (2011) relate variation regarding years of French presence across administrative and territorial units with a reform index and the urbanisation rate in key years (1850, 1875, and 1900). The effect of French presence on the urbanization rate is negative in 1850 and only turns positive in the second half of the nineteenth century. Whereas is cannot be excluded that French rule had economic effects in the very long run this article does not contribute to explaining Germany's transition to the post-Malthusian era in the early nineteenth century (Kopsidis and Bromley 2016). Keller and Shiue (2020) find that wheat price differentials between towns that had been under French rule and experienced liberal reforms were smaller than wheat price differentials between other towns in 1820–1880. Prima facie this suggests than institutional reforms undertaken under French influence, particularly the reform of business law, promoted market integration. But, a similar regional pattern of price differentials as the pattern prevailing from 1820 may already have existed prior to the Napoleonic era. Indeed, Albers and Pfister (2020) find that the French presence was weakly related to changes in bilateral differences in rye prices between German towns from the 1780s to the 1820s. In sum, whereas qualitative evidence suggests that reforms of institutions surrounding business and trade occurred more rapidly and were more profound in the regions annexed by France than elsewhere in Germany, this does not demonstrate that they contributed significantly to Germany's transition to the post-Malthusian age that took place after the end of the war. It also implies that Germany's experience during the Napoleonic Wars cannot serve as a historical experiment to assess whether reforms imposed from outside are more or less effective than reforms initiated from within by independent governments.

5.5 *The Olsonian View as Defensive Modernization*

The war period opened a window of opportunity for far-flung reforms not only for the territory annexed by France and—to a lesser extent—for the satellite states created by Napoleon, but for most other parts of Germany as well. In order to satisfy French demands and to bear the costs of military campaigns, most states came under pressure to carry out fiscal reforms and to enlarge the tax base through economic reforms that created a new and greater potential for economic growth. These reforms also served to forestall intervention by Napoleon and to provide the prevailing political order with a minimum of legitimacy. Outside pressure thus acted in an Olsonian way to weaken the power of particularistic interest groups and thereby turned market-oriented reforms into an element of defence against French pressure. In this sense, German states located outside immediate French control experienced programmes of defensive modernization (term coined by Wehler 1987, 363–454; see also Fehrenbach 1974, 2001; Klein 1965; Nolte 1990; Wegner 2016; Weis 1973). In many cases, the measures taken were not of an entirely new character but built on policies initiated earlier during the era of Enlightened absolutism. Pressure from France simply amplified and dynamized reform processes that had been under way for several decades (Tilly and Kopsidis 2020, 69–78).

A major focus of new reforms initiated during the Napoleonic Wars was on the reorganization of central government, the reform of regional administration and the development of modern fiscal regimes. In the economic sphere, two directions of reform stand out (Tilly and Kopsidis 2020, 78–84): First, the initiation of agrarian reforms, which abolished personal bonds between peasants and lords and introduced individual property rights in land. Second, individual and corporate privileges as well as barriers with respect to economic opportunities were by and large abolished. In Bavaria, this occurred under the new constitution of 1808 and was contained in a policy directed against noble prerogatives. In Prussia, the transformation to an open access order with inclusive markets occurred in several steps. The first was the introduction of a civil law code (the so-called *Allgemeine Landrecht*) in 1794. The famous October Edict of 1807, enacted within a year after the devastating defeats at Jena and Auerstedt, removed barriers between estates concerning the choice of marriage partners, occupation and the possession of large estates. Existing scholarship considers this edict as pivotal in creating inclusive markets. Finally, edicts enacted in 1810/11 abolished guilds and established freedom of trade. Liberalization of access to handicraft production and industry—so-called *Gewerbefreiheit*—occurred early in Prussia. Smaller states, whose bureaucracies were less developed and where corporate interests wielded more power, were slower in establishing inclusive markets. Only with the trade regulations of 1869/72 was the principle of *Gewerbefreiheit* established nationwide (Fischer 1962, 72–83, Henning 1978; Kaufhold 1982; Vogel 1983; Ziekow 1992, 327–531).

To what extent can the reforms that were initiated during wartime both in areas under French rule and in German states account for Germany's transition to the post-Malthusian age after 1815? A brief consideration of agrarian reforms provides a tentative answer. Summary treatments of the reforms undertaken during the Napoleonic era usually accord primacy to agrarian reforms among the measures explicitly addressing economic issues. An older historiography considered them to be important preconditions for agricultural growth and industrialization. If social reforms undertaken during the first two decades of the nineteenth century contributed to Germany's transition to the post-Malthusian era, then the agrarian reforms initiated during these decades should have had positive effects on agricultural growth (Acemoglu et al. 2011, 3291–92; Fehrenbach 2001, 90–93, 116–19; Harnisch 1984; Kiesewetter 2004, 100–01, 116–18; Wehler 1987, 378–80, 409–28).

Agrarian reform embraced at least four issues, namely, the dissolution of personal bonds between peasants and lords, the redemption of manorial obligations together with the introduction of individual property rights, the division of common land, and the dissolution of open field systems which included the removal of easements on real estate, provisions for the consolidation of fragmented farmland and the construction of service roads. In some states at least, several of these issues were dealt with in comprehensive reform packages. In others, reforms and their implementation occurred gradually (for surveys, see Dipper 1980; Schneider 2010).

In Prussia from the late eighteenth century peasants on royal domains were given options to improve their position by redeeming specific obligations. The October Edict of 1807 abolished serfdom but also removed state protection for peasant farms. Edicts promulgated in 1811, 1816 and 1821 regulated the redemption of all dues, including corvée labour, and land property rights for different types of peasants. Separate laws enacted in 1811 and 1821 provided a framework for the termination of the open field system and the division of common land, respectively. All these measures consisted of enabling rather than compulsory legislation, which implies that either peasants or proprietors of manors had to initiate specific procedures. Since the value of peasant obligations was determined on the basis of the prices prevailing during the previous twelve years the price depression after 1817 provided little incentive for peasants to initiate redemption procedures. Hence, only in the 1830s, when grain prices recovered, did implementation gain in momentum. In the provinces east of the Elbe the overwhelming part of peasant obligations had been redeemed by the early 1840s, and in many regions the open field system was abolished in the process (Harnisch 1984, 1986; Eddie 2013).

Saxony provides a contrasting case. Late but comprehensive reforms to rural property rights came in the wake of the revolution of 1830 in the form of a package of laws enacted in 1832. Since there were no other exogeneous variations around this time, it should be possible to isolate the economic effects of this institutional reform. Output of principal food crops in Saxony did not, however, react in a perceivable way to the reform, at least not during the 1830s and 1840s (Figure 4.3). There are two broad explanations for this finding: First, the redemption of feudal obligations, which stood at the heart of the reform of 1832, primarily changed the flow of income streams, rather than incentives. Moreover, most redemption acts were only completed during the 1850s and 1860s so that farmer's incomes benefitted only in the last quarter of the nineteenth century. Second, pre-reform agrarian institutions were sufficiently flexible to allow renegotiation over rights to land usage when and where this had been required for the introduction of land-saving innovations, such as the cultivation of clover and other fodder crops, or potatoes (Kopsidis and Pfister 2013, 11–12, 43–46; Pfister and Kopsidis 2015, 284–90).

Whereas the combination of property rights reform and the abolishment of the open field system may have contributed to agricultural growth in the central and eastern parts of Prussia by the 1830s and 1840s, evidence for Saxony and the western parts of Prussia do not testify in favour of an important effect of agrarian reforms on agricultural output, particularly around the time when Germany entered the post-Malthusian era, that is, the 1810s (Kopsidis et al. 2017; Tilly and Kopsidis 2020, 62–65). Taken as a whole, the reforms undertaken during the first two decades of the nineteenth century should not be considered as one-off institutional changes that altered economic incentives. Rather, pressure from France and exigencies connected with warfare improved economic policies by opening up new options, heightening the position of states vis-à-vis privileged individuals and particularistic interest groups, and increasing state capacity with respect to the implementation of legal norms. All this may have rendered markets more inclusive and reduced transaction costs. Above all the change in policy formulation and implementation took place in a gradual way. State capacity mattered crucially in this process, and state capacity, apart from its fiscal foundations, is related to the size of states.

5.6 *Effects of State Size, Increased State Autonomy and Growth in State Capacity*

What follows pursues the argument that the changes of territorial boundaries that took place during the Revolutionary and Napoleonic Wars increased state size, which increased the capacity to provide public goods (Alesina and

Spolaore 1997). This effect was amplified by a transformation of the political order, sanctioned by the Vienna settlement in 1815, as a result of which governments now ruled over sovereign states, rather than semi-autonomous estates within the framework of the former Empire. To the extent that organizational differentiation is correlated with size, public authorities in the enlarged states of the post-1815 era were more capable of pursuing and implementing state policies by resisting pressure from interest groups and other Imperial estates than there had been during the Old Regime. Increased state capacity may not have fundamentally altered economic institutions. In that sense, the present argument remains agnostic with respect to the interaction among interest groups, institutions, and growth. Rather, larger state bureaucracy with heightened autonomy amplified the scope of policies aimed at political development and improved the quality of policy formulation and implementation (Banerjee and Duflo 2012).

Agrarian reform discussed above stands for the increasing sophistication of policy formulation and implementation, while measures designed to foster market integration epitomize the enlarged scope for state action. War reduced political fragmentation and created relatively large states. In 1815, 60 per cent of the German population were citizens of one of the two largest states, Prussia and Bavaria. The changes in territorial boundaries thus created a potential for internal market development, whose exploitation was aided by state policies. Market integration within enlarged state boundaries deepened regional specialization along lines of comparative advantage. This in turn increased the efficiency of factor allocation and facilitated the spatial concentration of economic activities and the rise of urban industries and services benefitting from the externalities of agglomeration. All this contributed to an expansion of labour demand. Increased state size and heightened state autonomy, which improved state capacity, may thus have been a relevant and possibly significant factor underlying Germany's transition to a post-Malthusian growth regime.

Two policies specifically promoted economic integration, namely, the introduction of unified systems of border tariffs and the construction of paved roads (*chaussées*). Until the beginning of the nineteenth century rulers, other privileged individuals and corporate entities such as towns imposed tolls on trade at locations they controlled. About 1800 toll regulations are said to have existed in Germany around 1790. Neither the amounts charged nor the structure of tariffs followed any systematic rules. Bavaria began to introduce a system of unified border tariffs in 1765, but its implementation in all territories ruled by the Wittelsbacher dynasty was hindered by Imperial law. Within the framework of the *Reichsdeputationshauptschluss* of 1803 France had achieved the abolition of the many tariffs on the river Rhine, which created a need for tariff reforms. After the creation of the Rhine Federation French desire for free access to the markets of its members led to plans for coordinated trade liberalization. To pre-empt the imposition of a common trade policy under French supervision individual member states undertook reforms that established a unified system of border tariffs administered by newly created units within the central government. They abolished all entitlements of agents apart from states and drastically reduced exemptions favouring particular groups or trading partners. Bavaria, Württemberg, Baden, the Grand Duchy of Berg and the Kingdom of *Westphalen* all introduced modern tariff regimes along these lines between 1806 and 1812. Prussia followed in 1818 in the context of the fiscal reform carried out in the aftermath of the war. The responsible minister, Hans von Bülow, could draw on his experience with tariff reforms that he had gained in his previous position as minister of finance of the Kingdom of *Westphalen* at the beginning of the 1810s. Accession of former estates to sovereign status following the dissolution of the Empire in 1806 was instrumental for the introduction of unified tariff regimes in German states (Berding 1980; Häberle 1974; Ohnishi 1973).

At least in some parts of Germany, internal market creation resulting from changes in territorial boundaries and the creation of modern tariff systems led to an increase in market integration: Gaps in rye prices between markets that belonged to different polities before the wars and that both became part of Bavaria fell by about 62 percent between the 1780s and the 1820s. City-pairs that belonged to Kingdom of *Westphalen* and became part of Prussia after the wars experienced a reduction of price differentials by about 41 percent (Albers and Pfister 2020).

Progress in the formation of effective states had market creating effects within newly established territorial boundaries. It may also have led to trade diverting effects with respect to interstate trade and thereby motivated the formation of the *Zollverein* of 1834. Unified external tariffs created the challenge of access to foreign markets, and liberalization of trade on the river Rhine in 1831 meant that more inland states became dependent on transit trade through Prussia. Access to sea ports and to the markets of other states were motives for smaller states to join the *Zollverein*, which was advocated notably by Prussia (Keller and Shiue 2014; Huning and Wolf 2019).

Infrastructure development, particularly in the form of the construction of paved roads or *chaussées*, facilitated the exploitation of the potential created by the introduction of unified border tariffs. Although Germany possessed virtually no roads of the *chaussée* type around 1800, most states undertook vigorous programmes of road construction after the Napoleonic era. In the decades following the war road construction constituted the single most important type of expenditure that was not related to core functions of the state. The roots of these programmes usually lay in the war period when governments established technical standards, administrative responsibilities and sometimes a plan of action. In this initial phase Baden was already well advanced by 1812. In Prussia it drew to a close by 1817 (Borchard 1968, 200–05, 214–05, 260–78; Müller 2000).

Infrastructure development promoted market integration. From the 1820s to the 1850s the magnitude of price differentials between Westphalian markets for the prices of wheat and rye depended upon the existence of paved roads between them (Uebele and Gallardo Albarrán 2016).

Market integration widened the potential for the development of regional export industries and promoted activities characterized by increasing returns. This is mirrored by urbanization and changes to the urban hierarchy that occurred over the first half of the nineteenth century. Whereas German population increased by 53 per cent between 1800 and 1850 the forty largest towns increased the number of their inhabitants by 91 per cent on average—broadly in line with the rate of expansion of total urban population (data from Pfister 2020). Towns located at the apex of urban hierarchy grew faster, however, and they often exerted political functions. In 1850, seven of the twelve largest towns were either capitals (Berlin, Munich, and Dresden) or administrative centres of Prussian provinces. Those six capitals that were already among the 40 largest towns in 1800 saw their populations increase by 135 per cent by 1850. At the same time, their share in the total population of the forty largest towns rose from 26 to 31 per cent. Thus, the process of state growth that took place during the Napoleonic period was followed by a marked increase in urban hierarchy.

The spatial concentration of political and administrative power produced the agglomeration characteristics from which the development and application of complex new technologies depended. This is borne out by the spatial distribution of engineering activities, which emerged towards the middle of the nineteenth century and remain a defining element of Germany's economy today. To be sure, market access was also an important locational factor. In 1846, more than half of all engineering firms active in the *Zollverein* states were located in Saxony, the leading cotton manufacturing region at that time. However, the production of heavy machinery, in particular of steam engines and locomotives, which developed rapidly from the 1840s, initially tended to be located in capitals, particularly in Berlin, but also in Munich, Hanover, Kassel, Karlsruhe and Stuttgart/Esslingen. Leading engineering firms of the late nineteenth century were predominantly recruited from these first movers founded before 1850, a clear indication of scale effects. The location of institutions for technical training in capitals provided for thick labour markets, and the tendency of ministries of trade to treat technological innovation as a public good created dense information networks. Finally, the role of governments in infrastructural development also meant that capitals provided good access to markets. Thus, the creation of relatively large territorial states during the Napoleonic period that contributed to market development through unified regimes of border tariffs and infrastructure investment laid the foundation for the emergence of economic activities that depended upon externalities of agglomeration (Kiesewetter 2004, 197–206; Martin 1913, 18–26; Schröter and Becker 1962, 67–69, 102–05, 124).

6 Conclusion

To the extent that they involved Germanic societies and lands, the Revolutionary and Napoleonic Wars were fought in poorly monetized economies. Hence, non-fiscal channels were important for the mobilization of resources for warfare. They included levies, direct contributions in kind and predation by marauding troops. Apart from the final phase of the war in the early 1810s, the share of military personnel in adult male populations remained small, and the adverse effect of the wars on incomes seems to have been of a minor order. Nevertheless, areas serving repeatedly as major theatres of war were seriously affected; Saxony, where the largest known battle before World War I took place (Leipzig 1813) suffered a human loss of 5 per cent measured as negative deviation of population in 1815 from its long-term trend. The poor development of organized state finance also meant that even modest levels of military expenditures engendered fiscal nightmares. Coping with financial disorder and surviving French pressure by way of extending the tax base were powerful motives underlying fiscal, administrative, social and economic reforms that most German states undertook in the framework of defensive modernization programmes during the first two decades of the nineteenth century.

Within a few years after the end of war in 1815 Germany entered a post-Malthusian regime of economic growth. The reaction of mortality to income fluctuations weakened so that harvest failures ceased to provoke excess mortality on a national level. Demand for labour increased so that population growth could accelerate without provoking a serious decline in material welfare.

A vast literature draws connections between war-related dislocation, the power of particular interest groups and distributional coalitions, economic institutions, and welfare. However, the institutional reforms initiated from the 1790s to the 1810s do not seem to have had immediate economic effects. The most important policies, such as land reform and the introduction of freedom of trade, took decades to implement. In the case of land reform, the fact that many peasants already enjoyed fairly secure rights of usage during pre-modern times also meant that reform changed income streams flowing from land rather than incentive structures. Institutional change certainly quickened in the wake of the political dislocations resulting from the wars, but its gradualist nature implies that it cannot comprehensively explain the structural break that occurred in the years around 1820.

The main channel through which the Revolutionary and Napoleonic Wars contributed to economic development seems to reside in the transformation of Germany's state system. The abolition of clerical principalities and Imperial towns in 1803 and the formation of the Rhine Federation under French hegemony in 1806 were major steps in this process, which was eventually sanctioned by the Congress of Vienna in 1815. A plethora of territories that were embedded in the superstructure of the Holy Roman Empire gave way to about 35 sovereign entities. Apart from Prussia they included about ten middle-sized units that were capable of pursuing policies of state building, including programmes of political and economic integration. The latter included the creation of a unified system of external tariffs and road construction. Both improved the integration of regional markets and thereby contributed to economic growth by deepening the division of labour between adjacent zones. This in turn promoted learning by doing, which created positive returns to scale and a potential for technological innovation. The Revolutionary and Napoleonic Wars brought suffering and hardship in the short run. In the long run, they promoted economic development through the creation of modern states.

References

Acemoglu, Daron, Davide Cantoni, Simon Johnson, and James A. Robinson. 2011. "The consequences of radical reform: the French Revolution." *American Economic Review* 101 (7): 3286–3307.

Acemoglu, Daron, and James Robinson. 2012. *Why nations fail: the origins of power, prosperity, and poverty*. New York: Crown.

Albers, Hakon, Ulrich Pfister, and Martin Uebele. 2018. "The great moderation of grain price volatility: market integration vs. climate change, Germany, 1650–1790." *EHES Working Papers in Economic History* 135.

Albers, Hakon, and Ulrich Pfister. 2020. "War, state growth and market integration in the German lands, 1780–1830." In "Empirical essays on agriculture in Germany: past and present", authored by Hakon Albers, 159–90. PhD diss., Martin Luther University Halle-Wittenberg. http://dx.doi.org/10.25673/32681.

Alesina, Alberto, and Enrico Spolaore. 1997. "On the number and size of nations." *Quarterly Journal of Economics* 112 (4): 1027–56.

Amend-Traut, Anja. 2009. *Wechselverbindlichkeiten vor dem Reichskammergericht: Praktiziertes Zivilrecht in der Frühen Neuzeit*. Köln: Böhlau.

Banerjee, Abhijit V., and Esther Duflo. 2012. *Poor economics: a radical rethinking of the way to fight global poverty*. New York: PublicAffairs.

Banken, Ralf. 2019. "Bergische Waren und englische Kaperer. Der Einfluss der Kontinentalsperre auf die Wirtschaftsentwicklung Westdeutschlands." In *Moderner Kapitalismus: Wirtschafts- und unternehmenshistorische Beiträge*, edited by Hesse, Jan-Otmar, Christian Kleinschmidt, Roman Köster, and Tim Schanetzky, 325–42. Tübingen: Mohr Siebeck.

Bartels, Christoph. 1992. *Vom frühneuzeitlichen Montangewerbe zur Bergbauindustrie: Erzbergbau im Oberharz 1635–1866*. Bochum: Deutsches Bergbaumuseum.

Baten, Jörg, Dorothee Crayen, and Hans-Joachim Voth. 2014. "Numeracy and the impact of high food prices in industrializing Britain." *Review of Economics and Statistics* 96 (3): 418–30.

Berding, Helmut. 1973. *Napoleonische Herrschafts- und Gesellschaftspolitik im Königreich Westfalen 1807–1813*. Göttingen: Vandenhoeck und Ruprecht.

Berding, Helmut. 1980. "Die Reform des Zollwesens in Deutschland unter dem Einfluss der napoleonischen Herrschaft." *Geschichte und Gesellschaft* 6 (4): 523–37.

Böhm, Max. 1995. *Bayerns Agrarproduktion 1800–1870*. St. Katharinen: Scripta Mercaturae.

Borchard, Karl. 1968. "Staatsverbrauch und öffentliche Investitionen in Deutschland 1780–1850." PhD diss., University of Göttingen.

Bracht, Johannes, and Ulrich Pfister. 2020. *Landpacht, Marktgesellschaft und Agrarentwicklung: Fünf Adelsgüter zwischen Rhein und Weser, spätes 16. bis 19. Jahrhundert*. Stuttgart: Steiner.

Denzel, Markus. 2015. "Vom Scheitern eines Modells: das Kontinentalsystem als europäischer Wirtschaftsverband." In *1813 und die Folgen für Europa: Entgrenzung und Einhegung*, edited by Aschmann, Birgit, and Thomas Stamm-Kuhlmann, 187–216. Stuttgart: Steiner.

Dethlefs, Gerd, Armin Owzar, and Gisela Weiß (eds.). 2008. *Modell und Wirklichkeit: Politik, Kultur und Gesellschaft im Großherzogtum Berg und im Königreich Westphalen*. Paderborn: Schöningh.

Diefendorf, Jeffry M. 1980. *Businessmen and politics in the Rhineland, 1789–1834*. Princeton: Princeton University Press.

Dincecco, Mark. 2009. "Fiscal centralization, limited government, and public revenues in Europe, 1650–1913." *Journal of Economic History* 69 (1): 48–103.

Dincecco, Mark. 2011. *Political transformations and public finances: Europe, 1650–1913*. Cambridge: Cambridge University Press.

Dipper, Christof. 1980. *Die Bauernbefreiung in Deutschland*. Stuttgart: Kohlhammer.

Dufraisse, Roger. 1989. "De quelques conséquences économiques et sociales de la domination française sur les régions du Rhin inférieur 1794–1814." In *Franzosen und Deutsche am Rhein: 1789—1918—1945*, edited by Hüttenberger, Peter, and Hansgeorg Molitor, 129–60. Essen: Klartext.

Dufraisse, Roger. 1992. *L'Allemagne à l'époque napoléonienne: questions d'histoire politique, économique et sociale*. Bonn: Bouvier.

Eddie, S. A. 2013. *Freedom's price: serfdom, subjection and reform in Prussia, 1648–1848*. Oxford: Oxford University Press.

Engels, Wilhelm. 1957. *Ablösungen und Gemeinheitsteilungen in der Rheinprovinz: ein Beitrag zur Geschichte der Bauernbefreiung*. Bonn: Röhrscheid.

Esser, Franz Dominic. 2020. *Der Wandel der Rheinischen Agrarverfassung. Der Einfluss französischer und preußischer Agrarreformen zwischen 1794 und 1850 auf die bäuerlichen Rechtsverhältnisse im Rheinland*. Köln: Böhlau.

Fehrenbach, Elisabeth. 1974. *Traditionale Gesellschaft und revolutionäres Recht: die Einführung des Code Napoleon in den Rheinbundstaaten*. Göttingen: Vandenhoeck & Ruprecht.

Fehrenbach, Elisabeth. 2001. *Vom Ancien Régime zum Wiener Kongress*. München: Oldenbourg.

Fertig, Georg, Christian Schlöder, Rolf Gehrmann, Christina Langfeldt, and Ulrich Pfister. 2018. "Das postmalthusianische Zeitalter: Die Bevölkerungsentwicklung in Deutschland, 1815–1871." *Vierteljahrschrift für Sozial- und Wirtschaftsgeschichte* 105 (1): 6–33.

Fiedler, Siegfried. 1988. *Kriegsführung im Zeitalter der Revolutionskriege*. Koblenz: Bernard & Graefe.

Fischer, Wolfram. 1962. *Der Staat und die Anfänge der Industrialisierung in Baden 1800–1850*. Berlin: Duncker & Humblot.

Glaser, Rüdiger, and Dirk Riemann. 2009. "A thousand-year record of temperature variations for Germany and Central Europe based on documentary data." *Journal of Quarternary Science* 24: 437–49.

Häberle, Eckehard J. 1974. *Zollpolitik und Integration im 18. Jahrhundert: Untersuchungen zur wirtschaftlichen und politischen Integration in Bayern von 1765 bis 1811*. München: Wölfle.

Harnisch, Hartmut. 1984. *Kapitalistische Agrarreform und industrielle Revolution*. Weimar: Böhlau.

Harnisch, Hartmut. 1986. "Peasants and markets: the background to the agrarian reforms in feudal Prussia east of the Elbe, 1760–1807." In *The German peasantry: conflict and community in rural society from the eighteenth to the twentieth centuries*, edited by Evans, Richard J., and W. R. Lee, 1–36. London: Croom Helm.

Henning, Friedrich Wilhelm. 1978. "Die Einführung der Gewerbefreiheit und ihre Auswirkungen auf das Handwerk in Deutschland." In *Handwerksgeschichte in neuer Sicht*, edited by Wilhelm Abel, 147–77. Göttingen: Schwartz.

Hinz, Frank Lothar. 1977. *Die Geschichte der Wocklumer Eisenhütte 1758–1864 als Beispiel westfälischen adligen Unternehmertums*. Altena: Freunde der Burg Altena.

Huning, Thilo R., and Nikolaus Wolf. 2019. "How Britain unified Germany: endogenous trade costs and the formation of a customs union." *CEPR Discussion Paper* 13634.

Juhász, Réka. 2018. "Temporary protection and technology adoption: evidence from the Napoleonic Blockade." *American Economic Review* 108 (11): 3339–76.

Kaufhold, Karl Heinrich. 1982. "Gewerbefreiheit und gewerbliche Entwicklung in Deutschland im 19. Jahrhundert." *Blätter für deutsche Landesgeschichte* 98: 73–114.

Keller, Wolfgang, and Carol H. Shiue. 2014. "Endogenous formation of free trade agreements: evidence from the Zollverein's impact on market integration." *Journal of Economic History* 74 (4): 1168–1204.

Keller, Wolfgang, and Carol H. Shiue. 2020. "Market integration and institutional change." *Review of World Economics* 156 (2): 251–85.

Kermann, Joachim. 1972. *Die Manufakturen im Rheinland 1750–1833*. Bonn: Röhrscheid.

Kiesewetter, Hubert. 2004. *Industrielle Revolution in Deutschland: Regionen als Wachstumsmotoren*. Stuttgart: Steiner.

Kiesewetter, Hubert. 2007. *Die Industrialisierung Sachsens: ein regional-vergleichendes Erklärungsmodell*. Stuttgart: Steiner.

Kirchhain, Günter. 1977. *Das Wachstum der deutschen Baumwollindustrie im 19. Jahrhundert: eine historische Modellstudie zur empirischen Wachstumsforschung*. New York: Arno.

Kisch, Herbert. 1989. *From domestic manufacture to industrial revolution: the case of the Rhineland textile districts*. Oxford: Oxford University Press.

Klein, Ernst. 1965. *Von der Reform zur Restauration: Finanzpolitik und Reformgesetzgebung des preußischen Staatskanzlers Karl August von Hardenberg*. Berlin: de Gruyter.

Klein, Ernst. 1974. *Geschichte der öffentlichen Finanzen in Deutschland (1500–1870)*. Wiesbaden: Steiner.

Klemann, Hein A. M. 2013. "The Central Commission for the Navigation of the Rhine, 1815–1914: Nineteenth century European integration." *ECHR Working Paper* ECHR-2013-1.

Kopsidis, Michael, Johannes Bracht, Friederike Scholten, and Ulrich Pfister. 2017. "Agricultural output growth in a proto- and early industrial setting: evidence from sharecropping in Western Westphalia and the Lower Rhineland, c. 1740–1860." *Rural History* 28 (1): 21–46.

Kopsidis, Michael, and Daniel W. Bromley. 2016. "The French revolution and German industrialization: doubtful models and doubtful causality." *Journal of Institutional Economics* 12 (1): 161–90.

Kopsidis, Michael, and Ulrich Pfister. 2013. "Agricultural development during early industrialization in a low-wage economy: Saxony, c. 1790–1830." *EHES Working Papers in Economic History* 39.

Kriedte, Peter. 2007. *Taufgesinnte und großes Kapital: die niederrheinisch-bergischen Mennoniten und der Aufstieg des Krefelder Seidengewerbes (Mitte des 17. Jahrhunderts–1815)*. Göttingen: Vandenhoeck & Ruprecht.

Kutz, Martin. 1974. *Deutschlands Außenhandel von der Französischen Revolution bis zur Gründung des Zollvereins*. Wiesbaden: Steiner.

von Lancizolle, Carl Wilhelm. 1830. *Übersicht der deutschen Reichsstandschafts- und Territorial-Verhältnisse vor dem französischen Revolutionskriege, der seitdem eingetretenen Veränderungen und der gegenwärtigen Bestandteile des deutschen Bundes und der Bundesstaaten*. Berlin: Dümmler.

Luterbacher, J., D. Dietrich, E. Xoplaki, M. Grosjean, and H. Wanner. 2004. "European seasonal and annual temperature variability, trends and extremes." *Science* 303: 1499–1503.

Martin, Kurt. 1913. *"Die deutsche Lokomotivbauindustrie."* PhD diss., University of Münster.

Marzagalli, Silvia. 1999. *Les boulevards de la fraude: le négoce maritime et le blocus continental, 1806–1813—Bordeaux, Hambourg, Livourne*. Paris: Presses Universitaires du Septentrion.

Müller, Uwe. 2000. *Infrastrukturpolitik in der Industrialisierung: der Chausseebau in der preußischen Provinz Sachsen und dem Herzogtum Braunschweig vom Ende des 18. Jahrhunderts bis in die siebziger Jahre des 19. Jahrhunderts*. Berlin: Duncker und Humblot.

Nipperdey, Thomas. 1998. *Deutsche Geschichte 1800–1866: Bürgerwelt und starker Staat*. München: Beck.

Nolte, Paul. 1990. *Staatsbildung und Gesellschaftsreform: Politische Reformen in Preußen und den süddeutschen Staaten 1800–1820*. Frankfurt: Campus.

North, Douglass C., John Joseph Wallis, and Barry R. Weingast. 2009. *Violence and social orders: a conceptual framework for interpreting recorded human history*. Cambridge: Cambridge University Press.

North, Michael. 2012. "Finances and power in the German state system." In *The rise of fiscal states: a global history 1500–1914*, edited by Yun-Casalilla, Bartolomé, Patrick K. O'Brien, and Francisco Comín Comín, 145–63. Cambridge: Cambridge University Press.

Ohnishi, Takeo. 1973. *Zolltarifpolitik Preußens bis zur Gründung des Zollvereins: ein Beitrag zur Finanz- und Außenpolitik Preußens*. Göttingen: Schwartz.

Olson, Mancur. 1982. *The rise and decline of nations: economic growth, stagflation and institutional rigidities*. New Haven: Yale University Press.

O'Rourke, Kevin H. 2006. "The worldwide economic impact of the French Revolutionary and Napoleonic Wars, 1793–1815." *Journal of Global History* 1: 123–49.

Pfister, Ulrich. 2017. "The timing and pattern of real wage divergence in pre-industrial Europe: evidence from Germany, c. 1500–1850." *Economic History Review* 70 (3): 701–729.

Pfister, Ulrich. 2020. "Urban population in Germany, 1500–1850." *CQE Working Paper* 90.

Pfister, Ulrich, and Georg Fertig. 2010. "The population history of Germany: research agenda and preliminary results." *MPIDR Working Paper* 2010-035.

Pfister, Ulrich, and Georg Fertig. 2020. "From Malthusian disequilibrium to the post-Malthusian era: The evolution of the preventive and positive checks in Germany, 1730–1870." *Demography* 57 (3): 1145–70.

Pfister, Ulrich, and Michael Kopsidis. 2015. "Institutions vs. demand: determinants of agricultural development in Saxony, 1660–1850." *European Review of Economic History* 19 (3): 275–93.

Pfister, Ulrich, Jana Riedel, and Martin Uebele. 2012. "Real wages and the origins of modern economic growth in Germany, 16th to 19th centuries." *EHES Working Paper* 17.

Planert, Ute. 2007. *Der Mythos vom Befreiungskrieg: Frankreichs Kriege und der deutsche Süden, Alltag—Wahrnehmung—Deutung 1792–1841*. Paderborn: Schöningh.

Reckendrees, Alfred. 2012. "Zur Funktion der Aktiengesellschaft in der frühen Industrialisierung." *Jahrbuch für Wirtschaftsgeschichte* 53 (2): 137–74.

Rothenberg, Gunther E. 2006. *The Napoleonic Wars*. New York: Harper Collins.

Saalfeld, Diedrich. 1987. "Die Kontinentalsperre." In *Die Auswirkungen von Zöllen und anderen Handelshemmnissen auf Wirtschaft und Gesellschaft vom Mittelalter bis zur Gegenwart*, edited by Hans Pohl, 121–39. Stuttgart: Steiner.

Schäfer, Michael. 2016. *Eine andere Industrialisierung: Die Transformation der sächsischen Textilexportgewerbe, 1790–1890*. Stuttgart: Steiner.

Schirmer, Uwe. 1996. "Der Bevölkerungsgang in Sachsen zwischen 1743–1815." *Vierteljahrschrift für Sozial- und Wirtschaftsgeschichte* 83 (1): 25–58.

Schneider, Karl Heinz. 2010. *Geschichte der Bauernbefreiung*. Stuttgart: Reclam.

Schröter, Alfred, and Walter Becker. 1962. *Die deutsche Maschinenbauindustrie in der industriellen Revolution*. Berlin: Akademie.

Schulte Beerbühl, Margrit. 2018. "Coping with chaos: Geographische Dimension und institutionelle Neuerungen während der weltweiten Spekulationsblase von 1799." In *Ordnung und Chaos: Trends und Brüche in der Wirtschafts- und Sozialgeschichte*, edited by Günther Schulz, 53–75. Stuttgart: Steiner.

Siegert, Rosmarie. 2001. *Steuerpolitik und Gesellschaft: Vergleichende Untersuchungen zu Preußen und Baden 1815–1848*. Berlin: Duncker & Humblot.

Spaulding, Robert Mark. 2015. "Rhine river commerce and the Continental system." In *Revisiting Napoleon's Continental System: local, regional and European experiences*, edited by Aaslestad, Katherine B., and Johan Joor, 114–32. Basingstoke: Palgrave Macmillan.

Spoerer, Mark. 2004. *Steuerlast, Steuerinzidenz und Steuerwettbewerb: Verteilungswirkungen der Besteuerung in Preußen und Württemberg (1815–1913)*. Berlin: Akademie.

Spoerer, Mark. 2010. "The evolution of public finances in nineteenth-century Germany." In *Paying for the liberal state: the rise of public finance in nineteenth-century Europe*, edited by Cardoso, José Luìs, and Pedro Lains, 103–31. Cambridge: Cambridge University Press.

Thiemeyer, Guido, and Isabel Tölle. 2011. "Supranationalität im 19. Jahrhundert? Die Beispiele der Zentralkommission für die Rheinschifffahrt und des Octroivertrages 1804–1832." *Journal of European Integration History* 17: 177–96.

Tilly, Richard. 1966. *Financial institutions and industrialization in the Rhineland 1815–1870*. Madison: University of Wisconsin Press.

Tilly, Richard H., and Michael Kopsidis. 2020. *From Old Regime to Industrial State: a history of German industrialization from the eighteenth century to World War One*. Chicago: University of Chicago Press.

Uebele, Martin, and Daniel Gallardo Albarrán. 2015. "Paving the way to modernity: Prussian roads and grain market integration in Westphalia, 1821–1855." *Scandinavian Economic History Review* 63 (1): 69–92.

Ullmann, Hans-Peter. 1982. "Badische Finanzreformen in der Rheinbundzeit." *Geschichte und Gesellschaft* 8: 333–66.

Ullmann, Hans-Peter. 1986. *Staatsschulden und Reformpolitik: die Entstehung moderner öffentlicher Schulden in Bayern und Baden, 1780–1820*. Göttingen: Vandenhoeck & Ruprecht.

Ullmann, Hans-Peter. 2005. *Der deutsche Steuerstaat: Geschichte der öffentlichen Finanzen vom 18. Jahrhundert bis heute*. München: Beck.

Vogel, Barbara. 1983. *Allgemeine Gewerbefreiheit: die Reformpolitik des preußischen Staatskanzlers Hardenberg (1810–1820)*. Göttingen: Vandenhoeck und Ruprecht.

Vonyó, Tamás. 2008. "Post-war reconstruction and Golden Age of economic growth." *European Review of Economic History* 12 (2): 221–41.

Wegner, Gerhard. 2016. "Defensive modernization in Germany and in the Habsburg Empire: a historical study of capitalist transformation." *Journal of Institutional Economics* 12 (2): 443–69.

Wehler, Hans-Ulrich. 1987. *Deutsche Gesellschaftsgeschichte, vol. 1: Vom Feudalismus des Alten Reiches bis zur Defensiven Modernisierung der Reformära 1700–1815*. München: Beck.

Weis, Eberhard. 1973. "Der Einfluss der französischen Reformen und des Empire auf die Reformen in den süddeutschen Staaten." *Francia* 1: 569–83.

von Witzleben, Alexander. 1985. *Staatsfinanznot und sozialer Wandel: Eine finanzsoziologische Analyse der preußischen Reformzeit zu Beginn des 19. Jahrhunderts*. Stuttgart: Steiner.

Wolf, Holger C. 1995. "Post-war Germany in the European context: domestic and external determinants of growth." In *Europe's post-war prosperity*, edited by Barry Eichengreen, 323–52. Cambridge: Cambridge University Press.

Ziekow, Jan. 1992. *Freiheit und Bindung des Gewerbes*. Berlin: Duncker und Humblot.

CHAPTER 5

Revolutionary Wars and Economic Change in the New State of the Netherlands, 1795–1815

Marjolein 't Hart and Johan Joor

The Dutch suffered disproportionally from Napoleon's war blockades and exactions. Historians agree that the economic shock was severe, not least for the country's traditionally open and exposed trade networks (Brugmans 1961; Buyst and Mokyr 1990; De Vries and Van der Woude 1997; O'Rourke 2006, 146).[1] But what impact did this have on Dutch economic development in the longer term? Economic historians have shown that Dutch GDP languished between 1815 and 1850 (Smits et al. 2000). A short post-war revival was followed by several decades of decline and stagnation. Dutch GDP only began to pick up in the 1860s, with the start of industrialisation. To what extent were the difficulties of these post-war decades caused by the revolutionary wars of 1795–1815?

This question is easy to pose, but hard to answer. The historical evidence is scanty and dispersed, due to the rapid and manifold administrative changes that occurred in this period, which hampers analysis that covers both the period before the wars and the time thereafter. Although we do have an excellent reconstruction of the Dutch National Accounts from 1807 onwards, this is based on data that provide an estimation for the national story. For the period before 1807, we are reliant on partial, long-term data from the Province of Holland alone. The conclusions from these data provide some of the answers, but they cannot explain how wartime experiences differed strongly from year to year, varied from one region to another, or afflicted different subsectors in differentiated ways. Data on such a complex issue have simply not survived.

In addition, the Dutch experience of 1815–1850 runs counter to the general assumption that wars tend to have only limited effects on highly commercialised, diversified economies such as the Netherlands. A number of comparative

1 A previous version of this paper was presented at a series of conferences funded by the Leverhulme Trust, convened by Patrick O'Brien, in Madrid (2015), Lisbon (2016) and London (2017), and the ENIUGH Conference in Budapest (2017). We thank the participants for their remarks. The research was funded by Leverhulme and by the FWO/NWO-grant 326–53-001 for the project "Managing the Crisis? The Resilience of Local Networks and Institutions within the Low Countries during the Napoleonic Period."

 | DOI:10.1163/9789004472754_006

studies, varying over place and time, have concluded that such economies usually manage to recuperate quickly after wars, thanks to the high variation in the available options and resources. Indeed, despite war-time losses, wars also tend to give rise to innovations, such as engaging in alternative economic opportunities, using underexploited resources, and improving state capacity through novel fiscal measures. In such cases, periods of war often appear to be short-lived dips (Barbera 1973; Kang and Meernik 2005; Torres-Sánchez et al. 2018).

Yet the Netherlands found itself on a different trajectory. Why did it take so long for the Netherlands to find its way onto a firm path of economic growth? Did the wars of 1795–1815 hurt its highly commercialised and diversified economy so badly that it failed to recuperate thereafter? Or are other factors to blame? Our analysis will focus on the territory of the present-day Netherlands even though we realise such choices are not always congruent with historical realities. We start with a short overview of the political context, which will be followed by sections that discuss the wartime complications and losses of territory and colonies, population and urbanisation, trade and financial services, industry, fisheries and agriculture, and state finances. The analysis of the post-1813 period focuses on the failed unification with the South and the inefficiency of the crown's financial policies, and evaluates mercantilist aims to reinforce industry and trade. In the conclusion, we return to the main question posed above.

1 From Federal Republic to Unified State

The Dutch entered the revolutionary period with a strong commercial and specialised economy. The extraordinary productivity of agriculture enabled specialisation and social stratification, whilst industry profited from advanced levels of technology and trade networks that enabled large-scale exports. Competing urban oligarchies supported by strong local and regional authorities furthered the maintenance of an outstanding service sector. Yet the openness of the economy also rendered the Dutch federation vulnerable in international terms. During the eighteenth century, the country gradually lost its leading position in shipping and trade, largely due to increased competition from Britain and France. Although Dutch fisheries and industry experienced increasing difficulties, agriculture improved and the financial sector also boomed between 1770 and the early 1790s, despite increasing competition from London in international finance (Riley 1980, 101ff.).

Compared to other countries that experienced revolutionary reforms in the 1790s and subsequent decades, the 'shock' to political culture was limited due to the earlier revolutionary Patriot Movement, which had dominated politics in the 1780s (Van Sas 2004). Dutch Patriots had harboured radical ideas regarding democratic representation and civic equality, which challenged the ossified urban oligarchies and the Orange Stadholderate. Political discourse gradually exchanged a more 'federal' focus for a more 'national' one. For example, the Economic Branch of the Holland Society of Sciences aimed to strengthen trade, agriculture, manufacturing and fisheries with a *nationwide* scope. The Patriots were defeated in 1787 after military intervention by Prussian troops, yet their ideas and networks persisted and became resurgent during the French invasion of January 1795, facilitating a 'homemade', 'velvet' revolution that resulted in the new 'Batavian Republic'.

After 1795, the French exerted profound influence on Dutch policies. They annexed parts of the former Dutch Republic and dictated a rigid offensive alliance, which immediately resulted in war with Great Britain and the subsequent loss of colonial settlements overseas (Colenbrander 1925, 299–300). French domination became more intense after Napoleon seized power in 1799, in particular after the regime change of 1801 (which ended most of the Dutch democratic experiments) and 1805 (which imposed Rutger Jan Schimmelpenninck as a single head of state). In his attempt to reinforce French supremacy on the continent, Napoleon abolished the Batavian Republic, proclaimed the Kingdom of Holland on 5 June 1806 and put his brother Louis Napoleon on the throne. After years of trouble between Napoleon and Louis – not least because of disputes regarding the Continental Blockade – the Kingdom was annexed to the French Empire in July 1810. During this incorporation, the Netherlands lost its independence completely, even though three-quarters of its territory continued to be administered as a separate entity under a French governor.

The Batavian-French Period ended on 21 November 1813 with the proclamation of a General Administration for the Netherlands in the name of Prince William of Orange, the son of the former stadtholder. Six days earlier, the French had lost power after a massive revolt in Amsterdam, which caused the state's principal officials to flee. As a consequence of the 1815 Vienna Treaty, the country became a kingdom and was unified with the Southern Netherlands. The political events of 1795–1815 thus resulted in a centralised state and the adoption of a constitution with civil rights and the principal elements of democracy. Undoubtedly, the new king of the Netherlands 'slept in the bed of Napoleon'.[2] Yet the newly-formed United Kingdom suffered from a 'structural flaw', since the demographical dominance of the Southern provinces was not

2 Adapted from Joseph Fouché's remark on King Louis XVIII.

proportionate to its political influence (Bornewasser 1983, 220). Religious disputes added to political instability and resulted in the secession of Belgium in 1830.

The years 1795–1815 had been profoundly turbulent: they had seen one revolution, three military coups, two regime changes without military interference, the loss of independence, the restoration of national sovereignty and finally two successive changes of constitution. The days of the former decentralised and oligarchic Dutch Republic evidently belonged to the past. Yet what had been the impact on the economy of the Netherlands?

2 Land and Population: Losses, Gains and De-Urbanisation

Wartime territorial losses had direct economic consequences, if only because of the reduction of the domestic market and the severing of trade connections. The outbreak of the Batavian Revolution in 1795 and the alliance with France led to war with England and, as a direct consequence of this, the loss of Dutch colonial settlements, notably Ceylon, South Africa, Surinam and the Dutch Caribbean isles. The French regulations that limited overseas shipping isolated the Dutch from much of global trade, all the more so when the British occupied the Dutch East Indies in 1811. Thereafter, the Dutch flag flew over only one or two fortifications in West-African Guinea and the small trading post of Deshima in Japan.

In Europe, British plans to invade the Netherlands loomed large, forcing coastal communities to live with and pay for increased militarisation. One invasion materialised in 1809 on the island of Walcheren (Zeeland). The French inflicted much greater damage. Their revolutionary troops occupied Breda in 1793, followed by other parts of Dutch Brabant, Dutch Flanders and Dutch-Limburg. Subsequent treaties resulted in the restoration of some of these territories, but Napoleon responded to the invasion of 1809 with a phased annexation of Louis' kingdom, starting with Walcheren. In 1810, the French implemented direct rule in the provinces of Zeeland, Brabant and Northern Limburg, which comprised some 500,000 inhabitants; a quarter of the former Kingdom of the Netherlands, no less! As 'Dutch Departments', the remaining three-quarters fell under the government of Governor-General Lebrun, and included East Frisia (part of Prussia), which had been added to the Kingdom of Holland in 1807. The latter addition entailed augmenting the population by some 125,000 inhabitants (Joor 2000, 61).

The territorial losses of the revolutionary period vastly outnumbered the East Frisian gains, however. The destruction of dikes, lands, buildings, vehicles, plants and equipment that accompanied warfare on Dutch territory added to the direct war costs. Data suggest that investment in machinery, transport and residential buildings did not make up for the destruction and depreciation of capital between 1800 and 1813 (Smits et al. 2000, 169).

In terms of direct war deaths, the numbers were relatively limited, in part thanks to the 'velvet' character of the 1795 revolution. The French invasions of the early 1790s cost approximately 1,000 lives; the sea battles with the British entailed a death toll of 1,500; the 1809 British invasion of Zeeland caused the death of around 5,500 Dutchmen; a relatively high number (14,500) of the c. 35,000 Dutch conscripts in 1811–1813 perished in Russia; and lastly, over 2,000 Dutch soldiers died at Waterloo in 1815 (Van Leeuwen 1998, 334).

In 1795, the number of inhabitants stood at 2.1 million; in 1815, the census recorded 2.2 million. This slow growth trend had been characteristic of much of the eighteenth century, and the revolutionary period thus saw no major change in this respect. The overall death rate during the Batavian-French period hovered between 26 and 33 per thousand, a rate that remained similar in the decades thereafter. After 1815, the population increased at a slightly higher rate, reaching 3.1 million inhabitants in 1849 (Smits et al. 2000, 109).

Behind these general demographic trends lay three interconnected and far-reaching phenomena: Amsterdam's losses, massive de-urbanisation, and a general relocation of economic activities from the maritime West towards inland regions (Brusse and Mijnhardt 2011, 24, 33). Although these trends had been set in motion before 1795, the Batavian-French period accelerated these developments and thus altered the traditional political economy in a dramatic way.

The maritime West of the Dutch Republic had always been characterised by high rates of urbanisation. Around 1750, Holland and Zeeland comprised 47 per cent of the population, with 45 per cent of people living in towns with over 2,500 inhabitants. A gradual decline set in during the eighteenth century, only to continue at a much faster rate during the Batavian-French period. By 1815, Holland and Zeeland were home to 42 per cent of the population, with an urbanisation rate of only 37 per cent. [3] This was largely due to the sharp decline of both Amsterdam and Middelburg, the foremost trading centres in their respective provinces.

In addition, urban dwellers suffered disproportionally from the war. During 1795–1800, the cost of living had increased, which particularly hurt the inhabitants of towns; the cost of living peaked in 1800, after which it declined. By

3 See also Centraal Bureau voor de Statistiek, Volkstellingen 1795–1971, accessed 28 January 2021: http://www.volkstellingen.nl/nl/volkstelling/jaartellingdeelview/VT179501/index.html.

1811, around 11 per cent of the Dutch population depended on (supplementary) poor relief. In general, towns in the inland provinces fared better than those in the maritime West. In 1807, the proportion of people receiving poor relief varied from 4.5 per cent of the total population of Overijssel (in the East) to 27 per cent in North Holland (Hofstee 1981, 124–25).

In 1795, Amsterdam accounted for around 10 per cent of the Dutch Republic's population, with 221,000 inhabitants. This number declined to 202,000 in 1809 and fell sharply thereafter. Between 1809 and 1812, Amsterdam's mortality rate averaged 41.7, much higher than the national average. Overall unemployment soared, especially in shipping and fisheries, and also in industry; the additional activities in the navy shipyards could not turn the tide. The number of beggars rose; reports indicate that 30 to 40 per cent of Amsterdam's inhabitants lived on or supplemented their income with charity in the years between 1807 and 1809. In comparison, this rate had been around 10 per cent in 1765 and 13.5 per cent in 1790. During the four years following 1809, out-migration exceeded in-migration for the first time since 1500, worsened further by the draft of 1811–1813. By 1815, 180,000 people were living in Amsterdam, or 8 per cent of the population of the Northern Netherlands; a trend that continued to 7 per cent in 1850 (Joor 2000, 340–42; Joor 2015, 266; Diederiks 1982, 19; Poell 2005, 491).

Middelburg faced the same problems as Amsterdam. The city fell into a sharp decline immediately after French revolutionary troops lifted the trade blockade on the Scheldt in 1792, which restored Antwerp's international position. As a result, Middelburg lost its intermediary role in the trade with the Austrian Netherlands. As in Amsterdam, high rates of out-migration constituted the major cause of the decline, with the population falling from 17,700 in 1795 to 11,400 in 1807 (Brusse 2010, 33, 63, 84).

This de-urbanisation affected the dynamics of the political economy, which had been highly dependent upon the agency of independent elites in the maritime towns. The coming of the centralised state exacerbated their downfall. The Treaty of Vienna promised compensation for the new unified nation, thanks to the persistent diplomatic efforts of Lord Castlereagh, the British foreign secretary, who favoured a strong buffer state against France (Zappey 1967, 104). In 1814, Britain agreed to respect the Dutch colonial position as set out in the Treaty of Amiens in 1802, in compensation for the Dutch agreeing to create a United Netherlands with the former Austrian Netherlands at Vienna. The Dutch East Indies, Surinam and the six former Dutch Caribbean Isles were returned, but Ceylon, the Cape Colony and three Guyanese settlements remained British. The new United Kingdom of the Netherlands was to include Limburg and the former Austrian Netherlands (today's Belgium), plus some minor adjacent areas, but not East Frisia. All in all, the Vienna settlement more than doubled the domestic market from 2.2 to 5.5 million inhabitants, which could be expected to stimulate the recovery of the Dutch economy.

Considering the evidence in this section, we can conclude that the losses should not be understood primarily in terms of population numbers or direct war deaths. Yet the (temporary) loss of Dutch colonies swept away age-old global networks that could not easily be restored. During the war, the British had managed to expand their global networks, which hindered the revival of former Dutch colonial trade. The colonial losses also caused a substantial shrinking of traditional Dutch export markets, worsened further by annexations of one quarter of Dutch territory in 1810. The slow but radical process of de-urbanisation in the West meant that traditional centres lost much of their dynamism, not least because the towns also lost their autonomous power. On the other hand, the de-urbanisation of the West was accompanied by a gradual improvement in the economic conditions inland.

3 Trouble in Trade and Finances

In 1806, the service sector made up 51 per cent of Holland's GDP, compared to industry at 31 per cent and agriculture at 18 per cent (Van Zanden and Van Leeuwen 2012, 125). As a result of this dependence upon international trade and finance, revenues fluctuated strongly from one year to the next. Trade was responsible for one-third of Holland's service sector, for which European trading relations had always been much more important than colonial ones. In the eighteenth century, only 2–5 per cent of all Dutch maritime shipping was engaged in colonial trade. Luxurious and exotic goods attracted other foreign trade and promoted the rise of Amsterdam as a centre of global finance and commerce. Although colonial trade was severed by the British occupation of Dutch colonies from 1793 onwards, by then the Dutch had already lost their foremost position in global trade. The 1720s had been the best years for the East Indian trade, and the volume of trade achieved in that period was never reached again. Mismanagement and increased international competition resulted in such a high level of debt that by the early 1790s, the once-powerful East India Company (VOC) was facing bankruptcy (Van Eyck van Heslinga 1988, 34).

The revolutionaries had immediately embarked on reforms to colonial trade and liquidated the VOC in 1799. Louis Napoleon replaced the privately-conducted East Asian trade with a government-based administration that catered to integrated national and colonial interests, and created a Ministry of Colonial Affairs that launched a modernisation programme for the colonies

(Zappey 1967, 96). Meanwhile, the US had started to replace much of the former Dutch colonial trade in the East and the West; among others, US vessels took over Dutch East Indian tea shipping between 1810 and 1813. In the 1780s, the Dutch had commanded 36 per cent of the European and American trade with Asia, compared to Britain's 31 per cent and France's 22 per cent. The Dutch share declined to a mere 12 per cent in 1820–1829, whereas Britain's proportion rose to 60 per cent and the French and US commanded 12 per cent each (Solar 2013, 649).

By the early 1790s, Holland's European maritime trade had also lost its seventeenth-century vanguard position. Exact figures are hard to come by, as the different ports maintained different trades and connections, and the analysis is further hampered by the increased level of smuggling during the Batavian-French period (Marzagalli 1999, 167, 208, 246, 253; see also Davis and Engerman 2006, 427). Table 5.1 summarises the situation in the main sectors before 1795 and after 1800/1815.

Numerous segments in Dutch-European shipping had witnessed setbacks during the Anglo-Dutch War of 1780–1784; Dutch merchants themselves contributed to this trend by diverting many of their ships towards Ostend. The opening up of the Scheldt River in 1792 led to increasing competition from Antwerp. The grain trade declined for military-logistic reasons and due to prohibitions (Brusse 2010, 78); the trade did continue, however, albeit at lower levels, and partly through smuggling. The implementation of the Continental Blockade in 1806 did not immediately result in a sharp drop, as control of the blockade was initially inefficient (Marzagalli 1999, 179). A truly disastrous period began in 1809/1810, when all neutral trade was banned. Napoleon adapted the custom regulations in additional blockade decrees, permitting limited trade under a discriminative and complicated system of trade licenses in 1810. As a direct result of the annexation, Dutch merchants had to pay 50 per cent of the worth of their colonial products as an additional levy (Joor 2015, 262).

Worst of all was the decline in what had previously been massive grain imports from the Baltic. This had constituted a core activity of the Dutch Republic, and has even been described as 'the mother trade'. By the mid-eighteenth century, the Baltic trade was accounting for around two-thirds of ship movements in Dutch ports, facilitating re-exports towards areas in Europe that faced crop failures (Knoppers 1979, 242). The declining trend particularly affected Amsterdam, a city that was also hurt disproportionally by setbacks in colonial trade. The early nineteenth century saw little by way of improvement, since Ukrainian grain flooded into Western Europe and diminished the importance of the Baltic connection altogether (Van Tielhof 2002).

TABLE 5.1 Trends in Dutch-European shipping overseas from the late eighteenth century up to the early decades of the 1800s, by tonnage and by trade region

Tons 1750	Region	Before 1795	After 1800/1815
72%	The Baltic	Gradual decline in proportion of ships through the Sound from 60 per cent in 1710s to 14 per cent in 1790s, due to British competition and 'direct' trade from France to the Baltics	Further decline; from 1800s, increasing competition from Odessa grain trade
	Norway	Strong trade between Norway and Amsterdam; remained on a high level	England had replaced the Netherlands by 1799; very little left in 1840s
	German coast and Denmark	Increasing competition from Hamburg/Bremen from 1750s	Clear dominance by Hamburg
4%	Archangelsk/ St. Petersburg	Decline from 1780s; increasing competition from Britain	Partial recovery 1815–1822; Britain remained dominant
1%	England	Increasing, in particular through Rotterdam	After 1815, substantial increase despite growing competition from Antwerp
10%	France	Increasing trade in French colonial goods; after 1780s, strong competition	Up to 1813, increasing Dutch exports to France; after 1813, still substantial
14%	Spain	From 1750s, increasing competition from Denmark and Sweden	Similar to pre-1795 trend
	Portugal	Remained on the same level	Sharp decline due to British rise
	Other Mediterranean	Growth until 1770s, then decline	Insignificant

KNOPPERS 1979, 227–61; HORLINGS 1995, 176

The wartime losses in international trade reverberated through the competitive financial sector. In contrast to shipping, however, the banking sector had remained robust prior to the 1790s. After the Anglo-Dutch War, the Amsterdam network suffered an obvious decline, although only in a relative sense with respect to London, since in absolute terms the banking sector remained extremely strong and expanded even further, especially in the field of foreign investments (Riley 1980, 15–16).

The revolutionary war period was another matter altogether, and Amsterdam's position as a major international financial market came to a definitive end when London halted the registration of bills exchanged between the two cities in 1807. Hamburg took over Amsterdam's role in international finance on the continent (Marzagalli 1999, 78). Despite the crisis, foreign governments still came to Amsterdam to finance their war efforts, and an agent trying to raise a loan for Prussia found numerous willing investors with plenty of available cash in 1808 (Fritschy and Van der Voort 1997, 92). Nevertheless, by 1811 foreign investment had dwindled to 210 million guilders. Numerous arbitrary levies, such as the forced loans and *dons gratuits* imposed by the Batavian and French regimes, discouraged financial elites; various businessmen decided to live as rentiers (Joor 2015 273). Although Governor-General Lebrun tried to support merchants and bankers, he could not prevent the flight of powerful banking houses, often to London (Buist 1974 68).

Interior trade fared better. The Batavian-French regimes abolished inland toll and guilds. The volume of goods transported by inland navigation more than doubled between 1800 and 1813, partly because this shipping could avoid connections with the open sea (Horlings 1995, 75–81, 100, 419). Trends diverged strongly at the local level, however. Compared to Amsterdam, which lost its dynamism along with its competitive colonial connections, Rotterdam managed reasonably well. The town also profited from Middelburg's decline and Amsterdam's downfall, and an existing, excellent network with British traders increased the possibilities for all sorts of covert trade ('t Hart and Greefs 2018).

Rotterdam also expanded its role in international trade along the Rhine and Meuse, at the expense of Amsterdam. Part of overseas trade shifted to the continental rivers. The French managed to lift tolls and other trade barriers between Switzerland and the Netherlands in 1804; upstream traffic became more dominant at the expense of Dutch-controlled downstream commerce (Spaulding 2015, 124). The occupation of numerous German territories by the French after 1806 resulted in the disappearance of major Dutch export markets due to the Empire's prohibitively high custom rates, with the Netherlands being regarded as a 'foreign' ally. This situation remained unchanged, even after the annexation of 1810.

This section has thus shown that whilst much of the decline in international trade was foreshadowed in the last decades of the eighteenth century, the revolutionary wars severely exacerbated these trends. The rapid decline in Baltic trade crippled Amsterdam in particular, and 1807 saw the deathblow for numerous powerful financial intermediaries in Amsterdam. The competition did not only come from London, but also from Hamburg and Antwerp. On the other hand, the Dutch financial sector proved resilient and remained a factor to be reckoned with; it simply lost its primacy. Interior trade remained quite strong, in addition to trade with France and the international river trade. Of all the major towns in the maritime West, resilient Rotterdam stood out, profiting as a new intermediary between British economic might and the rise of industry in the German hinterland.

4 Challenges in Other Sectors

The traditionally open economy of the Netherlands proved extremely vulnerable to blockades and prohibitive high tariffs. In this sense, comparative studies on wartime economic effects that stress the resilience of highly commercialised societies tend to overlook the serious threat that such effects pose to countries with generally low levels of protectionism, such as the Netherlands. Even then, some sectors profited from the revolutionary dissolution of internal barriers and the ban on British imports, while others suffered disproportionally from the obstacles to foreign trade in general.

On the whole, agriculture did well. Between 1720 and 1800 the trend had been been positive, with a growth rate of 0.28 per annum (Van Zanden and Van Leeuwen 2012, 126). The Batavian-French period enabled many farmers to profit from high prices for their produce, which stimulated an advanced degree of specialisation. French rule led to the dissolution of the commons and their reallocation into privately-owned farms, especially in the inland provinces. Farming became more intense with more efficient means of exploitation, specialising in potatoes, flax, madder, and animal husbandry. The effects were less far-reaching in the maritime West, which was already extremely specialised. These farmers noticed a backlash when they found it difficult to access export markets for their livestock and dairy produce. Overall, however, the growth trend in agriculture that had started in the 1750s continued unabated throughout the nineteenth century (Van Zanden and Van Riel 2004, 281).

Some industries also profited from the impediments to foreign trade. Inland, cotton gained from increased protectionism against English imports. Madder profited from the French regulations; printing experienced high demand, leading to the introduction of the rotation press; and beer profited from the decline in tea and coffee imports. Tilburg woollens enjoyed the advantage of French army clothing orders and mechanical wool-spinning was even introduced during this period. Sectors that were oriented towards the domestic market only, such as clothing and shoemaking, did not generally experience major difficulties.

For numerous industries, however, the Batavian-French period ushered in a substantial decline, if not in quantity then in quality. The luxury woollens that had previously been exported were replaced by low-quality woollens produced mainly for the domestic market. This trend had started in the eighteenth century, but it was strengthened substantially. Likewise, the luxury tannery and leather industry shifted towards low-quality leather products when the import of foreign hides plummeted and export markets shrank. In addition, the production of high-quality paper dropped with the decline in foreign trade. In all three cases – woollens, leather and paper – there was a shift towards locations in the inland provinces, further exacerbating de-urbanisation in the maritime area. Impediments to trade also hurt metallurgy, sugar, tobacco, oils, dye and soap, which depended on specific imports such as iron ore, coal or colonial goods, while gin and brandy suffered substantially from declining exports (Buyst and Mokyr 1990, 69; Jansen 1999, 415).

Overall, the disadvantages outweighed the advantages. It was not easy to make up for the loss of numerous export markets. Prior to the 1790s, the luxury woollen, soap and tobacco industries had shown declining trends. British products had already been highly competitive in the late eighteenth century. Innovation played a minor role: cotton was of limited importance; the mechanisation in woollens in Tilburg remained a rare phenomenon; and beet sugar was still unable to replace traditional sugar-making. Before the 1790s, steam machinery had been employed in water management only; because of shrinking markets, steam had little to offer the already advanced windmill technology, which had proved so profitable in the oil-industry, for example. On the whole, Dutch industry remained dominated by small artisan workshops.

Shipbuilding had constituted a productive and crucial sector throughout the eighteenth century, although rising prices for timber and iron had started to cause stagnation in the 1790s (Van Zanden and Van Tielhof 2009). The restriction of overseas trade during the Batavian-French period generated a sharp drop; few ships were being built, apart from vessels for the marine and river trades. Figure 5.1 shows the disastrous development of the available tonnage in Dutch shipping from 1800 onwards.

The reduced tonnage also had a negative impact on the fisheries. Although herring-fishing had long been one of the most vibrant branches of the Dutch

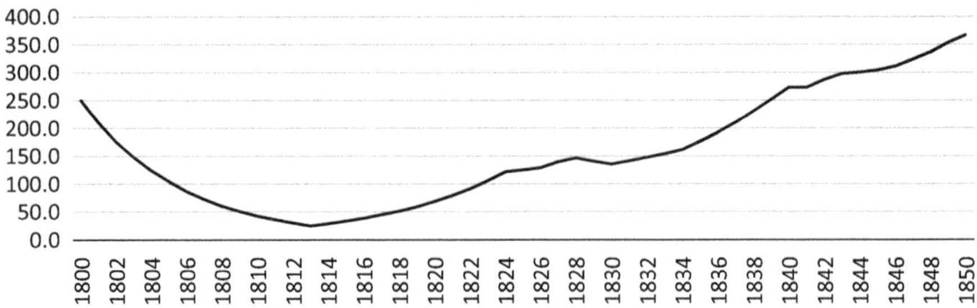

FIGURE 5.1 Gross tonnage of Dutch shipping, thousand tons, 1800–1850
SOURCE: DUTCH NATIONAL ACCOUNTS, HTTPS://NATIONALACCOUNTS.NIWI.KNAW.NL/TABLE/EXPENDI1.HTM

economy, this sector experienced sharply declining trends throughout the eighteenth century. Between 1750 and 1795, the tonnage used in fisheries had already dropped from 100 to 60 (Van Bochove 2004, 27). The causes were mainly 'external', related to the relocation of the herring population towards the Norwegian coast. Restrictive French regulations that aimed to reduce smuggling brought the sector to virtual standstill, although some loopholes remained, especially with regard to the illegal transport of correspondence and passengers by fishing vessels.

Once again, this section concludes with a mixed picture. In contrast to continuing growth in agriculture, there were serious losses in fisheries and in industrial export markets. Some of these developments had started in the eighteenth century, but they were reinforced by the revolutionary wars. The decline in exports held back the number of industrial innovations. Several industrial sectors started to exploit hitherto underused resources with a shift towards the inland provinces, moving away from export-led luxury products to lower-quality merchandise for the domestic market. In Dutch shipping, the dramatic decrease in gross tonnage would substantially hinder the post-war recovery in international trade.

5 Financial Burdens and Centralisation

The arrival of French troops in 1795 proved a challenge for the Dutch financial market: the troops immediately demanded 100 million guilders in war indemnities, an amount equal to three times the annual revenues of the conquered Dutch Republic. The French demands were met by cash payments, supplies to the French troops, and issues of bills drawn on merchants and guaranteed by the Dutch government. By far the largest part consisted of promissory notes (*Bataafse rescripties*) that carried a 4 per cent rate of interest. These bonds fluctuated in value and flooded the Dutch securities market, causing speculation. In addition, Dutch citizens were forced to shoulder the costs of the occupying forces, which consisted of 25,000 French troops each year. The worthless paper *assignats* used by the French to pay for military supplies endangered the monetary system.

The Dutch political economy showed a high degree of resilience in responding to these financial difficulties. The new Batavian authorities immediately decreed that all *assignats* could be exchanged for guilders by the local authorities, which would then be compensated by the central government. Although this policy cost 10.5 million guilders, it prevented a financial crisis (Fritschy and Van der Voort 1997, 74).

It was not possible to meet the new demands with ordinary tax revenues; indeed, as much as 40 per cent of state income between 1798 and 1805 came from extraordinary levies and forced loans. Attempts to return to the traditional system of voluntary loans in 1803 (when peace was expected) ended in failure. The new loans burdened the state budget, leaving almost no tax funds for purposes other than debt-servicing (see Table 5.2). Interest rates shot up from 2 to 4 per cent in 1788–1793, and then from 4 to 6 per cent in 1806–1809 (Pfeil 1998, 392, 543–47).

Tax revenues expanded only slowly. The government began to construct a universal and unified system of taxation in 1798, but it was not completed until 1806. The system included progressive direct taxes; the tax burden on property, for example, increased substantially. Alexander Gogel, the foremost financial expert in the revolutionary and Napoleonic years, who first served as Agent of Finances in 1798–1801, and later as Secretary of State, Minister and Intendant, was a supporter of high, progressive rates. He had to restrain his ambitions, however, because the French rulers were afraid to alienate the financial elite from the regime. Meanwhile, the yield from customs duties fell dramatically due to the war and the blockade. Excises continued to afflict the economy with high prices; the aspiration to reduce the burden failed, because the state was in dire need of these revenues (Postma 2017, 133, 137, 152, 254).

Nevertheless, the unification of the government in 1798 constituted a radical improvement on the federated structures of the past. Tax revenues did increase overall, from 35 million guilders in 1805 to 43 million in 1806 and 45 million in 1807 (Pfeil 1998, 465). King Louis Napoleon's beneficial reforms included the introduction of the metric system and the repeal of inland tolls and privileges. Budgets were made public in 1806, creating greater transparency in government (Pfeil 1998, 524). The annexation in 1810 again undermined the government's ability to raise tax revenues, however; these declined from 43 million guilders in 1810 to 33 million in 1811, because standard French tariffs were considerably lower than Dutch ones (Postma 2017, 283).

The expectation that state formation would lead to greater efficiency was not met immediately. The cost of provincial administration in the former Dutch Republic had been relatively low. Instead of the expected fall in the cost of government, the regime changes had the opposite result, bringing new laws and regulations. The alteration of provincial boundaries, along with administrative structures, hindered the implementation of new rules during the Batavian-French period. The departmental system established in 1810 represented a radical transformation of governance. New departments became engaged in a turf war over competences; Finance and Justice, for example, fought over the Continental System under King Louis Napoleon.

These extra administrative costs added to the government's financial woes. The annual costs of the revenue-collecting agency rose from 1.5 million guilders in 1799–1803 to 4 million guilders in 1807–1810, much higher than under the Dutch Republic (Pfeil 1998, 472, 554). The financial situation gradually became unsustainable. In 1809, King Louis Napoleon defaulted on interest payments. In 1810, Napoleon imposed new financial burdens in the form of a payment for 20,000 French troops plus an unknown number of French custom officers and the costs of maintaining a navy, including nine heavily-armoured warships. His decision of 1810 to *tierce* the public debt (by paying only one-third of the interest due to the state's creditors) revealed that the Netherlands was bankrupt. The Dutch financial elite no longer trusted the government; the price of government securities fell to an all-time low of 10–12 per cent of the original value (Pfeil 1998, 551). This represented a radical change from the situation in

TABLE 5.2 Public loans contracted in the Netherlands annually 1780–1810, in millions of guilders

Period	Total in loans	Percentage of tax revenues needed to service debt
1780–1794	36.8	66%
1795–1799	45.5	99%
1800–1804	42.5	98%
1805–1810	25.5	86%

SOURCE: PFEIL (1998, 49, 122, 209, 349, 554)

the Dutch Republic, when voluntary loans had been the rule and the investing public had always shown a high degree of trust in the financial system.

In sum, the massive financial demands made by the French crippled the wartime state. The partial bankruptcies of 1809 and 1810 represented a radical departure from the former trustworthy relations between the fiscal state and its creditors. Despite this, the monetary market as a whole remained resilient; the higher interest rates were still rather low from a European perspective. Furthermore, thorough government centralisation was a badly-needed measure that would increase the transparency of Dutch governance in the future.

6 The Failed Restoration of State Finances and Unsuccessful Unification

Between 1795 and 1813, the society and economy of the Netherlands had been severely undermined by rising and unavoidable levels of expenditure and a shrinking fiscal base for the appropriation of taxes. The Vienna peace settlements promised a firm restoration of power within an expanded territory. Central power was consolidated by the former Batavian political leaders and Napoleonic administrators, who continued in their posts under King William I's new regime. The new departments of Water Management and Colonial Affairs remained in place and pursued effective policies. An enduring process of judicial centralisation and unification was launched, and a clear and formal separation of the administrative and judicial powers came into effect, followed by the formation of a professional civil service and reform of the police.

Although the new kingdom was officially a constitutional monarchy, King William I in fact exerted absolute powers. Parliament exercised virtually no control over the budget or income that flowed into the royal institution (the Amortisation Syndicate) charged with dealing with the country's debts, reforming the mint and financing the construction of canals. The king also revived the former brokers' guild of Amsterdam that charged high fixed rates on all kinds of transactions (Van Zanden and Van Riel 2004, 155).

Amsterdam's financial sector enjoyed a post-war boom, but was soon hindered by the 1816 Currency Act, which overvalued gold over silver and the Belgian franc over the guilder. The internal border with Belgium presented an obstacle, with highly fluctuating exchange rates (Jonker 1997, 95–96), and public finances also continued to be problematic. The *tierce* of the debt had reduced the burden of debt-servicing by two-thirds in 1810, but not the debt itself (see Table 5.3). In an effort to soothe the financial elite, the king declared these amounts to be 'deferred debt', to be solved by the Amortisation Syndicate.

Soon, however, new debts were contracted and debt-servicing reached enormous levels again (Fritschy and Van der Voort 1997, 76).[4] Meanwhile, the traditionally high excises persisted; they made labour expensive and reduced the living standards of the many unemployed. Above all, the high excises caused massive discontent in the newly-added Southern provinces, which had been used to much lower duties. Although Southerners contributed 50 per cent of revenues to the new state, 80 per cent of these revenues were allocated to policies that benefitted the North (Van Zanden and Van Riel 2004, 128). In the meantime, the yields from customs duties remained low, because trade did not recover as expected. Trying to run with the hare and hunt with the hounds, King William I followed an inconclusive tariff policy in an attempt to satisfy both the demands of merchants in the North and industrialists in the South. From an international perspective, the Netherlands remained extremely liberal between 1815–1850, with tariff rates at roughly half of those in Britain, a sixth or seventh of those in France, and less than a tenth of those in Belgium (after 1830) (Horlings 1995, 136). However, import duties on some products, such as foreign steel, were raised to protect Southern industry, much to the chagrin of Amsterdam's merchants, who had been used to low tariffs, a hallmark of the erstwhile Republic. The outmoded ambition of re-establishing the Amsterdam staple market continued to dominate economic policy in the North for more than three decades in post-Napoleonic Holland. Fiscal capacity remained far below the standards of pre-1800 Holland; deficits were roughly eight times larger than revenues, a situation that also compared negatively to the country's European competitors (Dincecco 2011, 55–56; 't Hart et al. 2018, 8).

Discontent flared up in the South, focused on a mix of religious and administrative issues. In 1830, the Belgians proclaimed independence and chose Leopold I as their king. The separation of the two kingdoms was recognised on 15 November 1831, but it took William I another eight years to accept that the situation was irreversible, at a great financial cost. All of the plans of the Amortisation Syndicate had come to nothing, with the costly war with Belgium and the accumulation of even more sovereign debt. Interest rates on the private capital market were relatively high, revealing the negative consequences of the continuing demand for government loans on the financial market. At the same time, exports failed to catch up, covering only 50 per cent of imports. This imbalance led to an outflow of capital, estimated at about 5 per cent of GNP in 1831 (Horlings 1995, 122–27, 379). The financial sector experienced

4 See also Cardoso and Lains 2010, 12.

a substantial downfall in 1830–1833. Once more, the Netherlands was facing bankruptcy.

Throughout this period, the financial elites did not trust William I, due to discontent over his financial management and the obscure Amortisation Syndicate. Interest rates on public loans persisted at the high level of 6 per cent, 2 per cent higher in real terms than in the 1780s. Overall distrust of the king's financial policies retarded the acceptance of the new central bank (Nederlandsche Bank) and its introduction of banknotes (Jonker 1997, 95–96). The servicing of public debt absorbed virtually all tax revenues (see Table 5.3); debt itself rose to over three times GDP (Dincecco 2011, 25). The threat of the bankruptcy was only avoided by the abdication of William I and the launching of a more transparent regime under William II in the 1840s. The more liberal government restored creditors' trust and, among others, lowered the burdensome fees charged by financial brokers by one third (Riemens 1937).

7 Failed Mercantilism

The regime's financial difficulties obstructed the ambitious policies of King William I. As mentioned above, he followed an inconclusive mercantilist strategy of reviving the staple trade in the North (Amsterdam) and stimulating industry in the South. The domestic market in the North and South was to be improved with a canal scheme.

Initially, the main aim of this scheme was to restore Dutch colonial trade. Britain was the main competitor, with its immense fleet and cargoes of cheap textiles to exchange for foodstuffs and raw materials. American vessels had started to control the Dutch East Indian tea trade, and continued to do so after 1815. Within Europe, Hamburg and Antwerp had emerged as major competitors for Amsterdam's former colonial trade. King William I favoured free trade, but the first years after the war revealed that he would never be able to defeat the British competition by following this strategy. In 1824, the king therefore established the Nederlandsche Handel-Maatschappij (NHM) to coordinate colonial trade, supported by government subsidies. At the same time, the NHM would stimulate Dutch textile production in order to carry tradeable domestically-produced goods to Java. The NHM would also shore up colonial shipping and engage in the rigid exploitation of colonial resources.

The scheme achieved major successes. Dutch textiles started to constitute 50–60 per cent of textile imports in Java, compared to only 5 per cent in 1823 (Horlings 1995, 144). Shipbuilding received a boost, shipping expanded, Dutch colonial companies thrived, and even the international river trade was

TABLE 5.3 Amount of debt and debt charges in millions of guilders, and nominal debt as percentage of Dutch national income (1795–1850)

Year	Debt	Debt-servicing	% Debt of NI
1795	766	22.7	160
1800	975	34.3	204
1805	1,145	33.9	240
1810	1,232	41.5	258
1815	1,726	14.7	341
1840	2,250	35.5	348
1850	1,230	35.0	199

SOURCE: PFEIL (1998, 351)

enhanced through the revival of colonial trade via Amsterdam. The new ministry for colonial affairs that had been established under the French served the new system of colonial exploitation extremely well, and the Netherlands had again become a major player in global trade by the 1830s. The NHM thus helped to promote an economic revival in several respects.

At the same time, however, the NHM pursued several traditional policies that caused adverse economic developments over the longer term. The NHM remained attached to the traditional ideal of the Amsterdam staple market acting as the initial importer. Auctions were held only once or twice per year, favouring a relatively small group of rich merchants willing to pay high prices. In the meantime, Hamburg, with its weekly auctions of colonial goods, became much more attractive as an intermediary. The Dutch market for colonial goods fell under the control of brokers who jointly determined the prices, reinforcing the exclusion of 'outsiders'. Due to the focus on one or two auctions per year, storage costs were high, too, pushing up the price of the goods. Furthermore, Hamburg had the advantage of railway links to the hinterland, whilst Amsterdam and Rotterdam relied on river trade. River trade was cheaper, but it was also slower, and additional port and toll duties (see also below) rendered these connections relatively expensive again (Horlings 1995, 161–62).

The NHM's policies also held back innovative developments in global shipping. Government subsidies included commissions for high freight prices, with the result that merchants let ships remain idle for up to two years, since the actual commission would make up for any loss in efficiency. There was no need for speed, steam shipping or full capacity utilisation. Nor did companies modernise in an organisational respect. There were only four public limited shipping companies, and the average number of vessels per shipping company was 1.7. Meanwhile, the subsidies entailed high insurance premiums, despite the reduction of risks at sea, and distorted the development of greater efficiency in this branch (Horlings 1995, 147).

William I's ambitious canal-building policies turned out to be both exorbitant and relatively unhelpful; they were aimed at strengthening powerful ports, instead of establishing connections with inland industrial centres. The new Noordhollands Kanaal, which was meant to boost Amsterdam's port, demanded high duties. In an effort to come to terms with the distrustful Amsterdam elite, William I also permitted the re-establishment of several guilds that had traditionally dominated much of the trade, including financial brokers and port personnel. As a result, transit duties and transaction costs in Amsterdam remained substantially higher than those, for instance, in Antwerp, Hamburg, Bremen or Le Havre. Amsterdam's storage costs were four times higher than Antwerp's (Horlings 1995, 164, 194). The renewal of pre-1795 privileges also applied to the fisheries. Government subsidies favoured some sections of the industry over others, yet this was of little aid when faced with fierce competition from Scottish fishermen (Van Zanden and Van Riel 2004, 132–34).

The king also annulled Napoleon's abolition of tolls along the Rhine, which led to a disastrous and long-lasting disagreement with Prussia. Although the Vienna Treaty had declared Rhine shipping to be free *jusqu'a la mer*, which implied as far as 'into the sea', William I interpreted this as referring to the point where tidal movements were still visible – that is, 30 kilometres inland – thus permitting sea ports to continue levying high duties and regulating privileges for Dutch river shipping. Trade along the Rhine increased by more than 50 per cent in the 1820s and even 100 per cent in the 1830s, yet earnings in this sector remained modest because of the high tariffs involved. In this system, shippers were promised commissions at regular intervals, which resulted in their failing to use maximum capacity. The shippers also vehemently opposed any transport improvement plans, not least projects for river steamship companies. The Act of Mainz of 1831 did away with the some of the duties, yet it took twenty years for the longstanding conflict to be settled once and for all (Bouman 1931, 242).

On the whole, the industrial sector enjoyed a post-war boom. This came to a halt in 1824–1826, and the level of industrial production of 1807 was only achieved again in 1829. Unemployment was recorded at 3 per cent in 1815 – a very low rate, thanks to the post-war building boom – but the percentage of unemployed soon rose, reaching 6 per cent in the 1850s. Certain sectors did well and mechanised, such as sugar and garancine, which gradually replaced madder. The NHM's policies boosted several industries in the 1830s. Yet the overall scale of this boost was conditioned by competition from England and the Southern provinces. Dutch labour productivity had traditionally been high, but increasingly lagged behind Britain (Smits 1999, 16) due to the slow degree of mechanisation. All government support for industry, such as imports of English machinery, flowed to the South, and stimulated Belgian industrialisation from the 1830s onwards. Such subsidies fell on fertile ground, since Southern industries had profited from the expanding continental market during the time of the French annexation, in contrast to their Northern neighbours. Industry in the North profited only from NHM subsidies for cotton textiles, yet this support was concentrated on small firms in an effort to maximise employment. The funds were poorly spent, as the smaller factories eventually went out of business. Larger firms, meanwhile, had to fend for themselves. The NHM cottons were exported to Java at a net loss, discouraging mechanisation in this sector. All in all, small-scale enterprise remained dominant. Low customs tariffs rendered the Dutch textile industry vulnerable to stiff foreign competition, and hurt the tobacco sector, too, along with other sectors. Industries such as flour-milling and beer-brewing failed to expand, because tax regulations required certain traditional production methods (Jansen 1999, 92, 140, 155, 254).

Shipbuilding responded to the overall developments in shipping and trade. Both recovered after 1815, and the NHM's policy of promoting colonial connections favoured this sector in the 1830s. The lifting of British Acts of Navigation that had prevented the Dutch from exporting non-Dutch goods to Britain boosted expansion in the 1840s. There was an increased use of steam-driven power, above all for inland shipping and subsequently for trains. Yet technological advancement at the wharves was held back by the NHM's policy of artificially propping up the sector. Iron was late to replace wood, which rendered Dutch wharves backward internationally. Overall tonnage in Dutch shipping only regained its 1800 level in the 1840s (see Figure 5.1) (Jansen 1999, 82, 257).[5]

William I's decision to pursue a liberal trade policy was not particularly helpful for the farming community, either. One solution was to turn towards even more intensive farming, and farmers focused on potatoes, madder, flax, and animal husbandry. The sector proved quite resilient, not least because

5 See also Dutch National Accounts, accessed 28 January 2021: https://nationalaccounts.niwi.knaw.nl/table/expend1j.htm.

it had weathered the Batavian-French period rather successfully. Ultimately, agriculture became even more specialised, not only in the maritime West, but also in the inland provinces. As a result, the Netherlands became a net exporter of agricultural products, in a reversal of the situation in the Republic, when Baltic grain had dominated Dutch imports (Van Zanden and Van Riel 2004, 125–26; Van Tielhof 2002).

All in all, William I did attempt to improve the economy of his new United Kingdom, but many of his policies failed, as the circumstances had changed utterly. The strategies that had been adopted in the pre-1795 Amsterdam market, favouring low duties to attract foreign merchants and relying on trump cards such as colonial relations and proven institutions such as guilds, failed to work, as other countries had done away with cost-increasing corporations, foreign merchants already controlled the shipping in Dutch ports, and foreign manufacturing turned out to be too competitive for Dutch industry. The ideal of re-establishing the collapsed staple market ultimately proved to be an illusion due to the technological improvements in rail and steam transport, which made an international system of concentrated supply, storage and brokering obsolete. The focus on Amsterdam prevented the king from making firm decisions on alternative strategies. Rotterdam's port was expanding, stimulated by its strengthened position in international river shipping. Although William I was not completely blind to Rotterdam's potential – as a matter of fact, his favourite entrepreneur was Anthony van Hoboken, who was a leading merchant from Rotterdam – he remained primarily concerned with Amsterdam's interests. He also failed to perceive the potential for the cotton industry in the Eastern Netherlands. By the 1840s, the overall growth rate in industry had dropped once more due to the decline in colonial trade, partly because demand in Java was also stagnating (Smits 1999, 18).

8 Conclusion

Wars tend to have a limited economic effect in advanced and highly diversified societies. The Dutch weathered numerous wars, including the Eighty Years' War with Spain, in a way that confirms this thesis ('t Hart 2014a, 171; 't Hart 2014b). The revolutionary wars of 1795–1815, however, proved to be an entirely different case altogether.

Although history does not lend itself well to counterfactual reasoning, we can nevertheless ask the following question: what if the Patriot Revolution of the 1780s had been successful (without foreign interference by Prussia), and been followed by a centralisation process under the Batavian Revolution of

1795 – without forceful occupation and annexation by France and without armed conflict with Britain? In that case, the Netherlands would probably have continued along its path of Smithian growth, at least until the 1830s. Particular trajectories would have remained in place: de-urbanisation, increased rivalry in international trade and finance, harmful foreign industrial competition, and the fisheries in extreme difficulty, just to mention the main ones. Yet these trajectories would have avoided the sharp falls and decline that they actually suffered in practice. Certainly, Dutch public finances would not have experienced such disarray and distrust. A stronger centralised regime might have adopted more efficient economic policies, although one cannot expect immediate miracles from new administrations. Industrialisation might have occurred somewhat earlier, with slightly stronger incentives for mechanisation than was actually the case.

In actual fact, the revolutionary wars of 1795–1815 caused the Dutch to follow a different trajectory. We should stress that this path did not end in complete disaster: the Netherlands continued to be one of the wealthiest countries in the world. Outright famine was avoided, thanks to agricultural growth. The path did entail strong divergence at the local level, though. The people of Amsterdam suffered extremely high unemployment rates, resulting in massive out-migration, causing de-urbanisation that was 'repaired' only in the mid-nineteenth century, when Amsterdam again reached its pre-1800 population level (Paping 2009). Rotterdam, by contrast, fared much better; its population expanded immediately after 1815. The real problem was that Amsterdam occupied such a central place in the Dutch economy. Throughout the eighteenth century, the Netherlands had undergone a process of 'internal contraction', which magnified Amsterdam's economic power at the expense of the rest of the country (although Rotterdam managed to keep up some sort of rivalry) (De Vries 1968, 40). The revolutionary wars shattered this development in the most radical fashion, robbing the country of its most powerful and dynamic economic centre (Joor 2015, 274).

The restoration that followed was a missed opportunity to move on from an ancient system that had experienced continuous 'persistent but not consistent' economic growth (Van Zanden and Van Leeuwen 2012). In the longer term, government policy neglected to prepare the Dutch for ongoing foreign competition; instead, it reverted to traditional solutions such as guilds and tolls, and the revival of the lost Amsterdam staple market. Moreover, the Batavian-French period had destroyed the most dynamic sector in the Netherlands, namely maritime trade. It took decades before shipping and foreign financial services were properly restored (Smits et al. 2000, 50). True stabilisation in the political economy came only in the 1840s, with William II's financial and governmental reforms.

The revolutionary steps that the government made towards unified taxation and integration, the re-orientation towards the river trade with the hinterland, the efficient exploitation of the East Indies that eventually resulted in a positive balance in the state budget: all were necessary phases that enabled the start of a period of true economic growth in the later 1860s. These measures were thus of profound importance for the economy in the longer term, yet the Dutch had to wait several decades before they could reap the fruits of revolutionary change.

Bibliography

Aerts, Remieg. 2006. "De maatschappelijke orde: Aanvaarding, verschil en onderlinge afhankelijkheid." *Geschiedenis van Amsterdam Vol. III,* edited by P. de Rooij and R. Aerts, 217–92. Amsterdam, SUN.

Barbera, Henry. 1973. *Rich Nations and Poor in Peace and War.* Lexington, MA: Lexington Books.

Bornewasser, J.A. 1983. "Het Koninkrijk der Nederlanden 1815–1830." In *Algemene Geschiedenis der Nederlanden Vol. 11*. Haarlem: Fibula-Van Dishoeck.

Bouman, P.J. 1931. *Rotterdam en het achterland 1831–1851*. Amsterdam: H.J. Paris.

Brugmans, I.J. 1961. *Paardenkracht en Mensenmacht: Sociaal-Economische Geschiedenis van Nederland.* Leiden: Martinus Nijhoff.

Brusse, Paul, and Wijnand W. Mijnhardt. 2011. *Towards a New Template for Dutch History. De-urbanisation and the Balance between City and Countryside.* Utrecht: Uitgeverij Waanders.

Brusse, Paul. 2010. *Gevallen stad; stedelijke netwerken en het platteland, Zeeland 1750–1850*. Zutphen: Uitgeverij WBooks.

Buist, Marten G. 1974. *At Spes Non Fracta: Hope & Co. 1770–1815*. The Hague: Martinus Nijhoff.

Buyst, Erik, and Joel Mokyr. 1990. "Dutch Manufacturing and Trade during the French Period (1795–1814) in a Long Term Perspective." In *Economic Effects of the French Revolutionary and Napoleonic Wars*, edited by E. Aerts and F. Crouzet, 64–78. Louvain: Leuven University Press.

Cardoso, José Luís, and Pedro Lains (eds.). 2010. *Paying for the Liberal State. The Rise of Public Finance in Nineteenth-Century Europe.* Cambridge: Cambridge University Press.

Centraal Bureau voor de Statistiek, *Volkstellingen 1795–1971*, accessed 28 January 2021: http://www.volkstellingen.nl/nl/volkstelling/jaartellingdeelview/VT179501/index.html.

Colenbrander, H.T. 1928. *De Bataafsche Republiek*. Amsterdam: Meulenhoff.

Colenbrander, H.T. 1925. *Koloniale Geschiedenis, Vol. I*. The Hague: Martinus Nijhoff.

Davis, Lance E., and Stanley L. Engerman. 2006. *Naval Blockades in Peace and War: An Economic History since 1750*. New York: Cambridge University Press.

De Vries, Jan, and Ad van der Woude. 1997. *The First Modern Economy: Success, Failure and Perseverance of the Dutch Economy, 1500–1815*. Cambridge: Cambridge University Press.

De Vries, Johan. 1968. *De economische achteruitgang der Republiek in de achttiende eeuw*. Leiden: Stenfert Kroese.

Diederiks, Herman. 1982. *Een stad in verval: Amsterdam omstreeks 1800*. Amsterdam: Universiteit van Amsterdam.

Dincecco, Mark. 2011. *Political Transformations and Public Finances: Europe, 1650–1913*. Cambridge: Cambridge University Press.

Dutch National Accounts, 1800–1913. Accessed 28 January 2021. https://nationalaccounts.niwi.knaw.nl/.

Fritschy, Wantje, and René van der Voort. 1997. "From Fragmentation to Unification." In *A Financial History of the Netherlands*, edited by Marjolein 't Hart, Joost Jonker and Jan Luiten van Zanden, 64–93. Cambridge: Cambridge University Press.

Hofstee, E.W. 1981. *Korte demografische geschiedenis van Nederland van 1800 tot heden*. Haarlem: Fibula-Van Dishoeck.

Horlings, Edwin. 1995. *The Economic Development of the Dutch Service Sector 1800–1850. Trade and Transport in a Premodern Economy*. Amsterdam: NEHA.

Jansen, Michael. 1999. *De industriële ontwikkeling in Nederland 1800–1850*. Amsterdam: NEHA.

Jonker, Joost. 1997. "The Alternative Road to Modernity: Banking and Currency 1814–1914." In *A Financial History of the Netherlands*, edited by Marjolein 't Hart, Joost Jonker and Jan Luiten van Zanden, 94–123. Cambridge: Cambridge University Press.

Joor, Johan. 2000. *De Adelaar en het Lam: Onrust, Opruiing en Onwilligheid in Nederland ten tijde van het Koninkrijk Holland en de Inlijving bij het Franse Keizerrijk*. Amsterdam: De Bataafsche Leeuw.

Joor, Johan. 2015. "Significance and Consequences of the Continental System for Napoleonic Holland, Especially for Amsterdam." In *Revisiting Napoleon's Continental System: Local, Regional and European Experiences*, edited by Katherine B. Aaslestad and Johan Joor, 259–76. Basingstoke: Palgrave Macmillan.

Kang, Seonjou and James Meernik. 2005. "Civil War Destruction and the Prospects for Economic Growth." *The Journal of Politics* 67: 88–109.

Knoppers, J.V.Th. 1979. "De vaart in Europa." *Maritieme Geschiedenis der Nederlanden Vol. III*, edited by F.J.A Broeze et al., 226–61. Bussum: De Boer Martitiem.

Marzagalli, Silvia. 1999. *Boulevards de La Fraude: Le Negoce Maritime Et Le Blocus Continental, 1806–1813: Bordeaux, Hambourg, Livourne*. Villeneuve d'Ascq: Presses Universitaires du Septentrion.

O'Rourke, Kevin H. 2006. "The Worldwide Economic Impact of the French Revolutionary and Napoleonic Wars, 1793–1815." *Journal of Global History* 1: 123–49.

Paping, Richard, 2009. *Urbanisatie en De-Urbanisatie in Nederland 1400–1850*. Groningen: Universiteit van Groningen. Accessed 28 January 2021, see http://www.rug.nl/staff/r.f.j.paping/urbanisatietilburg2009powerpoint.pdf.

Pfeil, Tom. 1998. *Tot redding van het vaderland, het primaat van de Nederlandse overheidsfinanciën in de Bataafs-Franse tijd 1795–1810*. Amsterdam: Amsterdam University Press.

Poell, Thomas. 2005. "Het einde van een tijdperk. De Bataafs-Franse tijd 1795–1813." In *Geschiedenis van Amsterdam Vol. II-2*, edited by M. Prak and W. Frijhoff, 429–99. Amsterdam: SUN.

Postma, Jan. 2017. *Alexander Gogel (1765–1821): Grondlegger van de Nederlandse Staat*. Hilversum: Verloren.

Riemens, H.K. 1937. "De finantieele politiek onder Koning Willem I." *De Gids* 101: 144–67.

Riley, James C. 1980. *International Government Finance and the Amsterdam Capital Market 1740–1815*. Cambridge: Cambridge University Press.

Smits, Jan Pieter, 1999. "Economische ontwikkeling 1800–1995." In *Nationaal goed. Feiten en cijfers over onze samenleving 1800–1999*, edited by Ronald van der Bie and Pit Dehing, 15–36. Voorburg: CBS.

Smits, Jan-Pieter, Edwin Horlings, and Jan Luiten van Zanden. 2000. *Dutch GNP and its Components, 1800–1913*. Groningen: University of Groningen.

Solar, Peter. 2013. "Opening to the East: Shipping Between Europe and Asia, 1770–1830." *The Journal of Economic History* 73: 625–61.

Spaulding, Robert Mark. 2015. "Rhine River Commerce and the Continental System." In *Revisiting Napoleon's Continental System: Local, Regional and European Experiences*, edited by Katherine B. Aaslestad and Johan Joor, 114–32. Basingstoke: Palgrave Macmillan.

't Hart, Marjolein, Pepijn Brandon, and Rafael Torres Sánchez. 2018. "Introduction: Maximising Revenues, Minimizing Political Costs. Challenges in the History of Public Finance of the Early Modern Period." *Financial History Review* 25: 1–18.

't Hart, Marjolein. 2014a. *The Dutch Wars of Independence. War and Commerce in the Netherlands 1580–1680*. London: Routledge, 2014.

't Hart, Marjolein. 2014b. "From the Eighty Years' War to the Second World War: New Perspectives on the Economic Effects of War." *The Low Countries Journal of Social and Economic History* 11: 261–79.

't Hart, Marjolein, and Hilde Greefs. 2018. "Sweet and Sour. Economic Turmoil and Resilience of the Sugar Sector in Antwerp and Rotterdam, 1795–1815." *BMGN - Low Countries Historical Review*, 133: 3–26.

Torres-Sánchez, Rafael, Pepijn Brandon, Marjolein 't Hart. 2018. "War and Economy: Rediscovering the Eighteenth-Century Military Entrepreneur." *Business History* 60: 4–22.

Van Bochhove, Christiaan. 2004. "De Hollandse haringvisserij tijdens de Vroegmoderne Tijd." *Tijdschrift voor Sociale en Economische Geschiedenis* 1:3–27.

Van Eyck van Heslinga, E.S. 1988. *Van compagnie naar koopvaardij. De scheepvaartverbinding van de Bataafse Republiek met de koloniën in Azië 1795–1806*. Amsterdam: De Bataafsche Leeuw.

Van Leeuwen, Marco. 1998. *De eenheidsstaat. Onderlinges, armenzorg en commerciële verzekeraars 1800–1890*. Amsterdam: NEHA.

Van Sas, N.C.F. 2004. *De metamorfose van Nederland: van oude orde naar moderniteit, 1750–1900*. Amsterdam: Amsterdam University Press.

Van Tielhof, Milja. 2002. *The Mother of All Trades: The Baltic Grain Trade in Amsterdam from the Late Sixteenth to the Early Nineteenth Century*. Leiden: Brill.

Van Zanden, Jan Luiten, and Milja van Tielhof. 2009. "Roots of Growth and Productivity Change in the Dutch Shipping Industry, 1500–1800." *Explorations in Economic History* 46: 389–403.

Van Zanden, Jan Luiten, and Arthur van Riel. 2004. *The Strictures of Inheritance. The Dutch Economy in the Nineteenth Century*. Princeton: Princeton University Press.

Van Zanden, Jan Luiten, and Bas van Leeuwen. 2012. "Persistent but not Consistent: The Growth of National Income in Holland 1347–1807." *Explorations in Economic History* 49: 119–30.

Zappey, W.M. 1967. *De economische en politieke werkzaamheid van Johannes Goldberg*. Alphen aan den Rijn: Samson N.V.

CHAPTER 6

Napoleon in Italy: A Legacy of Institutional Reform?

Mark Dincecco and Giovanni Federico

1 Introduction

Napoleon conquered Italy twice, first in 1796–1797, and then again, after a successful Austro-Russian counter-offensive, in 1800–1801.[1] At the end of his first campaign, the Treaty of Campoformio (1797) between Napoleon and the Austrian Emperor carved up the Republic of Venice. Both the city and the Veneto were annexed to the Habsburg Empire, while Eastern Lombardy, the Duchy of Milan (formerly Austrian), the Papal domains in Emilia-Romagna (called the Legazioni) and the Duchy of Modena and Reggio became the Repubblica Cisalpina, a de facto French satellite polity. The following year the French (sans Napoleon, who was fighting in Egypt) invaded the rest of Italy and established republics in Liguria, Tuscany, Rome, and the continental South. With the support of large-scale peasant rebellions, the Austrians abolished these "Jacobin" republics in 1799. The French victory at Marengo and subsequent Treaty of Luneville (1801) reestablished French control in Northern Italy. Piedmont and the small Duchy of Parma and Piacenza were annexed to France, and the Repubblica Cisalpina was resurrected as the Repubblica Italiana, to be renamed the Regno d'Italia (with Napoleon as king) in 1805. French victory at Austerlitz (December 1805) sparked another round of expansion: Napoleon annexed Liguria to France and Veneto to the Regno d'Italia, and defeated the Kingdom of Naples (which had joined the Third Coalition just after Austerlitz) and made his brother Joseph king. Tuscany was annexed to France in 1807, with the exception of the city of Lucca, which was ruled by Napoleon's sister, Elisa. The year after, the French army invaded the Papal States and arrested the Pope. The Marche territories on the Adriatic coast were annexed to the Regno d'Italia, while Umbria and Lazio (including Rome) became French departments.

1 Woolf (1991 and 1979) provides an overview of the Napoleonic Empire and a history of pre-unification Italy.

 | DOI:10.1163/9789004472754_007

Thus, from 1808 onward, France either directly or indirectly ruled the whole of the Italian peninsula, except for the islands of Sardinia and Sicily, to where the exiled Savoy and Bourbon dynasties, respectively, had fled under the protection of the British Navy. The Congress of Vienna (1814–1815) restored the previous Italian dynasties: the Savoy in the Kingdom of Sardinia (which we refer to hereafter as "Piedmont"), the Bourbon in Naples (renamed the Kingdom of the Two Sicilies), and the Pope in Central Italy. Liguria was annexed to Piedmont, while Lombardy and Veneto were joined in a newly-formed Kingdom which was a de facto province of Austria.

The economic consequences of French rule in Italy remain unclear. Recent GDP estimates suggest that the early 1800s were characterized by a short-lived rebound that interrupted a long-run decline from the 1720s to the 1870s. In this chapter, we will evaluate the extent to which French rule can help explain this rebound. Similarly, we will study to what extent economic policy during the post-1815 "Restoration" era can explain the return to a downward economic trajectory. Finally, we will analyze the legacy of institutional reforms initiated during the Napoleonic era for modern economic growth in the late nineteenth century.

Our analysis will draw a distinction between the short run and the long run. The evidence suggests that the short-run economic and social costs of French rule in Italy outweighed any economic gains. By improving the underlying institutional environment, Napoleon's economic legacy may however have been beneficial to long-run development, but only after several decades *and* the establishment of further institutional reforms, pioneered from 1848 onward by Piedmont, and adopted throughout Italy after the political unification of the peninsula in 1861.

We structure this chapter as follows. In the next section, we review the evidence for Italy's economic performance under Napoleon. In Section 3, we discuss the short-run economic costs and benefits of French rule. In Section 4, we describe the institutional reforms that Napoleon made in Italy. In Section 5, we analyze Napoleon's long-run economic legacy in Italy. Section 6 concludes.

2 Economic Performance under Napoleon

We know relatively little about the Italian economy during the Napoleonic era. Historical works include basic information on French institutional reforms and economic policies, but the only comprehensive work on the economy, the *History of Economic Life in Italy under Napoleon,* by the Russian historian Yevgeny Tarle, was written in 1916 and translated into Italian in 1950 (Tarle

1950). Since then, economic historians have mostly neglected the Napoleonic era, with the exception of a specific issue, the sales of Church lands, which they have characterized as an important step in the development of the agrarian bourgeoisie.

The existing literature has not reached any consensus about the economic consequences of Napoleonic rule. Tarle's view is highly negative. He claims that the French used trade and fiscal policies to transform Italy into an "economic colony of the French Empire" (Tarle 1950, 32). Other scholars, such as Zaghi (1986) are more sanguine, highlighting some industrial progress. This more optimistic take fits with the traditional view of long-run economic trends in Italy (Caracciolo 1973; Felice 2015, 35–40), which claims that Italian commerce and manufacturing had been in decline since the sixteenth century, due both to the European discovery of the Americas and institutional sclerosis. From the mid-eighteenth century onward, however, absolutist rulers on the Italian peninsula attempted, with some success, to stave off this decline with institutional reforms inspired by the Enlightenment. Napoleon aggressively built upon their efforts, thereby promoting economic development.

This conventional view is largely based on works by Enlightenment-era reformers and on scattered anecdotal evidence. The available per capita GDP estimates for the Center-North of Italy (Malanima 2010), however, suggest a rather different story (Figure 6.1). Namely, per capita GDP was higher in the Center-North of Italy than in England and Wales as late as the 1720s (Broadberry et al. 2015), although it remained below its mid-fifteenth century peak. From 1720 to 1796, per capita GDP in the Center-North declined by about one-sixth (approximately -0.20% per year). Malanima (2002, 346–8) links this eighteenth-century economic "crisis" to demographic pressures on scarce land resources. Per capita GDP recovered in the early nineteenth century, with a peak in 1835 that was roughly 10% lower than a century earlier, and then declined again back to 1790s levels. The Napoleonic era coincided with the start of this recovery (Figure 6.2). From 1801 to 1809, per capita GDP grew by around 10%; most of these economic gains were lost during the last years of Napoleonic rule.

Malanima's demand-side estimate of GDP proxies for changes in income with real wages from the construction trade in Milan and for agricultural laborers in Vercelli (in Piedmont). He does not estimate GDP for the South, but elsewhere he has published series of real wages for building workers in Naples and agricultural laborers in Molfetta (in Puglia) (Malanima 2013). Over the long run, they display similar trends for Northern wages, but during the Napoleonic era, they simply fluctuated rather than rose. Nominal wages remained broadly constant everywhere. Thus movements in real wages depended mostly on

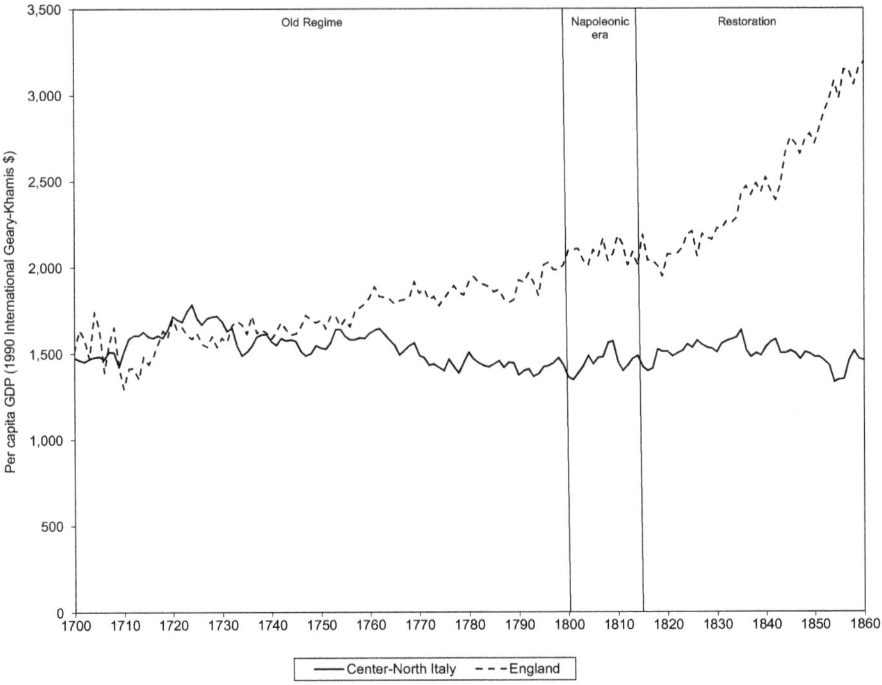

FIGURE 6.1 Per capita GDP in the Center-North of Italy, 1700–1860
SOURCES: MALANIMA (2010) FOR CENTER-NORTH OF ITALY; BROADBERRY ET AL. (2015) FOR ENGLAND (INCLUDING WALES)

prices (Malanima 2015). The available data on wheat prices show a sharp decline from a peak in 1801 to 1809, and then a rebound in the following years.[2] A downward trend in prices, combined with a constant population, and without evidence for increased imports, suggests – at the very least – constant agricultural output.[3] Indeed, the (not wholly reliable) official data for cereal production increased in all key agricultural areas in Lombardy (Cova 1977, tab. 2.1). After reviewing the (limited) evidence, De Biasio (2013, 167) cautiously

2 The average price of wheat fell from 142.7 grams silver/hl to 56.7 grams across the six sample markets within the Regno d'Italia; from 148.2 to 81.7 across the four sample markets that were annexed French departments; and from 102.7 to 62 across the two Southern markets (Federico et al. 2018).

3 The Center-North's population was 11.4 million in 1800 and 11.6 million in 1814, while the South's population was 5 million (1800) and 5.1 million (1814) (Malanima, personal communication).

FIGURE 6.2 Per capita GDP in the Center-North of Italy under French Rule
SOURCE: MALANIMA (2010)

suggests that cereal output was also on the rise in the South. However, one cannot rule out the possibility that these movements reflected random fluctuations in weather conditions. Summer temperatures in Switzerland and Central Europe, the closest proxy that we have to contemporaneous Italian weather data, were mild throughout the 1800s and well below average in the first years of the 1810s (Kelly and O'Grada 2014).

3 Short-Run Costs and Benefits of Napoleonic Rule

3.1 *Costs*

While Italy had been a key battleground during the Wars of the First and Second Coalitions of the 1790s, it remained relatively unscathed from 1800 onward. The military superiority of the French army relative to Bourbon and Papal troops was enough to make the subsequent conquest of Italy quite bloodless. The Center-North remained peaceful during the Napoleonic era, while the French army ruthlessly repressed uprisings in parts of the South. In 1814, the French withdrew their troops from Italy, and the Italian army disbanded, without much fighting. Nonetheless, Italians bore heavy burdens under French rule.

3.1.1 Conscription

First and foremost, Italians were subject to military conscription, which became mandatory in Piedmont, Tuscany, and Umbria-Lazio upon French annexation, in the Repubblica Italiana in 1802 (Zaghi 1986, 534), and in the South in 1807 (Galasso 2007a, 1085). Conscription ratios varied by polity, however. In the Regno d'Italia, the number of military conscripts increased from 16 draftees per 1,000 inhabitants in the early 1800s to 36 by 1813 (Zaghi 1986, 554). In the latter year, the Regno d'Italia had 114,000 troops, equivalent to just 5% of the male workforce (aged 15–65), but to 20% of males subject to conscription (aged 20–29).[4] In the South, by contrast, there was only 1 draftee for every 1,000 inhabitants initially, though this ratio doubled in 1809 (Galasso 2007a, 1110). In 1813, the South enlisted just 30,000 people – 3.5% of males aged 20–29, and 1.4% of the workforce. Overall, roughly 500,000 Italians (including Italian draftees from French departments and Southerners) were enlisted during the Napoleonic era, out of a total peninsular population of approximately 15 million (Zaghi 1986, 539).[5] Under the French, the Italian military fought in Germany, Russia, and Spain, and endured approximately 65,000 war-related deaths (Zaghi 1986, 536). Most draftees were illiterate peasants, although losses among officers deprived the country of valuable human capital. Yet, according to some scholars, the large human costs had a silver lining. Zaghi (1986, 554) suggests that those years of conscription helped Italians develop a national identity, while Tarle (1950, 54) and Trezzi (1992) suggest that wartime shortages of manpower increased wages. As described in Section 2, however, movements in real wages were determined mostly by price changes.

3.1.2 Taxation

Beyond the sheer costs in terms of human capital, French rule was expensive. At the beginning of their rule, the French imposed "predatory" tributes on all conquered regions – for example, Lombardy and Emilia paid 55 million lire in 1796–1797 (Marcelli 1967, 39–57). Thereafter, the French compelled the Italians

4 We rely on the age structure of the population according to the 1861 Italian census (MAIC 1861).

5 To this amount, we should add the sizeable number of draftees who failed to report for duty, which numbered 15–20% of the potential conscripts in Piedmont (Notario and Nada 1993, 32), and roughly 20,000 in the Regno d'Italia in 1810 (Zaghi 1986, 555).

to fund their own military forces as well as French troops stationed in their territories. Out of total expenditures of 136 million lire in 1809, for example, the Regno d'Italia spent 42 million on its own army (31% of the total), 30 million in tribute to France, 18 million on debt interest, 18 million on law enforcement, and 6 million for the civil list of the king (Napoleon himself) and the viceroy (Tarle 1950, 48).

Table 6.1 and Figures 6.3 to 6.5 present data on total and per capita revenue (in silver grams) from the mid-eighteenth century to political unification.[6] Given changes in political borders over time (along with data limitations), these data should be taken as rough proxies for tax levels rather than as precise measures. Figure 6.3 plots taxation per capita separately for Piedmont (including Savoy and Sardinia) and the Republic of Genoa before 1796, and jointly for all these areas after 1815, and compares them with taxes per capita for France (including occupied Piedmont) during the Napoleonic era. Similarly, we compare the Duchy of Milan and the Republic of Venice before 1790 to Lombardy-Veneto after 1815, and with the Regno d'Italia (including large swathes of Emilia and Marche) between 1803 and 1811 (Figure 6.4). The data for the South (Figure 6.5) include Sicily before 1790 and after 1815, but not during the Napoleonic era. While we do not include a figure for the Papal States, which were split between different states at different times during the Napoleonic era, per capita taxation also increased there (Caravale and Caracciolo 1978, 587).[7]

What these data make clear is that French domination increased taxation relative to the Ancien Régime across most of Italy, with the possible exception of Piedmont. High taxation during the Napoleonic era was a source of complaints. Further research is necessary to understand whether this high tax burden was distributed equitably or not. Notario and Nada (1993, 98) suggest that individuals in Piedmont adapted well to taxation under the French, since all taxes were quite high, and thus the regime was not perceived as favoring any particular social group. Furthermore, individuals were accustomed to a high level of taxation under the Savoy dynasty (Figure 6.3). In the Regno d'Italia, direct and indirect taxes appear to have increased at the same rate (Zaghi

6 The basic revenue trends depicted in Table 6.1 remain similar if we deflate by the price index in Malanima (2013) or by wheat prices according to Federico et al. (2018).

7 As described in Section 1, the pre-revolutionary Papal States were divided between the Repubblica Italiana/Regno d'Italia (the 'Legazioni' since 1797 and the Marche since 1808) and France (Lazio and Umbria, since 1808). Thus, per capita revenue for the Papal States under the Ancien Régime (Table 6.1) should be compared to levels for the Regno d'Italia and for France.

TABLE 6.1 Tax revenue in Italy, 1750–1860

Panel A: Average total tax revenue (millions of silver grams)

	1750–90	1800–15	1825–1847	1848–58
Piedmont	115		255	420
Genoa	23			
Lombardy-Veneto	145		101	143
Tuscany	38		66	109
Papal States	56		161	247
Two Sicilies	93	323	394	544
"Italy"	78		195	293
Regno d'Italia (1803–11)		540		
France (1800–15)		4004		

Panel B: Average per capita tax revenue. silver grams)

	1750–90	1800–15	1825–1847	1848–58
Piedmont	90		67	101
Genoa	50			
Lombardy-Veneto	44		21	28
Tuscany	39		46	63
Papal States	24		58	80
Two Sicilies	20	65	49	60
"Italy"	45		48	66
Regno d'Italia (1803–11)		114		
France (1800–15)		134		

Notes: The 1750–90 data for Piedmont do not include the Republic of Genoa. We present the 1750–90 Genoa data separately. We scale the 1750–90 per capita data for Piedmont and Genoa by their respective populations. By contrast, the 1825–58 data for Piedmont do in fact include Genoa. See Section 1. We thus scale the 1825–58 per capita data by the population of Piedmont plus Genoa. The 1750–90 data for Lombardy-Veneto sum the individual data for the Duchy of Milan and the (mainland) Republic of Venice, and thus scale the per capita data by the summed populations. The pre-1815 data for the Kingdom of the Two Sicilies uses the individual data for the (mainland) Kingdom of Naples (as data for the Kingdom of Sicily are not available). By contrast, the 1825–58 data for the Kingdom of the Two Sicilies include both Naples and Sicily. The per capita data are scaled accordingly. The Napoleonic-era data were converted from ducats into silver grams for the Kingdom of the Two Sicilies, and from lire into silver grams for the Regno d'Italia. The 1825–58 data were converted from gold grams into silver grams. The Regno d'Italia includes Lombardy, Veneto, and Emilia-Romagna (see Section 1). "Italy" averages the data across the Italian peninsula.

TABLE 6.1 Tax revenue in Italy, 1750–1860 (*cont.*)

SOURCES: THE 1750–90 DATA ARE FROM CHILOSI (2014), EXCEPT FOR THE 1772–87 DATA FOR THE KINGDOM OF THE TWO SICILIES, WHICH ARE FROM VILLANI (1964, 12). THE 1807–14 DATA FOR THE KINGDOM OF THE TWO SICILIES ARE FROM BIANCHINI (1834, 601–13). THE 1803–11 DATA FOR THE REGNO D'ITALIA ARE FROM TARLE (1950, 48, 57). THE 1800–15 DATA FOR FRANCE ARE FROM DINCECCO 2011. THE 1825–58 DATA ARE FROM DINCECCO ET AL. (2011). THE SILVER/GOLD RATIO DATA ARE FROM OFFICER AND WILLIAMSON (MEASURINGWORTH.COM). THE NAPOLEONIC-ERA DATA IN LIRE WERE CONVERTED INTO SILVER GRAMS BASED ON THEIR SILVER CONTENT (WITH ONE LIRA EQUAL TO ONE FRENCH FRANC).

1986, 526), while in the South, indirect taxes increased more than the land tax (Bianchini 1835, 594–610).

3.1.3 Trade

Tarle (1950, 67) claims that trade policy was the main tool of French exploitation: "The Kingdom [of Italy] was the playing field where French industry could freely compete with domestic producers, as the Empire remained closed to all foreign manufactures." By definition, French manufacturers had free access to the annexed Italian departments (and vice versa), while elsewhere in Italy they enjoyed different levels of protection according to the country of origin of their competitors. Trade with England was forbidden, except under special authorization, while commerce with neutral states such as Prussia and Switzerland was subject to high duties. Trade between France and its satellite states was regulated by bilateral treaties. The first treaty (1798), with the Repubblica Cisalpina (see Section 1), capped duties on bilateral trade at 6% (Cova 1988, 117). The French were not satisfied with this agreement, however, claiming that it allowed German and Swiss producers to sell their wares in France disguised as Italian products. The new 1808 treaty between France and the Regno set duties on bilateral trade to half the duties of the general tariff and stipulated that this cut should not be applied to imports from other French satellite states such as the Confederation of the Rhine (Tarle 1950, 221). The French trade system began to collapse in 1814, when the King of Naples allowed English goods to enter with sharply-reduced duties in order to gain British political support.

Italian merchants and manufacturers complained about Napoleonic trade policy, and indeed there is ample evidence of crises at port cities due to trade restrictions. Leghorn (Livorno) had prospered before 1807 as an entry point for British goods, but annexation to France and the British blockade caused trade to collapse and its population to shrink by one-sixth from 1806 to 1813 (Filippini

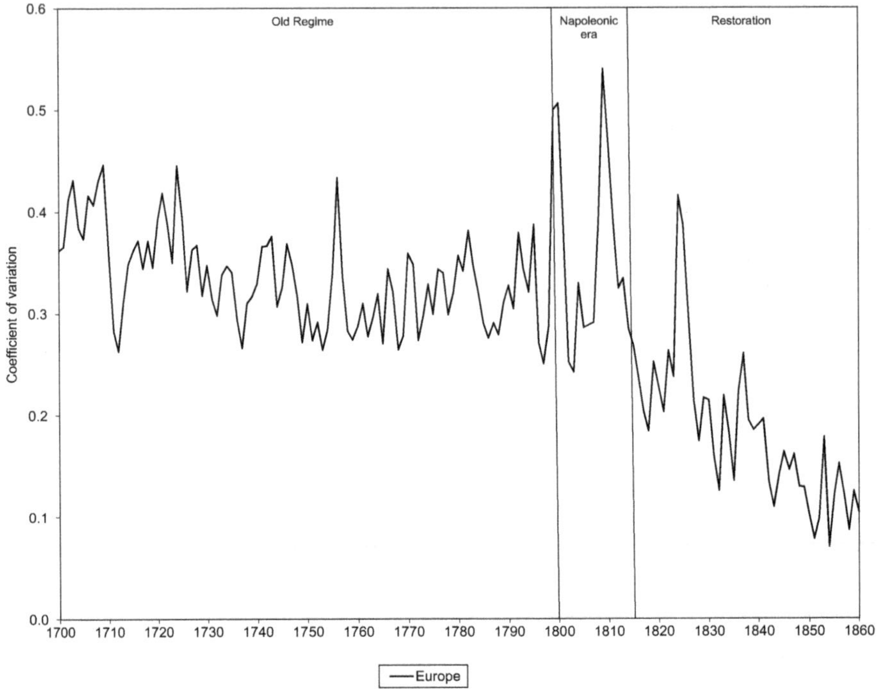
Old Regime
Napoleonic era
Restoration
Coefficient of variation
0.6
0.5
0.4
0.3
0.2
0.1
0.0
1700
1710
1720
1730
1740
1750
1760
1770
1780
1790
1800
1810
1820
1830
1840
1850
1860
Europe

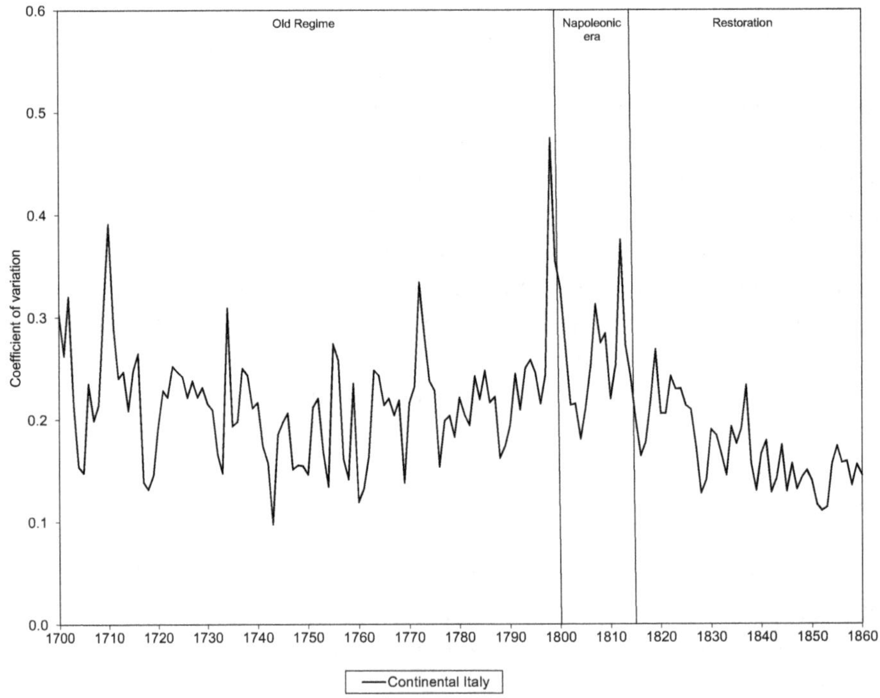
Old Regime
Napoleonic era
Restoration
Coefficient of variation
0.6
0.5
0.4
0.3
0.2
0.1
0.0
1700
1710
1720
1730
1740
1750
1760
1770
1780
1790
1800
1810
1820
1830
1840
1850
1860
Continental Italy

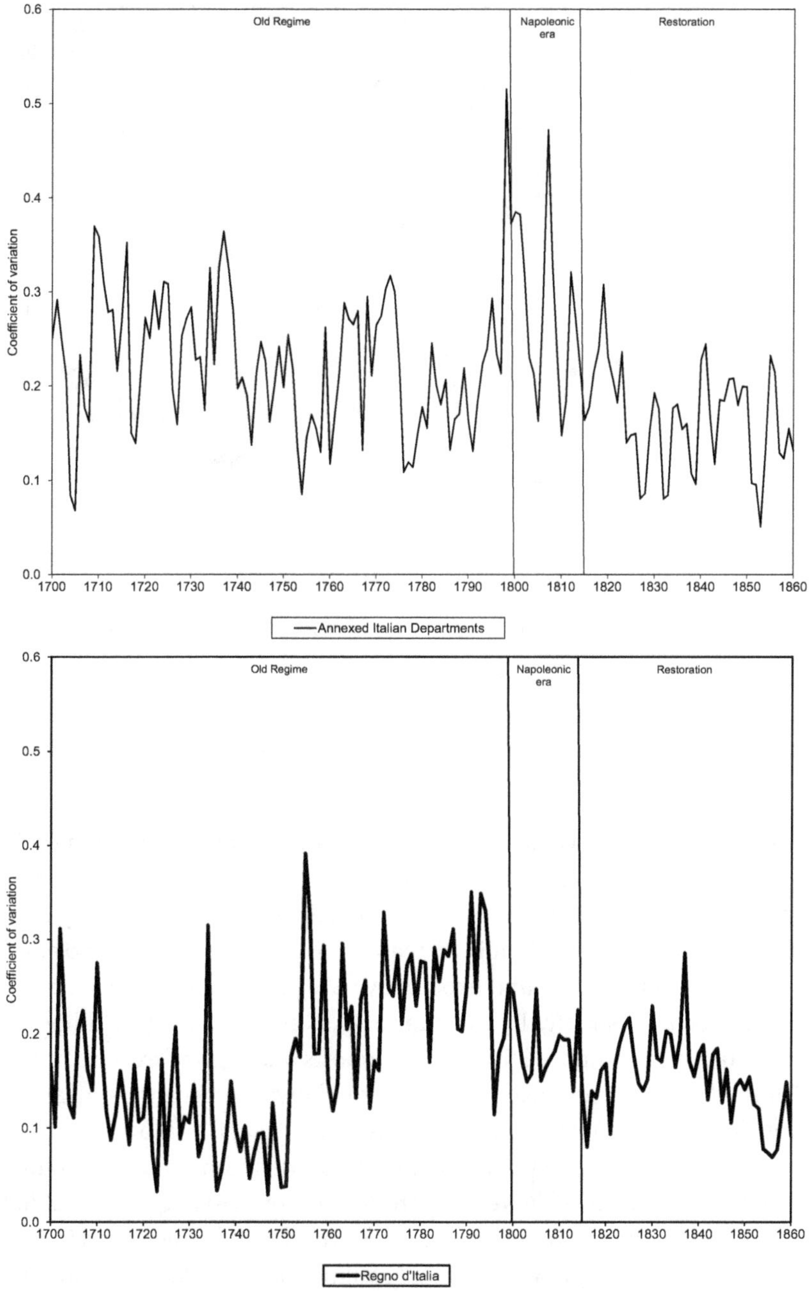

FIGURE 6.3 Changes in price dispersion of wheat, 1700–1860
Notes: The panel for Europe includes 84 markets; the annexed Italian departments include 4 (Florence, Pisa, Rome, Vercelli); the Regno d'Italia includes 6 (Brescia, Mantua, Milan, Padua, Rovigo, Udine), and continental Italy includes the French departments and the Regno d'Italia as described above, plus Naples and Acquaviva delle Fonti (in Puglia).
SOURCE: FEDERICO ET AL. (2018)

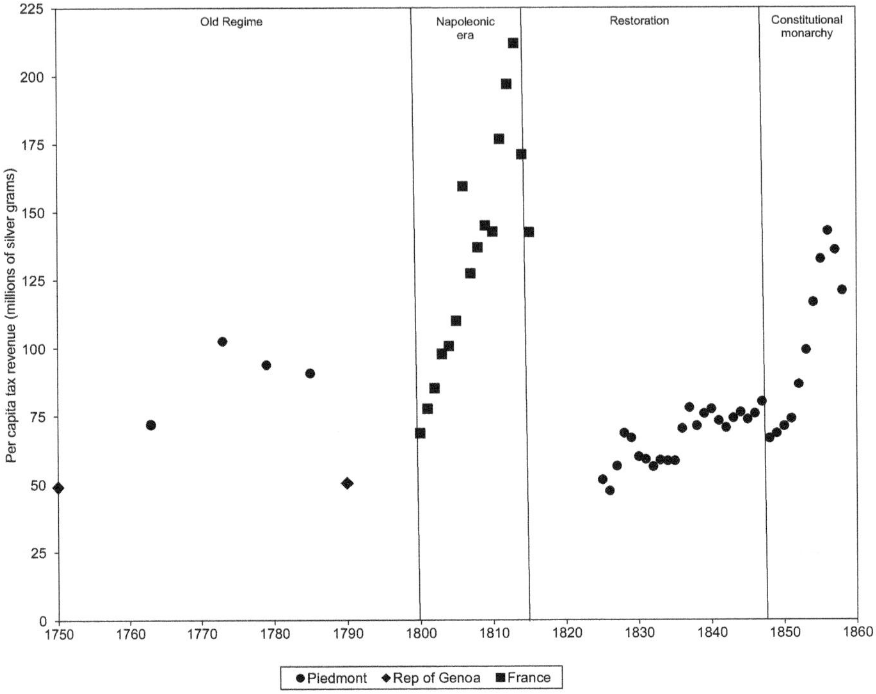

FIGURE 6.4 Per capita tax revenue in Piedmont, 1750–1860
Notes: See Table 6.1 for construction methods and source materials.

1985; Coppini 1993, 119–26). Genoa suffered even more, as the reduction in trade was accompanied by huge losses on financial assets from the renegotiation of French debt and the near default on local public debt (Doria 1969, 4). By contrast, total trade by the Regno d'Italia increased significantly between 1807 and 1810 (imports went up by 18%, and exports by 28%) according to official trade statistics, but declined slightly by 1812 (Tarle 1950, 240). France (including its Italian departments) accounted for 58% of imports and 55% of exports of the Regno. These data are to be taken with caution, however, because smuggling was very widespread, in spite of official efforts to eradicate it (Grab 2015).

The effects of French trade policy on consumption and production in Italy are even more difficult to evaluate. The prohibition of British goods shielded domestic producers from Europe's most competitive firms, but deprived Italian consumers of the relatively low (and rapidly falling) prices of British industrial products. Manufacturers in Lombardy, moreover, gained additional protection against firms located in other parts of the Austrian Empire. Still, Italian manufacturers had to face French competition, with low duties (in the Regno

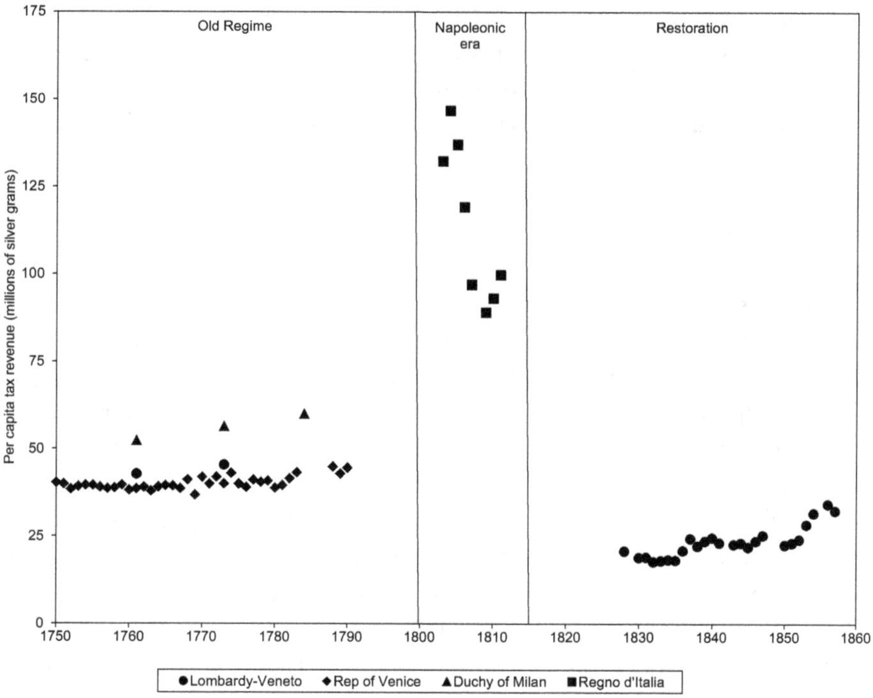

FIGURE 6.5 Per capita tax revenue in Lombardy-Veneto, 1750–1860
Notes: See Table 6.1 for construction methods and source materials.

d'Italia and later in the South) or none at all (in the annexed Italian departments). The effects of the Napoleonic trade regime may have been more severe in the South, since prior to 1806 local production had been protected against all imported manufactured goods. Italian consumers experienced additional welfare losses due to the British counter-blockade, which prompted a shortage of colonial goods which were not easily substitutable, with the exception of sugar from beets (O'Rourke 2007).

Exporters were allegedly in deep trouble under the Napoleonic trade regime. The French market did not need cheese or wheat from Lombardy, while its demand for silk, the main staple of the Center-North of Italy, may have been insufficient to fully absorb Italian production (Moioli 1992, 210). Exports of silk to Central Europe had to pay a duty from 1803 onward, which tripled in 1810, and exports to Britain were officially forbidden. However, substantial quantities were smuggled via Germany and Switzerland (Moioli 1992, 210). Indeed, total British silk consumption grew by one-third between 1800–1804 and 1810–1814, while the share of "Italian" silk (which may have included some silk from the Levant) only declined from 63% to 57% (Federico 1994, tabs. XXXI-V). Taken together, these figures suggest that Italian silk exports to Britain increased by one-quarter. This evidence, though limited, suggests that the complaints of Italian industrialists about the Napoleonic trade regime should be taken with a grain of salt.

3.2 *Benefits*

The abolition of trade barriers and market integration are thought to be the main drivers of economic growth in pre-industrial Europe (e.g. Epstein 2000; Persson and Sharp 2015). French conquest entailed a major simplification of the political map on the Italian peninsula, from ten independent states in 1796 to three major ones (France, the Regno d'Italia, and the Kingdom of Naples) and three minor ones (Lucca, Sardinia and Sicily) by 1810. Furthermore, the King of Naples abolished all internal trade duties in 1810 (Bianchini 1835, 598). Last but not least, the French invested heavily in road-building for military purposes – approximately 72 million lire in ten years for roads within the Regno itself, and 22 million lire for roads across the Alps (Zaghi 1986, 426–34).

The basic evidence for price convergence is a reduction in the coefficient of variation over time for time-invariant samples (Federico, 2012a). Figure 6.6 plots these coefficients for wheat prices in the annexed Italian departments (1809 borders; four markets), the Regno d'Italia (six markets), and continental Italy as a whole (including two Southern markets), as well as for Europe-wide (84 markets).[8]

Although the results of this analysis differ somewhat by sub-sample, overall they do not suggest major market integration. The coefficients of variation fluctuated widely for the annexed Italian departments and for continental Italy as a whole. Similarly, there is no evidence of price convergence for the European-wide market. By contrast, the coefficient of variation within the Regno d'Italia fell from 0.28 in 1789–95 to 0.20 in 1796–1800.[9] It is tempting to attribute this drop to the invasion by France, but the causal link should be further investigated – was it the abolition of trade barriers, the increase in information flows, or a combination of the two that really mattered? In the early 1800s, price dispersion within the Regno remained relatively constant, without apparently benefiting from domestic stability or road construction. Given

8 These markets are: Florence, Pisa, Rome, and Vercelli for the annexed Italian departments; Brescia, Mantua, Milan, Padua, Rovigo, and Udine for the Regno d'Italia, and Acquaviva delle Fonti (Bari) and Naples for the South. All data are from Federico et al. (2018).

9 A Bai-Perron (2003) test confirms the significance of this drop – the year 1796 being the sole structural break over the entire 1700–1860 period.

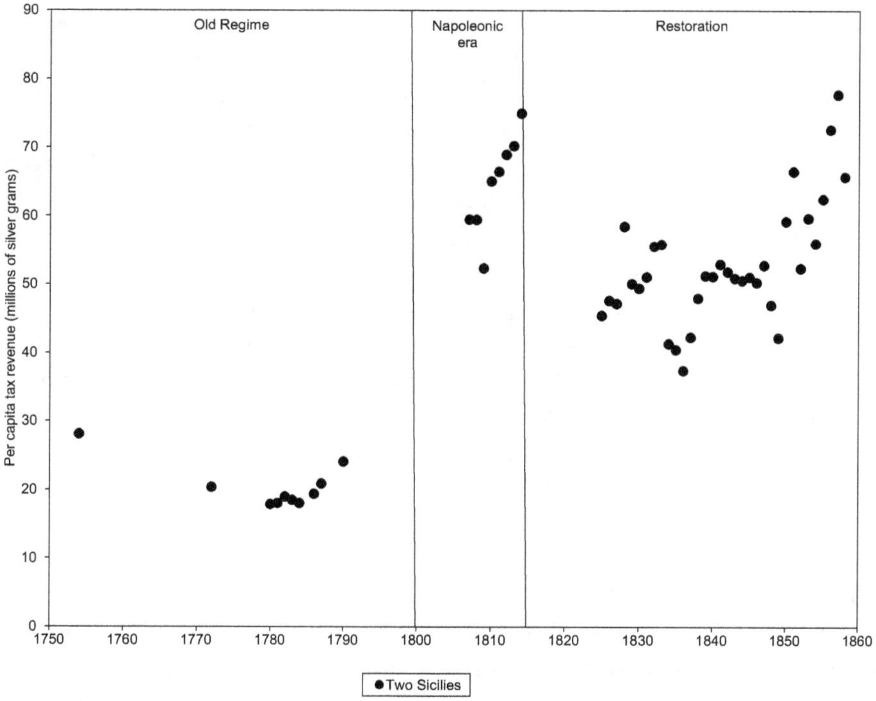

FIGURE 6.6 Per capita tax revenue in the South, 1750–1860
Notes: See Table 6.1 for construction methods and source materials.

that the Regno's markets were located inland, moreover, they should not have been subject to the British coastal blockade. Of course, one might argue that wheat is not representative, and indeed it would be useful to double-check these results against price data for other goods (including manufactures). Unfortunately, such data are not available.

Economic historians have singled out two specific French policies as beneficial for the Italian economy. First, Romani (1982, 39–40) and Zaghi (1986, 528) have argued that higher government expenditures fostered short-run economic growth in the Regno d'Italia. This argument, however, cannot refer to deficit spending, as the budget was nearly always balanced. The deficit peaked in 1811 when it amounted to approximately 10% of revenue, and thus likely to less than 1% of GDP.[10] Zaghi concentrates on public procurements of

10 Malanima (2010) does not estimate GDP at current prices. However, public revenue was approximately 7% of GDP and expenditure approximately 10% in the early 1860s (Federico 2009). It appears implausible that such shares were higher during the Napoleonic era.

industrial goods. Such procurements were not that large, as most public expenditures went toward food, lodging, and salaries for the troops. State purchases of "materiali" grew from 1.1 million lire in 1805 to a peak of 5.7 in 1811 – in other words, from just 1.1% to 3.7% of total public expenditures (Cova 1988, tab. 11). Italian producers generally supplied their own ammunition and textiles. The French army was reluctant to buy Italian major weapons because they seldom met its quality standards (Moioli 1992, 287).

Second, Italian agriculture is said to have benefited from the expropriation and sale of Church lands (which were renamed "beni nazionali"). This policy was not unprecedented, as the Duchy of Milan and the Venetian Republic had seized and sold a good deal of monasterial lands in the 1770s and 1780s to reduce the Church's power (Marcelli 1967, 21–37).[11] The French extended this policy to other regions, both out of revolutionary zeal and in order to settle the long-standing public debts of Ancien Régime polities, which were absorbing substantial amounts of revenue.[12] Repudiating these debts would have jeopardized French relations with local elites, and thus the French decided to re-issue approximately half of them, and to convert the other half into special bonds which debt-holders could only redeem through the purchase of beni nazionali, with or without an additional cash payment.[13] Though not all Church lands were seized and sold, the quantities were nonetheless substantial, amounting to (at least) 5% of total land in the Repubblica Cisalpina and Repubblica Italiana, 4.25% in the South, 2.7% in Piedmont, and 1.5% in Tuscany and Venetia.

Most scholars deem this transfer to have been beneficial to agricultural development (Villani 1964, 37; Mineccia 1985, 543; Zaghi 1986, 573; Coppini 1993, 148; Notario and Nada 1993, 68). The new landowners allegedly introduced

11 The Grand Duchy of Tuscany had distributed most of its land to small debt-holders from 1769 onward (Giorgetti 1966), while the King of Naples had seized and sold various Church estates to fund reconstruction efforts after an earthquake in 1783 (Villani 1964, 16).

12 See Notario (1980) for Piedmont, Marcelli (1967) for both the Repubblica Cisalpina and the Repubblica Italiana, Calzavarini (1992) for Veneto, Bassetti (1985) and Mineccia (1985) for Tuscany, and Villani (1964) for the Kingdom of Naples. De Felice (1960) describes the planned, but never implemented, Church land sale by the Repubblica Romana in 1798–1799, but there is no quantitative analysis of post-1810 French sales (Candeloro 1958, 341). Genoa was an exception, perhaps because the Church lands to be seized were not valuable enough relative to the outstanding debt of the Banco di San Giorgio.

13 Church lands were organized in large estates, which the French had no time or interest to divide before sales. Thus, the sales were generally a bargain for substantial creditors, who could purchase land at prices below their long-run valuations, and with generous terms of payment. Small creditors, by contrast, often had to sell their bonds at heavy discounts.

better agricultural technologies, intensified cultivation, and forced laborers to work harder in order to increase land rents and pay off their investments.[14] The evidence for such improvements is limited, however, and the argument seems to rely on a somewhat mechanistic contrast between sluggish land management by the Church versus aggressive modern management by new agrarian capitalists.

3.3 *Section Summary*

Given the available quantitative evidence, we remain doubtful to say the least that the short-run economic benefits of French rule emanating from government expenditures, land transfers, infrastructure investment, and market integration were large enough to outweigh the economic and social costs of occupation including military conscription, war-related deaths, high taxation, and (perhaps) trade destruction. French rule did offer peace and stability after 1800, but most of the Italian peninsula had already been peaceful since the end of the War of the Austrian Succession in 1748.

4 Institutional Reforms

A large literature argues that institutional reforms have been vital to long-run economic development.[15] Dincecco and Katz (2016), for example, show evidence for a significant long-run relationship between national-level fiscal reforms – oftentimes related to Napoleonic conquests – and economic development across Western Europe. Similarly, Acemoglu et al. (2011) claim that institutional reforms caused the French-dominated areas (i.e., the Confederation of the Rhine) to grow faster than other parts of Germany over the second half of the nineteenth century.[16]

Italian institutions in 1796 were not uniformly archaic. Feudal rights had long disappeared in the most advanced parts of the Center-North, and absolutist monarchs throughout the peninsula had attempted – with varying levels of success – to modernize their governments over the eighteenth century (Candeloro 1956; Wolf 1979). Dauchy, the French plenipotentiary in Tuscany, deemed local institutions almost as advanced as French ones (Coppini 1993, 108). Elsewhere,

14 Recently, Heldring et al. (2015) have put forward a similar argument for the abolition of monasteries in England by Henry VIII.

15 Dincecco (2017) provides an overview of this literature.

16 Kopsidis and Bromley (2016), however, challenge this view.

TABLE 6.2 Years of Napoleonic-era reforms in Italy

	Piedmont	Regno d'Italia	Tuscany	Papal States	Continental South
Equality before law	1801	1797	1805		
Guild abolition	1801	Pre-1796	Pre-1796		
Abolition of feudal rights	1801	Pre-1796	Pre-1796	Pre-1796	1806
Abolition of majorat	1801	1797	1805	1805	1807
Code Napoléon	1805	1806	1808	1809	1808

Notes: Blank cells indicate that data were not available; "Pre-1796" indicates that the institution in question had already been reformed prior to 1796.
SOURCES: BIANCHINI (1835); ZAGHI (1986); WOOLF (1991); NOTARIO AND NADA (1993)

however, antiquated institutions remained, and the French implemented a vigorous reform agenda. Indeed, it almost appears as if the French policies were taken from World Bank prescriptions – albeit a late eighteenth-century version – about the implementation of "good institutions." They included the following: citizen equality before the law (versus discrimination against minority groups including Jews); guild abolition; the abolition of (any remaining) feudal rights; the adoption of the French legal system (the Code Napoléon); the abolition of fiscal privileges (whether by region or class including the Catholic Church); the abolition of restrictions to inheritance (fidecommissum and majorat); the standardization and simplification of the tax system, with three main sources of revenue (taxes on land, on income from trade, and on consumption, including duties); and bureaucratic reorganization according to the French model (namely, governance by similarly-sized local departments, with strong control by the central government).

In Table 6.2 we list the approximate dates of the adoption of French reforms in different Italian polities.[17] Historians have been more concerned with the political process of institutional change than with its nitty-gritty details, and

17 The Chaptal Law of 1802, which the French extended to Italy, improved literacy by expanding access to primary education and unifying diverse curricula (Postigliola and Rota 2020).

in any case singling out a specific date for each reform is not straightforward. In some cases, the bulk of the reform had been adopted before the arrival of the French, who only finished things off. In other cases, actual implementation was delayed or only partial. Last but not least, in quite a few cases, reforms had first been adopted by the "Jacobin" republics (see Section 1) and were overturned by the Austro-Russians in 1799. As a rule, we neglect these short-lived attempts, reporting the date of adoption after the second French conquest.

The timing of institutional reforms was heavily dependent on military events. The French generally imposed a standard set of institutional reforms soon after they conquered a given territory, without much effort to build local consensus. This policy was especially ruthless in the annexed territories (Broers 2005), but was also adopted in the satellite polities. For example, feudal rights were abolished in the Kingdom of Naples in August of 1806 – just three months after the Bourbon military ended its resistance (and just six months after the proclamation of Joseph Bonaparte as king).[18]

Napoleonic-era reforms were not only modernizing, but were also uniform across Italian states. For example, Napoleon ignored the draft of new tort laws that had been prepared by local experts in the Regno d'Italia, opting instead to have the Code Napoléon translated and approved (Zaghi 1986, 344). In principle, standardization should have produced economic benefits: the universal adoption of the Code Napoléon across the Italian peninsula, for example, should have reduced the transaction costs of trade.

Nonetheless, it is doubtful that French institutional reforms can explain the relatively good economic performance of the Center-North during the Napoleonic era (see Section 2). Wage and GDP growth had begun before the institutional reforms took place, and peaked just after their adoption. Such reforms required a major reorganization of the civil service, a time-consuming process. For example, the abolition of feudal rights in the South required among other things the appointment of a committee which, over the course of two years (1808–1810), adjudicated on more than 5,000 cases (Galasso 2007a, 1138–46). Thus, we would not expect to observe any immediate economic effects of the French institutional reforms.

---

18 Feudal rights were abolished by the Bourbon king in Sicily in 1812 as part of a constitutional reform inspired by the British (Candeloro 1956, 351–3), while in Sardinia they remained until the reforms of the 1830s.

5 Napoleon's Legacy

5.1 *Economy*

After 1815, all states except for Tuscany reverted to pre-revolutionary trade policies, attempting to promote domestic manufacturing with high duties and other measures including subsidies, public management, and the granting of temporary monopolies (Romani 1982, 66–77; Pescosolido 1998, 61–6). According to the conventional wisdom, such policies caused market disintegration and thus economic losses.

The available evidence, however, does not support this view. First, the series on GDP and wages do not indicate any particular downward shock in 1815 (see Section 2). The Italian economy continued to grow, although slowly, for at least fifteen years after the Restoration. Unusually cold weather due to the explosion of the volcano on Mount Tambora in Indonesia caused wheat prices to soar in 1816–1817 throughout the Western hemisphere, but they then collapsed, triggering a protectionist reaction in most European countries (Federico 2012b). There is no evidence for the disintegration of Italian wheat markets; the dispersion of prices across the Italian peninsula in the mid-1820s was actually lower than during the Napoleonic era (see Figure 6.6). Due to declining transportation costs, price dispersions fell further in both Italy (and the rest of Europe) over the first half of the nineteenth century (Federico 2007 and 2011). Wheat, however, may have not been representative, as barriers to grain trade were comparatively low. All states apart from the Kingdom of Sardinia were either self-sufficient or net grain exporters (Federico 2012a). Indeed, Piedmont, along with other European importers, reacted to the threat of grain imports from Russia by augmenting duties to approximately 50 percent of the world wheat price in 1822.[19]

Simple logic, moreover, suggests that the effects of Restoration-era trade policy relative to the Napoleonic era may not have been as negative as the conventional view claims. Post-1815 protectionism increased on imports from France and other Italian polities, but it may have decreased on imports from Continental Europe, while the end of the Continental Blockade abolished the ban on imports of colonial goods and on British manufactures. Furthermore, Italian exports of silk and other primary products were freed from duties or prohibitions. Put differently, while French hegemony may have increased intra-European trade, it reduced trade with the British and the rest of the world.

19 Note, however, that the case for wheat does not rule out a negative effect of trade policy on market integration for manufactures.

The post-1815 Restoration reversed both policies, and the economic benefits of British and world trade may have eventually outweighed the costs of French and Italian protectionism. Nonetheless, Italian producers may have failed to properly exploit their newfound trade freedom. From the 1820s to political unification in 1861, Italian silk lost shares on both the British and French markets (Federico 1994, tab. XXXV), and total Italian exports increased by less than world trade (Federico and Tena 2016). This decline points to supply-side problems.

Relative to the pre-revolutionary era, total tax revenue after 1815 was higher than under the Ancien Régime in all Italian polities except for Lombardo-Veneto (Table 6.1). This evidence suggests that the simplification of the tax code and the abolition of traditional tax privileges by the French were conducive to higher overall taxation. Furthermore, after 1815 per capita taxation increased in the Papal States and in the South, where it had been very low under the Ancien Régime, and (to a lesser extent) in Tuscany. In the North, by contrast, per capita taxation was lower after 1815 than prior to French conquest, and this difference was particularly large in Lombardo-Veneto. We interpret this strategy of reduced tax demands on individuals as one at least partially inspired by ruler anxiety. Restoration-era leaders (along with their Austrian protectors) feared overthrow, and not without justification: conspiracies, riots, and revolts were frequent and widespread between 1815 and 1860, with major waves in 1820–21, 1830–31, and most significantly in 1848 (Dincecco et al. 2011, 894). Keeping taxation low was a simple way to secure stability and reduce popular support for revolutionary ideas. This method was particularly valuable for the Austrians in Lombardo-Veneto, who were perceived as foreigners and had experienced first-hand in Milan in 1799–1800 how high taxes could alienate the local population (Zaghi 1986, 243). Furthermore, the post-1815 political situation on the Italian peninsula may have reduced the need for revenue. As under the Ancien Régime, most expenditure (net of interest on the public debt) went toward the military.[20] Yet Austrian hegemony in Italy made a large military establishment redundant. While the military was still necessary to repress popular unrest, its loyalty was by no means assured. Officers who had been trained during the Napoleonic era could harbor revolutionary ideas. Indeed they sparked many of the revolts during the 1820s and 1830s.

20 For example, the army, navy, and police absorbed one third of total expenditures and about two-thirds of expenditures net of debt service in the Kingdom of Two Sicilies in 1816–1825 (Ostuni 1992: Appendix V, tab. II).

Piedmont was an important exception (Dincecco et al. 2011). It had a strong military tradition, and sought an independent foreign policy aimed explicitly at territorial expansion in the Po Valley. Meanwhile, the acquisition of Genoa at the Congress of Vienna enabled it to fund a larger military with a lower level of taxation per head than under the Ancien Régime. Through the mid-1840s, military spending accounted for about two-fifths of Piedmont's total expenditure, and debt service for an additional one-sixth (Felloni 1959). After defeat by Austria in 1848–1849, Piedmont continued to spend heavily on the military, but also undertook a far-reaching process of economic liberalization and modernization. It abolished duties (including those on wheat) and invested heavily in railways and other infrastructure of up to one-fifth of total state expenditure (Felloni, 1959). Tax revenue alone was not sufficient to cover both butter and guns, and so Piedmont had to borrow large sums. Interest payments soared in the mid-1850s to about one-fourth of total expenditure. Thus, this strategy was financially risky, but it eventually paid off, as Piedmont's debt was recognized by the newly unified Italy in 1861 (Dincecco et al. 2011).

5.2 *Institutions*

While official rhetoric emphasized the return to the pre-revolutionary past after 1815, the (limited) available information suggests that for a mix of expediency and politics the bulk of the Napoleonic-era institutional reforms survived the Restoration. There were substantial ideological differences among rulers, but none of them could afford to completely alienate pro-Napoleonic elites, out of fear that they would then ally with revolutionary zealots. The rulers thus pursued an "amalgam" policy that attempted to bring together core supporters and pro-Napoleonic elites into a new ruling class (Riall 1994). For this reason, no Restoration regime dared return the "beni nazionali" to the Church, as the new landowners were too numerous and powerful to be challenged. These returns were limited to lands which had not yet been sold, either in full, as in Piedmont and in the South, or partially, as in Tuscany (Biagianti 1985).

The King of Sardinia (i.e., Piedmont) and the Duke of Modena made the most thorough efforts to re-establish Ancien Régime institutions. King Vittorio Emanuele I issued a decree formally abolishing all Napoleonic legislation the day after he returned to Turin (Romeo 1974). He reduced the civil rights of Jews, made majorat legal again, abolished French administrative divisions, and implemented the pre-1789 laws, including Church privileges. Furthermore, he retained the trade barriers between Piedmont's traditional domains and the newly-acquired territories in Liguria. This policy damaged the economy and earned the Savoy a reputation for being the most reactionary Italian regime.

Yet even the Savoy dynasty was unable to fully turn the clock back to 1789, as changes in Piedmontese society were too deep, and Genoa remained politically restless.

Other Italian states, and the Austrians in Lombardo-Veneto, were much less conservative than the Savoy. Formally, all Italian states abolished the Code Napoléon, while simultaneously adopting "national" civil codes that replicated its most important clauses, with the notable exception of divorce (Candeloro 1958, 24; Caravale and Caracciolo 1978, 597; Zaghi 1986, 384). The "national" code for the South was extended to Sicily, which had never adopted the Code Napoléon (Galasso 2007b 14, 122–9). Similarly, all Italian states beyond Piedmont retained French-style governance structures (namely, similarly-sized local departments subject to strong centralized control), though they made minor name changes and border modifications, and often replaced professional French bureaucrats with local aristocrats (Meriggi 1994, 130–41).[21] The Austrian government resisted requests by the local nobility for a return to Ancien Régime political institutions (Meriggi 1987, 27–44). The French administrative system, besides being more rational, offered the Austrians much greater control over society than the pre-revolutionary one, which had hampered the reform plans of previously "enlightened" absolutist monarchs (Riall 2009, 55).

6 Conclusions

Overall, our analysis suggests that we should distinguish between the short-run and long-run implications of Napoleonic rule in Italy. According to the available evidence, the costs of French rule outweighed the benefits over the short run. The French imposed military conscription, presided over a large number of war-related deaths, raised taxes, and adopted a protectionist trade policy. It is therefore not clear how Napoleonic rule can explain the economic rebound in Italy between 1801 and 1810.

Over the long run, the institutional reforms introduced by the French can be represented as a major improvement over the Ancien Régime, and most of them survived the Restoration. Nonetheless, GDP per capita and real wages declined or stagnated until the 1870s (see Figure 6.1). While post-1815

21 For example, the Papal States switched from 13 departments to 14 "delegazioni" (Caravale and Caracciolo 1978, 592).

Restoration economic policies were less than ideal, the available evidence suggests that they were not as harmful as the conventional wisdom would have us believe.

We thus conclude that, although the Napoleonic reforms were a useful first step towards the modernization of the Italian economy and society, sustained economic growth arguably called for even bolder reforms, which were surprisingly first undertaken by Piedmont (Romeo 1974; Coppini 1994). There, the initial reactionary policies were abandoned in the 1830s, but the real turning point was the military defeat by Austria in 1848–1849. Unlike other Italian rulers, King Vittorio Emanuele II decided to retain the liberal 1848 constitution (Statuto Albertino), which subjected both the budget and trade policy to regular parliamentary control. Beyond its positive revenue implications (see Figure 6.3), this move was politically smart. Piedmont became a beacon of modernity and freedom for the rest of the peninsula, and eventually succeeded in defeating the Austrians and unifying the whole of Italy (with the help of the French army, ably secured by Piedmont's Prime Minister Cavour). After political unification in 1861, Piedmont's "good institutions" were extended throughout the Kingdom of Italy.

In our view, therefore, the most compelling argument for long-run economic development in Italy should revolve around the Savoy kings, Carlo Alberto and Vittorio Emanuele II, and Cavour, rather than Napoleon. While the reforms that Napoleon introduced into Italy may have been necessary to clear out the institutional "undergrowth" left over from the Ancien Régime, they were not in themselves enough to provide Italy with modern growth-enhancing institutions. For that, Italians had Piedmont's leaders to thank.

References

Acemoglu, Daron, Davide Cantoni, Simon Johnson, and James Robinson. 2011. "The Consequences of Radical Reform: the French Revolution." *American Economic Review*, 101: 3286–307.

Bai, Jushan and Pierre Perron. 2003. "Computation and Analysis of Multiple Structural Change Models." *Journal of Applied Economics*, 18: 1–22.

Biagianti, Ivo. 1985. "La soppressione dei conventi in età Napoleonica," *La Toscana nell"età rivoluzionaria e napoleonica*, edited by Ivan Tognarini, 443–69. Firenze: Olschki.

Bassetti, Maurizio. 1985. "La vendita dei beni nazionali in Toscana: il dipartimento dell"Arno," *La Toscana nell"età rivoluzionaria e napoleonica*, edited by Ivan Tognarini, 471–509. Firenze: Olschki.

Bianchini, Lodovico. 1835. *Della storia delle finanze del Regno di Napoli, vol. III.* Naples: Tip. Flautina.

Broadberry Stephen, Bruce Campbell, Alexander Klein, Mark Overton, and Bas van Leeuwen. 2015. *British Economic Growth.* Cambridge: Cambridge University Press.

Broers, Michael. 2005. *The Napoleonic Empire in Italy.* Basingstoke: Palgrave.

Candeloro, Giorgio. 1956. *Storia dell"Italia moderna, vol. I.* Rome: Feltrinelli. 2nd edition, 1975.

Candeloro, Giorgio. 1958. *Storia dell"Italia moderna, vol. II.* Rome: Feltrinelli. 2nd edition, 1975.

Calzavarini, Mirella. 1992. "La vendita dei beni nazionali nei dipartimenti veneti dal 1806 al 1814," *Veneto e Lombardia tra rivoluzione giacobina ed età napoleonica*, edited by Gianluigi Fontana and Antonio Lazzarini, 133–63. Milan: Cariplo-Laterza.

Caracciolo, Alberto. 1973. "La storia economica," *Storia d'Italia Einaudi, vol. III*, edited by Ruggiero Romano, 509–693. Turin: Einaudi.

Caravale, Mario and Alberto Caracciolo. 1978. *Lo stato pontificio da Martino V a Pio IX.* Turin: UTET.

Chilosi, David. 2014. "Risky Institutions: Political Regimes and the Cost of Public Borrowing in Early Modern Italy." *Journal of Economic History*, 74: 887–915.

Coppini Romano, Paolo. 1993. *Il Granducato di Toscana. Dagli "anni francesi" all"Unità.* Torino: UTET.

Coppini Romano, Paolo. 1994. "Il Piemonte sabaudo e l"unificazione. 1849–1861)," *Storia d'Italia, vol. I*, editedy by Giovanni Sabbatucci and Vittorio Vidotto, 339–431. Bari: Laterza.

Cova, Alberto. 1977. *Aspetti dell"economia agricola lombarda dal 1796 al 1914.* Milan: Vita e Pensiero.

Cova, Alberto. 1988. "Tradizione e innovazione nel mutato contesto politico e territriale dell"età francese," *Storia dell"industria lombarda, vol. I*, editedy by Sergio Zaninelli, 104–97. Milan: Il Polifilo.

De Felice, Renzo. 1960. *La vendita dei beni nazionali nella Repubblica Romana del 1798–99.* Rome: Edizioni di Storia e Letteratura.

Di Biasio, Aldo. 2013. "Produzione e consumo di cereali nel Regno di Napoli," *Il Mezzogiorno prima dell"Unità*, edited by Nicola Ostuni and Paolo Malanima, 145–96. Soveria Mannelli: Rubbettino.

Dincecco, Mark. 2011. *Political Transformations and Public Finances.* Cambridge: Cambridge University Press.

Dincecco, Mark, Giovanni Federico, and Andrea Vindigni. 2011. "Warfare, Taxation, and Political Change: Evidence from the Italian Risorgimento." *Journal of Economic History*, 71: 887–914.

Dincecco, Mark and Gabriel Katz. 2016. "State Capacity and Long-Run Economic Performance." *Economic Journal*, 126: 189–218.

Dincecco, Mark. 2017. *State Capacity and Economic Development*. Cambridge: Cambridge University Press.

Doria, Giorgio. 1969. *Investimenti e sviluppo economico a Genova alla vigilia della prima guerra mondiale, vol I.* Milan: Giuffre.

Epstein, Stephen. 2000. *Freedom and Growth*. London: Routledge.

Felice, Emanuele. 2015. *Ascesa e declino: Storia economica d'Italia*. Bologna: Il Mulino.

Federico, Giovanni. 1994. *Il filo d'oro*.Venice: Marsilio.

Federico, Giovanni. 2007. "Market integration and Market Efficiency: The case of Nineteenth-Century Italy." *Explorations in Economic History*, 44: 293–316.

Federico, Giovanni. 2009. "Always on the Brink: Italy, 1861–1914," *Paying for the Liberal State*, edited by J.L. Cardoso and P. Lains, 186–213. Cambridge: Cambridge University Press.

Federico, Giovanni. 2011. "When Did the European Market Integrate?" *European Review of Economic History*, 15: 93–126.

Federico, Giovanni. 2012a. "How Much Do We Know About Market Integration in Europe?" *Economic History Review*, 65: 470–97.

Federico, Giovanni. 2012b. "The Corn Laws in Continental Perspective." *European Review of Economic History*, 16: 166–87.

Federico, Giovanni and Antonio Tena-Junguito. 2016. "World Trade, 1800–1938: A New Dataset." EHES Working Paper in Economic History 93.

Federico, Giovanni, Max-Stephan Schulze, and Oliver Volckart. 2018. "European Goods Market Integration in the Very Long Run: From the Black Death to the First World War." LSE Economic History Working Paper 87184.

Felloni, Giuseppe. 1959. "Le spese effettive e il bilancio degli stati sabaudi dal 1825 al 1860." *Archivio economico dell''unificazione italiana, serie I, vol. IX*.

Filippini, Jean-Pierre. 1985. "Le coneguenze economiche e sociali della dominazione francese sulla vita del porto di Livorno," *La Toscana nell'età rivoluzionaria e napoleonica*, edited by Ivan Tognarini, 321–38. Firenze: Olschki.

Galasso, Giuseppe. 2007a. *Il Regno di Napoli: Il Mezzogiorno borbonico e napoleonico. 1734–1815*. Turin: UTET.

Galasso, Giuseppe. 2007b. *Il Regno di Napoli. Il Mezzogiorno borbonico e continentale. 1815–1861*. Turin: UTET.

Giorgetti, Giorgio. 1966. "Per una storia delle allivellazioni leopoldine." *Studi Storici*, 7: 245–290, 515–584.

Grab, Alexander. 2015. "The Kingdom of Italy and the Continental Blockade," *Revisiting Napoleon's Continental System*, edited by Katherine Aalestd and Johan Joor, 98–113. Basingstoke: Palgrave.

Heldring, Leander, James Robinson, and Sebastian Vollmer. 2015. "Monks, Gents, and Industrialists: The Long-Run Impact of the Dissolution of English Monasteries." NBER Working Paper 21450.

Kelly, Morgan and Cormac O'Grada. 2014. "Change Points and Temporal Dependence in Reconstructions of Annual Temperature: Did Europe Experience a Little Ice Age?" *Annals of Applied Statistics*, 8: 1372–94.

Kopsidis, Michael and Daniel Bromley. 2016. "The French Revolution and German Industrialization: Dubious Models and Doubtful Causality." *Journal of Institutional Economics*, 12: 161–90.

Malanima, Paolo. 2002. *L"economia italiana. Dalla crescita medioevale alla crescita contemporanea.* Bologna: Il Mulino.

Malanima, Paolo. 2010. "The Long Decline of a Leading Economy: GDP in Central and Northern Italy, 1300–1913." *European Review of Economic History*, 15: 169–219.

Malanima, Paolo. 2013. "Prezzi e salari," *Il Mezzogiorno prima dell"Unità*, edited by Nicola Ostuni and Paolo Malanima, 339–72. Soveria Mannelli: Rubbettino.

Malanima, Paolo. 2015. "Cibo e povertà nell"Italia del Sette ed Ottocento." *Ricerche di Storia Economica e sociale*, 1: 15–39.

Marcelli, Umberto. 1967. *La vendita dei beni nazionali nella Repubblica Cisalpina.* Bologna: Patron.

Meriggi, Marco. 1987. *Il Regno Lombardo-Veneto*. Turin: UTET.

Meriggi, Marco. 1994. "Società, istituzioni e ceti dirigenti," *Storia d'Italia, vol. I*, edited by Giovanni Sabbatucci and Vittorio Vidotto, 119–228. Bari: Laterza.

Mineccia, Francesco. 1985. "La vendita dei beni nazionali in Toscana: il dipartimento dell"Arno," *La Toscana nell"età rivoluzionaria e napoleonica*, edited by Ivan Tognarini, 511–50. Firenze: Olschki.

Moioli, Angelo. 1992. "L'economia lombarda fra tradizione ed innovazione: le manifatture," *Veneto e Lombardia tra rivoluzione giacobina ed età napoleonica*, edited by Giovanni Luigi Fontana e Antonio Lazzarini, 179–244. Milan: Cariplo-Laterza.

Notario, Paola. 1980. *La vendita dei beni nazionali in Piemonte nel periodo napoleonico. 1800–1814.* Milan: Banca Commerciale.

Notario, Paola and Narciso Nada. 1993. *Il Piemonte Sabaudo: Dal periodo napoleonico al Risorgimento*. Turin: UTET.

O'Rourke, Kevin. 2007. "War and Welfare: Britain, France, and the United States, 1807–1814." *Oxford Economic Papers*, 59: 8–30.

Ostuni, Nicola. 1992. *Finanza ed economia nel Regno delle Due Sicilie*. Naples: Liguori.

Postigliola, Michele and Mauro Rota. 2020. "Institutions and Literacy Rates: The Legacy of Napoleonic Reforms in Italy." Forthcoming, *European Review of Economic History*.

Pescosolido, Guido. 1998. *Unità nazionale e sviluppo economico*. Bari: Laterza.

Persson, Gunnar and Paul Sharp. 2015. *An Economic History of Europe*. Cambridge: Cambridge University Press.

Riall, Lucy. 1994. *The Italian Risorgimento: State, Society, and National Unification*. London: Routledge.

Riall, Lucy. 2009. *Risorgimento: The History of Italy from Napoleon to Nation-State*. New York: Palgrave MacMillan.

Romani, Mario. 1982. *Storia economica d'Italia nel secolo XIX*. Bologna: Il Mulino.

Romeo, Rosario. 1974. *Dal Piemonte Sabaudo all'Italia liberale*. Bari: Laterza.

Tarle, Yevgeny. 1950. *La vita economica dell'Italia napoleonica*. Turin: Einaudi.

Trezzi, Luigi. 1992. "Attività minerarie e metallurgiche in Valcamonica durante il Regno d'Italia," *Veneto e Lombardia tra rivoluzione giacobina ed età napoleonica*, edited by Giovanni Luigi Fontana e Antonio Lazzarini, 344–67. Milan: Cariplo-Laterza.

Villani, Pasquale. 1964. *La vendita dei beni dello Stato nel Regno di Napoli*. Milano: Banca Commerciale.

Woolf, Stuart. 1979. *A History of Italy, 1700–1860*. London: Methuen.

Woolf, Stuart. 1991. *Napoleon's Integration of Europe*. London: Routledge.

Zaghi, Carlo. 1986. *L"Italia di Napoleone dalla Cisalpina al Regno*. Turin: UTET.

CHAPTER 7

The Napoleonic Wars: A Watershed in Spanish History

Leandro Prados de la Escosura and Carlos Santiago-Caballero

1 Introduction

The Napoleonic Wars are usually depicted as a major juncture in European history. Historians' assessments of the Peninsular War (1808–1814) tend to emphasise its negative impact. In this essay, we survey the short-term effects of war but also look beyond to and consider its long run consequences. The French invasion had severe consequences for the economy of Spain in the short run. The actions of French and Allied armies had a higher demographic impact, larger than any other military conflict, including civil wars, in Spanish modern history. Confiscations of crops and destruction of livestock hindered agriculture, while shrinking demand, disrupted trade, and a shortage of inputs hampered industry and services. Moreover, the loss of the American mainland colonies, a by-product of the French invasion, severely harmed absolutism, challenging its viability. In the long run, however, the Napoleonic Wars contributed to the removal of Ancien Régime institutions and interest groups. Freed from their constraints, the economy experienced a far from smooth transition towards a liberal society. The Napoleonic Wars may be deemed, then, a watershed in Spanish history.

2 The Short-Run Impact

The invasion of Spain by the Napoleonic armies was initially a peaceful process that took place with the complete agreement of the Spanish authorities.[1] However, as soon as Napoleon forced Charles IV's abdication, insurrection broke out, starting in Asturias and quickly spreading throughout the country.

1 On March 16th 1808, Charles IV issued a proclamation, "Breath calmly: know that the army of my good ally the emperor of the French passes through my kingdom with ideas of peace and friendship. Its purpose is moving to the points threatened by an enemy landing ..."(Queipo de Llano, 2008, 1202).

 | DOI:10.1163/9789004472754_008

By then, Napoleon had already stationed large contingents of soldiers at key points in Spain and was ready to face Spanish and allied forces in the upcoming war. How large was the damage inflicted on the economy? The direct effects of the war are hard to reckon. In the following paragraphs we will survey different social and economic dimensions of its impact.

2.1 *Population*

Losses due to military operations in Spain, a major battleground of the Napoleonic Wars, have been estimated around 300,000 (Urlanis 1971), probably a figure on the high side. Most of the casualties took place, however, among the civilian population. The confiscation of food, the violence of Napoleonic and Allied armies, and the spread of diseases, as large contingents of soldiers moved all over the country, were its main causes. In the shire of Valdeorras, only one ninth of the Spanish casualties were military (Canales 2018). French troops followed a very clear strategy in dealing with local resistance, namely bloodbath and terror to avoid further insurrections. After the siege, Zaragoza was completely destroyed and 54,000 people lost their lives (Gates 1986, 129). Equally brutal were the sieges of Badajoz, Ciudad Rodrigo and the complete destruction of San Sebastián at the hands of the Allied forces.

The increase in mortality rates can be exemplified by comparing the cases of Ávila, where resistance to the French troops was moderate, with Albacete, sacked several times during the war for resistance to occupation (Figure 7.1). In Ávila mortality remained at the same level before and after the war, except during the second occupation by the French army in 1812–13. In Albacete, mortality increased by more than 50 per cent in 1808–09 and 1811–13.[2]

The negative effects of the war were also clear in the marriage strategies of the populations of Albacete and Ávila. Figure 7.2 shows the evolution of marriages in both cities between 1801 and 1819. The rapid increase during the first years of the century suffered a sudden stop followed by a reversal at the beginning of the war. The number of marriages decreased by 35 per cent between 1808 and 1814. Figure 7.2 also shows the importance of the war for indirect effects such as the reduction in fertility -a consequence of young male casualties.

More significant are the losses resulting from deviations from the demographic trend. Fraser (2006) suggested that Spain's potential population

2 As Sánchez Albornoz (1911) wrote, "during this period when most of the Spanish cities adorn their history with heroic deeds, not a single one is carried out in the Ávila of the Loyalists and the Knights, a single act that would made the Avulenses of that time worthy descendants of the hidalgos from medieval Ávila".

FIGURE 7.1 Monthly mortality in the cities of Albacete and Ávila, 1807–1816 (Jan-Dec 1807=100)
SOURCE: OWN ESTIMATES FROM THE RECORDS OF THE PARISH OF SAN JUAN BAUTISTA (ALBACETE) AND THE PARISHES OF SAN JUAN BAUTISTA, SANTIAGO AND SAN PEDRO (ÁVILA) RETRIEVED FROM FAMILYSEARCH.COM

decreased by around 0.8 million inhabitants during the first fifteen years of the nineteenth century. Although the casualties of the war did not exceed 375,000. Canales (2018) reckons that excess mortality reached 0.6 million during 1809–13. These figures are not far apart from contemporary estimates suggesting an overall war toll of about one million (Muñoz Maldonado 1833). Pérez Moreda (1985, 2010) considers this figure plausible, provided it includes the effects of the subsistence crisis of 1803/05 on the number of births. Thus, adding up direct casualties and losses resulting from excess mortality a total loss of nearly one million people can be suggested (Figure 7.3).

Regional consequences were unevenly distributed. In the south and the interior, most of the increase in mortality took place before the war, as a result of the subsistence crisis of 1803/05. It was in the periphery that the effects of the conflict were considerably larger, particularly in Catalonia and the northern regions (Figure 7.4). Madrid was especially hard hit in 1812, as consequence of the poor harvest of 1811 and supply difficulties arising from warfare (Fraser 2006, 203). Thus, those regions that had already experienced a significant

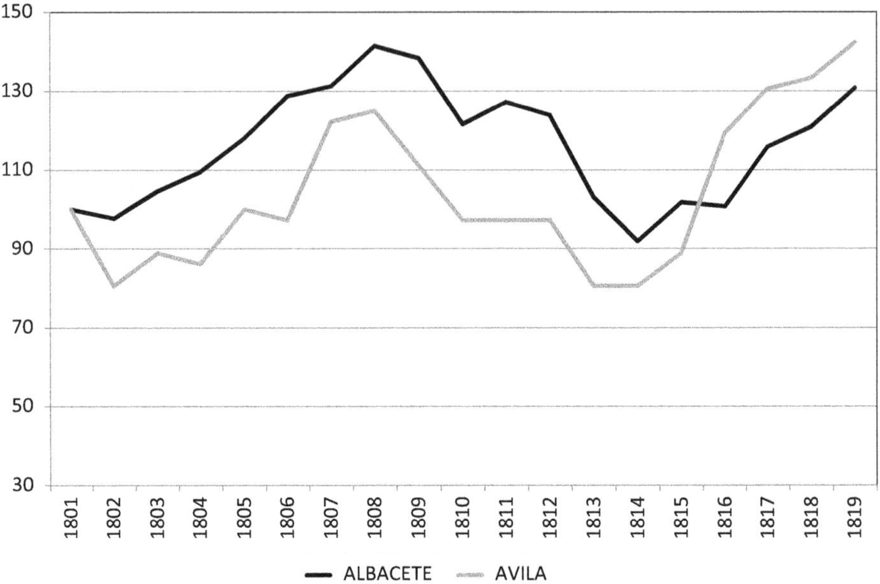

FIGURE 7.2 Marriages in the cities of Albacete and Ávila, 1801–19 (5-year moving average 1801=100)
SOURCE: SAME AS FIGURE 7.1

FIGURE 7.3 Population conjectures: Spain, 1780–1820 (million)
SOURCE: PRADOS DE LA ESCOSURA ET AL. (2020)

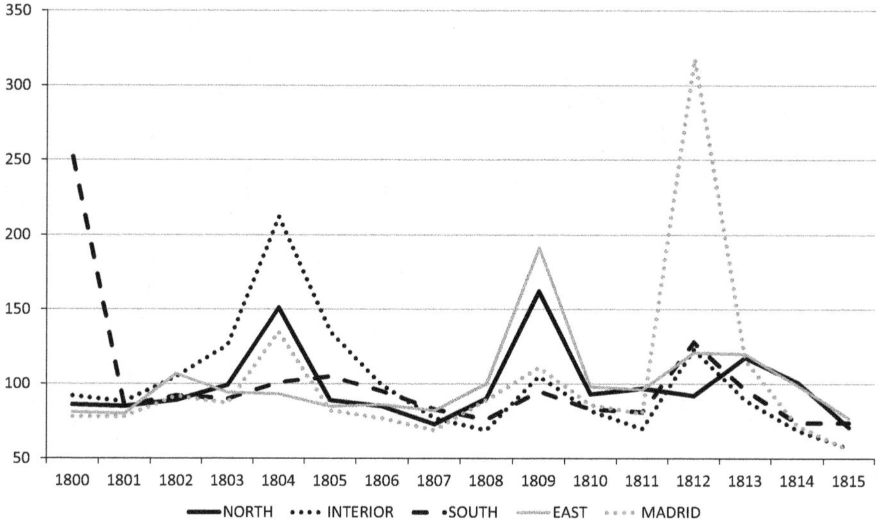

FIGURE 7.4 Mortality in Spanish regions, 1800–1815 (1800–1815=100)
SOURCE: CANALES (2018)

population contraction during the previous subsistence crisis suffered a milder demographic impact during the Peninsular War.

2.2 *Agriculture*

The Peninsular War had deep and widespread effects on the agricultural sector. Plundering and confiscation by French and Allied armies imposed a considerable toll on producers. The war also affected Ancien Régime institutions that had conditioned the secular behaviour of farmers and peasants.

Napoleonic troops relied on supplies from France to carry out their military operations, but guerrilla attacks on their supply lines led to requisitions from local producers (Gates 1986, 41). The British expeditionary force also relied on requisitions but promised to pay for the expropriated produce.[3]

Confiscations of livestock were particularly significant and had two significant effects. First a decline in the amount of meat and dairy products consumed by the population. Secondly immediate and long term reduction in capital stock used for ploughing and transportation. Confiscatory taxation had

3 However, payments rarely occurred because farmers had to travel to Lisbon and wait for weeks to receive the money. Many of them sold the bills at considerable rates of discount (Fraser 2006, 761).

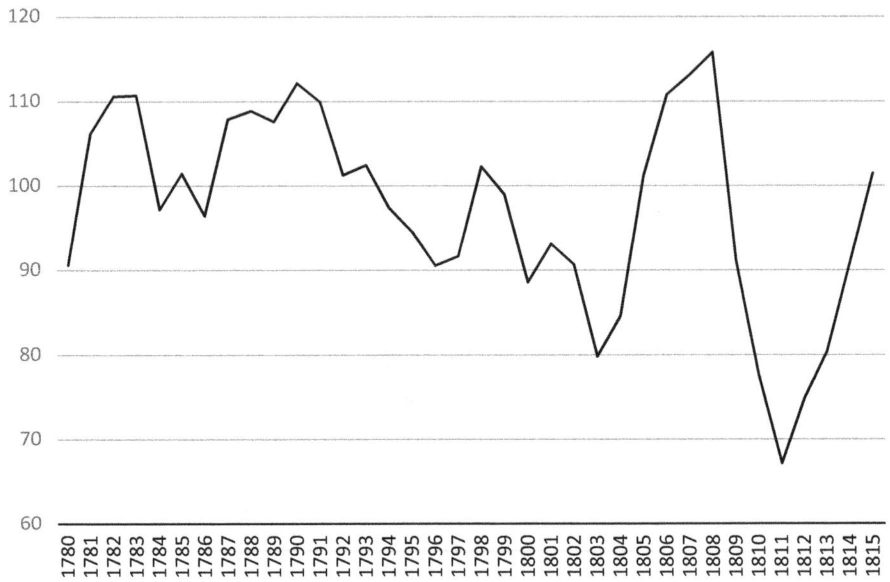

FIGURE 7.5 Real agricultural output per head, 1780–1815 [1790/99=100)
SOURCE: PRADOS DE LA ESCOSURA ET AL. (2020)

similar effects. In Catalonia. For example, the French administration collected more than 100 million Reales from landlords and farmers.

French invaders reformed Ancien Régime institutions. For example, they repealed the tithe, a religious tax that, in principle, represented 10 per cent of total production. Municipal laws restricting land cultivation at the extensive margin ceased to be enforced and thereby extended the frontier of land available for cultivation (Santiago-Caballero 2013). *Desamortización* (namely, the confiscation and public sale of landed property owned by religious and communal institutions, took place during Joseph Bonaparte's rule in order to finance the French army (Rueda Hernanz 1997). Although the area affected was limited and confiscation was partially reversed after the war, the transformation of commons and church lands into private property became irreversible. This was not the first episode of disentailment. *Desamortización* had taken place in 1798, as a way of funding the war against the French Republic and the United Kingdom (Herr 1971). Our estimates based on data related to tithes suggest a severe contraction occurred during the war followed by a rapid recovery (Figure 7.5).

Output in preindustrial agriculture was highly dependent on climatic conditions and the Napoleonic Wars coincided with a period of instability. The Maldá Anomaly or oscillation, that simultaneously increased droughts and

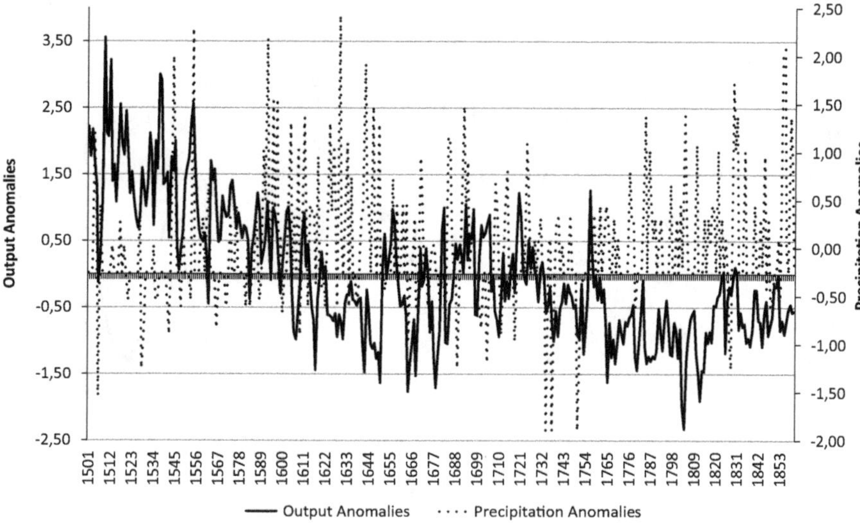

FIGURE 7.6 Agricultural output and precipitation anomalies 1500–1860
SOURCES: AGRICULTURAL OUTPUT, ÁLVAREZ-NOGAL ET AL. (2016); PRECIPITATION, RODRIGO ET AL. (1999)

floods, coincided with the first Dalton Minimum -a phase of low solar radiation between 1790 and 1830-, and the eruption of the Tambora volcano in 1815, that increased atmospheric (CO2) concentration, brought with it high climatic irregularity and hydrologic extremes. These climatic anomalies were matched by severe output fluctuations (Barriendos and Llasat 2003 and Barrera-Escoda and Llasat 2015).

Figure 7.6 shows agricultural output and seasonal rainfall anomalies – measured as yearly deviations from the historical average relative to the standard deviation-. An inverse association between output and rainfall variations can be predicated, with wet periods associated to negative output fluctuations.

The exogenous shock brought by the war and climatic anomalies impacted on returns to factors of production. The extension of land under cultivation depressed land rents. They fell by nearly 50 per cent between 1808 and 1812 and never re-gained pre-war levels (Figure 7.7). Real wages suffered a more intense reduction during the war but returned to pre-war levels by 1817.

Comparing land rents and real wages allowed us to draw trends in income distribution. Returns from land ownership are imore unevenly distributed than returns from wages. Thus, the rent-wage ratio provides a measure of changes in income inequality. The ratio displays a tendency to decline from 1800 onwards a tendency that was not reversed at the end of the war except for two peaks

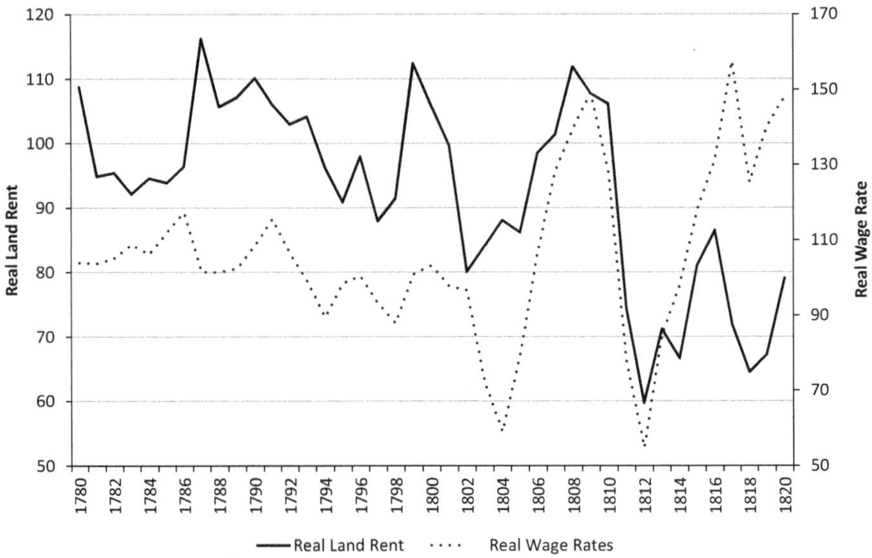

FIGURE 7.7 Real land rent and wage rates, 1780–1820 (1790/99=100)
SOURCE: ÁLVAREZ-NOGAL AND PRADOS DE LA ESCOSURA (2013)

during the pre-war subsistence crisis (1804) and in the Peninsular War (1812) (Figure 7.8).

2.3 *Industry*

The effects of war on the industrial sector included the reduction of internal and external demand, scarcity of inputs, and heavy taxation. In addition, producers faced unrestricted competition from French and British goods.

For example, in the woollen factory of Astudillo, one of the main centres of textile production in Old Castile, the price of wool more than tripled between 1808 and 1814. The requisition of animals and the increase of transport costs were probably behind these changes, while the invasion of common municipal lands and their use for cultivation also reduced available pastures to feed sheep. Producers were forced to cut prices and profit margins (Hernández García 2004, 171).

In the case of the cotton industry, mainly located in Catalonia, inputs scarcity severely restricted production. For example, Erasmo de Gómina's factory in Barcelona interrupted inputs purchases (cotton and dyes) during the Peninsular War (Figure 7.9).

Heavier taxation to finance the war effort by both French and Allied authorities drained resources from productive activities and reduced incentives for

FIGURE 7.8 Inequality trends: Real land rent/wage rate ratio, 1780–1820 (1790/99=100)
SOURCE: ÁLVAREZ-NOGAL AND PRADOS DE LA ESCOSURA (2013)

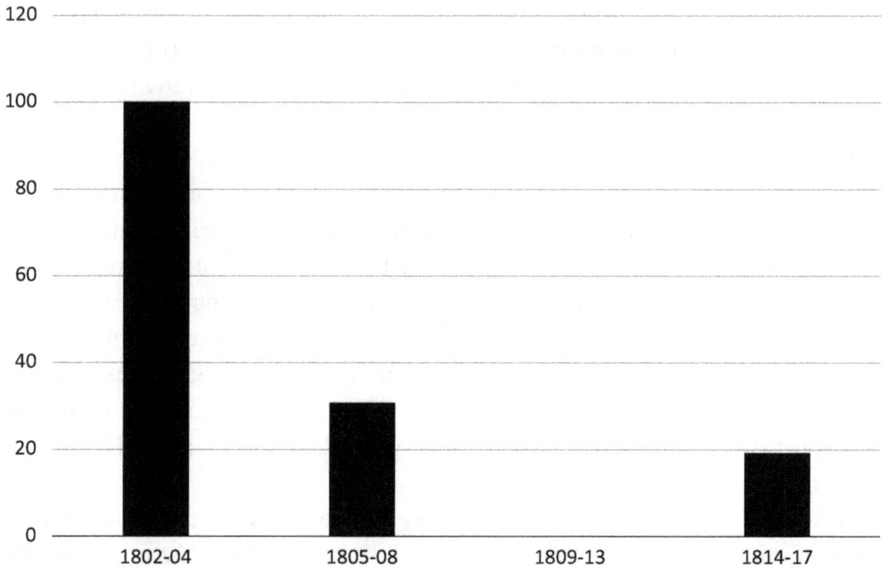

FIGURE 7.9 Inputs bought by Erasmo de Gómina's cotton textile company (1802–04=100)
SOURCE: SÁNCHEZ (2010)

economic activity. In Astudillo, textile producers were charged with additional taxes for the city to fund the French invaders (Hernández García 2004, 162). In Murcia, after the French took the city on April 25th 1810, General Sebastiani obtained a ransom of 34,560 Reales for not sacking the city that was mainly paid by local businesses (Melendreras Gimeno 2000, 64).

The so-called Royal Factories (*Reales Fábricas*) also suffered the effects of the war and never recovered. They had been established to reduce the importation of valuable goods such as porcelain, glass, and fine textiles and to upgrade the technologies used by local producers (La Force 1965). However, their impact remained limited and they virtually ceased to exist after the end of the Peninsular War (Benaul and Sánchez 2004). The Royal Factory of Porcelain in Madrid was completely destroyed by English troops in 1812 (Martínez Caviró 1973).

Although the immediate effects of the war were probably similar across industries, while traditional industries collapsed, modern industries continued to adopt new technologies. The recovery, however, was not immediate and in the Catalan cotton industry pre-war (1783–97) nominal levels of investment were only recovered in the 1830s (Sánchez 2000, 502).

An additional problem for domestic industry wrought by the war was the high level of smuggling. Net imports experienced exponential growth during the war, and one-third were smuggled through Gibraltar and Portugal (cotton textiles and tobacco, in particular) (Figure 7.10). In addition, the Napoleonic authorities allowed French traders to flood Spain with French manufactures.

2.4 *Trade*

One of the most obvious effects of the war was the immediate disruption of both internal and international trade. Markets had gradually integrated during the eighteenth century as the fall in the price differential for wheat between coastal and interior regions suggests (Llopis Agelán 2010) (Figure 7.11). The war provoked a reversal, and a return to pre-Peninsular War levels of integration had to wait until the mid-nineteenth century (Peña and Sánchez-Albornoz 1984). Market disintegration was negative for economic activity it increased transport costs and restricted the supply of goods to urban centres (Ringrose 1970, 1983).

Transport costs increased due not only to rising insecurity but also shortages of manpower. Muleteers dominated short and mid-distance internal trade. French and Allied armies forced muleteers to service them and reduced regular transport services (Ros 1999, 195). Furthermore, guerrillas confiscated grain supplies, including supplies for Madrid in 1813 (Fraser 2006, 697).

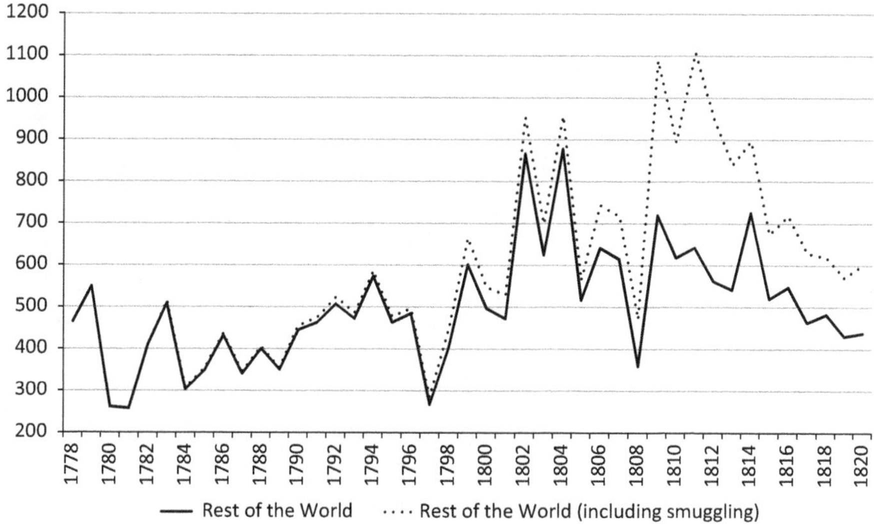

FIGURE 7.10 Spanish net imports from the rest of the world (excl. Spanish America), 1778–1820: with and without smuggling (000 1808 Reales)
SOURCE: PRADOS DE LA ESCOSURA (1993)

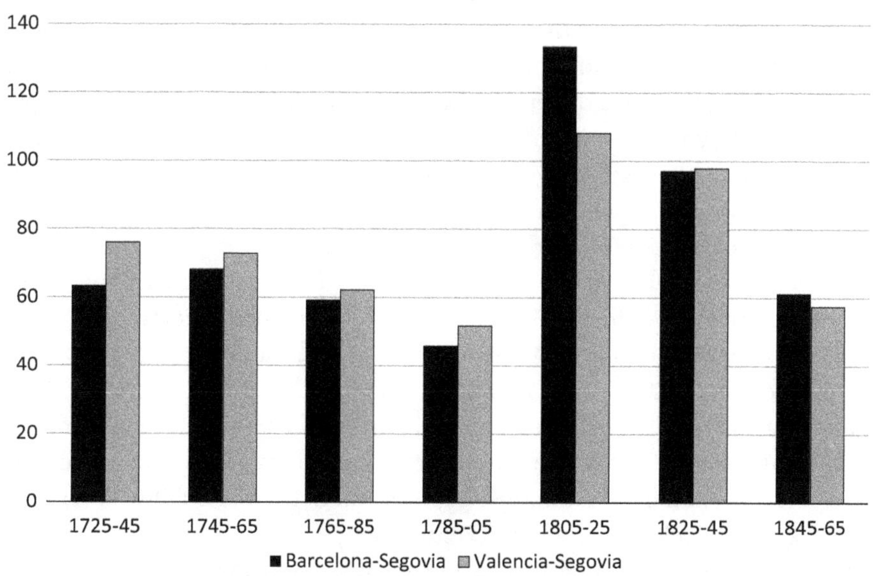

FIGURE 7.11 Market integration: average wheat price differentials (%)
SOURCE: LLOPIS AGELÁN (2010)

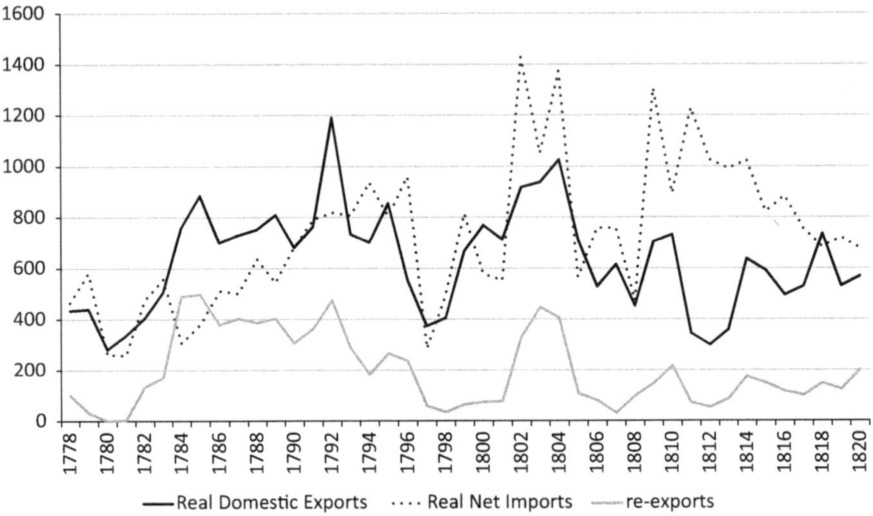

FIGURE 7.12A Real domestic exports, net imports, and re-exports, 1778–1820 (1808 reales)
SOURCES: TRADE, PRADOS DE LA ESCOSURA (1993)

International trade increased during the eighteenth century, promoting monetisation and market orientation at a time of expanding population and rising land rents. This trend suffered a reversal during the Napoleonic Wars. For almost two decades since the break out of the war with Britain in October 1796, Spain maintained almost no links with its colonies. The French invasion contracted trade further and triggered the struggle for independence in Spanish America (Grafe and Irigoin 2012, 368).

Trade fell dramatically after the outbreak of war in 1797, briefly recovering after the Amiens peace (1802) and shrank again as war resumed (1805–1808) (Figure 7.12a). The Peninsular War reduced real domestic exports again. They experienced a trough in 1812. While real re-exports declined to very low levels, imports retained for domestic consumption recovered during the war (1809–11), largely due to allied supplies, but they experienced a steady decline thereafter. Relative to the size of the economy, the contraction of the trade sector is even more dramatic, with domestic exports and net imports falling after 1802 and re-exports declining after 1793 (Figure 7.12b).

Trade with Spanish American colonies stimulated industry and services because protectionist legislation made Spanish manufactures artificially competitive. Industrial exports were concentrated in two sectors, textiles and food (36.6% and 22.3% of total domestic exports in 1792) followed by paper and iron (4.4% and 3.2%). Some of these industries represented advanced

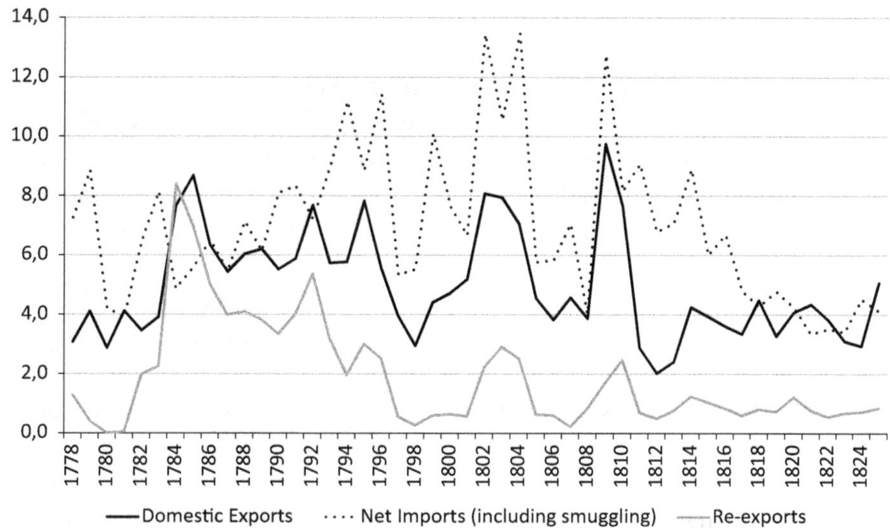

FIGURE 7.12B Trade shares: Domestic exports, net imports, and re-exports, 1778–1820 (% GDP)
SOURCES: TRADE, PRADOS DE LA ESCOSURA (1993) AND GDP, PRADOS DE LA ESCOSURA ET AL. (2020)

manufacturing sectors that had important effects on the development of particular regions. Shipbuilding and its associate activities (iron, cordage, and timber industries) were favoured by Spanish navigation laws. At most, exports of domestic manufactures to the colonies made a 5% contribution to industrial value added before the Napoleonic Wars (Prados de la Escosura 1993).

The composition of colonial trade suggests that the possibility of increasing production by reallocating resources was small, and that most gains probably resulted from changes to consumption patterns. By 1792, over 60% of retained imports consisted of cocoa and sugar. Furthermore, Spain's dependence on the colonies for raw materials was very small (raw cotton and dyestuffs represented only 4% of retained imports in 1792) (Prados de la Escosura 1993). Since these colonial products could have been acquired on international markets, gains from colonial trade could only occur if Spain acquired the same commodities at lower prices. Furthermore, the low dependence on colonial raw materials provides a measure of the weakness of domestic manufacturing. In the Catalan cotton textile industry, European cotton yarn imports were more important than colonial raw cotton imports which suggests that the spinning industry was weak.

The subsequent decline in domestic exports (some 25% between 1784/96 and 1815/20) can be attributed almost exclusively to the fall in colonial commerce (which shrank by 60%). This marks the end of a long-standing distribution of domestic exports between colonial and European markets (roughly one-third and two-thirds, respectively), and the establishment of a new pattern that continued throughout the nineteenth century (with foreign markets absorbing four-fifths of domestic exports). Retained imports of colonial goods for domestic consumption (which had represented one-fifth of total retained imports) fell to 15%. Again this was offset by imports from Europe. The collapse of trade with the empire was particularly significant for the service sector (finance, insurance, and transportation). Total real re-exports collapsed to 40% of the pre-war levels and re-exports to Latin America by three-fourths between 1784/96 and 1815/20. Spain's balance of trade also felt the effects of colonial independence. Before the loss of empire, Spain had a deficit on current account with foreign countries that was balanced by a corresponding surplus in colonial trade. With colonial emancipation that balance disappeared, with deflationary consequences for the domestic economy. Fortunately, a favourable shift in the terms of trade vis-à-vis Europe compensated for the deterioration of the terms of trade with the colonies and increased the purchasing power per unit of exports by nearly 40% between 1784/96 and 1815/20. This allowed Spain to avoid a further deterioration on its current account balance.

A conjectural estimate of the real cost to Spain from the loss of her colonies questions the generally accepted view that the cost was significant (Prados de la Escosura 1993). It is based upon assumptions that the resources embodied in exported commodities and services had alternative uses in the domestic economy. In contrast to other trades exports to the colonies were transported in Spanish ships. Thus, the decline of Spanish American trade led to a contraction in Spanish income from shipping services. Furthermore, the loss in state revenues from the cessation of precious metal shipments, and the reduction of customs duties resulting from colonial independence have been taken into account by assuming that public revenues from the colonies were productively used in the domestic economy. Thus, the upper bound estimate of Spanish losses implied by these assumptions comes to around 6% of national income. And while it could be argued that the profits from colonial trade represented a high proportion of the funds used to finance investment in Spain, an upper bound estimate of their contribution made to total capital formation was already below 15% by 1784/96. These estimates, derived from a static framework, are consistent with Palma's (2016). He used a dynamic model to suggest that intercontinental trade raised real wages by 6.2% and urbanization by 3.9 percentage points which are relatively low figures in a European perspective (Palma 2016).

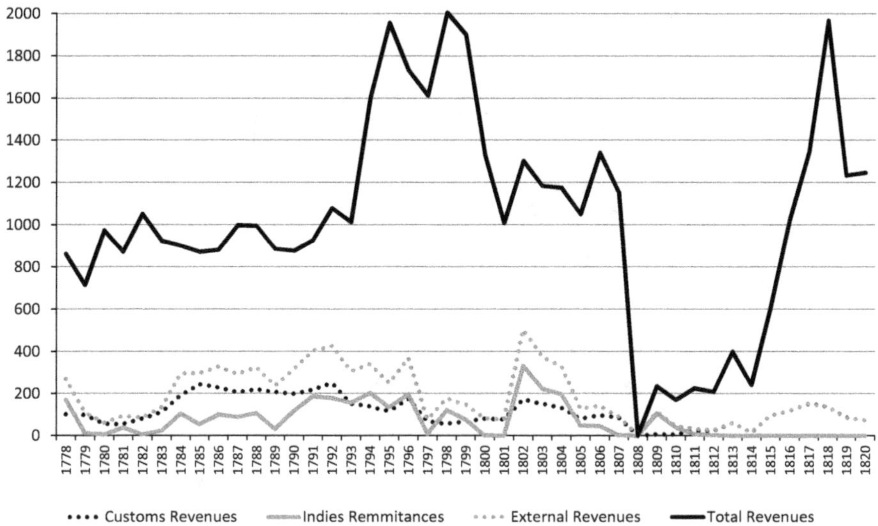

FIGURE 7.13 The evolution of public revenues, 1778–1820 [million reales, 1808 prices)
SOURCE: PRADOS DE LA ESCOSURA (1993)

2.5 *Finance*

In addition to the contraction of external public revenues (customs revenues plus Indies' remittances, namely, surpluses from colonial administration), as a result of the sharp decline of international and colonial trade, the Peninsular War led to the collapse of all government revenues to one-fifth of pre-bellum (1784–96) levels, which amounted to about one-tenth of normal levels (Figure 7.13). To offset this collapse, between 1808 and 1815, the British Government made advances of £7.8 million in money, weapons, and supplies that Spain never repaid (Sherwig 1969).

Finally, the war also introduced distortions into the monetary system. For example, it provided the French authorities with an opportunity to extract precious metals from Spain via monetary manipulation. French currency was allowed to circulate and to be accepted for payments in Spain. An *ad hoc* Commission established exchange rates that assigned the same purchasing power to French coins with lower intrinsic metallic content, than Spanish coins. On average, the differential was about 10 per cent for the most commonly used coins (de Vadillo 1846). As a consequence, in occupied territories Spanish coins disappeared and only French currency circulated (Queipo de Llano 2018, 1136). The situation was not easily reversed and French coins remained in circulation after the war (Sardá 1948). These monetary costs not only implied a loss of silver, but also contributed to macroeconomic instability.

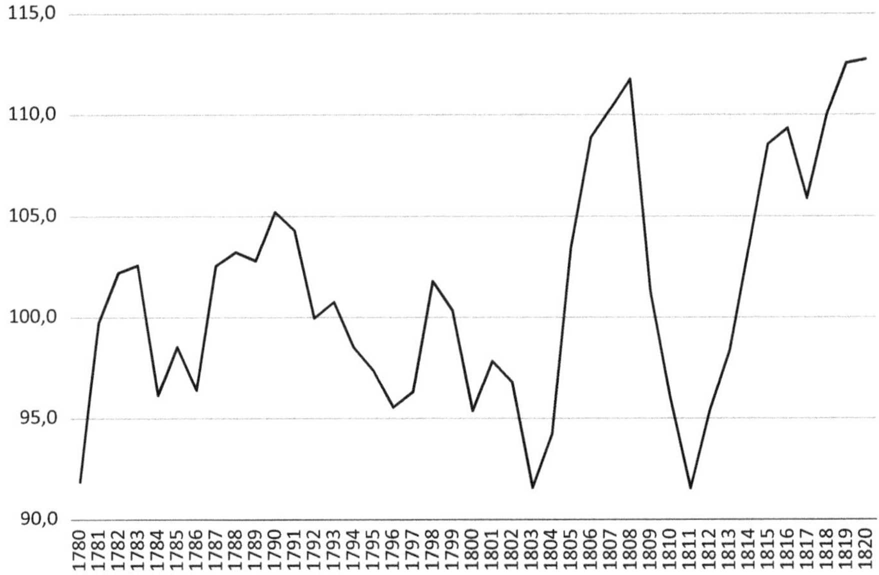

FIGURE 7.14 Real GDP per head, 1780–1820 (1790/99=100)
SOURCE: PRADOS DE LA ESCOSURA ET AL. (2020)

2.6 *Summing Up*

The Peninsular War had deep and negative economic consequences for Spain. The demographic impact, direct and indirect, can be represented a disaster. Population fell one million short of its potential level. The half a million casualties or so represents around 5 per cent of the population, which is more than double the ratio recorded for the 1936–39 Civil War. The Peninsular War was the bloodiest conflict in Spain's modern history. Its short-term effects on agriculture are ambiguous. On the credit side, the suspension of pre-war laws with respect to tithes allowed farmers to increase the area of cultivated land and to pay reduced rents. On the negative side, confiscations of livestock reduced the stock of agricultural capital. The war afflicted the industrial sector in different ways. An impoverished population reduced its consumption of manufactures. Military operations increased transport costs and input prices. Heavier taxes diverted capital from productive investment. Services were also disrupted. International trade experienced a dramatic collapse. Government revenues also collapsed and the outflow of silver had a deflationary impact on the economy. As a consequence, GDP per head fell during the Peninsular War, a relative decline that was only surpassed by the severe subsistence crisis of 1803/05 (Figure 7.14), even though its regional effects were very unevenly distributed.

The Peninsular War also ignited the fight for independence in Spanish America and their institutional consequences were far from negligible. The empire had strengthened Spain's absolutist monarchy. Colonial revenues promoted, consolidated, and concentrated the powers of the state (Yun Casalilla 1998). Prior to the Napoleonic Wars, the Crown revenues from the colonies (including the surpluses from colonial chests and customs duties) represented one-fourth of the total (Cuenca 1981). This reduced the monarchy's need to raise taxes and to bargain over fiscal policies with its subjects thereby reducing the state's need to increase taxation on the metropolis population. The colonial empire consolidated and stabilised traditional institutions and structures of power. The emancipation of the American colonies thereby contributed to the end of the Ancien Régime (Fontana 1991), and opened the way to a trajectory of liberal reform.

3 The Liberal Revolution

The liberal reforms included a redefinition of property rights that changed the status of Spain's population status from subjects to citizens equal before the law, the liberalization of commodity and factor markets, and the Parliamentary control over public revenues and expenditure. Nevertheless this was a long process fraught with difficulties and reversals.

The first step involved intellectual property rights. After the short-lived patent act of1820, legislation that regulated property rights for innovation was introduced in 1826 (Sáiz González 1995, 90). The number of patents rose steadily, especially between 1843 and 1864 (Saiz González 1996, 14).

The second and more significant step came with the modern Code of Commerce in 1829, which concentrated commercial matters into a single unified legal framework which reduced uncertainty and transaction costs. The Code of Commerce, the creation of the Bank of San Fernando, and the establishment of the stock market in Madrid in 1831, provided for the institutional transformation of the financial system (Tedde 1994; Artola 1983, 307).

The liberalization of commodity and factor markets implied major changes. The gradual suppression of the tithe increased disposable income. The tithe was halved in 1821, and though formally abolished in 1837, the First Carlist War delayed its definitive elimination until 1841. In 1834, the internal market for primary products was liberalised and taxes on the exportation of grains exports abolished (Artola 1983, 297).

Guilds that restricted the formation of relevant skills and the participation of women in industrial work activities were suppressed. The Cádiz Parliamentary

Assembly (Cortes) decreed in 1813 that establishing a factory or carrying out an industrious activity did not required previous approval, or membership, of any guild (Spain. Real Decreto CCLXII 8th June 1813). However, in 1814, the absolutist government repealed the decree, and the elimination of guild privileges became only effective in the mid-1830s (Spain. Real Decreto 20th January 1834; Spain. Real Decreto 6th December 1836).

The liberalization of the land market included the elimination of mayorazgo (an institution that had permitted the accumulation of assets as property that could not be alienated or divided at inheritance) and the introduction of *desamortización* (disentailment), that is, the confiscation and sale of ecclesiastical, communal, and public land. The change from mayorazgo and entailed property to absolute property rights reduced transaction costs, increased the amount of land in the market, and provided incentives for its exploitation. *Desamortización* was also motivated by government's need to increase its revenues. Although 'old' taxes disappeared, broadening the fiscal base at a time of rising demand for public services among the new citizens was difficult and fiscal reform was delayed until 1845 (Tedde 1994 and Comín 1988, 1990).

Reformed property rights also implied the abolition of the privileges enjoyed by the Mesta. These privileges had imposed severe limitations on the ability of landowners to enclose their properties (García Martín 1988, 123). The laws passed in 1813, and reinstated in 1834, explicitly allowed enclosures and reinforced owners' property rights.

The redefinition of land property rights was, however, not a smooth process. The upper nobility took advantage of a weak state to transform their jurisdictional rights over given territories into rights of ownership by expropriating the rights of the local peasants (de Moxó 1965). A stream of the literature has claimed that the *desamortización* did not change the ownership structure of landed property as only the affluent could afford to buy confiscated land property (Herr 1971 and 1989). A careful assessment of the literature has, however, revealed a more mixed regional outcome (Rueda Hernanz et al. 1986 and Rueda Hernanz 1997).

Recently, the view that the diffusion of liberal property rights to land led to efficiency gains (Rueda Hernanz et al. 1986) has been challenged by some historians. They argue that the elimination of communal property represented a heavy blow to peasants' living standards and that village communities were undermined by the spread of markets coupled with fiscal demands for cash at a time of deflation (Beltrán Tapia 2015, Fontana 1978 and Torras 1976). These reforms provoked an anti-liberal Carlist reaction among peasants and gentry whose grievances were augmented by the virtual disappearance of public goods such as *pósitos* and hospitals that the church and other institutions had provided under the Ancien Régime but the new liberal regime could no longer afford.[4]

We conclude that the institutional changes were initiated by and followed upon the Peninsular War. They were part of an ongoing liberal reform movement. Warfare acted as a catalyst for the development of liberal economic policies, even before the French invasion. In its wake new property rights emerged in Spain that reduced information and transaction costs, and led to the re-distribution of wealth and income.

4 The Long-Run Impact

So far our focus has been on the short-term consequences of the Napoleonic Wars. However, their long run consequences, largely neglected by historians, deserve consideration. A glance at the post-Napoleonic Wars era reveals a distinctive pattern, when compared to the pre-war era, for key dimensions of social and economic activity. Thus, over the years 1820–60 demographic expansion accelerated. The natural rate of increase nearly doubled compared to the second half of the eighteenth century (from 0.42 to 0.76% yearly) (Pérez Moreda 1999, 8). By 1860, the size of the population was 50% per cent larger than in 1787 (Figure 7.15).

Furthermore, the geographical location of the population also continued to change. Te tendency to concentrate on the Peninsula's periphery intensified. More significant from an economic point of view was the increase in the rate of urbanization (0.4%) in the early nineteenth century. The share of population living in towns of 5,000 and over, and excluding those dependent on agriculture shows that, by 1857, almost one-fourth of the population (22.9%) had ceased to depend upon agriculture for subsistence, a significant change compared to 1787 (17.4%) (Figure 7.16).

Agricultural consumption per person increased during the 1820s, fell during the Carlist War (1833–39) and, then, exhibited a growing trend until the early 1850s (Figure 7.17). From a long run perspective, the early nineteenth century can be represented as a break in the declining trend of consumption per head. It improved at yearly rate of 0.33 per cent between the 1810s and the 1850s (Álvarez-Nogal and Prados de la Escosura, 2013). It is worth noting also that, after the Peninsular War, there was an upward shift in the level of

4 Positos were municipal institutions, destined to store cereals for their loan to the peasants in times of scarcity.

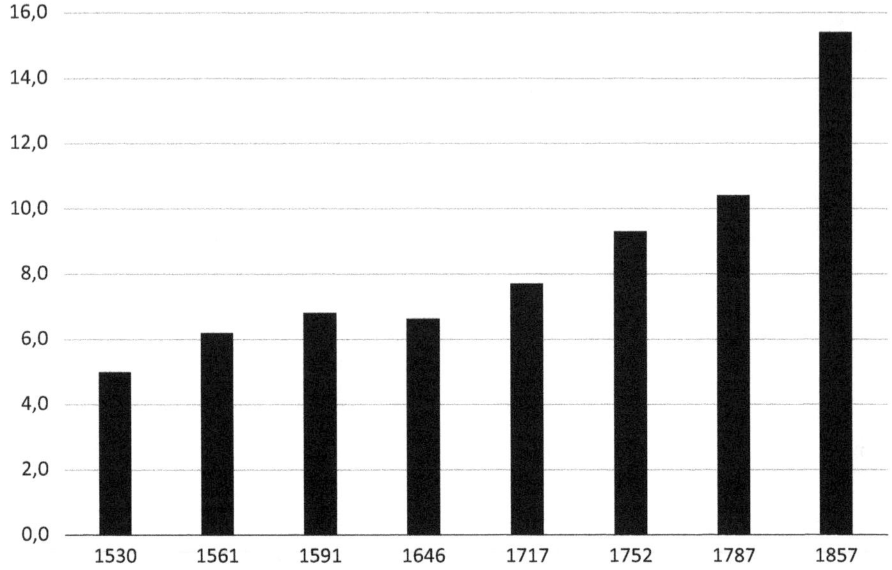

FIGURE 7.15 Population, 1530–1857
SOURCES: PRADOS DE LA ESCOSURA ET AL. (2020)

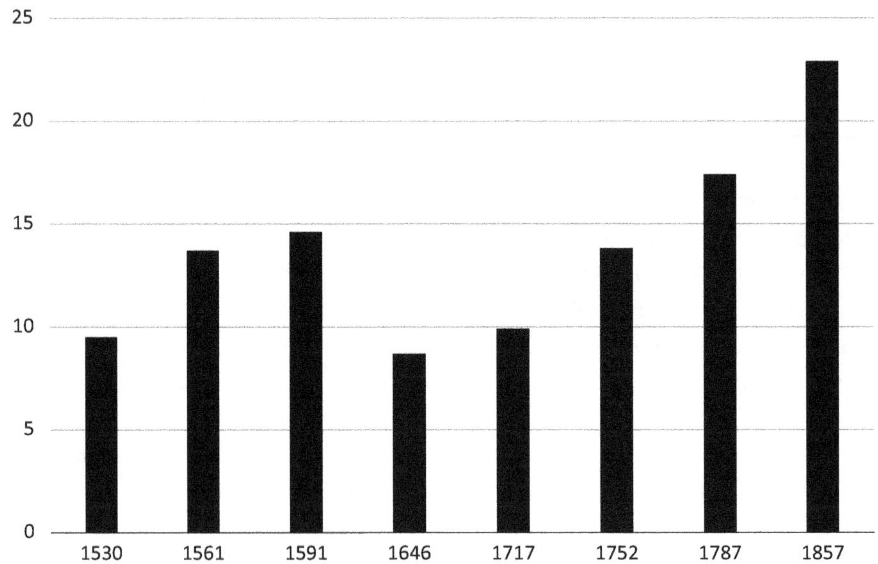

FIGURE 7.16 Adjusted urbanization rates (less population living on agriculture) 1530–1857 (%)
SOURCES: PRADOS DE LA ESCOSURA ET AL. (2020)

FIGURE 7.17 Real consumption per head in agriculture, 1815–1850 (1850/9=100)
SOURCES: ÁLVAREZ-NOGAL AND PRADOS DE LA ESCOSURA (2013)

efficiency (total factor productivity) in agriculture in Andalusia and Old Castile (Figure 7.18).

The increased variety of goods and services provided by the market and the reform of land property rights that broadened access to property, favoured a new trajectory in which increasing real wage rates went up along with an intensification of work. [5] Thus, during the first half of the nineteenth century while the economically active population in agriculture multiplied by 1.5, the area of cultivated land rose 2.4 times (Bringas Gutiérrez 2000, 86).

As regards manufacturing, although the immediate effects of the war were probably similar across industry, traditional industries collapsed, but modern industries continued to adopt new technologies. While the long-term consequences for industry of the loss of the colonies depended on the flexibility and dynamic nature of the industry concerned.

The decline in exports that flowed from the loss of the colonies illustrates a lack of competitiveness across Spanish industries. They could not offer the Latin American consumers either the prices or the quality provided by their

5 Thus, by 1850, economically active population in agriculture worked an average of 240 days per year (García Sanz 1979–80) compared to around 170 days in the eighteenth century (Álvarez-Nogal and Prados de la Escosura 2013).

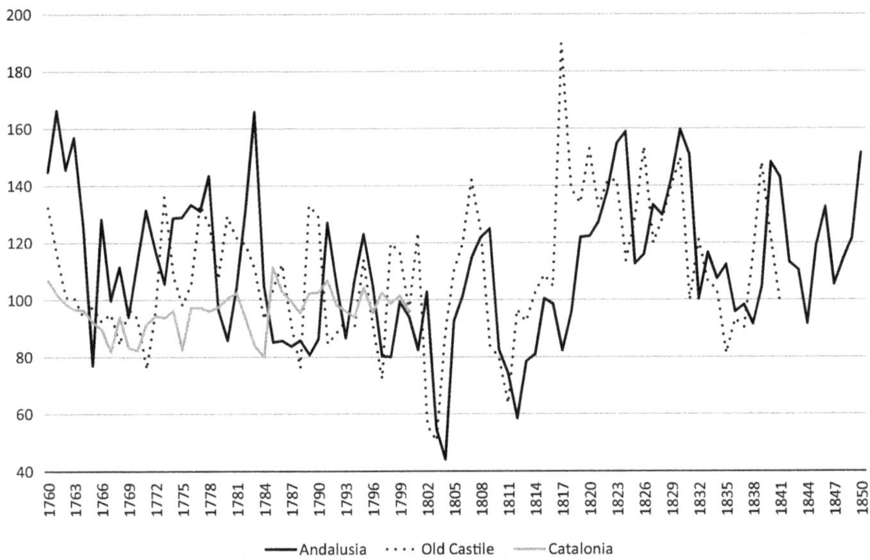

FIGURE 7.18 Total factor productivity in agriculture, 1760–1860 (1790/9=100)
SOURCES: ÁLVAREZ-NOGAL AND PRADOS DE LA ESCOSURA (2007)

Western European competitors. For example, the Basque iron and steel industry (which had sold at least a third of its output to colonial markets at the end of the eighteenth century) became uncompetitive from the 1770s onward. A similar situation afflicted the Valencia silk industry. Between the 1790s and the 1820s net exports of raw silk rose and net imports of silk textiles increased. Catalan shipping was yet another industry which had grown under colonial protection and suffered thereafter. While cotton textiles continued expanding after the loss of the colonial market. After the war the production of textiles in Catalonia recovered and mechanized, a process that was particularly intense in spinning, which absorbed three quarters of the increase in investment after 1814 (Sánchez 2000, 502). As Figure 7.19 shows, the numbers of water-frames and mules increased (in thousands) from 12.9 in 1807 to 77.3 in 1829 and 622.9 in 1850. These machines represented just 13 per cent of all spinning frames in 1807 but rose to represent more than 77 per cent by 1850 (Sánchez 2000, 508). As Rosés (1998) has shown, in the Catalan cotton industry, high levels of skills facilitated the adaptation of foreign technologies, while efficiency gains in spinning and weaving contributed one-fourth and one-third, respectively, to increases in output between 1830 and 1860.

The more competitive and flexible sectors of the economy eventually adapted to new circumstances, particularly commercial agriculture, which

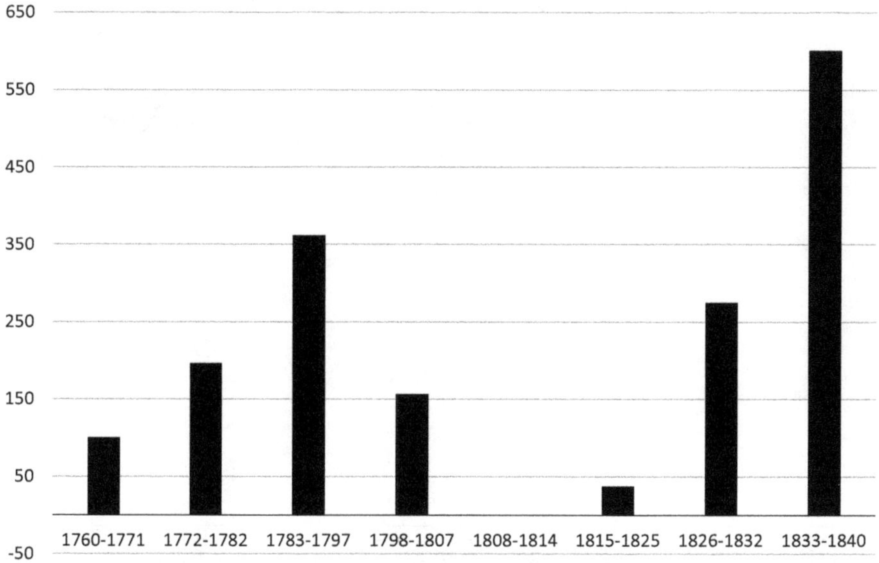

FIGURE 7.19 Investment in Catalan cotton textiles, 1760–1840 (1760–1771=100)
SOURCE: SÁNCHEZ (2000)

turned towards exporting to growing markets in Western Europe. France and Britain became the leading markets for Spanish exports, accounting for more than half of Spain's sales abroad until the end of the nineteenth century. The terms of trade moved favourably for Spanish primary producers. Technological progress lowered the prices of industrial goods and growing demand raised agricultural prices. As a result, the purchasing power in terms of imports per unit of exports trebled (Figure 7.20). Meanwhile, Latin American markets never recovered the significance they had before emancipation. At best (particularly Cuba) one fourth of all exports from Spain.

On the whole, the economy expanded steadily during the early nineteenth century (except during Carlist War 1833–1839), and population growth was accompanied by a sustained increase in GDP per head. For some European countries that would imply escape from the Malthusian trap. This was, however, not the case in Spain, a frontier economy, in which population and per capita income had evolved together over time (Figure 7.21). The novelty was that both population and per capita GDP growth had intensified, with yearly rates of 1.0 and 0.5 %, respectively, over 1815–1850, compared to 0.4 and 0.3 % during the period 1714–1808. On the downside, despite exhibiting faster growth and higher levels of per capita income than ever before, Spain fell gradually

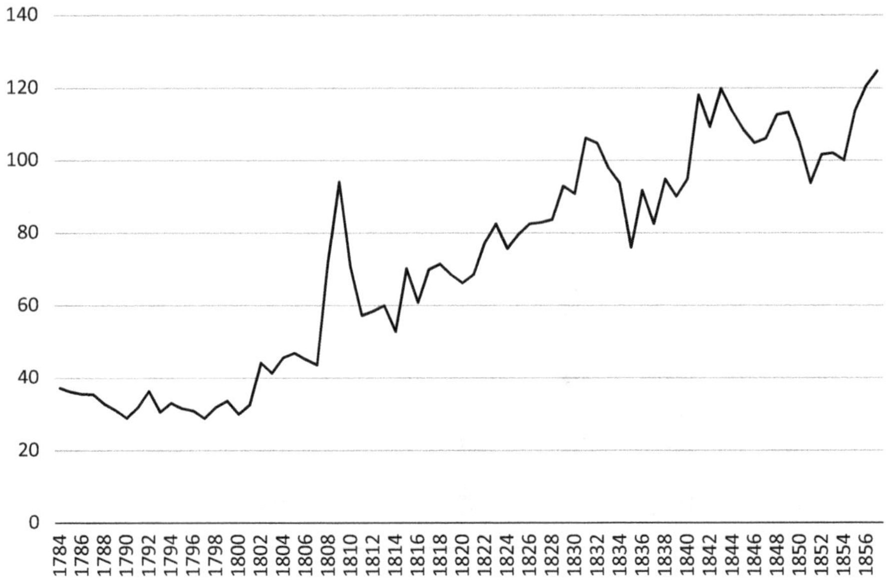

FIGURE 7.20 Terms of trade between Spain and Britain, 1784–1857 (1854=100)
SOURCES: PRADOS DE LA ESCOSURA (1994)

behind north western European countries, particularly Britain and France (Prados de la Escosura et al. 2020).

How was this progress distributed? Real wage rates increased in the 1820s, but fell steadily during the Carlist War, and recovered through to the 1840s (Figure 7.22). Real land rents, in turn, rose to the beginning of the Carlist war but showed a declining tendency thereafter. The ratio between land rents and wages provides a measure of income distribution that suggests a long-term decline in inequality punctuated, nonetheless, by reversals in 1825 and at the beginning and end of the Carlist War (Figure 7.23).

4.1 *Were the Napoleonic Wars a Watershed?*

The empirical evidence on the post–war era marshalled here suggests that the Napoleonic Wars constituted a conjuncture in Spanish history. This might however simply be an *ex post ergo propter hoc* argument. The relevant question seems to be: in the absence of war, would an enlightened elite have reformed Spain's absolutist state and initiated a gradual transition towards a liberal society? Historians have published evidence to support this hypothesis. They refer to the sound public finances of Charles IV prior to the war (Barbier and Klein 1985; Cuenca 1981; Merino 1987; Tedde 1990) to Spain's integration in the international financial world through Cádiz and Madrid stock exchanges

FIGURE 7.21 Real GDP per head and population, 1815–1850 [1850/59=100)
SOURCES: PRADOS DE LA ESCOSURA ET AL. (2020)

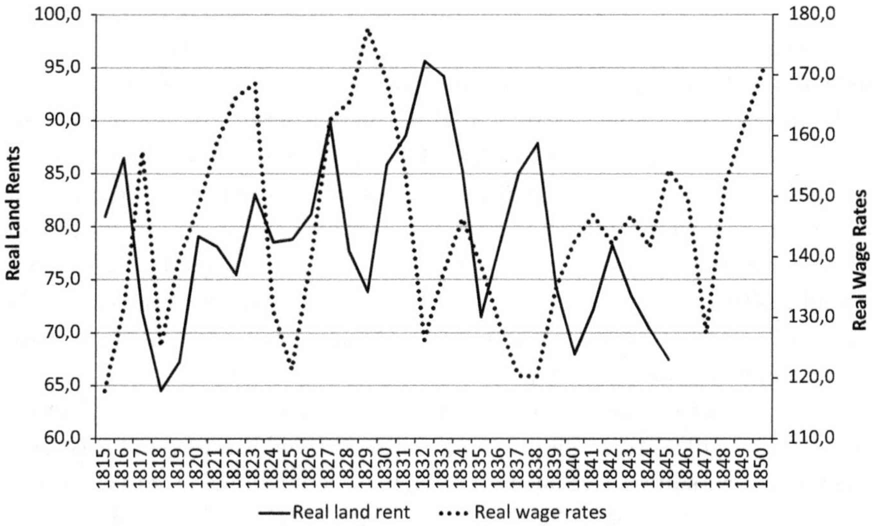

FIGURE 7.22 Real land rent and wages, 1815–1850 (1790/99=100)
SOURCE: ÁLVAREZ-NOGAL AND PRADOS DE LA ESCOSURA (2013)

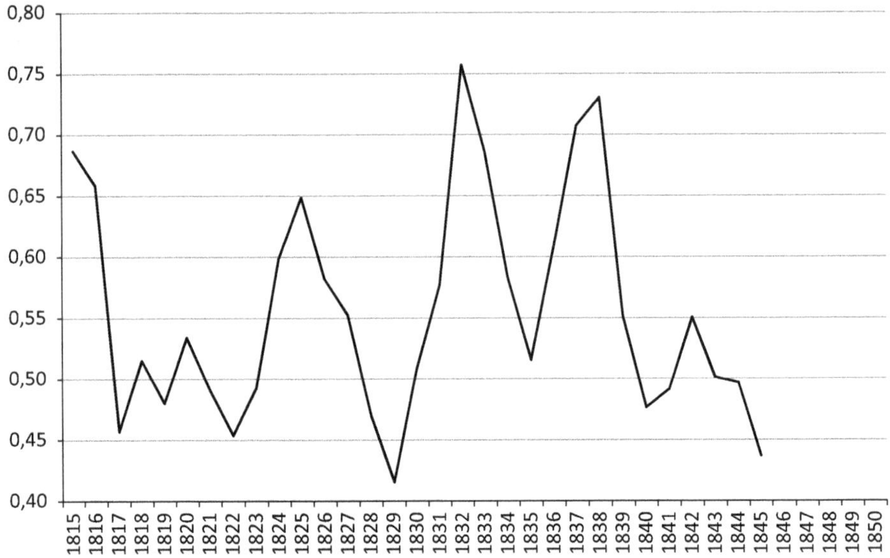

FIGURE 7.23 Inequality trends: Real land rent/wage rate ratio, 1815–1845 (1790/99=100)
SOURCE: ÁLVAREZ-NOGAL AND PRADOS DE LA ESCOSURA (2013)

which were closely connected with those of Amsterdam, London, and Paris (Tedde 1988) and to Spain's active involvement in the Anglo-French trade liberalization plans of the 1780s, which were never implemented because war broke out (Ehrman 1962). Finally, the best minds in Spain as Jovellanos and Campomanes, contributed to the liberal ideas spreading throughout Western Europe (Anes 1995; de Castro 1996; Llombart 1992). Nevertheless, there are also arguments against this interpretation. The colonial empire reinforced absolutism and only the war brought that to an end (Yun Casalilla 1998). Furthermore, the difficulties and reversals faced by the liberal reformers undermine the notion of a potentially gradual transition from absolutism to liberalism in the absence of war (vide Chapter 3 on France).

Pursuing these lines of enquiry and specifying heuristic counterfactuals involves a complete research programme way beyond the scope of this essay. As a provisional solution we have ventured to put our hypothesis to a cliometric test. Our exercise consists of ascertaining if structural breaks can be detected in the series of the economic variables previously discussed. Of course, this exercise falls short of a proper historical explanation but, if breaks are present in the data, we propose to conclude that our narrative is potentially feasible.

We have therefore tested our data for real GDP per capita, agricultural consumption, wages, land rents, the rent/wage ratio, and agricultural prices for

TABLE 7.1 Structural breaks in main economic variables, 1750–1850

	Coefficient	Year 1	Coefficient	Year 2
Per Capita GDP	4.1***	1783	9.8***	1814
Agricultural Consumption per Head	9.6***	1762	6.0***	1817
Agricultural Prices	7.5***	1785	-6.2***	1811
Wages	-15.8***	1761	22.7***	1818
Land Rent			-14.6***	1809
Rent/Wage Ratio			-18.8***	1811

Note: *** statistical significant at 1%; ** at 5%; * at 10%;

structural breaks, either in the trend or the level, over the century from 1750 to 1850 1750–1850. But a caveat is needed. Rather than exogenously choosing the dates at which the series are tested for structural breaks, we allowed the data to endogenously identify where the breaks, if they can be detected in the data, appear.

Since there could be more than just one structural break we used the Clemente-Montañés-Reyes unit root tests that allow us to establish the existence of one or two structural breaks.[6] Table 7.1 summarises our results. In the case of Land Rent and the Rent/Wage Ratio only one structural break was found and, therefore, the specific test designed to identify only one break was preferred.

The breaks found before the war reveal an increase in per capita GDP growth, but also decreasing wages, increasing inequality, falling agricultural consumption per person, and a rise agricultural prices. After the war, per capita GDP growth accelerated with a break point around 1814. Real wages also increased rapidly after the conflict, with a break around 1818. The end of the war also meant an improvement in agriculture, with consumption expanding and prices decreasing, as the break points around 1817 and 1811, respectively, show. While land rent showed a decrease at the beginning of the French invasion with a break point around 1809. Inequality measures also declined

6 We computed two different specifications of the tests, but finally opted for the innovational outlier unit root test that allows for more gradual changes rather than for the additive outlier unit root, which is more adequate to capturing very sudden variations in the series (Clemente et al. 1998).

with the beginning of the war, showing a break point for the Rent/Wage ratio around 1811.

Using the structural break points located in the series, we can now compute the trends of the different variables before the war and extrapolate them to the post-war period and compare, then, the counterfactual values to the actual values. This way, we can get a crude idea of whether the war represented a discontinuity in economic trends.

Table 7.2 presents the actual and counterfactual values at the end of the considered period and the implied change with respect to the pre-war trend projection. We can observe that GDP per capita levels were 12 per cent higher by mid-nineteenth century than what they would have been had pre-war trends prevailed. Also, real wages were 139 per cent higher and land rents 30 per cent lower. There was also an improvement in social equality. The Rent/Wage ratio emerges as two-thirds lower than a pre-war projected value. Agricultural consumption per head increased by nearly one-third and prices more than halved compared to the predicted levels with pre-war trends.

Thus, it can suggested that there were important gains that would not have been achieved had pre-war trends persisted in the early nineteenth century and that, consequently, the war can be plausibly represented as a defining conjuncture for the development of the Spanish economy.

TABLE 7.2 Main economic variables: post-war counterfactual and actual levels

	Counterfactual	Actual	% Change	% Yearly Rate	Year
Per Capita GDP	883	985	12	0,3	1850
Agricultural Consumption per head	83	107	29	0,7	1850
Agricultural Prices	196	82	-58	-2.5	1850
Wages	71	171	139	2.5	1850
Land Rent	96	67	-30	-1.2	1845
Rent/Wage Ratio	128	44	-66	-3.6	1845

5 Conclusions

The economic consequences of the Peninsular War in Spain were clearly negative in the short term. The immediate demographic effects of the war were harder than any other conflict in the history of the country. Agriculture was affected in different ways. While forced expropriations had a clear negative effect, the elimination of the Ancien Régime controls made it possible to increase production and provided a more flexible institutional framework favouring economic growth. Industry was hampered by the impoverishment of the population and the disruption of trade that increased the cost of inputs. War represented a heavy blow for traditional and inefficient industries. International trade suffered a severe contraction. GDP per head fell during the Peninsular War, with its effects unevenly distributed.

The loss of the American colonies, another by-product of the Napoleonic Wars, had short-run negative effects on capital formation, trade, and manufacturing industry, and Government revenues, but the overall impact on GDP was much lower than previously posited in qualitative assessments, and was concentrated in particular regions and economic sectors. Furthermore a direct link has been exposed between Spanish America independence and the fall of the Ancien Régime. Thus, the loss of the colonies would have contributed significantly to the transition to liberalism in Spain.

In the long run, the Napoleonic Wars triggered a complex transition from an absolutist empire to a modern nation. The liberal reforms redefined property rights, making all citizens equal before the law, freed commodity and factor markets, and introduced new legislation and regulation for economic activities. Moreover, liberalism represented control of the executive through parliament. The long-term consequences were a more efficient allocation of resources and sustained economic growth. Needless to say, serious obstacles emerged on the way, with civil wars and military takeovers as major setbacks that deferred the transition. Our view is that the Napoleonic Wars may be plausibly depicted as a watershed.

Acknowledgements

We gratefully acknowledge participants in the Waterloo Network and, in particular, Jaime Reis, Nuno Palma, Guido Alfani, Alejandra Irigoin, and most especially, Patrick O'Brien for their comments and suggestions.

References

Álvarez-Nogal, Carlos, and Leandro Prados de la Escosura. 2007. "The Decline of Spain (1500–1850): Conjectural Estimates." *European Review of Economic History* 11, no. 3: 319–366.

Álvarez-Nogal, Carlos, and Leandro Prados de la Escosura. 2013. "The Rise and Decline of Spain, 1270–1850." *Economic History Review* 66, no. 1: 1–37.

Nogal, Carlos, Leandro Prados de la Escosura, and Carlos Santiago-Caballero. 2016. "Spanish Agriculture in the Little Divergence." *European Review of Economic History* 20, no. 4: 452–477.

Anes, Gonzalo. 1995. *La Ley Agraria.* Madrid: Alianza.

Artola, Miguel. 1983. *Antiguo Régimen y Revolución Liberal.* Barcelona: Ariel.

Barbier, Jacques A., and Herbert S. Klein. 1985. "Las prioridades de un monarca ilustrado: el gasto público bajo el reinado de Carlos IV." *Revista de Historia Económica* 3, no. 3: 473–495.

Barrera-Escoda, Antonio, and M. Carmen Llasat. 2015. "Evolving flood patterns in a Mediterranean region (1301–2012) and climatic factors-the case of Catalonia." *Hydrology and Earth System Sciences* 19, no. 1: 465–483.

Barriendos, Mariano, and M. Carmen Llasat. 2003. "The Case of the `Maldá' Anomaly in the Western Mediterranean Basin (AD 1760–1800): An Example of a Strong Climatic Variability." *Climatic Change* 61:191–216.

Beltrán Tapia, Francisco. 2015. "Commons and the Standard of Living Debate in Spain, 1860–1930." *Cliometrica* 9: 27–48.

Benaul, Josep Mª., and Alex Sánchez. 2004. "El legado industrial del Antiguo Régimen." In *El legado del Antiguo Régimen en España,* edited by Enrique Llopis, 187–228. Barcelona: Crítica.

Bringas Gutiérrez, Miguel Ángel. 2000. *La productividad de los factores en la agricultura española (1752–1935).* Madrid: Banco de España.

Canales, Esteban. 2018. "1808–1814: demografía y Guerra en España." Retrieved from https://previa.uclm.es/ab/humanidades/profesores/descarga/manuel_ortiz/crisis regimen.pdf.

Clemente, Jesús, Antonio Montañés, and Marcelo Reyes. 1998. "Testing for a Unit Root in Variables with a Double Change in the Mean." *Economics Letters* 59, no. 2: 75–182.

Comín, Francisco. 1988. *Hacienda y Economía en la España Contemporánea, 1800–1936.* Madrid: Instituto de Estudios Fiscales.

Comín, Francisco. 1990. *Las cuentas de la Hacienda preliberal en España (1800–1855).* Madrid: Banco de España.

Cuenca, Javier. 1981. "Ingresos netos del Estado español, 1788–1820." *Hacienda Pública Española* 69: 183–208.

de Castro, Concepción. 1996. *Campomanes. Estado y reformismo ilustrado.* Madrid: Alianza.

de Moxó, Salvador . de 1965. *La disolución del régimen señorial en España.* Madrid: CSIC.

de Vadillo, José Manuel. 1846. *Reflexiones sobre la urgencia de remedio a los graves males que hoy se padecen en España por causa de muchas monedas que circulan en ella.* Cádiz: Imprenta de D. Manuel Bosch.

Erhman, John. 1962. *The British Government and Commercial Negotiations with Europe, 1783–1793.* Cambridge: Cambridge University Press.

Fontana, Josep. 1978. "La crisis agraria de comienzos del siglo XIX y sus repercusiones en España." *Hacienda Pública Española*, 55: 177–190.

Fontana, Josep. 1991. "La crisis colonial en la crisis del Antiguo Régimen español.", In *El sistema colonial en la América española,* edited by Heraclio Bonilla, 305–20. Barcelona: Ariel.

Fraser, Ronald. 2006. *La Maldita Guerra de España: Historia Social de la Guerra de la Independencia, 1808–1814.* Barcelona: Crítica.

García Martín, Pedro. 1988. *La ganadería mesteña en la España borbónica (1700–1836).* Madrid: Secretaría General Técnica, Ministerio de Agricultura, Pesca y Alimentación.

García Sanz, Ángel. 1979–80. "Jornales agrícolas y presupuesto familiar campesino en España a mediados del siglo XIX." *Anales del CUNEF*, 49–71.

Gates, David. 1986. *The Spanish Ulcer: A History Of Peninsular War.* London: Allen & Unwin.

Grafe, Regina, and Alejandra Irigoin. 2012. "A Stakeholder Empire: the Political Economy of Spanish Imperial Rule in America." *Economic History Review* 65, no. 2: 609–651.

Hernández García, Ricardo. 2004. "La Guerra de Independencia y su incidencia en la fábrica textil de Astudillo." *Investigaciones históricas: Época moderna y contemporánea* 24: 159–176.

Herr, Richard. 1971. "Hacia el derrumbe del antiguo régimen: crisis fiscal y desamortización bajo Carlos IV." *Moneda y Crédito*, 118: 37–100.

Herr, Richard. 1989. *Rural Change and Royal Finances in Spain at the End of the Old Regime.* Berkeley: University of California Press.

La Force, James Clayburn. 1965. *The Development of the Spanish Textile Industry, 1750–1800.* Berkeley and Los Angeles: University of California Press.

LLombart Rosa, Vicent A. 1992. *Campomanes, economista y político de Carlos III.* Madrid: Alianza.

Llopis Agelán, Enrique. 2010. "El impacto de la Guerra de la Independencia en la agricultura española." In *La guerra de Napoleón en España: Reacciones, Imágenes, Consecuencias,* edited by Emilio La Parra López, 333–378. Alicante: Universidad de Alicante.

Martínez Caviró, Balbina. 1973. *Porcelana Del Buen Retiro: Escultura Volumen 49 de Artes y Artistas. Colección artes y artista.* Madrid: CSIC.

Melendreras, Gimeno, Maria del Carmen. 2000. *La Economía en Murcia Durante la Guerra de la Independencia.* Murcia: Universidad de Murcia.

Merino, José Patricio. 1987. *Las cuentas de la Administración Central española, 1750–1820.* Madrid: Instituto de Estudios Fiscales.

Muñoz Maldonado, José. 1833. *Historia política y militar de la Guerra de la Independencia de España.* Madrid: Imprenta de D. José Palacios.

Palma, Nuno. 2016. "Sailing Away from Malthus: Intercontinental Trade and European Economic Growth, 1500–1800." *Cliometrica* 10: 129–149.

Peña, Daniel, and Nicolás Sánchez-Albornoz. 1984. "Wheat Prices in Spain, 1857–1890: An application of the Box-Jenkins methodology." *Journal of European Economic History* 13, no. 2: 353–373.

Pérez Moreda, Vicente. 1985. "La evolución demográfica española en el siglo XIX (1797–1930): tendencias generales y contrastes regionales.2 In *La popolazione italiana nell'Ottocento*, edited by SIDES, 49–51. Bologna: Societá Italiana di Dimografia Storia.

Pérez Moreda, Vicente. 1999. "Población y economía en la España de los siglos XIX y XX." In *Historia Económica de España, Siglos XIX y XX*, edited by Gonzalo Anes, 7–62. Barcelona: Galaxia Gutemberg.

Pérez Moreda, Vicente. 2010. "Las crisis demográficas del periodo napoleónico en España." In *La Guerra de Napoleón en España. Reacciones, imágenes, consecuencias*, edited by Emilio la Parra López, 305–332. Alicante: Editorial Universidad de Alicante-Casa de Velázquez.

Prados de la Escosura, Leandro. 1993. "La pérdida del imperio y sus consecuencias económicas en España." In *La independencia americana: consecuencias económicas*, edited by Leandro Prados de la Escosura and Samuel Amaral, 253–300. Madrid: Alianza.

Prados de la Escosura, Leandro. 1994. "Terms of Trade and Backwardness: Testing the Prebisch Doctrine for Spain and Britain During the Industrialization." Economic History and Institutions Working Papers, Universidad Carlos III de Madrid, WP04-65.

Prados de la Escosura, Leandro, Carlos Álvarez-Nogal, and Carlos Santiago-Caballero. 2020. "Growth Recurring in Preindustrial Spain: Half A Millennium Perspective." EHES Working Paper in Economic History no. 177.

Queipo de Llano y Ruiz de Saravia, Jose María. 1839, 2008. *Historia del levantamiento, guerra y revolución de España.* Madrid: Imprenta del Diario.

Ringrose, David. 1970. *Transportation and Economic Stagnation in Spain, 1750–1850.* Durham N.C.: Duke University Press.

Ringrose, David. 1983. *Madrid and the Spanish Economy, 1560–1850*. Berkeley and Los Angeles: University of California Press.

Rodrigo, Fernando S., María Jesús Esteban-Parra, David Pozo-Vázquez, and Yolanda Castro-Diez. 1999. "A 500-Year Precipitation Record in Southern Spain." *International Journal of Climatology* 19: 1233–1253.

Ros Massana, Rosa. 1999. *La industria textil lanera de Béjar (1680–1850). La formación de un enclave industrial*. Valladolid: Junta de Castilla y León.

Rosés, Joan R. 1998. "Measuring the Contribution of Human Capital to the Development of the Catalan Factory System (1830–61)." *European Review of Economic History* 2: 25–48.

Rueda Hernanz, Germán, José Ramón Díez Espinosa, and Pablo García Colmenares. 1986. *La desamortización de Mendizábal y Espartero en España*. Madrid: Cátedra.

Rueda Hernanz, Germán. 1997. *La desamortización en España: un balance (1766–1924)*. Madrid: Arcolibros.

Saiz González, J. Patricio. 1995. *Propiedad Industrial y Revolución Liberal: Historia del Sistema Español de Patentes (1759–1929)*. Madrid: Oficina Española de Patentes.

Saiz González, J. Patricio. 1996. "Las patentes y la economía española:(1826–1878), Oficina Española de Patentes y Marcas." Oficina de Patentes y Marcas, Universidad Autónoma de Madrid, Documento de trabajo 9606.

Sánchez, Alex. 2000. "Crisis económica y respuesta empresarial. Los inicios del sistema fabril en la industria algodonera catalana, 1797–1839." *Revista de Historia Económica* 18, no. 3: 485–523.

Sánchez, Alex. 2010. "Guerra e industria: Consecuencias de la Guerra de la Independencia en la industria manufacturera española." In *La guerra de Napoleón en España: Reacciones, Imágenes, Consecuencias*, edited by Emilio La Parra López, 333–378. Alicante: Universidad de Alicante.

Sánchez-Albornoz, Claudio. 1911. "Ávila desde 1808 hasta 1814." *Nuestro Tiempo*, 519–540.

Santiago-Caballero, Carlos. 2013. "The Rain in Spain? Climate versus Urban Demand as Causes of Agricultural Stagnation in Eighteenth Century Spain." *European Review of Economic History* 17, no. 4: 452–470.

Sardá Dexeus, Juan. 1948. *La política monetaria y las fluctuaciones de la economía española en el siglo XIX*. Madrid: Instituto Sancho de Moncada, CSIC.

Sherwig, John M. 1969. *Guineas and Gunpowder: British Foreign Aid in the Wars with France, 1793–1815*. Harvard: Harvard University Press.

Spain. Real Decreto 20th January 1834, declarando que las asociaciones gremiales no gozan fuero privilegiado, y que no se podrá formar ninguna que monopolice el trabajo. Retrieved from: http://www.boe.es.

Spain. Real Decreto 6th December 1836, mandando guardar, cumplir y ejecutar el de las Córtes que restablece otro de las generales y extraordinarias, fecha 8 de Junio de

1813, por el que ordenaron la libertad en el establecimiento de fábricas y ejercicio de cualquiera industria útil. Retrieved from: http://www.boe.es.

Spain. Real Decreto CCLXII 8th de June 1813, sobre el libre establecimiento de fábricas y exercicio de qualquier industria útil. Retrieved from: http://www.cervantes virtual.com.

Tedde, Pedro. 1988. *El Banco de San Carlos (1782–1829)*. Madrid: Alianza-Banco de España.

Tedde, Pedro. 1990. "Política financiera y política comercial en el reinado de Carlos III." In *Actas del Congreso Internacional "Carlos III y la Ilustración"*, edited by Ministerio de Cultura, 129–217. Madrid: Siglo XXI.

Tedde, Pedro. 1994. "Cambio institucional y cambio económico en la España del siglo XIX." *Revista de Historia Económica* 12, no. 3: 525–538.

Torras Elías, Jaume. 1976. *Liberalismo y rebeldía campesina, 1820–1823*. Barcelona: Ariel.

Urlanis, Boris. 2011. *Wars and population*. Moscow: Progress.

Yun Casalilla, Bartolomé. 1998. "The American Empire and the Spanish Economy: An Institutional Perspective." *Revista de Historia Económica* 16, no. 1: 123–156.

CHAPTER 8

Portugal's French Wars: Cost, Loss, Missed Opportunities? 1793–1850

Cristina Moreira, Jaime Reis and Rita Martins de Sousa

> The French invasions had some direct impact on the Portuguese economy [...] but the exact extent of such consequences have not yet been measured by economic historians.
>
> COSTA et al. 2016, 232

∴

1 Introduction[1]

The impact of large-scale warfare is an attractive subject for comparative historians. Not only does the stress suffered by participants reveal much regarding their economic, social and institutional fundamentals. It is also a guide to understanding the legacy of war. In the case of the Revolutionary and Napoleonic Wars (RNW), this is all the more significant given that they overlapped with an epochal turning point in the life of the nations in question.

During these twenty-three years of belligerency, Europe experienced massive social and economic disruption and political and institutional transformation. In the present chapter, we consider how Portugal fared by looking at three topics. The first is the essential interrogation concerning all wars: the overall cost and how this was defrayed? The second regards the impact of the war on

1 The authors wish to thank José L. Cardoso, José M. L. Cordeiro, Leonor F. Costa, the participants in the three conferences held by the Project on the Economic Outcomes Flowing from the Revolutionary and Napoleonic Wars, 1793–1815, respectively in Madrid, Lisbon and London, for comments. They are grateful to José Carlos Neto for research assistance. This work was supported by FCT, I.P., the Portuguese national funding agency for science, research and technology, under Project UIDB/04521/2020. The support of the Interdisciplinary Centre of Social Sciences of Minho University is also appreciated.

 | DOI:10.1163/9789004472754_009

the economy as a whole, as well as on its principal sectors. The third focuses on the implications of the era and whether they cleared a long-term path to higher levels of prosperity and well-being.

In the following pages we seek answers to these queries. In some instances, we offer revisions of the conventional wisdom, in others we corroborate it. We confirm that the war caused substantial hardship to Portugal, yet was less protracted, devastating and costly than has been supposed by many. We note that it did not cause the huge financial strain which some other states endured and which led to major fiscal reforms (O'Brien 1988). On the geo-political side, the outcome was mixed. Portugal, a more than seven-hundred-year-old state, retained full autonomy under its traditional reigning family and avoided incorporation into its arch-rival Spain. On the other hand, it suffered the amputation of Brazil, its richest colony. Lastly, it adopted most of the institutional changes inspired by Napoleonic rule and generally perceived as the foundations of modern Liberal Europe. However, these growth-stimulating reforms were adopted comparatively late and hesitantly and this may have delayed the speed of its development. The country failed to make the transition to the modern society and effective institutions required by emerging industrial capitalism. The nineteenth century was not the time in which Portugal decisively joined the train of modern economic growth.

2 The Napoleonic Invasions

The RNW started, for Portugal, in 1793 with the war of the First Coalition against Republican France, which ended in 1797. A small Portuguese army entered the Roussillon but this yielded neither diplomatic, nor land gains. A decade of low-intensity belligerency ensued. This was interspersed with phases of neutrality during which Portugal armed itself for future conflicts and was amply rewarded by its active participation in international trade (Pedreira and Costa 2009; Cruz 2015; Eloranta et al. 2018). In 1801, another minor "war of the Oranges" led to a brief Spanish invasion supported by France and to a slight territorial loss for Portugal (Ventura 2008).

By the early 19th century there were important diplomatic and economic reasons for the outbreak of full war. One was Portugal's pursuit of neutral status at the same time as covert collaboration with the British. This would infringe the Continental Blockade but a break in Anglo-Portuguese relations could precipitate a British blockade of Portuguese ports. This would entail, for Portugal, the loss of Britain's naval shield in the Atlantic, the starvation of the country, and a separation from its protected trade with Brazil.

TABLE 8.1 Portugal's French invasions, 1807–1811

Dates	Leader	French army size (men)	Duration (months)	Conquest of Lisbon	Occupation of Portugal
1807/8	Junot	28,000	9	Yes	Yes
1809	Soult	23,900	4	No	No
1810/11	Masséna	65,000	9	No	No
Total			22		

SOURCES: SEE TEXT

British naval supremacy was another important worry for Napoleon. The Royal Navy had 148 "ships of the line" compared to France's 79 and a greater capacity to fire broadsides (Roberts 2015; Modelski and Thompson 1988). This required a secure network of friendly ports from which Britain could police the seas, harass enemy shipping, and unload supplies and soldiers into hostile territory. Lisbon's deep all-weather harbour and strong defences made it eminently suited to the needs of the Navy (Glover 2001, 59) and an essential asset for furthering British aims.

In 1807, the years of "armed peace" came to an end. Portugal entered the era of high stakes and furious conflict which has been termed "total war" (Bell 2007). What prompted this onslaught? Despite the leonine conditions imposed at Tilsit (1806), Napoleon continued to need foreign revenues, wider protected markets and fines on conquered populations (Esdaile 2002, 10). By then, however, not so much was left on the Continent to conquer. Russia was too large and too far and Britain seemed impregnable (Roberts, 2015). Iberia emerged as attractive since it might even yield an empire for France in South America as well.[2]

In late 1807, the opportunity for a French invasion became tempting (see table 8.1). Spain allowed French troops to cross its territory. A quick dash by them across the Peninsula would yield two vital results. One was the capture of the Prince Regent of Portugal (later, John VI) who, under intense British pressure, was preparing to escape to Brazil and avoid becoming the head of

2 Under the treaty of Fontainebleau (October 1807), France and Spain declared that "all islands, colonies and other overseas properties of Portugal" would be divided between them. The king of Spain would become the Emperor of the two Americas. See Birmingham (1993, 97).

a French puppet regime in Portugal.[3] The other was the seizure of Lisbon, the confiscation of the Portuguese fleet and the breach of the British blockade. Both met with total failure. The Regent and a host of followers got away and set up a new government in Rio de Janeiro, leaving a regency in charge of the metropolis (Pedreira and Costa 2009). The Portuguese navy escaped and the Tagus was blockaded by the British. By summer 1808, the French were facing two dangerous opponents. A nation-wide, anti-French popular uprising left the country ungovernable (Valente 2007). Meanwhile, the arrival of a British force of some 21,800 men led to the defeat of the occupying army at Vimeiro, helped by Portuguese forces.[4] The outcome was a humiliating French surrender and evacuation in September (Broers 2015, 156).

The next two incursions did no better. In fact, they did worse. Both failed to achieve mastery of the country or to reach Lisbon. The first of them, in 1809, was a minor part of a grand design to subdue Spain, conquer Lisbon and put Joseph Bonaparte on the throne in Madrid. It entered via the north, aiming to conquer Porto and Lisbon, but never got beyond Porto. Five months later, it exited Portugal in complete disarray, pursued by Anglo-Portuguese troops and Portuguese militias and guerrillas, leaving behind all its artillery, cavalry and 6,000 casualties (Soriano 1866–90, II, 272).

The third invasion, in 1810, tried the western route, from Ciudad Rodrigo (Glover 2001, 128). It was the swan song of France's attempts on Portugal. A much larger army this time fought a battle at Buçaco, which went undecided, but then the trouble started. The French Grande Armée du Portugal found the only road to Lisbon blocked by a defensive system of trenches and redoubts manned by 130,000 Anglo-Portuguese line troops and militiamen, and equipped with 240 cannons (Soriano, II, 209–10). The lines of Torres Vedras, which took a year to dig in secret and absorbed £200,000 sterling, simply could not be breached. In a vast area around them and to the south of Lisbon, the population was evacuated and the land scorched. The French army was utterly demoralized and starved and left for Spain, never to engage in operations on Portuguese soil again.

3 According to Marques (1973 I, 576, the plan to send the royal family to Brazil, maintain the British alliance and allow the French to conquer mainland Portugal was a part of internal political debate ever since at least the Seven Years War.

4 Roberts (2015, 478) estimates the British contingent was only 13,000 strong. Reliable military statistics for the Peninsular War are hard to obtain, as discussed by Glover (2001, 12–3). We use here his appendix 5, ("orders of battle") for British and Portuguese data, and Soriano (1866–90, passim) for French ones.

For Portugal, this was not the end of the war. Half of its army went on to fight for another three years in Spain and then in France. In the first half of 1812, French forces in the Peninsula still numbered 230,000 and there was concern over a possible fourth invasion (Serrão 2002, VII, 98). A year later, these 25,000 Portuguese soldiers continued to play a crucial role as part of the Anglo-Portuguese forces employed by Wellington to drive Napoleon out of southern Europe.

This summary raises an interesting conundrum, while seeking to explain why Portugal's experience of occupation was comparatively short and left so light a military imprint. Theoretically, it should have been an easy prey for the empire. The ratio of populations alone was an immense 14:1 and the French war machine was truly daunting.[5] In all of Europe it comprised more than 600,000 well-equipped and battle-hardened men, of which between 250,000 and 300,000 were stationed in Spain for most of the time. It was led by a highly experienced officer corps and its commanders in Portugal were generals of the highest calibre.[6] In contrast, in 1807 the Portuguese army was not only diminutive (20,000 men) but had experienced only slight fighting experience. Its officer corps was poorly trained and in the hands of the 'old' nobility. It was hardly a match for the Napoleonic behemoth (Newitt and Robson 2004; Teixeira et al. 2017).

How was this turned around? One factor was the alteration in the balance of military manpower. This was a result of a rapid growth in the size of the permanent allied forces in Portugal, which started with the arrival of 25,000 well-armed British soldiers in mid-1808 and continued, with the creation of a Portuguese force of similar size, to replace the pre-war army disbanded by Junot. In 1809, a further 25,000 Portuguese troops were incorporated, bringing the total of regular Portuguese soldiers to approximately 50,000. Meanwhile, informal, ill-equipped bodies of irregulars started to play a significant part alongside the troops of the line. Likely estimates of more than 40,000 militiamen (*milícias*) and even larger numbers of guerrrilas (*paisanos*)[7] led to an

5 As Napoleon pithily put it, "who can withstand the soldiers who conquered at Austerlitz, at Jena, at Eylau ?" (Glover 2001, 51).

6 Junot was made a general at the age of 32. Soult became, in 1804, the first "Marshall of the Empire". Masséna, a general at the age of 35, was called by Napoleon "the greatest name of my military Empire".

7 A quarter of French casualties in Spain was due to guerrilla action (Roberts 2015, 494). We assume that in Portugal the efficiency would have been similar, though Broers (2015, 205) argues that the Portuguese guerrillas were more effective than their Spanish counterparts.

Anglo-Portuguese striking force of over 100,000 combatants. At this time, the largest French army to enter Portugal numbered less than 80,000 men.

Napoleon always claimed that Portugal could be captured by less than 100,000 French soldiers. He therefore insisted on sending too few troops there, contrary to the judgement of both British and French generals (Eisdale 2002, 124; Soriano 1866–90, II, 94), a mistake due to his disregard for the dimension of "patriotic" feeling in the Peninsular War. As a result, Spain's conquest was soon found to represent an overwhelming drain on human resources, aggravated by the difficulty of communications and supply transport, which tied down one fourth to one third of all French military personnel in the Peninsula.[8]

The third factor which jeopardized French military efforts was the "remarkable metamorphosis" of the Portuguese army which occurred between 1809 and 1811. It was achieved by a British military mission, agreed upon by the two allies and consisting of 300–400 British officers, under a British commander-in-chief, with full powers over the new Anglo-Portuguese army (Barata and Teixeira 2003; Newitt 2009). The goal was to create a new army along British military lines, with a tight system of discipline and a capacity to follow modern tactics on the battlefield. The men were armed and clothed by British standards and the officer corps was composed of British volunteers and younger Portuguese officers recruited by merit. Thus, from a mediocre, defensive fighting force, the Portuguese army became known to be the only one in Europe capable of "consistent victories over the French" (Broers 2015).[9]

3 The Cost of War

It is often remarked that the sinews of war are men and money.[10] In the previous section, we touched upon the former. In the present one, we try to establish how much of the latter was needed for Portugal to achieve liberation.

The Napoleonic wars have been held to be hugely exorbitant, although accurate estimates are not easy to come by. Measuring the direct cost of war poses a number of problems. One of them arises out of how the direct cost of

---

8 Communications between Portugal and Britain took place in one fourth of the time it took for a French message to reach Bayonne.

9 At the battle of Buçaco, Masséna was led to believe that the Portuguese army facing him was in fact the British one (Soriano 1866–90, II, 180).

10 Cicero focused on one only – money; Machiavelli added "men"; Hemmingway's list included also "materials, maintenance and morale". See *The Oxford Dictionary* of Quotations (1986).

war is defined. Standard notions speak of "adding up the *actual* [our emphasis] war expenditures for each year" [of war] (Goldin and Lewis 1975, 300); or, of "calculating the flow of spending by government on the prosecution of the war" (Broadberry and Harrison 2005, 22). It considers that, beyond this, the correct result requires deducting from these yearly amounts "all military costs which would have been incurred in the absence of war" (Goldin and Lewis 1975, 304).[11] In the present analysis, we take a different view, namely that the direct cost of war must incorporate all military inputs used by belligerents, irrespective of what might have been spent had there been no fighting.

A second difficulty is caused by the scarcity of reliable statistics during this period regarding state activities and, in particular, defence. In the case of Portugal, the lack of historical data for national military expenditure has long been a barrier and has only been overcome thanks to two circumstances. One is the possibility of using now the "enlightened" fiscal reform of the marquis of Pombal which created, in 1761, a modern, centralized Royal Treasury (Erário Régio) (Tomaz 1988). This provides detailed and consistent yearly information concerning all financial aspects of state activity. The other is the recent scholarly effort to breakdown aggregate flows of income, by fiscal source, and of expenditure, by categories of expenditure. Figure 8.1 displays these data for the three variables which are of greatest interest to us here: aggregate expenditure and revenue, and military expenditure.[12] They allow us to quantify spending on military activity, as well as to contextualise it against the backdrop of aggregate economic activity and the resources of the state.

A third challenge facing cost-of-war calculations stems from the fact that during the RNW, Great Britain provided Portugal with substantial free-of-obligation military aid in cash, kind and men.[13] This raises a need to distinguish between two different approaches depending on the origins of the resources employed. One refers to the total value of military outlays drawn only from the country's own resources. We call this the "national-cost-of-war". The second is based on all war expenditures, however or by whomever incurred. We

11 The logic is that peace-time defence spending is not employed in waging war and therefore should not be taken on board in this calculation.

12 For a number of earlier but less comprehensive studies, see Caetano (2013), Capela (1993), Cardoso and Lains (2010), Costa (2008), Costa et al. (2016), Moreira (2007; 2011), Moreira and Eloranta (2012), Silveira (1987). For the present chapter, we have compiled exhaustively all the data from Livros da Receita e da Despesa Corrente do Tesoureiro Mor do Erário Régio, Arquivo Histórico do Tribunal de Contas, Lisboa.

13 During this period, Portugal was among more than thirty states receiving this kind of help from Britain. See Sherwig (1969, 365–8).

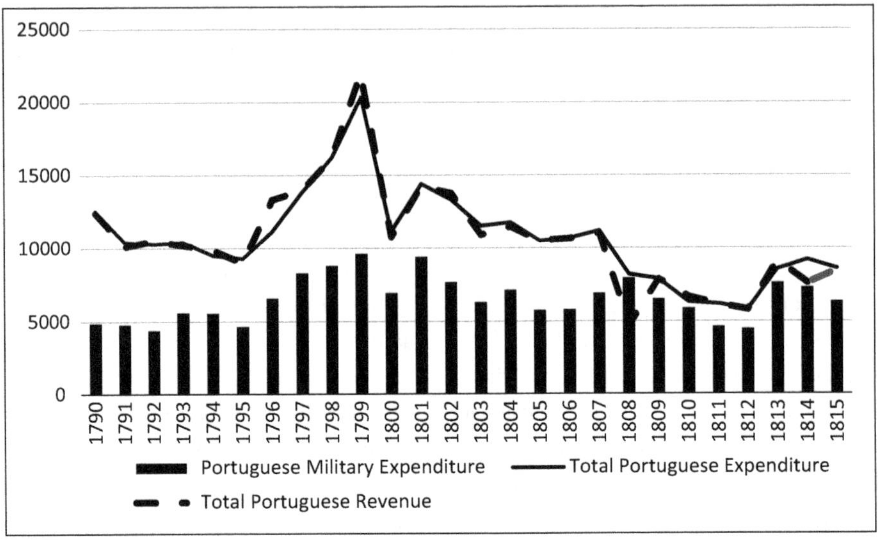

FIGURE 8.1 Total state expenditure and revenue, and military expenditure, 1790–1815 (at 1800 prices) (in *contos*)
SOURCE: LIVROS DA RECEITA E DA DESPESA CORRENTE DO TESOUREIRO MOR DO ERÁRIO RÉGIO, *ARQUIVO HISTÓRICO DO TRIBUNAL DE CONTAS*. FOR THE PRICE DEFLATOR, SEE PALMA AND REIS (2019).

designate it as the "full-cost-of war". It includes the "national-cost-of-war" and foreign contributions.

A common form of assistance to allies was the British practice of raising non-British armies in foreign countries at a lower financial and political cost than if they had mobilized similar numbers of British troops and shipped them instead. By 1815, the total disbursement on account of this policy across Europe had reached the remarkable figure of £65 million sterling. Portugal was the second largest recipient in absolute terms and the largest in per capita terms. This item could constitute a significant source of error in cost-of-war accounting given that the sums were considerable and that the system for implementing them did not always function transparently.[14] British aid was concerned

14 Sherwig (1969, passim) discusses the difficulties of reaching accurate and comparable estimates for the subsidies received. These include multiple accounting practices, problems with converting prices of supplies into cash values, and variations in discount rates on bills of exchange. The estimates for Portugal's total subsidies vary among scholars: £ 11,071,271 - Sherwig, passim; £8,228,852 - Caetano (2013, 129); and £10,678,000 - Costa (2008, 17). Sherwig's figure is calculated directly from British Treasury sources and is therefore the one preferred here.

only with military operations and was channelled through the British Military Commissariat of Wellington's army. These are not traceable therefore via the Portuguese treasury's accounts displayed in figure 8.1.

The British expeditionary force, which arrived in 1808 and stayed four and a half years, was decisive in all battles against the invader and also highly dissuasive of invasion attempts as long as it was on or close to Portuguese soil. Its cost was also defrayed by the British Treasury. Direct quantification of this contribution is not easy and we resort therefore to an indirect approximation based on two indicators. One is the size of the force, which was *circa* 30,000 men. The other is the mean cost of maintaining and paying a British soldier on the continent on a war-footing. In 1815, this was put at £65 per combatant per year. For the entire war, this input for Portugal will have amounted to 31,284 contos.[15]

The historiography of the RNW in Portugal has not given much attention to quantifying the total military Allied effort to end the French presence. It has resorted instead to qualitative assessments, referring vaguely to "enormous sums" (Costa et al. 2016), "outrageously steep" costs (Paquette, 2013), which left the country "prostrate" (Broers 2015), "impoverished" (Birmingham 1993) or "exhausted" (Serrão 2002). Table 8.2 compiles an itemized list of the different war costs associated with Portugal's liberation and provides us with a first "full-cost-of-war" estimate. The result is a bill for Portugal and its Allies for these 23 years of conflict of 221,184 contos (line 4 col. 6) at 1800 prices, the equivalent of £62 million sterling. [16]

This was an enormous sum but was it on a par with the great disasters of this epoch, as suggested by the literature? One way of answering this is to set it against the material consequences of other major calamities.[17] For Portugal, the obvious yardstick is the Lisbon earthquake of 1755, which destroyed "one of the largest and richest European cities" and took 30 years to reconstruct (Pereira 2009). Assessing this loss has been variously estimated at between 70,000 and 150,000 contos (Cardoso 2007, 168) and, for the sake of argument,

15 We take the former from Wellington's estimate cited in Soriano (1870, II, 484). For the latter, see Sherwig (1969, 338). The Portuguese monetary unit was the *real* (plural, réis) and for large amounts, the *conto* was employed. One *conto* was equal to a million réis and to £280.5 sterling.

16 This is a lower-bound result. It does not comprise provisions, horses, habitations and the like, which many soldiers on either side lived off, but never paid for, and which are not accounted.

17 For a comprehensive list of calamities in Portugal since the 14th century, see the PWR-Portugal data base: http://pwr-portugal.ics.ul.pt/wp-content/uploads/Chronology_of_Calamities.pdf.

we assume an intermediate value of 100,000 contos. This is close to half the "full cost of war" of the RNW at 1800 prices between 1793 and 1815.

A question of comparability is raised here, however, since the duration of these events is hardly the same. A better solution is to draw parallels between the average yearly cost of war and yearly economic magnitudes, such as GDP, or per household earnings of labour. In this optic, an average year's full cost of war (9,616 contos over 23 years) is equivalent to 5.2 percent of GDP (at 1800 prices); and, per household, as roughly a burden of 65 days a year of the labour of a male unskilled worker.[18] These results are substantial but perhaps less than the crushing nature assumed by the qualitative literature noted above.

Table 8.2 can also take us one step beyond these findings by narrowing the scope of our analysis to that of the "national cost of war", as defined above. It thus focuses on the contribution by the Portuguese nation alone. This has two advantages. It provides a clear measure of the sacrifice exacted by the state from the national population to this end. Secondly, it gives us the amount which the state had to mobilize, out of its income and other sources, in order to meet the French threat. The relevant variable is displayed in table 8.2 under the title "National cost of war" (line 1). It is defined as the sum of all military outlays originating in domestic sources for purposes of defence between 1793 and 1815 at 1800 prices. The total is 155,577 contos. As above, we draw parallels with other variables in order to get a clearer sense of these magnitudes. The average yearly cost of the war (1793–1815) to the Portuguese treasury, at 6,764 contos, was equivalent to 3.7 percent of GDP; and, in per household terms, to roughly the value of 43 days of the labour of an unskilled male worker. Here too, very large sums were at stake and implied individual and collective sacrifices on a significant scale, yet they cannot be said to have represented the overwhelming liability which some have claimed.

The most striking implications to emerge from the analysis of table 8.2 are those concerning the years of "total war", that is 1807–1815. This was the time during which total military costs per annum more than doubled (from 7,115 contos to 17,349 contos), British armed intervention was at its peak, and yet victory appeared uncertain. It was also when Portugal's share of total allied expenditure was at its lowest ebb – a mere 36.5 percent - leaving the remaining almost two thirds to be carried by Great Britain. We must conclude that without the latter's assistance, Portugal could never have entertained any serious hope of successfully defying the threat of conquest by mighty France. For this

18 Real wages for unskilled labour are from Palma and Reis (2019). The estimate of households in Portugal is from Palma et al. (2020).

TABLE 8.2 Full and national costs of the Anglo-Portuguese war against the French in *contos* (1800 prices)

	1762–1792 peace time	1793–1807 "armed peace"		1808–1815 "total war"		1793–1815
Period	**Annual average (1)**	**Total (2)**	**Annual average (3)**	**Total (4)**	**Annual average (5)**	**Total cost (6)**
National cost of war (1)	5,291	104,921	6,995	50,656	6,332	155,577
British aid (2)	-	1,797	120	32,526	4,065	34,323
British expeditionary army (3)	-	-	-	31,284	6,952	31,284
Full cost of war (4)	5,291	106,718	7,115	114,466	17,349	221,184

SOURCES: SEE TEXT

Note: Sterling values converted at £1= 3,565 reis.

to be possible, Portugal would have had to be capable of expanding dramatically the financial resources needed for settling the conflict. In this case, however, it would have had to tackle the financial and monetary dislocation that other nations had to face when they tried to resist Napoleon without having the means for it. As we shall see, thanks to its Oldest Ally's deep pockets and a better capacity for financial management than many have admitted, Portugal avoided such contingencies.

4 Defraying the Cost: A Financial Crisis?

According to many, the worst legacy of the Portuguese Napoleonic war was a protracted financial crisis which extended throughout this period and well into the nineteenth century (Broers 2015). For some, this problem was endemic to the Ancien Régime, in Europe. It was a result of the major 18th century states having taken on responsibilities for the conduct of wars without the sufficient wherewithal to pay for them (Hespanha 1982, cited by Silveira 1987). For others, the problem was more recent and gained root during the RNW (Fernandes 2005, 394). The basic cause was the inordinate rise in military spending on permanent armies compounded by the inability to generate revenues to match such a situation. The outcome was fiscal deficits of "unprecedented levels" (Costa et al. 2016, 223). This led to a spiralling public indebtedness to pay for interest and amortization on earlier debt; and often, concurrently, an inflationary process was fuelled by the emission of un-backed paper money. According to Mata and Valério (1994, 132), in Portugal, these difficulties reached a pitch such that, had they not occurred, "the economic and demographic consequences of war could have been easily surmounted".

Reality, in fact, was much less dire than these diagnoses would have us believe and, while far from easy to manage, do not seem to have amounted to "a profound financial crisis" (Silva 2005, 257). The Portuguese economy did indeed face financial challenges but these did not attain the intensity which has often been asserted. The key to our revision is displayed by the data in figure 8.1. This shows that over the entire war period the Royal Treasury, was not only able to avoid large deficits, but was even capable of keeping surpluses in sufficient size and number so that the total negative balance for the entire period of conflict (1793–1815) was only 1,395 contos.[19] How was this possible? An important reason was that when revenues fell, as between 1808 and 1815 because of a decline in customs and Crown patrimonial income, non-military expenditure was drastically cut as well, and thus national war-spending could be kept up. The other was that the greatly augmented military effort between 1808 and 1815 was accompanied by massive British aid, which precluded the need for large budget deficits. Altogether, this "gift" came to 34,323 contos, which was roughly the equivalent to five years of full-cost-of-war expenditure (see table 8.2, line 1).

Besides being adept at finding ways to compress non-military expenditure, the treasury also made efforts to create new taxes or improve the efficiency of existing ones. Two of these were well-known and debated both in Portugal and abroad. A stamp duty was approved in 1800 with little effect. An Extraordinary Defence Contribution came into force in 1803, putting an end to exemptions enjoyed by the nobility and the clergy with respect to the income tax (*décima*) (Cardoso and Lains 2010, 257). Between 1808 and 1815, this Extraordinary Defence Contribution represented 11 percent on average per year of total

19 This is corroborated by Caetano (2008, 96–126)'s data for the years 1812–1817. Costa et al.'s (2016, 223) claim concerning "enormous" war-time deficits is fragile given it is founded on three exceptional years only – 1800, 1801 and 1802.

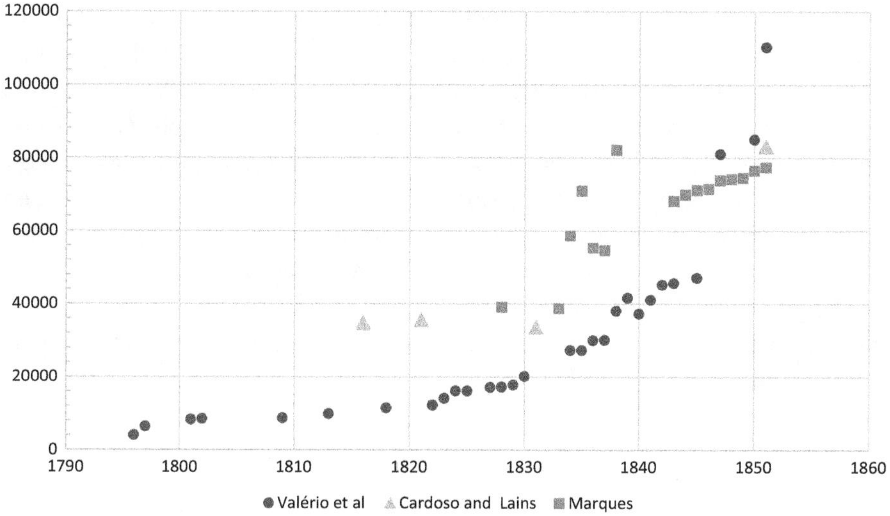

FIGURE 8.2 Consolidated public debt (1796–1851) (in *contos*, nominal values)
SOURCES AND METHODS: SEE APPENDIX TABLE 8.4

revenue. The result of these changes overall was essentially neutral, however, given that revenue from other duties declined in the meantime.

In spite of these efforts, the Portuguese treasury was impelled at times to innovate in order to deal with some of the fiscal strain, just as other countries did.

One of these new measures was the issue of bonds in the years 1796–7, 1801 and 1812 in the market at various rates of interest, for a total value of 9,828 contos nominal (Valério et al. 2001; see figure 8.2). The financial impact of these operations is best gauged by calculating the Portuguese public-debt-to-GDP ratio, which fluctuated between 2 and 5 percent. This was amongst the smallest in Europe and therefore unlikely to support the hypothesis of a grave financial disruption in Portugal.[20]

A similar tale may be told regarding the issue of inconvertible paper money in Portugal for the first time during a period of financial urgency. Most of it occurred between 1797 and 1799 and, by 1802, had reached a net total in

20 The Portuguese ratio is based on GDP data from Palma and Reis (2019) and appendix table 1.1. For France in 1815 the ratio was 16 percent, Sweden 's was 20 percent, Prussia's was 40 percent, and the Netherlands, during the years 1795 to 1815, went from 160 to 341 percent. Data for these countries are from the relevant chapters in Cardoso and Lains (2010, passim), except for the Netherlands which are from the relevant chapter in the present work.

circulation of 10,126 contos nominal.[21] Given the heavy discount on the face value of these notes – 12 to 60 percent during the RNW – and their normal circulation only in Lisbon and Porto, this would probably not have represented more than a 12 percent increment of the country's money supply[22] and would not solve the nation's financial problems. On the other hand, this was unlikely to unleash a "raging inflation lasting until the 1820s" for which it has been blamed (Macedo et al. 2001, 225). The inflationary surge in Portugal, which took place from 1790 to 1814, came mostly from Great Britain, Portugal's main trading partner. A glance at the London and Lisbon CPIs shows that in these years they moved along parallel tracks, except during the turbulent war years of 1810–1812.

5 The Economic Impact of War

It is difficult to stress sufficiently the extent of the harm suffered by the countries involved in the tragedy of the RNW. Yet the scale of human sacrifice, loss of output and destruction of physical assets that they endured may have diverged among them by not a little. While some underwent longer lasting conflicts, others experienced greater intensity and cost of war. Some nations were better endowed to resist the ravages of the conflict; others were less well provided for it. In this section, we try to unravel these threads and gain a clearer view of the effects of the conflagration on Portugal's economy by focusing on how its main sectors responded.

5.1 *Population*

As in all conflicts, an important aim of the RNW was to cause the greatest number of injuries or deaths to enemy forces, as well as to civilians who became involved in military operations. Aside from these two causes of population decline, a third was society's demographic reaction to conflict leading to lower propensities to marry and to procreate. All three made themselves felt on a substantial though varying scale. Calculating them with precision raises difficulties, however. To establish their respective magnitudes, we begin by assessing the first two and then infer the third as a residual.

21 Issued paper money is recorded in Godinho (1955, 210). The amount in circulation in 1802 can be found in Doc. 23, Caixa 83, Cartórios Avulsos, Erário Régio, Arquivo do Tribunal de Contas, Lisboa.

22 At the end of the 18th century the money supply was about 56,000 contos, according to Sousa (2006). For the discount rate, see Madureira (1997, 291–2).

Military casualties had particularly serious repercussions, the most obvious one being the loss of welfare associated with death and bereavement. A second was the cost of specific human capital which had to be replaced and trained afresh for the battle-field. A third stemmed from the fact that soldiers were adult males, mostly in the prime of life, and their deaths implied a severe negative premium in terms of labour supply. From 1808 to 1815, Portugal suffered a death toll on the battle field of some 43,990 men, of which two thirds were "deaths in action".[23] This total represented 1.5 percent of the entire population and 8 percent of the agricultural male labour force, and was quite a severe blow to the nation.[24] Such a rate of decimation – the equivalent per annum of a sixth of the front-line army – would appear to reflect the expected high intensity of conflictuality on Portuguese battlefields. In fact, only a third of these fatalities originated on the home front. The remaining two thirds perished in the course of field actions abroad, in Spain and France, following the expulsion of the French army from Portugal in 1811. Thus, paradoxically, the country which owed its independence so much to the assistance of foreign mercenaries, experienced its heaviest military losses on foreign battlegrounds in a mercenary capacity too.

Civilian casualties are much harder to quantify. Their causes - mainly disease, starvation, exposure, atrocities, friendly fire, public disorder, sackings and executions - are highly scattered throughout chronicles, local histories, archives, field reports and autobiographies. They are therefore much more difficult to compile.[25] The bulk of this multiplicity of events was on a minor scale but some were shockingly large, like the "carnage" of Évora (5,000 deaths), the sacking of Coimbra (3,000 deaths) and the crossing of the river Douro at Porto (8,000 deaths). Most harrowing of all was the demise of *circa* 80,000 rural non-combatants, in the provinces of Beira and Estremadura, as a result of Wellington's scorched earth policy during the third French invasion (Esdaile 2002).

Evidently, assembling such dispersed and heterogeneous records is not a satisfactory approach to the issue of non-military casualties. Some historians have sought to circumvent it by subtracting the country's stock of residents

23 Clodfelter (2017, 152–8). As a term of comparison, military action during the earlier War of Independence from Spain (1640–68) cost Portugal 12,300 lives.

24 The agricultural labour force of all ages on the eve of the war numbered circa 525,000 men (Reis 2005). If we consider a smaller base, however, consisting only of single men, between 16 and 30 years of age and legally subject to recruitment (Costa 2008, 7–8), this ratio would be 36 percent.

25 For an illustration in a single province (Beira), see Oliveira (2002, chapter 3).

at the end of the war from the one at the beginning as the means of obtaining an appropriate statistic. They have arrived at numbers ranging from 200 to 300,000 individuals for the period in question and we assume here an intermediate figure of 250,000 civilian deaths.[26] Although imprecise, it points to two conclusions. One is that the sacrifice of non-combatants vastly outnumbered that of combatants, which confirms the singular brutality often attributed to the Peninsular War. The other is that violent deaths on the Portuguese side altogether came to some 300,000 individuals, representing a staggering tenth of the country's inhabitants.

The demographics of war can yield further results on an annual basis thanks to recent new estimates of long-term Portugal's population (Palma et al. 2020). We start by considering two sets of annual statistics for this epoch (1808–15): actual and presumed peace-time yearly stocks. Given that in the previous half century the former fitted well a linear trend, it seems reasonable to use data from the latter to represent counterfactually the population in the absence of war. The next step is to calculate the differential between the two of them in war-time and thereby gauge the yearly total demographic decline comprising military mortality, civilian mortality and averted births due to socio-economic dislocation.

Figure 8.3 displays the results of this exercise and therefore allows a better understanding of the demographic decline during the war. A first conclusion is that in its eight years the RNW imposed an overall reduction of 685,950 inhabitants on Portugal.[27] In other words, population in these years went altogether off-trend by this amount. This was a brutal shock as it implied a drop of almost of a quarter of the national population (23.7 percent), and the disappearance on average of close to 100,000 persons per year. The second is that the larger part of this loss must be attributed to indirect demographic effects (57 percent) rather than to the direct consequences of bloodshed (43 percent). This supports the commonly heard notion that a severe disruption of human relations was inflicted by war on Portuguese society and stalled its reproductive potential considerably. The third is the unequal distribution over this period of the drop in population. During the first and most bitterly

26 Our sources are Broers (2015); Esdaile (2002); Godinho (1955); Gray (2011); Paquette (2013); and Payne (1973 vol.2). We have ignored two outliers: Marques (1973) and Serrão (2002) for, respectively, 500,000 and 400,000. National population at the time was around 2.885 million inhabitants (Palma et al. 2020).

27 In total, the three components were 44,900 military deaths, 250,000 civilian deaths and 391,000 non-births.

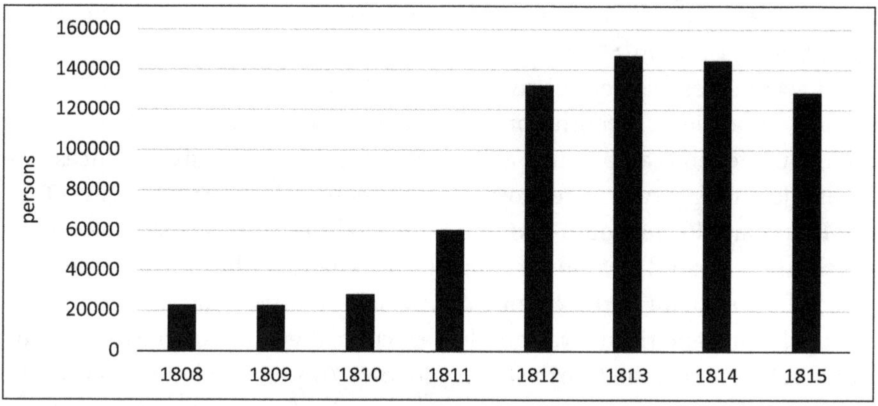

FIGURE 8.3 Yearly population losses (number of persons), 1808–1815
SOURCES: PALMA ET AL. (2020); AND TEXT

fought half of the struggle (1808–1811), around 134,000 lives were lost. These were probably mostly deaths by violence, since in the following four years military activity and public disorder were much less significant.[28] In the second half of the RNW, population fell by 551,000 but less as a consequence of actual demises than because of demographic shortfall imposed by falling marriage and fertility rates.

5.2 *Agriculture*

There is a strong consensus that the negative impact of the RNW on the economy of Portugal was felt principally in agriculture (Birmingham 1993; Caetano 2009; Costa et al. 2016; Marques 2002; Pedreira, 1987; Serrão 2002). It was the largest sector, employing some two-thirds of the labour force and, undoubtedly, satisfying the largest share of the nation's expenditure. At the same time, husbandry had become a critical element in international conflict, both as a source of supply to keep armies moving and fighting, and, as a major military goal, to weaken enemy capability on and off the battle field. As a result, the sector endured massive destruction, pillage and confiscation, and substantial losses and displacement of its workforce. At the end of the war, in the words of the Council of the Regency, all that was left was an "universal devastation of fields, crops, cattle and tools, owing to the destruction

28 There is no way of estimating the quantity of deaths arising from banditry and unstructured rural violence.

or theft of everything the peasants had possessed, as well as to the deaths of a great many of them".[29]

An accurate assessment of such a bleak picture of waste and desolation is not easy to achieve, a central problem being that the impact of war was far from homogeneous across time and space. Of the country's six provinces, two - Alentejo and Algarve - were mostly spared these ordeals. Another two - Trás-os-Montes and Entre-Douro-e Minho - were only affected during the comparatively short second Invasion (see table 8.1). The main brunt of the destruction fell upon Beira and Extremadura, which endured most of the fighting during the first and third invasions. In particular, they suffered the devastation wrought by the scorched earth strategy followed during the latter. None of the six provinces can therefore serve as an exemplar for the rest and there is a risk of the most harrowing depictions of the impact of war overestimating the actual losses experienced by agriculture.[30]

Some cases of this are worthy of consideration. Port wine, Portugal's principal export, was one of them. In spite of significant military action in Trás-os-Montes, where its production was concentrated, none of the three invasions caused "any more than minimal physical and economic suffering" (Bennett 1992, 17).[31] Several factors account for this. One was the broken terrain of the region and its miserable roads, which kept the French away from the vineyards. Another was the absence, in spite of the conflict, of labour shortages owing to minimal recruitment requirements for the local militias of the relatively peaceful Upper Douro Valley. A third was the tradition of seasonal labour from Galicia, which shielded port farmers from labour dislocation. Finally, port wine sales, despite its international commodity status, were sustained thanks to increased consumption by the British expeditionary force and by increased demand in the parts of the country where vineyards had been ravaged.

Two further illustrations of how qualitively-based conjectures can be quantitatively misleading are olive oil and livestock.[32] The former was a perenial crop with a wide but unequal presence throughout the country. Balbi (1822

29 From the proclamation of 30th March, 1811, at the end of the last invasion. Cited in Serrão (2002 VII, 95).

30 We follow here the accounts of military action and its consequences by Serrão (2002 vol.VII, 241–59) and Soriano (1866–90, passim). The detailed description of the war in the province of Beira by Oliveira (2002) illustrates the high level of suffering of this region but does not allow an extrapolation to the rest of the country.

31 Vintage totals suitable for shipment averaged 52,590 pipes in 1781–1806 compared with wartime 52,917 pipes in 1807–1815 (Bennett 1992, 29).

32 A mid-nineteenth century estimate puts the total share of these two sectors of agriculture at 35 percent of gross output (Reis 2000, 39).

[2004] I, 148) observed that many olive trees had been uprooted by soldiers from both sides in search of fuel, suggesting an important sector which was razed country-wide during the French wars. In fact, most of Portugal's olive oil did not come from the most war-torn provinces but from Alentejo and Algarve, which were spared this fate. A strong contraction of this commodity seems unlikely and potentially distortive of the national picture.

With livestock, the backbone of the agrarian system and a key target in wartime, a similar analysis is possible. By all accounts, oxen, donkeys, horses and mules became scarce and this represented a serious obstacle to trade, transport and agricultural outpt. Unusually for this time, some data are available and allow an assessment of how great was this "devastation". At the time of the first invasion, the country's stock of oxen was estimated at 400,000 units, of which two-thirds were used for traction and the remainder consumed as meat. By 1813, it had suffered a nation-wide decline of 64,000 teams (i.e. 128,000 units). This was a severe blow, but the remaining 272,000 heads of cattle left at the end of the war can hardly correspond to the "total destruction" which Campos e Mesquita (1990 [1825?], 317), a high official at the time, spoke of in his "Memoir on the Present Destruction of our Herds of Cattle".

The best way to overcome these problems is by means of a demand-function approach. This technique combines market-price and wage series[33] and allows us to estimate with some accuracy yearly variations in per capita gross agricultural output. The result for Portugal 1750–1850 is displayed in figure 8.4. It shows both gross production at constant prices (hard line), but also its long-run trend line (dotted line). Given its good overall adherence, we assume that the latter represents fairly well the underlying structural behaviour of Portuguese agriculture. Together, they depict the historical reality of a century of steady decline and the impact of non-systemic shocks, such as climate, extraordinary market events and war.

We begin by concentrating on the last of these factors. From 1808 to 1815, other things being equal, the consistently negative difference, in each year, between the trend and the production lines, represents the loss to the primary sector arising from the devastation of war in that interval. For further clarity, these differentials are reproduced in figure 8.5 as percentages of total yearly output. They enable us to reach several conclusions. The most important is

33 The methodology rests on the assumption that food consumption will roughly equal food production. For a discussion of its application to Portugal in the interval 1500 to 1850, see Reis (2017). Reasons for not resorting in our case to the alternative quantitative approach, based on tithe data, are considered there too. See Alvarez-Nogal et al. (2016) for the latter approach in the case of Spain.

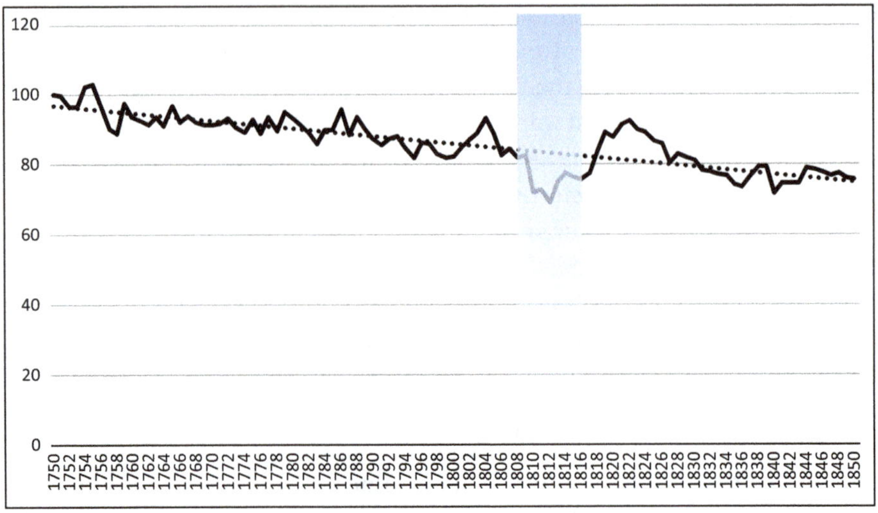

FIGURE 8.4 Real gross agricultural output per capita (1750 =100) (1750–1850)
Note: linear trend, dotted line. Shadowed Area = War Period
SOURCE: REIS (2017)

that the size of the aggregate loss accumulated over the entire eight-year war period comes to the equivalent to 1.35 years' worth of annual agricultural output. It confirms that, although the country may not have been entirely razed to the ground during the RNW, as so often claimed, it suffered considerable devastation nevertheless. Secondly, we must note that there were production shortfalls in every year of war but, not surprisingly, their extent varied quite significantly, with the intensity of the conflict. The worst years of war - 1810, 1811 and 1812 - correspond to the largest material damages.[34] These were double or triple the size of the losses suffered in 1808 and 1809, the far milder years of the first two French invasions. In 1813, 1814 and 1815, in the absence of significant military action within Portugal, levels of destruction retreated considerably. Our third finding is that this steady lessening of war damage, from 1813, opened the way to a fairly early return – by 1818 - of Portuguese agriculture to its pre-war trend.[35]

Bearing in mind variations in meteorological conditions and their influence on farming results, we have now to consider whether our indicator of war

34 This is corroborated by the particularly heavy imports of foodstuffs in 1811 and 1812. See Pedreira (1994, 572).

35 According to Serrão (2002 VII, 74–5), this prompt agricultural recovery was possible because it did not require massive amounts of capital. Most of the area under cultivation in Portugal was not of perennial crops, and therefore did not call for heavy investments.

FIGURE 8.5 Annual agricultural losses as percentage of output (1808–1815)
SOURCE: REIS (2017)

losses ought to be modified as a consequence. Although data for average rainfall and temperature exist for the whole period (Freire and Lains 2017, appendices A1 and A2), we are unable to estimate with any precision their effects on production. Based on contemporary reports, we can only distinguish, agriculturally "good years" from "bad" ones and make the appropriate adjustments. In figure 8.5, the latter - five years - would be graphically smaller than as represented, while the former – three years - would be the opposite.[36] As a result the corrected appearance of figure 8.5 would look somewhat less pronounced.

5.3 *Industry*

In the late eighteenth century, manufacturing occupied a subordinate position in the economy of Portugal but was flourishing. According to historiographic tradition, a few years later the French invasions and "fatal" trade policies imposed by Britain had ruined it for a long time to come (Balbi 1822; Sideri 1978). Subsequent research by Lains (2005), Madureira (1997) and Pedreira (2005), however, has challenged this pessimistic and inaccurate view of events.

Although lack of data precludes any rigorous assessment, the approximate 156,000 workers then employed in industry - the equivalent of 15 percent of total labour - gives support to the notion of this limited scale (Reis 2005, 123). Most of industry used simple technology, was structured around domestic

36 Consensually, the "bad" years were 1807–12 and the "good" ones, 1813–15. See Serrão (2002, VII, 149); Oliveira (2002, 288); and Sherwig (1969, 229)).

and workshop forms of organisation and satisfied the needs of a low income, small-town or rural population. In contrast, the minority of urban, well-off or noble consumers satisfied their needs mainly by importation or by resorting to domestic substitutes.

A "modern" component consisting of protected "royal factories" had begun to emerge in the 1760s under a vigorous mercantilist program of state intervention. From a total of 56 in the 1770s, they reached 412 establishments during the 1790s (Pedreira 2005). The aim was to encourage some import-substitution, mainly of luxury goods, large scale enterprises with high capital intensity, and encourage technical progress (Madureira 1997; Pedreira 2005; Costa et al. 2016). By prohibiting manufactures in overseas territories and closing their markets to foreign goods, exports of Portuguese goods from this sector to the colonies boomed. At their peak, in 1799 (Pedreira 2000, 847) this flow reached a value of 5,700 contos, or roughly 3 percent of GDP. At this date, factories were employing close to 10 percent of industrial labour. Another 15 to 40,000 workers were in workshops, and home-based production probably absorbed the remaining 80 to 120,000.[37]

The war had several negative consequences for Portuguese industry. The most important was allegedly the destruction of physical capital carried out by the enemy, but at times also by allied forces and, even by civilian marauders. Whether an act of belligerence or of self-interest, reputedly many manufacturing plants were dismantled, demolished or torched, and tools, stocks of raw materials and finished goods were stolen and sold. (Soriano 1866–90; Marques 2002; Serrão 2002). Examples abound and their distribution is quite uneven. The region of Estremadura is often cited in this respect. With its 24 factories producing leather, iron goods and cotton textiles at locations not far distant from Lisbon, it was among the hardest hit. In the district capital of Santarém, where Massena set up his headquarters for a while, only 3 out of 17 tanneries survived. Nearby in Alcobaça, one of the country's largest textile mills was burnt to the ground by the same French troops (Custódio 1996). Further north, into Beira, the principal industrial buildings of Covilhã, the chief centre for industrial woollen production in Portugal, were similarly devastated.[38]

The heterogeneity and dispersion of the industrial sector inevitably make the evaluation of this wave of destruction problematic. Production data are unavailable but occasional reports provide tallies of factories and assessments

37 These calculations are based on Pedreira (2005) and Reis (2005) and must be used with caution.

38 Other industrial centres around the country which suffered similar fates are described in (Pedreira 1994, 320–3).

TABLE 8.3 Factories in Portugal and their condition in 1811–13

Condition	Number
Progressive	140
Decadent	252
Stationary	36
Inactive	14
Burnt-down	1
Start-up	5
No account	72
Total	520

SOURCE: NEVES (1984)
Note: The meanings of the "conditions" are described in the text.

of their respective conditions, which are helpful since they are official and reasonably reliable. The results of the one shown in table 8.3 were compiled between 1811 and 1813, when the war was at its height, and list 520 establishments in Portugal at that time. They allow two conclusions to be drawn. The first is that the number of factories in existence by the end of the invasions was similar or possibly larger than the stock before the conflict began. This is surprising considering the historiography, and suggests either that the depredations of war were less intense than has been claimed, or that they were relatively easy to recover from. In any case, either hypothesis contradicts to some extent the traditional narrative.[39] The second finding is the lack of economic health displayed by these firms once the fighting was over. Only one third of them were doing well ("progressive"). The remaining two-thirds were either "decadent", "stationary" or "inactive". The issue this raises is whether this poor performance was a consequence of the destruction of physical capital, or should be attributed instead to other negative side-effects of the war, which raised production costs and reduced output.

We begin by considering two indirect cost-raising constraints on output which have often been to the fore in the literature, namely input shortages. The first was lack of manpower caused directly by the war and indirectly by the

39 Interestingly, only one burnt-down factory is mentioned in the list, again a contradiction with the traditional view.

fear of military recruitment, reinforced, in the case of artisans, by their flight to Brazil with the Royal Court.[40] Evidence is scarce but two clues raise doubts regarding this influence. One is that of the 380 factories listed in table 8.3, which were "decadent" or worse, only 4 attributed this to a lack of workers. The other is the evolution of the real wage of skilled operatives. This was 20 percent lower between 1808 and 1814 than in the half dozen years preceding the onset of the French invasions. The implication is that industry's problem may not have been one of short labour supply.[41] The second constraint was the scarcity of imported raw materials, also reportedly a common cause of trouble for industries beset by international conflict. In the case of Portugal, the index of their import prices relative to that of imported manufactures during the war was on average 70 percent of the mean of the preceding peacetime figure.[42] Thus, in both cases there was actually a relative abundance and cheapness of inputs and, if anything, this should have been beneficial to industrial performance.

We turn now to the adverse impact of war as viewed by the demand for industrial products. One aspect is the collapse of sales of Portuguese manufactures to the Brazilian market, which had become highly significant for the home industry before 1808. This, it has been claimed, was the consequence of two war-time economic adjustments imposed by Britain on her ally. One was the opening of Brazilian ports to friendly nations, in 1808, which ended the colonial pact. The other was the Luso-British treaty of 1810, conceding British goods most-favoured-nation status and therefore exposing less competitive Portuguese textiles, hats and ironmongery to them (Balbi 1822 I, 444; Costa 2016, 232). In reality, the momentous reduction in these exports had started long before the start of the RNW and reached its nadir of 1600 contos, in 1807, as hostilities broke out. Thereafter, this variable stabilized for the duration of the war (Pedreira 2000, 847). The conclusion to be drawn is that it was neither the war, nor associated shifts in trade policy which eroded Brazil's demand for the products of Portuguese industrialization. Rather it was growing British technological and commercial advantage which dealt this decisive blow and overwhelmed Portuguese competition, as some have argued (Macedo 1990, 238; Madureira 1997, 319; Cordeiro 2003, 658).

40 According to Marques (2002, 114) this movement reached a total of 40,000 people. See also Soriano (1866–90 vol.II, 444).

41 Based on data for four main cities in the PWR-Portugal data base. Similar evidence has been collected by Madureira (1997).

42 Calculation based on Madureira (1997, appendix to chapter 8). The materials considered for this index are skins, raw wool, linen and silk, leather, coal and iron.

The most important influence in causing a slump in industrial performance appears, however, to have been the reduction of domestic demand (Pedreira 1987, 572; Lains 2005, 264). This related, directly, to the contraction of GDP at this time and, secondly, to the parlous state of internal commercial circuits owing to the dislocation of war. How these factors are quantified is discussed below, in sections 5.4 and 6.2, respectively. In the meantime, and assuming a constant income-elasticity of demand over the period, we may suppose that between 1808 and 1815 industry probably fell, in tandem with GDP, by at least an average 7 percent a year. Such a strong impact would have been even greater if distributional inefficiencies had arisen. In reality, they did not, as we shall see below. Imports of foreign goods, would have had a similar detrimental effect on industry, but the available evidence suggests that this did not displace domestic production significantly, contrary to expectation.[43]

Altogether, industry remained a small part of the economy and the harm done to it during the Peninsular war does not seem much out of line with what happened to the rest of the economy. This finding is based, however, on the activity of "factories", which did not represent the sector as a whole. Yet Lains (2005) and Pedreira (1994) have come to the view that in fact there was no great divergence between all three subsectors, either during wartime, or during the slow but steady post-war recovery of Portuguese manufacturing. It would seem that pre-war levels were reached by 1818 (Pedreira, 1987).[44]

5.4 *Transport and Trade*

Difficulties with internal transport and trade have long been considered a major problem for Portugal's economy. On the eve of the war, French engineers recognized this when preparing the overland invasion, and Napoleon warned that the state of the roads threatened the advance of his troops (Vicente, 1983). Both the latter and the Allied armies went on to make matters a great deal worse by obstructing rivers and roads with spoils and broken carts, destroying bridges and warehouses, and requisitioning labour, draught animals and vehicles (Serrão 2002 VII, 249). Historians have concluded that, by the end of the RNW, the infrastructure was "severely damaged" (Paquette 2013, 92), "almost

43 This is based on a national volume index of imported manufactures for two periods - 1803–7 and 1809–1815 - estimated by Madureira (1997, 473). It does not mean that there were no significant regional differences. For example, Porto's industry suffered a lot from British competition according to Cordeiro (2003, 669–70).

44 Notwithstanding, Pedreira (1994, 326) holds, confusingly, that industry suffered a "collapse".

impossible to rebuild" (Broers 2015, 213) and "domestic trade had practically reached a point of paralysis" (Pedreira 1994, 323).

Evidence for such obstacles and their economic impact is mostly anecdotal and difficult to treat systematically. Nevertheless, commodity market convergence across the country is amenable to quantification and provides a measure of national economic efficiency. Recent research (Federico, Schulze and Volckart 2021) has tracked this indicator across Europe for the long term, using the coefficient of variation (CV) of wheat prices in a variety of markets. We emulate this for Portugal's main wheat markets - Lisbon, Porto, Coimbra and Évora - with the results being presented in figure 8.6.

It is important to note that, in the early years of the RNW (1793–1800), this index remained fairly stable and was similar to the long second half of the eighteenth century. We conclude that during these years the infrastructure was unchanged and, thanks to the country's neutrality, coastal shipping, a key factor in the domestic circulation of goods, was not harassed by hostile shipping (Matos 1980; Pedreira 1994, 123–4). In contrast, during the run-up to the French invasions (1801–1807), market disintegration rose considerably as expressed by a 34 percent rise of the CV index. Since the road network still remained unchanged and unaffected by war on land, we presume this increase was due to the disturbance of coastal shipping. During the 1808–1815 "total war" epoch, our statistic rose considerably, by a further 18 percent. By this time, the Royal

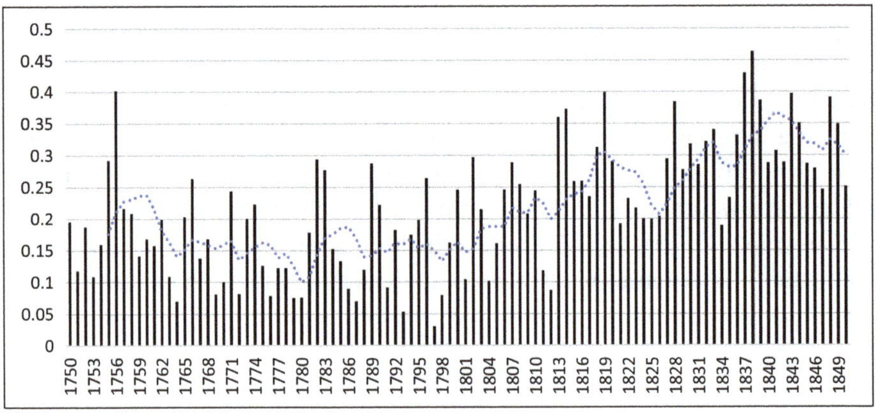

FIGURE 8.6 Coefficient of variation of wheat prices (1750–1850)
Note: the cities represented are Lisbon, Porto, Coimbra and Évora. Dotted line = 5-year moving average.
SOURCES: WHEAT PRICES FROM PWR-PORTUGAL DATA BASE: HTTP://PWR-PORTUGAL.ICS.UL.PT/?PAGE_ID=31

Navy was protecting Portugal's shores, and so the disturbance of internal communications must be ascribed to disruption of overland communications. The annual data confirm the historical narrative produced by Serrão from official announcements (2002 VII, 102–19). By the end of the war, heavy infrastructural damage had reportedly accumulated cross the country and the CV for the price of wheat, a bulky commodity, had risen to a level 44 percent above the start of the war.

Towards the end of the Ancien Regime, Portugal's external trade soared. Exports and imports roughly quadrupled (nominal values) between the 1770s and a peak in 1801.[45] At the latter point, their respective average ratios to GDP attained remarkable levels for the time - 14.7 and 12.6 percent - and Portugal enjoyed its first surplus of the eighteenth century on current account.[46] Two factors contributed significantly to this performance. Portugal's neutrality favoured its international trade and Brazil responded fully to the strong European demand for cotton, sugar and tobacco (Cruz 2015). By the turn of the century, the economic impact of the empire on the metropolis had become substantial and has been calculated recently as equal to 22 percent of the real wage of Portugal (Costa et al. 2015).[47]

It has often been held that the RNW shook Portugal's trade to its foundations. Indeed, between 1808 and 1815, "war period" exports plus imports fell on average to 45 percent of their "neutrality" level (1796–1807), a decline of 27,400 contos or 15.0 percent of GDP. The causes and consequences of this reversal have been the object of much debate, particularly with regard to the roots of the country's economic backwardness (Alexandre 1993; Costa et al. 2016; Pedreira 1994; Caetano 2008). To understand this causality, we break down the impact of its determinants, focusing on exports alone, where the inter-action between war and foreign trade is easier to perceive.

The first moment in this train of events was the extension of the Berlin decree to Portugal and the attempt to subject the country to the Continental

45 All values in this section are nominal. Despite the excellent work on deflation of exports and imports by Madureira (1997), this cannot be used in the present exercise.

46 All foreign trade data are from Alexandre (1993), Costa et al. (2016), Pedreira (2000), and also kindly supplied by Leonor Freire Costa. GDP is from Palma and Reis (2019). "Exports" here include: Portuguese exports to other nations; re-exports of Brazilian commodities to other nations; and re-exports from Portugal to Brazil (comprising agricultural products, manufactures from other nations sent via Portugal and Portuguese manufactures). "Imports" includes domestic imports from other nations and imports from Brazil for re-export. For a description of sources for Portuguese foreign trade, see Moreira (2013, 2015).

47 Using the same yardstick, the next most successful nation was England, with a figure of 16 percent. In 1750, the figure for Portugal was 17 percent.

Blockade (Pedreira and Costa 2009). This implied two actions by France. One was that no part of Europe under Napoleonic rule or influence should import either Portuguese products or re-exports from its American colony. Although French rule over Portugal never went far, this imposition was effective because the former kept control throughout the continent over the points of entry for Brazilian goods. The second was to deny access to Portugal's coast and thus prevent trade by France with Britain and Brazil. This proved unsuccessful, however, even while France occupied Portugal territorially, owing to Britain's naval might.[48] Sales by Portugal of mostly Brazilian commodities to continental states were denied to these markets and consequently plummeted. This loss can be measured by the difference between their average export flows in the "neutrality" and the "war periods", respectively. It comes on average to 7,800 contos a year and represents 4.3 percent of GDP, or 69.2 percent of its pre-1808 level.

The second war-related change in Portugal's foreign trade framework was the drastic recasting of Anglo-Portuguese relations between 1808 and 1810. Portugal relinquished its colonial pact and Britain gained long term direct access to the Brazilian market.[49] Unrestricted entry into all Portuguese ports was granted to "friendly nations" for shipping and for goods. Greatly reduced tariffs were applied on equal terms and freedom of circulation and establishment for the nationals of these states were allowed too. These arrangements were considered deeply asymmetric by Portugal but may have been less skewed than appeared. The reason is that, in return, Britain had to commit, in perpetuity, to maintain Portugal's independence in Europe and South America and keep the House of Bragança on the throne. It also pledged exceptionally generous subsidies to help defray the cost of Portugal's current war against France.[50]

The repercussions of these changes can be calculated as was done above regarding the Continental Blockade. We consider five categories of exports. In the case of direct commercial links with "other powers" - largely Britain - there was hardly any alteration. Food products sent to Brazil also resisted the

48 O'Rourke's (2007) test to verify the effectiveness of naval blockades during this era is useful here. Portuguese price data confirm that, like Britain, it enjoyed a high degree of international market integration during 1808–1815 and was thus not much affected by the French blockade.

49 The main legal instruments here comprised the 1808 declaration opening the ports of Brazil; and the 1810 Anglo-Portuguese Treaties for Trade and Navigation, and Friendship and Alliance. See Soriano (1866–90, I, 576–8 and II, 416).

50 See above, section 3. Significantly, at the Vienna Congress, Britain blocked a threat to hand Portugal over to Spain so that Russia might receive territory in Italy in exchange. Pedreira and Costa 2009, 288).

storm well, with a yearly export loss of just under 500 contos, representing a drop of 30 percent on the "neutrality period" average. In contrast, owing to Britain's discrimination in favour of its own colonial commodities, Brazilian re-exports to its ally suffered a fall of 70 percent relative to the pre-war level. This amounted to 2,100 contos, or 1.1 percent of GDP.[51] Finally, competition in the newly opened Brazilian market for manufactures was where Portugal suffered the most owing to Britain's industrial superiority (Cardoso 2013). This occurred in two ways. One was a drastic shrinkage of 70 percent between the two sub-periods in the rubric "products of the factories of the Kingdom", totalling 2,280 contos a year.[52] The other was a decline in Portuguese re-exports of British manufactures to Brazil which formerly, under the colonial pact, had been obliged to proceed via the metropolis. Between 1808 and 1815, this category of re-exports fell precipitously, to 15 percent of the pre-war period, and the corresponding shortfall of 2,549 contos was equivalent to 1.4 percent of GDP.[53]

Altogether, "this disintegration of its colonial system", represented for Portugal annual export losses of 16,050 contos, half of which due to hostile French action and the other half, to diplomatic pressure from Britain. This was close to a tenth of GDP and over a half (59 per cent) of the country's exports during the prosperous years preceding the onset of the conflict. Amongst all the burdens of war, was this the greatest of them all? According to recent research (Costa et al 2016), the impact of Portugal's trade concessions, eventually leading to the independence of Brazil in 1822, was enormous and "probably" greater than the value of all the demographic, military, agricultural and other damages inflicted by the RNW. Although undoubtedly a considerable figure, it is impossible that it reached such a level. Merely in terms of global military expenditure by Allied forces during the war years (see table 8.2 above), the two amounts come close, but military expenditure (17,349) was greater. If we take into account only Portugal's share in the total military expenditure, namely 6,332 contos a year, then the country's foreign trade losses emerge, impressively, as about two and a half times greater. This does not, however, save the earlier point.[54]

51 Before 1808, Brazilian commodities were shipped via the metropolis, rather than directly to European ports, which made them dearer by 40 percent.

52 Portuguese manufactures were losing market share in Brazil significantly already in 1805, before ports became "free". This suggests that even if the colonial pact had continued, they might not have resisted.

53 Immediately upon the opening of the ports, a swarm of British merchants rushed to Brazil, backed by 90 ships. In 1810, this rose to 442 ships (Cardoso 2013, 96).

54 A major issue in the historiography of Anglo-Portuguese relations during the RNW is which of the partners reaped the most from the trade-off? In purely economic terms,

A different approach is proposed by Pedreira (1994, 362–6). Instead of assessing each calamity by matching them with sectoral yardsticks, as in several instances above, it adopts a macroeconomic perspective and treats the problem counterfactually. The question is by how much would Portuguese GDP have increased had there been no fall in exports? The 8 percent result of this estimation is not implausible in the context of such studies (Palma 2016), but has limitations. The chief one is methodological. The model employed is static and fails to give the more accurate answer that a dynamic one would. Indeed, the problem is that dynamic models for the RNW period have not been developed for this context and suitable data for doing so are probably unavailable.[55] A further objection concerns the period of analysis, which encompasses far more than the war years, in fact 1796–1808 *versus* 1827.

6 Conclusions

During the great wave of social, economic and political change which swept Continental Europe from the Ancien Regime to the establishment of the Liberal era, the response of RNW belligerents varied considerably. Macroeconomically, some (France, Germany and Sweden) performed well, while others (Italy and Spain) did so only moderately. Portugal languished and under-performed.[56] In the critical matter of institutional change, its achievement was also less than impressive, both as a late comer and because of the relative unsuccess of these reforms.

6.1 *Portugal's Total War Damage*

The economic losses caused by the Napoleonic conflict have long been considered decisive for understanding Portugal's long-term development. Estimating them in the aggregate must therefore be our next objective. We use as a yardstick the real per capita GDP series provided by Palma and Reis (2019), which covers the years of the war, as well as the pre-and post-bellum epochs. Figure 8.7 displays the profile of this variable from the mid-18th to the mid-19th centuries,

the present findings allow us to conclude that the winner was Portugal. Whilst Britain's yearly gains in the Brazilian market after 1808 totalled around 4,800 contos on average, Portugal received in return a yearly average of 11,017 contos in cash and military aid, i.e. twice as great.

55 The dynamic model employed by Costa et al (2015) and Palma (2016) for similar purposes was borrowed from Allen (2003) but cannot be applied to the time frame we are considering here.

56 These national growth evaluations, in international GK dollars, are from Palma and Reis (2019, 500).

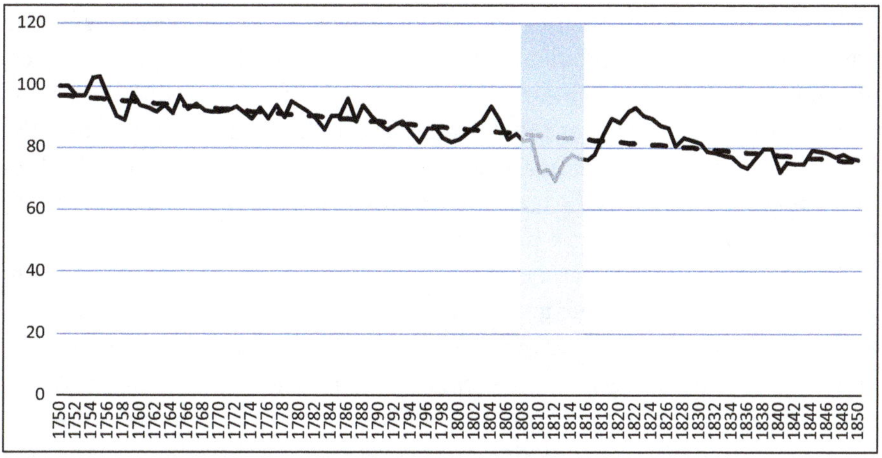

FIGURE 8.7 Portuguese real GDP per capita (1750=100) (1750–1815)
Note: linear trend, dotted line. Shadowed Area = War Period.
SOURCE: PALMA AND REIS (2019)

as well as its trend line. Worthy of note are its long-run downward sloping structural trend and the significant episode of war-induced disruption between 1808 and 1815 (shaded in the figure). The negative impact of the conflict can thus be clearly perceived although not rigorously quantified.

To achieve the latter, we measure the impact on the economy of a year of military struggle as the difference between each year's actual output, which is available to us, and that which would have materialized had peace prevailed. There are two approaches to the latter. One is to take year-on-year changes in

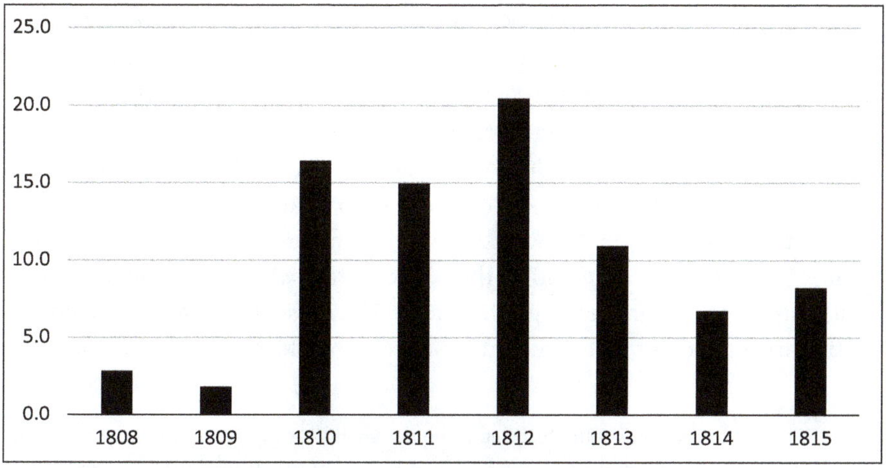

FIGURE 8.8 Annual losses from war as a percentage of GDP (1808–1815)
SOURCES: PALMA AND REIS (2019)

real per capita GDP and assume that they correspond to the variations in output due to warfare. The problem with this method is that it ignores the effects of combat carried over from earlier years. This would entail an underestimate. The alternative is to use, for the duration of war, the annual figures from the GDP pc trend as a proxy for non-wartime output. Subtracting historical values from these should give us the measure we seek.[57] The differentials obtained are then normalized by reference to actual GDP pc.

Adding up the yearly parcels for the duration of the conflict allows us to conclude that the aggregate damage inflicted on the Portuguese economy was equivalent to nearly a full year's real pc GDP (82 percent), i.e. close to 10 percent annually. This was a huge setback – probably unparalleled in the country's history - and one made all the harder by the extreme ups-and-downs endured for almost a decade by the population. Figure 8.8 displays these fluctuations: the light damage of the early years (1808 and 1809); the worsening consequences of the war (1810 and 1811), the escalation to a severe 20 percent loss in a single year (1812), and the ensuing winding down towards peace (1813, 1814 and 1815).

To evaluate the seriousness of this eight-year impact, we resort to the same standard as was employed in section 3 based on the negative effect of the Lisbon 1755 earthquake. The eight years between 1757 and 1764 are the term of reference we consider now. The cumulative loss sustained from this natural calamity can be gauged roughly as 20.0 percent of a year's real GDP pc. Over the same interval, the impact of the man-made RNW tragedy was thus four times greater than the outcome of the "most shattering natural phenomenon to disturb Europe's peace of mind in the eighteenth century" (Birmingham 1993, 73).

6.2 *A Missed Opportunity, 1815–1825?*

In the early post-war years, expectations regarding Portugal's future had reason to be pessimistic. As the regency informed the absent king in 1818 the country was "bankrupt", had suffered an extraordinary flight of capital and the crown's coffers were "exhausted".[58] The merchant marine was "void" of ships, trade was profoundly "decadent" and industry was "bereft" of skilled labour which, in the meantime, had fled overseas. Thousands of farm and manufacturing hands were without occupation. Notwithstanding, the first decade of peace displayed clear signs of reversal, indicating that, by contrast with earlier times, significantly better opportunities might lie ahead. The most challenging was the revolutionary movement which set out, in 1820, to transform the country's ancient

57 We consider this procedure justified given the good long-run fit between the trend and the output variable; and the absence, until 1815, of other structural shocks besides the war.

58 Cited in Caetano (2008), 38–41.

form of government into a modern liberal monarchy. Its founding fathers (the *vintistas*) sought to recover two things: the ancient freedoms of the Portuguese nation, long smothered by Absolutism; and the country's past prosperity, for centuries stifled by the straightjacket of the Ancien Regime (Cardoso, 2005). Following two years of frantic legislation – 1821 and 1822 - by an independently elected assembly, a modern constitution was approved. It vested sovereignty in the nation, conferred full equality before the law for all, and reduced the monarch to a mere head of the executive, on a par with the legislative and judicial branches. In the meantime, a stream of ordinary laws endeavoured to wipe out seigneurialism, invigorate the economy and subject it to the discipline of market forces.[59]

The beneficial effects of these transformations have yet to be properly assessed. In any case, in the 1820s they were probably going to be of limited impact by comparison with the gains of the many states of Europe which joined the wave of Napoleonic reforms some ten to twenty-five years earlier than Portugal (Hill 1936). Whilst these had time to consolidate such institutional improvements, the case of Portugal was entirely different owing to the special nature of its war with France. Having been subjected to no more than a short and cursory occupation, Portugal missed out on the "French treatment" which many other nations underwent and which endowed them with robust alien modern institutions.[60] Instead, from 1808 to 1820 it was a British protectorate, strongly influenced by Tory officers and diplomats who favoured the "old order" and wished to postpone "any serious attempt at renewed revolution" (Birmingham 1993, 105).

In the absence of a strong central power, the Portuguese constitutional outcome, in 1822, could be no more than a fragile equilibrium of conflicting social, ideological and economic forces let loose by an eight-year-long bitter war. Unavoidably, it was a patchwork of contradictions, incapable of imposing radical change. The Liberals had to accept that tithes and Church lands, for them a key issue, would remain intact; and that entail would be preserved, to ensure the economic might of the high nobility in the service of the traditional

59 The Portuguese constitution of 1822 was inspired by the radical Cadiz one of 1812, and has been described by Marques (2002, 240) as "quasi republican".

60 The "French treatment" described by Acemoglu et al (2011) was the set of revolutionary reforms of territories invaded by or ruled through satellite states by France for different periods between 1793 and 1815. The authors conclude that the longer such occupations lasted, the better the economic consequences from them.

monarchy.[61] Despite these and other concessions, in less than a year, the constitutional Liberal reforms had been fully repealed by the king, under pressure from internal reactionary forces and from France and absolutist Spain (Marques 2002, 564–6; Monteiro 2013, 60–2, 193). It had not taken long for Portugal to return to the Ancien Regime, from which it was to emerge again, in a far more radical guise, in the 1830s (Amaral 2012).

The positive experience enjoyed by the Portuguese economy during this initial phase of peace was no less important than its institutional reforms. Despite obvious handicaps, it now embarked on a clear upward trend, with GDP per capita at constant prices rising steadily at 1.28 percent a year during the time span under consideration. This compared well, both internationally and relatively to previous Portuguese growth episodes: 0.3 percent growth a year from 1793 to 1807; and, during the Napoleonic epoch, at -1,2 percent (Palma and Reis 2019).[62] Given the length and intensity of the preceding war, it seems likely that this brisk recovery was essentially a catch-up process led by the primary sector but with little productive intensification. Given the country's notorious scarcity of physical and human capital, this would be unsurprising.[63]

Much of this agriculture-based recovery was due to a significant re-absorption by this sector of large amounts of land abandoned in the course of the war. After the departure of the French, the authorities encouraged this trend, which involved thousands of erstwhile cultivators in every region (Serrão 2002, 98–112 and 257–63). Undoubtedly it also helped the impressive 20 percent gain in food output per capita achieved in these ten years (Reis 2017, 209–10). This was stimulated also by trade policies, which did not infringe Portugal's recent treaties, to protect farming with tariffs which stimulated production of grain, flour and, animal products. These were of little use, however, to wine producers, a critical sector for Portugal (Ferreira 1991; Justino 1986; Martins 1998).

The pacification of rural Portugal, after the turmoil of the war, has not attracted much the attention of historians, yet it was a significant factor of

61 On the other hand, many Liberals were adamantly against bi-cameralism and giving the King the right of veto on laws approved by Parliament, both of which were cherished by traditionalists.

62 This positive view of post-war Portuguese growth revises the long-standing historiographic consensus based on price movements and Annales-type cyclical history. According to the latter, the 1820 revolution occurred in the midst of a severe economic crisis and a sharp decline in prices. See Godinho (1955); Marques (2002); Mendes (1985); and Justino (1986).

63 Balbi (1822), a well-informed Italian observer who wrote in 1821, never mentioned either productive difficulties or structural changes during this post-war agricultural revival.

agricultural progress, although a hard one to appraise.[64] By limiting uncertainty, it encouraged investment in farming, made markets more efficient and reduced transport costs. All of this is easily gathered from the data in figure 8.6 which reflect with clarity the rapid integration during these years of internal commodity markets. In the first five years of peace, social appeasement, not surprisingly, seems to have been harder to attain. After 1820, on the other hand, conditions clearly improved in this respect, particularly since transport infrastructure hardly changed. The 30 percent fall in the wheat CV-index just before the Liberal regime began to crumble provides robust evidence of this.

Other salient aspects of the real economy, counted for little in the present calculus regarding Portugal's long-term economic prospects. Manufacturing continued to serve mostly the domestic market, having lost a large part of the Brazilian one, and modern factories continued to be few and externally uncompetitive (Costa et al. 2016). As a result, foreign trade did not recover from the losses caused by the opening of colonial markets (Madureira 1997).

Finally, public finance sounded a worrying note, despite the absence of major wars or occupying armies. Although this was not yet irreparable, heavier burdens of public deficits and public debt were pointing in this direction. The former, which had averaged circa 300 contos between 1796 and 1815, rose now to a mean of over 1,000 contos yearly in 1815–25.[65] The consolidated debt, although still modest, had risen in the meantime by 40 percent (see table 8.4 in the appendix).

This shift was a worrying harbinger of what was to come and, inevitably, the verdict of contemporaries became more and more negative. Already on the day of the 1820 revolution, "the reserves in the Treasury vault were found to be less than those of any mediocre businessman in town", according to the great Liberal leader Fernandes Tomás (Tomás, 2020 [1820], 128). More recently, and possibly with less hyperbole too, this perspective still holds and is summed up by the diagnostic that "the Liberals of the 1820s were quite unable to solve their financial legacy" (Fernandes 2005, 394).

6.3 *The Great Fracture, 1826–1850*

The issue raised in these final pages concerns how Portugal's long-term growth was shaped by its involvement in the RNW. Could it have emulated

---

64 This was carried out very much under the auspices of the army, at that time still a disciplined body, with its top echelons largely in the hands of British officers. See Newitt and Robson (2004, 102).

65 The available data for budgets after 1815 are intermittent but a good deal higher and clearly on a rising trend. See Marques (2002, 151–2).

the long-term economic achievements of fellow-belligerents, such as France, Germany, Sweden or Italy? Could the country's post-war conditions of recovery described above have lasted long enough to make this possible? A simple projection of Portuguese GDP per capita sheds light on this question (figure 8.9). Our starting point is 1800, at which point this variable was at a respectable 916 GK dollars. Between then and the end of the war, the economy declined by 9 percent, reaching 833 GK dollars. Yet, following the first ten years of peace, by 1825 it was back again to an encouraging level of 944 GK dollars. Although an apparently modest figure, if kept up subsequently, this could have raised Portugal's economy to a per capita GDP level of 1,297 GK dollars by mid-century. This result would have been better than Spain (1,178) and Sweden (1,255) at that moment and not far below Germany (1,428). Only the numbers for France (1,597) and Italy (1,481) would have remained still distant (Palma and Reis 2019). Arguably, this would have placed the country in a favourable position for joining the international drive for long term growth which was then under way. At this point, however, Portugal was still at a level of around 923 GK dollars per capita, where it had remained roughly for two and a half decades and had thus become one of the most backward of Napoleon's erstwhile enemies in western Europe.

The key to why this happened is complex and cannot be scrutinized in a few pages. We address here only two highly negative consequences of the RNW which marked lastingly the second quarter of the 19th century and erected unsurpassable barriers to the country's long-term growth. The first was the

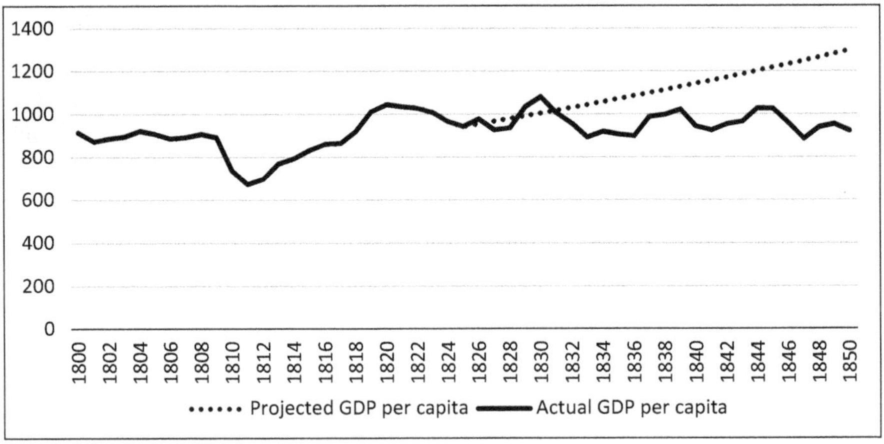

FIGURE 8.9 Portugal's real GDP per capita, 1800–1850: Actual and projected (in GK dollars)
SOURCES: PALMA AND REIS (2019)

continuation of war in the form of a civil version of bitter, internecine strife which swept the country for twenty-five years. Its origin lay in the long-festering rivalry for the throne of Portugal between Pedro and Miguel, John VI's two sons; and for the right to impose a favoured system of government – either Liberal, or based on the divine right of kings. For six years (1828–34) the country was split in a rancorous conflict without quarter. The war mobilized over 100,000 combatants in two main armies, numerous guerrilla brigades, naval forces and foreign mercenaries and officers. During this "most violent political fracture of Portuguese history" (Monteiro and Pedreira (2013, 19), tens of thousands were imprisoned, 50,000 were exiled, and numerous confiscations of property and executions were perpetrated. Casualties on eight battle fields totalled 20,000, and two pivotal naval expeditions were fought in the Atlantic (Dixon and Sarkees, 2015). Ultimately, France, Britain and Spain guaranteed the peace, banished Miguel, and put his brother in charge.

Having settled the dynastic issue, another wound opened up, the constitutional one, and the country went to war with itself again. This was intermittent but long drawn-out, indeed lasting until the 1851 Regeneration pact which finally pacified Portugal. In the meantime, eighteen uprisings of varying degrees of intensity succeeded each other, some of them veritable civil wars (1844 and 1846–7).[66] Some were urban, others were peasant protests, all involved different military factions with their own particular grievances. The crux was an 1822 radical-type of constitution versus a moderate 1826-type of Constitutional Charter (Birmingham 1993, 116–20). "A general breakdown of public authority, widespread banditry, mass escapes from jail, arbitrary suspensions of civil rights, the pillaging of entire towns by guerrillas and the kidnapping of government officials" ensued (Marques 2002, 600). Direct measures of the turmoil of this age are lacking but the indicator in figure 8.6 regarding domestic market integration is suggestive. Having started low in the mid-1820s, by the mid-1840s it had almost doubled, clearly reflecting the rise of the disorder which reigned in the country and the parlous state of its transport system (Matos 1980).

The second negative factor of the RNW legacy was the financial penury into which Portugal lapsed from the mid-1820s. This had several facets. One was the aphorism concerning money being the sinews of war, which now returned with a vengeance. It is difficult to quantify the cost of all the civil wars and successive uprisings, yet their military dimension outlined above leaves little

66 For a review of insurrections and revolts during the first half of the nineteenth century, see Vargues (1985).

doubt that it was a heavy burden.[67] Another was that Portugal no longer had access to the windfall of British aid which had made its finances viable during the French invasions. The third was that a radical program of dis-amortization of Crown and Church assets after the Liberal victory in 1834 fell far short of the pressing needs created by the civil war (Silva 1989). The fourth was the decline of the state's revenue-gathering capacity owing to the many hurried and radical reforms of the 1830s, coupled with its considerable loss of authority and efficiency.[68]

The only possible response was borrowing heavily, to cover the accumulation of steeply rising budget deficits. The Portuguese consolidated debt rose vertiginously, first in Paris, then in London. From a total of 17,175 contos in 1828, by the mid-1830s, it had almost doubled, and then, gone on to reach 240 percent of this amount by the end of the next decade (see appendix table 8.4).[69] As a result, the country's debt-to-GDP ratio shot up from 11 to 68 percent in two decades, reaching a level of 70 percent above those of France and Austria-Hungary (Cardoso and Lains 2010).

In the present state of research, we cannot say for certain whether a debt on such a scale was sustainable. It seems highly probable that it was not (Esteves 2005, Drelichman and Voth 2008). Countries under such conditions incline to suffer from low growth and high interest rates and find it difficult to break this vicious circle. In the case of Portugal between 1826 and 1850, this imposed two critical constraints on its economic growth. One was insufficiency of resources to enable governments to restore enduring and costly peace and harmony. The other was a lack of means to endow the economy with a modern infrastructure which it had never had and which its rivals were now rapidly acquiring. Undoubtedly, these two were not the only obstacles in the way of Portugal catching up on the rapidly developing countries of Europe but they were decisive and a part of the extended legacy of the RNW.

67 The only reliable estimate of this kind is the cost of suppressing the Patuleia civil war in 1846–7, which was above 30,000 contos (Marques 2002, 615). At the time, this was equivalent to more than 30 percent of the consolidated debt.

68 For staggering examples, see Reis (1996).

69 The national debt is measured here by the stock of Portuguese consols. This is an underestimate since we should also include the floating debt and other short-term instruments. These are difficult to identify correctly and are highly volatile. We thus assume the consolidated debt as a suitable trend value for this analysis.

Appendix

Portugal's Public Debt during the First Half of the Nineteenth Century: An Explanatory Note

The differences amongst authors concerning the value of the stock of Portuguese consolidated public debt arise as a result of the diversity of concepts used by them regarding the nature of the public debt.

Column 1 is the most complete of all three and comprises data from Valério et al. (2001). It contains only non-floating debt, although some of the stock represented may have arisen from consolidations of pre-existing floating debt. The figures for each year have been determined by adding to the data of the previous year any newly issued consolidated stock and subtracting amortizations.

Marques (2002), as well as Cardoso and Lains (2010), include in their calculations for yearly total debt the following items: funded debt, floating debt, paper money (*papel moeda*) and current debt, namely postponed payments. This is the reason why, prior to 1833, the values of columns 2 and 3 are often greater than those in column 1, which do not comprise these components. This inclusion, in our view, is in spite of the fact that neither "paper money" nor "current debt" can be properly considered as "public debt".

As regards "papel moeda", some authors have considered it a form of floating debt. This is incorrect because by definition the latter should have a life span of less than one year and should pay interest to the bearer. Neither criteria apply in this case.

"Papel moeda" came into existence on the 13th July 1797 in the form of notes of less than 50,000 réis, which would circulate freely and without endorsement or payment of interest, as if convertible. In all transactions, whether in payments to the State or to private entities, they had to be received at face value up to half the amounts due. In practice, these small notes circulated at a discount with no endorsement and should be received as "cash". In other words, they should not be likened to "debt".

As regards "current debt", although this was a state obligation, in reality, it was a form of arrears, which paid no interest and had no assignee. Technically, it was a form of treasury management.

TABLE 8.4 Portuguese consolidated public debt (nominal values) (in *contos*)

Year	Valério et al (1)	Cardoso and Lains (2)	Marques (3)
1796	4,000		
1797	6,367		
1798			
1799			
1800			
1801	8,235		
1802	8,468		
1803			
1804			
1805			
1806			
1807			
1808			
1809	8,707		
1810			
1811			
1812			
1813	9,828		
1814			
1815			
1816		34,757	
1817			
1818	11,428		
1819			
1820			
1821		35,601	
1822	12,182		
1823	14,104		
1824	16,104		
1825	16,104		
1826			
1827	17,104		
1828	17,175		39,100
1829	17,764		
1830	20,164		
1831		33,700	

TABLE 8.4 Portuguese consolidated public debt (nominal values) (in *contos*) (*cont.*)

Year	Valério et al (1)	Cardoso and Lains (2)	Marques (3)
1832			
1833			38,698
1834	27,294		58,651
1835	27,294		70,900
1836	30,038		55,280
1837	30,143		54,618
1838	38,075		82,040
1839	41,640		
1840	37,307		
1841	41,042		
1842	45,192		
1843	45,640		68,115
1844			69,880
1845	47,040		71,093
1846			71,419
1847	80,954		73,802
1848			74,192
1849			74,420
1850	84,954		76,405
1851	110,250	83,082	77,364

SOURCES:
(1) VALÉRIO, NUNO (COORDINATOR), NUNES, ANA BELA, BASTIEN, CARLOS AND EUGÉNIA MATA (2001). *AS FINANÇAS PÚBLICAS NO PARLAMENTO PORTUGUÊS. ESTUDOS PRELIMINARES*. LISBOA: ASSEMBLEIA DA REPÚBLICA, PP. 129–131, 160–165. AUTHOR'S CALCULATIONS
(2) JOSÉ LUÍS CARDOSO AND PEDRO LAINS (EDITORS) (2010). *PAYING FOR THE LIBERAL STATE. THE RISE OF PUBLIC FINANCE IN NINETEENTH-CENTURY EUROPE*. CAMBRIDGE UNIVERSITY PRESS, PP. 273–4
(3) MARQUES, OLIVEIRA (2002). *PORTUGAL E A INSTAURAÇÃO DO LIBERALISMO*. LISBOA: EDITORIAL PRESENÇA, VOLUME IX, PP. 154 AND 157

Notes:
(1) One *conto* equal to a million réis.
(2) When values are in sterling, we converted them into *réis*. Until 1822, £1 sterling equal to 3,565 réis. After 1822, £1 sterling equal to 4,150 réis.

References

Acemoglu, Daron, Cantoni, Davide, Johnson, Simon and James A. Robinson. 2011. "The consequences of radical reform: the French revolution", *American Economic Review* 101, 3286–307.

Alexandre, Valentim. 1993. *Os Sentidos do Império. Questão Nacional e Questão Colonial na Crise do Antigo Regime Português*. Porto: Afrontamento.

Allen, Robert. 2003. "Progress and poverty in Early Modern Europe. *Economic History Review* LVI, 403–43.

Álvarez-Nogal, Carlos, Prados de La Escosura, Leandro and Carlos Santiago-Caballero. 2016. "Spanish agriculture in the little divergence". *European Review of Economic History*. 20, 452–77.

Amaral, Luciano. 2012. "Institutions, property and economic growth: Back to the passage from the Ancien Régime to Liberalism in Portugal". *Análise Social*. XLVII, 28–55.

Balbi, Adrien. 1822, [2004]. *Essai Statistique sur le Royaume de Portugal et d'Algarve*. Lisboa: Imprensa Nacional, 2 vols.

Barata, Manuel T. and Teixeira, Nuno S. (eds). 2003. *Nova História Militar de Portugal*. Lisboa: Circulo de Leitores, 3 vols.

Bell, David. 2007. *The First Total War: Napoleon's Europe and the Birth of Warfare as We Know it*. New York: Houghton Mifflin Harcourt.

Bennett, Norman. 1992. "The Vignerons of the Douro valley and the Peninsular War." *Journal of European Economic History* 7, 7–29.

Birmingham, David (1993). *A Concise History of Portugal*. Cambridge: Cambridge University Press.

Broadberry, Stephen and Mark Harrison. 2005. "The economics of World War I: An overview.' In *The Economics of World War* I, edited by Broadberry, Stephen and Harrison, Mark, 3–40. Cambridge, Cambridge University Press.

Broers, Michael. 2015. Europe under Napoleon. London: Tauris.

Caetano, António A. 2008. *A Economia Portuguesa no Tempo de Napoleão. Constantes e Linhas de Força*. Lisboa: Tribuna da História.

Caetano, António A. 2009. "A agricultura de Portugal nos alvores de Oitocentos: Insuficiente grau de desenvolvimento (Ensaio de Cliometria)". Unpublished manuscript.

Caetano, António A. 2013. *Os Socorros Pecuniários Britânicos Destinados ao Exército Português 1809–1814. Subsídios para a História da Guerra de Libertação Nacional*. Lisboa: n.p.

Capela, José V. 1993. *Política, Administração Pública, Economia e Finanças Públicas Portuguesas, 1750–1820*. Braga: Universidade do Minho.

Cardoso, José L. 2005, "A legislação económica do vintismo: Economia política e política económica nas Cortes Constituintes". *Análise Social* XXVI, 471–488.

Cardoso, José L. 2007. "Pombal, o terramoto e a política de regulação económica". In *O Terramoto de 1755: Impactos Históricos*, edited by Cardoso, José L., Araújo, A., Monteiro, Nuno G., Serrão, José V. and Walter Rossa, 165–81. Lisboa: Livros Horizonte.

Cardoso, José L. 2013. "Lifting the Continental Blockade: Britain, Portugal and Brazilian Trade in the Global Context of the Napoleonic Wars". In *A Global History of Trade and Conflict since 1500*, edited by Coppolaro, L. and F. McKenzie, 87–104. Basingstoke: Palgrave Macmillan.

Cardoso, José L. and Pedro Lains. 2010. "Public finance in Portugal, 1796–1910". In *Paying for the Liberal State. The Rise of Public Finance in Nineteenth-Century Europe*, edited by José L. Cardoso and Pedro Lains, 251–78. Cambridge: Cambridge University Press.

Clodfelter, M. 2017. *Warfare and Armed Conflicts: A Statistical Encyclopedia of Casualty and other Figures, 1492–2015*. McFarland: Jefferson, North Carolina.

Cordeiro, José M. L. 2003. "Fontes para a história da indústria portuense: O mapa das fábricas de 1820". *Cadernos do Noroeste*. 20, 649–711.

Costa, Fernando D. 2008. "Army size, military recruitment and financing in Portugal during the period of the Peninsular War – 1808–1811". e-Journal of Portuguese History, 6, 1–27.

Costa, Leonor F., Palma, Nuno and Jaime Reis. 2015. "The great escape? The contribution of the empire to Portugal's economic growth, 1500–1800". *European Review of Economic History* 19, 1–22.

Costa, Leonor F., Lains, Pedro and Susana M. Miranda. 2016. *An Economic History of Portugal, 1143–2010*. Cambridge: Cambridge University Press.

Cruz, Miguel D. 2015. "Neutral shipping and Portuguese economic relations with the Atlantic World (1793–1814)". In *Neutrals and Neutrality in the Atlantic World during the Long Eighteenth Century (1700–1820). A Global Approach,* edited by Éric Schnakenbourg, 317–48. Paris: Les Perséides.

Custódio, Jorge. 1996. "A vila de Santarém ao tempo da invasão de Massena: Testemunhos e realidades. In *Sá da Bandeira e o Liberalismo em Portugal, 1795–1910* 157–237. Santarém: Câmara Municipal de Santarém.

Dixon, Jeffrey S. and Meredith R. Sarkees. 2015. *A Guide to Intra-state Wars: An Examination of Civil, Regional, and Intercommunal Wars, 1816–2014*. London: Sage.

Drelichman, M. and H.J.Voth. 2008. Debt sustainability in historical perspective: The role of fiscal repression". *Journal of the European Economic Association*. 6, 657–67.

Eloranta, Jari, Golson, Eric, Hedberg, Peter and Cristina Moreira (eds.). 2018. *Small and Medium Powers in Global History: Trade, Conflicts and Neutrality from the 18th to the 20th Centuries*. London: Routledge.

Esdaile, Charles. 2002. *The Peninsular War. A New History*. Oxford: Penguin.

Esteves, Rui P. 2005. "Finanças públicas". In *História Económica de Portugal. Vol.II. Século XIX,* edited by Lains, Pedro and Álvaro F. Silva, 305–335. Lisboa: Imprensa de Ciências Sociais.

Federico, Giovanni, Schulze, Max-Stefan and Oliver Volckart (2021). "European goods market integration in the very long run: From the Black Death to the first world war". *Journal of Economic History*. 81, 276–308.

Fernandes, Paulo J. 2005. "Política económica". In *História Económica de Portugal. Vol.II. Século XIX*. Edited by Lains, Pedro and Álvaro F. Silva, 393–419.Lisboa: ICS.

Ferreira, Jaime. 1991. "Proteccionismo e contrabando cerealífero, 1821–22". *Análise Social* XXVI, 489–511.

Glover, Michael. 2001. *The Peninsular War 1807–1814. A Concise Military History*. London: Penguin Books.J.

Godinho, Vitorino M. 1955. *Prix et Monnaies au Portugal 1750–1850*. Paris: Librairie Armand Colin.

Goldin, Claudia D. and Lewis, Frank D. 1975. "The economic cost of the American civil war: Estimates and implications". *Journal of Economic History*, 35, 299–326.

Gray, Anthony. 2011. "The French invasions of Portugal 1807–1811: Rebellion, reaction and resistance". M.A. thesis, University of York.

Hespanha, António M. (1982). História das instituições: épocas medieval e moderna. Imprenta: Coimbra, Almedina.

Hill, Henry B. 19Sc36. "The constitutions of Continental Europe, 1789–1813". *Journal of Modern History*, 8, 82–94.

Justino, David. 1986. *Formação do Espaço Económico Nacional. Portugal 1810–1914*. Lisboa: Veja, 2 vols.

Lains, Pedro. 2005 "A indústria". In *História Económica de Portugal. Vol.II Século XIX*, Edited by Lains, Pedro and Silva, Álvaro F., 259–81. Lisboa: Imprensa de Ciências Sociais.

Macedo, Jorge B. de. 1990. *O Bloqueio Continental. Economia e Guerra Peninsular*. Lisboa: Gradiva, 2nd edition.

Macedo, Jorge B., Silva, Álvaro F., and Rita M. Sousa. 2001. "War, Taxes and Gold – The Inheritance of the Real". In *Transferring Wealth and Power from the Old to the New World – Monetary and Fiscal Institutions in the 17th through the 19th Centuries*, edited by Bordo, Michael D. and Roberto Cortés-Conde, 187–228. Cambridge: Cambridge University Press.

Madureira, Nuno L. 1997. *Mercado e Privilégios: A Indústria Portuguesa entre 1750 e 1834*. Lisboa: Estampa.

Marques, A. H. de Oliveira. 1973. *História de Portugal*. Lisboa: Ágora, 2 vols.

Marques, A. H. de Oliveira. 2002. *Portugal e a Instauração do Liberalismo. Nova História de Portugal*. vol.IX. Lisboa: Presença.

Martins, Conceição A. 1998. "Vinha, vinho e política vinícola em Portugal. Do Pombalismo à Regeneração". Ph. D. dissertation, Universidade de Évora, 3 vols.

Mata, Eugénia and Nuno Valério. 1994. *História Económica de Portugal. Uma Perspectiva Global*. Lisboa: Presença.

Matos, Artur T. 1980. *Transportes e Comunicações em Portugal, Açores e Madeira (1750–1850)*. Ponta Delgada: Universidade dos Açores, 2 vols.

Mendes, José A. 1985. "Portugal no século XIX: Uma economia em transição". In *História de Portugal*, Vol. V, edited by José Mattoso, 395–421. Lisboa: Círculo de Leitores, 8 volumes.

Mesquita, João M. de C. 1990 [1825?]. "Extracto da memória sobre o destroço actual das criações de gado vaccum, apresentado à Academia Real das Ciências de Lisboa". In *Memórias da Academia das Ciências de Lisboa*, edited by José Luis Cardoso, IV, 315–320. Lisboa: Banco de Portugal.

Modelski, George and William R. Thompson. 1988. *Seapower in Global Politics, 1494–1993*. Houndmills: Macmillan.

Monteiro, Nuno and Jorge Pedreira. 2013. *O Colapso do Império e a Revolução Liberal. 1808–1834*. Lisboa: Objectiva.

Moreira, Cristina. 2007. "Tracking signs of the Portuguese fiscal military state 1762–1816". In *War, State and Development. The Fiscal Military States during the Eighteenth Century*, edited by Rafael Torres Sanchez, 251–75. Eunsa.

Moreira, Cristina. 2011. "Portuguese state military expenditure: British support of the Peninsular War efforts of Erário Régio (Royal Treasury) from 1809 to 1811". In *The Spending of the States. Military Expenditure during the Long Eighteenth Century: Patterns, Organisation and Consequences, 1650–1815*, edited by Conway, S. and R. Torres, 109–28. Saarbrücken: VDM Verlang.

Moreira, Cristina. 2013. *Relaciones Comerciales Luso-Españolas (1774–1860)*. Riga: Editorial Académica Española.

Moreira, Cristina. 2015. "Portugal, 1775–1831". *Revue de l'OFCE* 140, 319–333.

Moreira, Cristina and Jari Eloranta. 2012. "Contracts and the role of the state: Portuguese military provisions supply system in the early nineteenth century". In *The Contractor State and its Implications: 1659–1815*, edited by Harding, Richard and Sergio S. Ferri, 199–221. Las Palmas de Gran Canaria: Universidad, Servicio e-Publicaciones.

Neves, José A. das. 1984. *Obras Completas*. Porto: Afrontamento, 3 vols.

Newitt, Malyn. 2009. *Portugal in European and World History*. London: Reaktion Books.

Newitt, Malyn and Martin Robson. 2004. *Lord Beresford e a Intervenção Britânica em Portugal, 1807–1820*. Lisboa: Imprensa de Ciências Sociais.

O'Brien, Patrick K. 1988. "The Political Economy of British Taxation, 1660–1815". *Economic History Review*. 41, 1–32.

O'Rourke, Kevin. 2007. "War and welfare: Britain, France, and the United States 1807–14". *Oxford Economic Papers* 59, 8–30.

Oliveira, João. 2002. *A Beira Alta de 1700 a 1840. Gentes e Subsistências* (2002). Coimbra: Palimage.

Palma, Nuno. 2016. "Sailing away from Malthus: Intercontinental trade and European economic growth, 1500–1800". *Cliometrica*, 10, 129–149.

Palma, Nuno and Jaime Reis. 2019. "From convergence to divergence: Portuguese economic growth, 1527–1850". *The Journal of Economic History*, 79, 477–506.

Palma, Nuno, Reis, Jaime and Mengtian Zhang. 2020. "Reconstruction of regional and national population using intermittent census-type data: The case of Portugal, 1527–1864". *Historical Methods: A Journal of Quantitative and Interdisciplinary History*, 53, 11–27.

Paquette, Gabriel. 2013. *Imperial Portugal in the Age of Atlantic Revolutions. The Luso-Brazilian World, c. 1770–1850*. Cambridge: Cambridge University Press.

Payne, Stanley G. 1973. *A History of Spain and Portugal*. Madison: University of Wisconsin Press, 2 vols.

Pedreira, Jorge. 1987. "Indústria e atraso económico em Portugal (1800–1825). Uma perspectiva estrutural. *Análise Social* XXIII, 563–93.

Pedreira, Jorge. 1994. *Estrutura Industrial e Mercado Colonial. Portugal e Brasil (1780–1830)*. Lisboa: Difel.

Pedreira, Jorge M. 2000. "From growth to collapse: Portugal, Brazil and the breakdown of the old colonial system (1760–1830)", *Hispanic American Historical Review* 80, 839–64.

Pedreira, Jorge. 2005. "A indústria". In *História Económica de Portugal. Vol.I. Século XVIII*, edited by Lains, Pedro and Álvaro F. Silva, 177–208. Lisboa: Imprensa de Ciências Sociais.

Pedreira, Jorge M. and Fernando D. Costa 2009. *D. João VI, o Clemente*. Lisboa: Temas e Debates.

Pereira, Alvaro S. 2009. "The opportunity of a disaster: The economic impact of the 1755 Lisbon earthquake". *Journal of Economic History*, 69, 466–99.

Reis, Jaime, 1996. *O Banco de Portugal. Das Origens a 1914*. Lisboa: Banco de Portugal.

Reis, Jaime. 2000. "How poor was the European periphery before 1850? The Mediterranean vs. Scandinavia". In *The Mediterranean Response to Globalization before 1950*, edited by Pamuk, Sevket and Jeffrey G. Williamson, 17–44. London: Routledge.

Reis, Jaime. 2005. "O Trabalho". In *História Económica de Portugal. Vol.II. Século XIX*, edited by Lains, Pedro and Álvaro F. Silva, 119–51. Lisboa: Imprensa de Ciências Sociais.

Reis, Jaime. 2017. "Gross agricultural output: A quantitative, unified perspective". In *An Agrarian History of Portugal, 1000–2000. Economic Development on the European Frontier*, edited by Freire, Dulce and Pedro Lains, 172–216. Leiden: Brill.

Roberts, Andrew. 2015. *Napoleon the Great*. London: Penguin.

Serrão, Joaquim V. 2002. *História de Portugal*. Lisboa: Verbo, 3rd edition, vols. VII–VIII.

Sherwig, John M. 1969. *Guineas and Gunpowder. British Foreign Aid in the Wars with France, 1793–1815*. Cambridge, MA: Harvard University Press.

Sideri, Sandro. 1978. *Comércio e Poder: Colonialismo Informal nas Relações Anglo-Portuguesas*. Lisboa: Cosmos.

Silva, Álvaro F. 2005. "Finanças Públicas". In *História Económica de PortugaL 1700–2000,* Vol. I. *Século XVIII* edited by Lains, Pedro and Álvaro F. da Silva, 237–61. Lisboa: Imprensa de Ciências Sociais.

Silva, António M. 1989. "Desamortização e venda dos bens nacionais na primeira metade do século XIX. Ph.d. dissertation, University of Coimbra.

Silveira, Luís E. 1987. "Aspectos da evolução das finanças públicas portuguesas nas primeiras décadas do século XIX (1800–1827)". *Análise Social,* XXIII, 505–29.

Soriano, Simão J.L. 1866–90. *História da Guerra Civil e do Estabelecimento do Governo Parlamentar em Portugal; Compreendendo a História Diplomática, Militar e Política deste Reino desde 1777 até 1824*. Lisboa: Imprensa Nacional, 19 vols.

Sousa, Rita M. 2006. *Moeda e Metais Preciosos no Portugal Setecentista (1688–1797)*. Lisboa: Imprensa Nacional-Casa da Moeda.

Teixeira, Nuno S., Domingues, Francisco C. and João G. Monteiro. 2017. *História Militar de Portugal*. Lisboa: Esfera dos Livros.

The Oxford Dictionary of Quotations. 1986. Oxford: Oxford University Press, 3rd edition.

Tomás, Manuel F. 2020. *Escritos Políticos e Discursos Parlamentares (1820–1822)*. Edited by José Luís Cardoso. Lisboa: ICS.

Tomaz, Fernando. 1988. "As finanças do estado pombalino, 1762–1776,". In *Estudos em Homenagem a Vitorino Magalhães Godinho*, 355–88. Lisboa: Sá da Costa.

Valente, Vasco Pulido. 2007. *Ir Pró Maneta. A Revolta contra os Franceses*. Lisboa: Aletheia.

Valério, Nuno, Nunes, Ana Bela, Bastien, Carlos and Eugénia Mata. 2001. *As Finanças Públicas no Parlamento Português. Estudos Preliminares*. Lisboa: Assembleia da República.

Vargues, Isabel N. 1985. "Insurreições e revoltas em Portugal (1801–1851). Subsídios para uma cronologia e bibliografia." *Revista de História das Ideias,* 7, 501–72.

Ventura, António. 2008. *Guerra das Laranjas 1801*. Lisboa: Academia Portuguesa de História.

Vicente, António P. (1983). *Manuscritos do Arquivo Histórico de Vincennes referentes a Portugal,* Paris: Fundação Calouste Gulbenkian, 3 vols.

CHAPTER 9

The Long-Term Effects of the French and Napoleonic Wars on the Global Economy

Peter M. Solar

To analyse the impact of the French Wars on the global economy is an impossible brief. Taken broadly, it would include much of what is dealt with in the country chapters as well as what happened in such faraway places as Peru, South Africa and China. In order to be manageable the scope of the enquiry needs some narrowing. It cannot be the world economy in the sense of production and consumption around the globe. Only the foolhardy and the late Angus Maddison would think of taking on such a task for a period before the twentieth century, and even for recent years such efforts are fraught with index number and other problems. The aim of this chapter will be much more limited, though still daunting. In the spirit of Ronald Findlay and Kevin O'Rourke's majestic *Power and Plenty* (2007), it will focus on the economic interactions between Europe and other major parts of the world.[1] Most of the discussion will be about shipping and trade in goods, but movements of labour, both voluntary and involuntary, will also be addressed. During this period intercontinental capital movements and transfers of technology and knowhow were of relatively little importance and will only be discussed incidentally. As Findlay and O'Rourke emphasize, these interactions need to be seen within their geopolitical context, especially in a period when war and colonialism were prominent features.

Another problem is how long is the long term. It may be reasonable to suppose that if the French wars did have long-term effects on the global economy, then these effects should already have manifested themselves in the first few decades after 1815. If they were indeed persistent, then the effects should still have had some influence by the mid-nineteenth century. Arbitrary though a mid-century stopping point may be, looking further into the nineteenth century, or even the twentieth century, increases the risk of confounding the effects of the wars with those of other economic and political changes,

1 This book and an accompanying article by Kevin O'Rourke (2006) deal quite thoroughly with the immediate impact of the wars, that is, the effects of the wars on economic activity during the war years.

 | DOI:10.1163/9789004472754_010

particularly the transition in the late 1840s from a still somewhat mercantilist international order to a more liberal one, a change incarnated in the repeal of the British Corn and Navigation Laws, and, somewhat later, a resurgence of European colonialism.

How will these long-term consequences be discerned? Potential candidates will be sought by looking at what happened during the wars and in the settlement that ended them. The question of whether significant changes did occur will be addressed by comparing the situation before the wars, mainly in the peacetime years of the 1780s, with that after the wars, in the 1820s, 1830s and 1840s. Whether the changes that did take place were indeed consequences of the wars, or whether they resulted from other developments, must then be tackled. Here a prime confounding factor was early industrialization, mainly in Britain but already underway in places such as Belgium, Saxony and the United States.

We start by surveying the major changes in the political landscape, notably the changes in colonial control of areas outside Europe, the demise of the East India companies, and the rise of British naval hegemony. Then we survey the development over the wars in shipping and intercontinental trade, paying particular attention to a number of key commodities. We also examine whether there were major changes in relative commodity prices and in intercontinental price differences, before finishing with a brief look at intercontinental movements of free and unfree labour and of capital.

1 Geo-Political Context

1.1 *Political Changes*

The exigencies of war in Europe and the inability of the continental powers to project their military power overseas led to a major wave of decolonization. Saint Domingue, France's most lucrative colony, revolted successfully. Although there had been some earlier agitation by whites for independence and by free blacks for legal equality, the revolution in France sparked a slave uprising in the 1790s that ultimately led to Haiti's de facto independence in 1804. The difficulties of defending Saint Domingue and its other American colonies and the chance of a financial windfall also led Napoleon to sell New Orleans and the vast Louisiana territory to the United States in 1803. In the post-war settlement France was only able to recover a few small islands in the Caribbean and the Indian Ocean as well as French Guiana on the coast of South America. The loss of French possessions in India may have facilitated Britain's increasing control over the sub-continent.

The wars also contributed to Spain and Portugal losing most of their colonies in South and Central America, though the struggle continued into the 1820s. Napoleon's conquest of Spain in 1808 launched a wave of independence movements in Spanish America that the restoration of the monarchy in 1814 could no longer control. By 1830 Spain retained only Cuba, Puerto Rico and the Philippines. During the Portuguese royal family's stay in Rio de Janeiro from 1807 to 1815, Brazilians acquired a taste for power and status that made it difficult for them to accept relegation to colonial status in the early 1820s. After the Brazilians' successful war for independence, Portugal's empire consisted only of a few outposts in Asia and along the coast of Africa.

The independence wars in South America showed the limits of European military technology. In conflicts with forces whose leaders were trained in similar tactics and whose soldiers were armed with comparable weapons, neither Spain nor Portugal were able to put enough troops on the ground to defeat the indigenous forces. They were unable to deal effectively with guerilla tactics. The insurgents also had the advantage of help from Britain.

More generally, wartime innovations did little to enhance European imperialism in the postwar world. As Daniel Headrick (1981, ch. 4) has argued, the colonial wars of the early nineteenth century were increasingly close-run affairs.[2] The French wars had produced no significant breakthroughs in weaponry or tactics, and it had become easier for anti-colonialists to achieve parity. The African continent still remained impenetrable, mainly because of its forbidding disease environment. Most men sent there died within a year or two. European weaponry also held no great advantage. Without horses, also subject to tropical diseases, cannon could not be used effectively in Africa, and European small arms were not decisive against African tactics. Nor were they sufficient when the Russians faced guerilla resistance in the Caucasus from the 1820s and when the British tried to conquer Afghanistan in the early 1840s. In other cases, Europeans came up against well-trained and armed indigenous forces, as did the French against Abd al-Qadir in Algeria from the late 1830s and the British did against the Sikhs in the late 1840s. Although Europeans retained control of the oceans, the second wave of colonial conquest, in which relatively small European forces would again be able to acquire vast territories, awaited the development, from the mid-nineteenth century, of more accurate and rapid-firing small arms, of quinine to prevent malaria, and of steam vessels to penetrate interior regions and control river traffic (Etemad 2007).

2 The French Revolutionary and Napoleonic wars thus constitute an exception to Philip Hoffman's (2015) longer-term story about the West's military dominance of the world.

Despite decolonization in much of the Americas, many parts of the world remained European colonies after the wars.[3] In the peace settlement the Dutch were fortunate to recover Surinam and a few islands in the Caribbean as well as most of their possessions in the Indonesian archipelago. Britain held onto all of its prewar possessions and added the Cape Colony (part of modern South Africa) and several islands in the West Indies and elsewhere that had previously been controlled by the French, Spanish or Dutch. The absence of the Dutch in Asia from the 1790s allowed the British to take Ceylon (now Sri Lanka).

Above all, Britain was able to consolidate its control of India during the wars. Although the French tried to carry the war to India, the logistics of maintaining significant forces in Asia were beyond them. Unlike the British, who had the dockyard at Bombay, the French had nowhere to maintain and repair their warships. Given British naval strength, the French also had difficulty supplying their ground forces and sustaining their indigenous allies. France's absence probably speeded up the extension of British power in India. In the Second Anglo-Maratha War (1803–5) the British, due more to their infantry tactics than to any superiority in small-arms technology, acquired much of western India, with yet more territory to be taken in the Third War (1817–8) (Satya 2018, 295). Elsewhere in India they continued their divide-and-conquer strategy with respect to local rulers.

These changes in the political map influenced postwar trading relationships. Trade to Latin America officially became open to merchants who were not Spanish or Portuguese, though the British and others had long found ways of circumventing earlier colonial restrictions. The new nations in the Americas could now set their own rules and many imposed high tariffs in order to raise revenue, a policy choice that served to limit the expansion of trade (Coatsworth and Williamson 2004). In Asia the restoration of Indonesia to the Dutch gave rise to conflicts of interest in the immediate postwar years, but the 1824 Anglo-Dutch Commercial Treaty effectively established spheres of influence for the two European powers. The effect was a sort of forced free trade regime within southeast Asia. Tariffs and other barriers to intra-Asian trade were low in the postwar years, facilitating a considerable expansion (Sugihara and Kawamura 2013; Sugihara 2009).

---

3 Etemad (2007, 106–107, 219–226) shows the area of European colonies falling from 24.2 to 8.2 million square kilometres between 1760 and 1830, but the population rising from 27.1 to 205.6 million people. This increase in population comes overwhelmingly from British control of India.

1.2 *End of the East India Companies*

The wars saw the winding down of the chartered monopolies that had controlled European trade to Asia since the sixteenth century. The French and Dutch East India companies were casualties of revolution and conquest; had they survived, their activities during the wars would have been severely limited by Britain's naval power. The English East India Company persisted well into the nineteenth century, but lost its monopoly on trade with India in 1813 and on trade with China in 1833.

Well before the wars the commercial activities of the English company had already come under various pressures (Hejeebu 2016). In India its increasing military and territorial presence from the 1750s created tensions within the Company that tended to undermine its trading activities. Parallel civilian and military authorities clashed over pay and conditions, revenue collection and political strategy with respect to local rulers. In Britain dissatisfaction with the Company's performance in India led to increased intervention by the government from the 1760s onward. Dividends were capped and the Company was required to reduce its indebtedness. In 1784 a Board of Control was established to oversee the Company's activities. With the Company, the relationships of trust between the Company and its servants deteriorated, with opportunistic behaviour becoming more common as the average length of service in India fell by about a half. All of these developments were making the Company a less efficient commercial enterprise.

The wars may have retarded, then accelerated the Company's eventual exit from trading activities. The Company's charter came up for renewal in 1793 and again in 1813. In 1793 a concern for stability in the face of the revolution in France and the imminence of war probably influenced the government's decision to renew the monopoly, though the Company had to make some concessions to private traders. By 1813, a number of developments, some war-related, led to the loss of the Company's monopoly on trade with India (Webster 2009). The costs of military activity in India had driven up the Company's indebtedness; no longer a cash cow, it had become a burden on the Exchequer. The exigencies of supply during wartime led to a shift in the government's stance toward privileged monopolies. Policy-makers became more concerned with meeting the needs of British industry, including opening new markets and securing supplies of cheap raw materials. This changing stance was supported by increasingly vocal lobbies of merchants and industrialists in provincial Britain and of merchants in India.

As the British opened up the India and China trades, the Dutch set about trying to reaffirm their control over production and trade in the Indonesian archipelago. The "culture system", which exacted tribute by imposing forced

TABLE 9.1 Naval strength of Western Powers (sailing fleets only; 1000 tons)

	1790	1810	1825	1845
United Kingdom	473	673	441	430
France	324	194	221	180
Spain	253	100	27	16
Netherlands	123	40	47	53
Portugal	41	46	25	20
USA	10	16	50	71

SOURCE: GLETE 1993, VOL. 2, APPENDIX 2

labour and collecting taxes in the form of export crops, was to prevail from 1830 to 1870 (van Zanden 2010).

1.3 *Naval Power*

The configuration of global naval power changed from multipolar in the eighteenth century to British predominance in the early nineteenth century. As can be seen in Table 9.1, although Britain did have the largest navy before the French wars, an alliance of France with either Spain or the Netherlands could match it in warship tonnage. After the wars the tonnage of the British fleet easily exceeded the combined tonnage of all the other major fleets. In addition, in the 1820s the British had a large reserve force of ships that had been laid up after 1815.

Ship numbers do not tell the whole story. The technology for building sailing warships was well-known and the costs, though expensive, were within the budgets of determined nations. What proved more difficult for eighteenth-century navies were the equally important tasks of maintaining and repairing the ships and recruiting, feeding and keeping their crews healthy, which were essential to keeping vessels at sea and on distant missions. During the eighteenth century Britain had developed the organizational capabilities necessary to project its naval power effectively (Baugh 2004; O'Brien and Duran 2011). The experience of the French wars only enhanced these capabilities, consolidating the naval hegemony shown by the warship numbers.

British naval hegemony meant that war at sea became much less likely, so the seas were safer for merchant vessels. In addition, the British navy devoted more resources to dealing with piracy and to keeping ports open for trade. This changing mission led Britain, and most other countries, to shift the balance of their naval forces from large battleships to smaller vessels, of 500–1500 tons.

British control of the seas and the absence of naval warfare benefited other countries during the prolonged peace after 1815. For example, marine insurance rates at Hamburg, which had more or less doubled during the wars, fell sharply afterwards and drifted further downward in the following decades (Denzel 2017). Commercial rivalry among nations persisted, but trade was largely a peaceful activity during most of the nineteenth century.

British hegemony was not challenged until the late 1840s when the French started to build a steam navy, provoking alarms in Britain about the adequacy of its own fleet. These concerns, which may have exaggerated the quality of French ships, sustained a substantial construction programme in the late 1850s and 1860s that would assure British primacy in the steam era (Lambert 1984).

In Asian waters the changes in the configuration of naval forces were similar, but with a twist (Solar 2013). In the eighteenth century, European navies only rarely ventured into the Indian Ocean. Instead, when wars broke out in Europe, the large, warship-like vessels of the East India companies served as their surrogates. In addition, such ships could easily outgun Indian or Chinese vessels. East Indiamen, being heavily-armed and heavily-manned, hence expensive to build and expensive to operate, could not, in peacetime, compete commercially with smaller, lightly manned merchant vessels, so the European powers had to grant the companies monopoly rights in order to sustain these quasi-navies. The demise of the continental East India companies and the emergence of British naval hegemony put an end to this system. After the wars, trade to Asia was carried on in smaller, much less heavily armed vessels, and the Royal Navy maintained a more permanent presence in Asia.

2 Shipping

The rise of Britain to naval hegemony was echoed in commercial shipping (Table 9.2). The tonnage of shipping registered in the United Kingdom roughly doubled over the wars, whilst the fleets of the other European powers shrank or grew only modestly. The result was that the U.K.'s share of European commercial shipping rose from a bit more than a third to over a half, and this dominance was maintained during the early nineteenth century. But a major development of this period was the rise of the United States as a shipping and trading nation. When American shipping is taken into account, the U.K. share rose over the wars but fell back subsequently. However, these statistics exaggerate the American presence in global trade, as a much larger share of the

TABLE 9.2 Merchant shipping fleets

	1786–7	1820	1850
	tons	tons	tons
United Kingdom	1278	2439	3565
France	729	500	688
Spain	149	200	245
Netherlands	398	150	433
Other western European	1107	1049	1839
United States	200	1280	3535
	per cent	per cent	per cent
UK share (exc USA)	35	56	53
UK share (inc USA)	33	43	35

SOURCES: 1786–7: ROMANO 1962, 575–591; 1788 (U.K.), 1820, 1850: MITCHELL 1992, 689–693, 708
Notes: The figures for France, Spain and the Netherlands in 1820 represent rough estimates based on figures from the late 1820s and early 1830s.

American fleet was devoted to inland or coastal shipping than was the case in Britain. Statistics for the tonnage of domestically-owned ships entered from abroad in the US and the UK indicate that the American mercantile fleet grew from 29 per cent of the British fleet in the early 1790s to 35 per cent in the early 1820s and 42 per cent around 1850.[4]

Flows of shipping to Asia confirm the rise of the United Kingdom over the wars. From the peacetime years of 1783–1792 to the 1820s annual tonnage bound for Asia from western hemisphere countries roughly doubled. Almost all of this increase was accounted for by the growth in voyages from the U.K., so that its share of the tonnage rose from 31 to 60 per cent (Solar 2013, 649).

The war also saw the appearance of a new and disruptive participant in Asian trade. Britain, fearing the entry of the United States on the side of France, concluded a "Treaty of Amity, Commerce and Navigation" with the

4 British figures for U.K. vessels entered from abroad from Parliamentary Papers; American figures for U.S. vessels entered from abroad from Carter 2006, Table Df594–605.

TABLE 9.3 U.K. imports by origin (£m; current prices)

	1784–86	1824–26	1834–36
Asia	4952	11019	11535
West Indies	4573	8577	7946
USA	1156	6061	13223
Canada	350	3081	3320
Latin America	8	3109	3380
Africa	148	681	2017
Australia	0	177	1232
TOTAL	11227	32705	42453

SOURCE: DAVIS 1979, 93

Americans in 1795. Among the provisions of the Jay Treaty were most-favoured nation status for American trade with Britain, limited rights for Americans in trade with the West Indies, and non-interference with American merchant vessels. As neutrals during most of the wartime period, the Americans expanded their trade with China and India. Since they were able to use smaller, cheaper vessels, American merchants were able to reap supernormal profits and put pressure on the prices at which the English company could sell its goods, and hence on its profits from trade. Fichter (2010) has argued that these supernormal profits were key to America's early industrial expansion.

3 Intercontinental Trade

3.1 *General Structure*

Although Bairoch and Etemad (1985) have assembled data on third world exports c. 1830, comparable late eighteenth-century trade statistics are wanting. A partial, but still revealing view can be had by examining the imports of the United Kingdom. Table 9.3 shows that the value of U.K. imports from other continents more or less tripled over the wars. The volume of trade would have roughly doubled since the price level increased by about 50 per cent between the 1780s and the 1820s and 1830s. The growth in intercontinental imports to the U.K. thus grew somewhat faster than British GDP, but not strikingly so.

The growth in U.K. imports thus corresponds quite well to the growth in U.K. commercial shipping tonnage, which would suggest that there was also a significant rise in the U.K.'s share of intercontinental trade. This shows up most obviously in the increase in direct imports from Latin America. The very low figure for the mid-1780s is somewhat deceptive since before the wars Britain was already importing some goods from Spanish America either legally via Spain and Portugal or illegally via the West Indies. Much of the large expansion of this British trade over the wars was just the other side of the fall by almost a half in Spain's direct imports from the New World (Cuenca Estaban 2008, 328).

The most striking change in British trade was the huge expansion of imports from North America, though it is difficult to attribute this to the wars. The fundamentals behind North American growth were abundant land, a rapidly growing population, and institutions favourable to production and trade. In the late eighteenth century settlement in North America had still been concentrated along the Atlantic coast and in the estuary of the St Lawrence River. Away from coastal areas and in the south, settlement was still relatively sparse, and vast areas remained for exploitation west of the Appalachian Mountains, augmented in 1803 by the purchase of the immense Louisiana territory. Americans were well fed and lived mainly in rural areas with favourable disease environments, except in parts of the south where malaria was endemic. As a result, they were not only among the tallest people in the world, they had both high fertility and low mortality, making for a very high rate of natural increase, around 25 per 1000 throughout the eighteenth century and the first decades of the nineteenth (Haines and Steckel 2000, 178, 700). This growing population, at least the part that was not enslaved, was also generally literate. Federal, state and local governments maintained private property rights (again for the white population) and were generally favourable to improvements in transport infrastructure that helped open up the interior and foster production and trade (Engerman and Sokoloff 2011). The rapid growth of the American economy was thus likely to have taken place in the absence of war.

The regional distribution of intercontinental trade certainly changed over the wars. It is more difficult to determine whether its *rate of growth* increased between the eighteenth and nineteenth centuries. For the pre-war period estimates are very rough, based as they are on shipping tonnages. De Vries (2010, 718–9) put the growth of trade between Europe and Asia at about 1.1 per cent per annum between the 1690s and the 1780s. He also estimated that transatlantic trade grew by at least 2.2 per cent. Since by the eighteenth century transatlantic trade was much larger than Asian trade, overall growth was probably closer to the transatlantic rate. For the period after Waterloo, Federico and Tena (2018) have put together statistics for the value of trade at constant prices. Their figures for Asia and America contain some trade between and within these regions, but most trade from these areas during early nineteenth century would have been with Europe. Between 1816–20 and 1846–50 this trade grew at 4.2 per cent per annum, about twice the eighteenth-century rate. However, some of this growth should probably be ascribed to post-war recovery. Federico and Tena's figures, which begin in 1800, show that trade from these regions grew hardly at all between that date and 1815. Nonetheless, there does seem to have been some acceleration in the growth of Europe's intercontinental trade. Whether it was due to the wars must remain an open question, particularly given the preceding discussion of the reasons for the growth in trade with the United States.

Intercontinental trade from the rest of the world to Europe involved a fairly limited range of commodities. Table 9.4 shows that imports to the United Kingdom were dominated by exotic foodstuffs and raw materials. These commodities accounted for over 90 per cent of the U.K.'s intercontinental imports and this mix of goods is likely to have been much the same in the imports of other European countries, except that the share of raw cotton would have been somewhat lower, reflecting the cotton industry's smaller presence elsewhere.

3.2 *Major Commodities*

Grouped by region of origin intercontinental trade looks even more rudimentary. As shown in Table 9.5, one or two commodities generally accounted for more than half of all imports from the major world regions. Trade in five of these commodities – sugar, tea, cotton, timber and indigo – will be examined in detail in order to try to isolate what features of wartime experience may have influenced longer-term trends. These five commodities accounted for 45 per cent of third world exports c. 1830 (Bairoch and Etemad 1985, 62).

3.2.1 Sugar

In the eighteenth century cane sugar was produced in tropical and semi-tropical regions throughout the world. Despite some initiatives by the English and Dutch East India companies, there was essentially no trade in sugar between Asia and the Atlantic world, and in Asia most cultivation was on a small scale and destined for local markets. Europe, by contrast, depended on imports of sugar cultivated by slaves on West Indian and South American plantations. Trade was channeled to European powers from their colonial possessions: Saint Domingue to France; Brazil to Portugal; Cuba to Spain; and Jamaica, Barbadoes and other Caribbean islands to Britain. Sugar was the key commodity grown in most of these areas, accounting for roughly half of the value of all exports.

After the wars, the geography of production had changed. Jamaica, Barbadoes and Brazil remained major producers, but sugar cultivation for export in Saint Dominque (now independent Haiti) had effectively disappeared and Cuba

TABLE 9.4 U.K. intercontinental trade by commodity (£ m, current prices)

	1784–6	1824–6	1834–6
Sugar	2614	6695	7068
Tea	2587	4121	3846
Cottons and silk cloth	1344	363	347
Cotton, raw	897	6747	14494
Silk, raw	568	1151	2113
Tobacco	536	594	735
Spirits	391	475	675
Other dyestuffs	348	1305	1171
Hides and skins	258	903	1278
Timber	221	2599	2918
Indigo	185	2974	1398
Spices	180	464	514
Coffee	158	1012	1013
Total	10287	29403	37321
Share in all Intercontinent trade (per cent)	95·9	95·5	92.6

SOURCE: DAVIS, *INDUSTRIAL REVOLUTION*, 110–121

had developed from a minor to a major player. New areas, notably Trinidad and British Guiana, had become important producers. Significant quantities of sugar also began to arrive from Mauritius and Réunion in the Indian Ocean. Trade in sugar still tended to flow along paths established by colonial relations. This was fostered in the United Kingdom by significant tariff preference given to sugar grown in its own colonies, though high tariffs on refined sugar discouraged processing at source. In Europe indigenous supplies began slowly to become available through cultivation of the sugar beet.

Figure 9.1 shows rough estimates for the growth of sugar output. It is difficult to discern the eighteenth century trend, particularly since some of the growth in the 1780s may have been recovery after the American Revolutionary War. Extrapolation from the pre-war peaks in 1775 and 1791 suggests that production did not return to trend until just after 1815. Growth was then more rapid during the 1820s before decelerating in the 1830s.

TABLE 9.5 Intercontinental trade: Major commodity imports to U.K.

Region	Share of total imports from the region (per cent) 1784–6	1824–6	1834–6
Asia	Tea	Tea	Tea
	54	39	34
	Cottons & silks	Indigo	Indigo
	28	27	12
West Indies	Sugar	Sugar	Sugar
	58	73	73
USA	Tobacco	Cotton	Cotton
	54	81	88
Canada	Hides & skins	Timber	Timber
	63	85	84
Latin America	Hides & skins	Cotton	Cotton
	83	47	49
Africa	Dyestuffs	Wine	Sugar
	93	27	47
Australia		Wool	Wool
		70	79

SOURCE: DAVIS, *INDUSTRIAL REVOLUTION*, 110–121

In the 1780s Britain imported about a third of total sugar production, of which between a fifth and a quarter was reexported. During the wars, Britain's import share rose to about two-thirds of output, of which a third or so was reexported. In the 1820s the British share fell back to around 45 per cent, with a bit less than a quarter of that being reexported.

Technological change in sugar production became more dynamic during the wars. Most growers replaced indigenous varieties of cane with the Otaheiti or Bourbon variety, which came originally from Oceania. A new roller technology was applied to crushing and these rollers started to be powered by steam. Boiling and refining started to be transformed after the wars by the use of the vacuum pan, invented in 1813.

Yet the major change in the industry was probably the beginnings of the long path to the abolition of slave labour. The slaves of Saint Domingue took their freedom in 1791, and the *trade* in slaves was abolished by most European countries during the 1790s and 1800s. But emancipation of slaves already in British colonies had to wait until 1832 and in French colonies until 1848. The

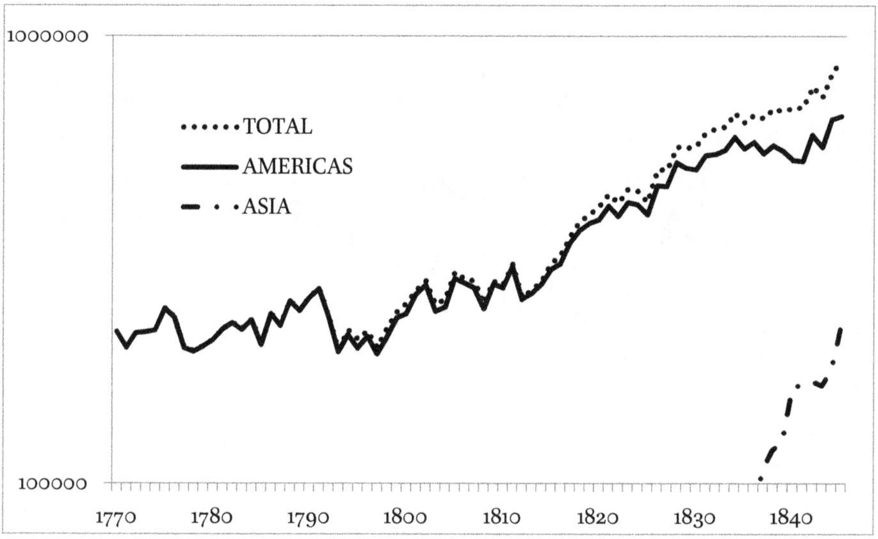

FIGURE 9.1 Sugar production, 1770–1845 (tons)
SOURCE: ESTIMATES, SOMETIME GUESTIMATES, ARE BASED ON THE FIGURES IN NOËL DEERR, *THE HISTORY OF SUGAR* (2 VOLS, LONDON: CHAPMAN & HALL, 1949)

effects of abolition on sugar cultivation depended very much on the local alternatives to plantation work.

What role did the wars play in the changes affecting the sugar industry? Revolutionary ideology, if not war, certainly figured in decline of sugar cultivation on Saint Domingue. Had there been no wars, the French would probably have been able to put down the revolt and San Domingue would have maintained or augmented its position in the sugar trade. As it was, the revolt there frightened planters in other areas, though it did provide a stimulus to the industry in Cuba. A more general fear of revolution may have delayed the abolition of the slave trade, although abolitionism as a movement was well underway before the wars. The reshuffling of colonial control during the wars and at the peace settlement in 1815 influenced the development of new producing regions, as British planters took advantage of opportunities to develop cultivation in Trinidad, Guiana and Mauritius. The sugar trade from Mauritius and Réunion in the Indian Ocean also benefited from the end of the monopoly companies and the reduction in shipping costs that ensued.

Certain changes in technology may have been stimulated by interruptions of trade during war. The French government provided support both for research on sugar beet cultivation and for the construction of the first factories. Although sugar beet growing collapsed after 1815, it started to spread

FIGURE 9.2 Tea exports from Canton (piculs)
SOURCE: HOSEA BALLOU MORSE, *THE CHRONICLES OF THE EAST INDIA COMPANY, TRADING TO CHINA, 1635-1834* (5 VOLS, OXFORD: CLARENDON PRESS, 1926-1929), VOLS. 4, 5

again from the 1820s, so that by the early 1840s it had come to account for about 5 per cent of world sugar production (Deerr 1949, II, 490). Other technological changes, such as the introduction of the Otaheiti variety and new roller designs and the use of steam power, probably owed more to the innovative culture associated with early industrialization than to wartime conditions.

3.2.2 Tea

Before the 1830s, when cultivation began in India, all tea imported to Europe came from China. Figure 9.2 shows the exports from Canton, the port to which the tea trade had been restricted by the Chinese government. The large fluctuations in the trade make it difficult to discern whether the growth in tea exports accelerated after the wars. But it does seem that the wars depressed the tea trade much less than it did that of sugar.

Two major developments took place in the countries which predominated in the tea trade (Table 9.6). First, the U.K. share rose during the wars and remained distinctly higher in the 1820s than it had been in the 1780s. Second, during the wars American merchants replaced merchants from continental Europe in the tea trade. Whilst during the 1790s some American ships may have been vessels of convenience for Dutch and other continental merchants, by the end of the wars this part of the trade was firmly in the hands of the Americans and it remained so in the 1820s.

TABLE 9.6 Tea exports from Canton by shipper (1000 piculs)

	1784–1792	1793–1815	1820–1832
U.K.	129	201	251
Other European	70	15	2
United States	9	35	77
U.K. share (per cent)	62	80	76

SOURCE: MORSE 1926–9, VOLS. 4, 5

3.2.3 Cotton

The scale and provenance of European cotton imports changed completely over the wars.[5] In the late 1780s Britain imported 64,000 bales of cotton annually, with 71 per cent coming from the West Indies and 20 per cent from Greece and Turkey. In the late 1820s imports were a far larger 582,000 bales per year, with the West Indian and Mediterranean shares reduced to 2 and 3 per cent, respectively. Imports from West Indies even fell absolutely, from 45,000 to 13,000 bales. In the late 1820s 75 per cent of British cotton imports came from the United States, 10 per cent from Brazil and 10 per cent from India (Ellison 1886, 86). Similar changes in the provenance of cotton imports occurred on the continent.

The transformation of the cotton trade had little to do with the wars. The increase in scale was driven by technological changes on both the demand and supply sides. The productivity improvements arising from the mechanization of spinning were well under way by the 1780s, with both jennies and water frames in widespread use. These were superseded by mules and throstles during the 1790s and 1800s. These macro-inventions and their subsequent, rapid improvement increased the demand for raw cotton and focused innovative activity on the mechanization of weaving (Maw, Solar, Lyons and Kane, 2021). Although the power loom had been invented in the 1780s, it was only perfected and brought into widespread use from the 1810s and, as such, further increased the demand for raw cotton (Allen 2018).

The supply of cotton was transformed by American ingenuity. Whitney's cotton gin of 1793 and subsequent improvements in ginning technology broke the

5 Much of the material on cotton in this and other sections draws on my ongoing work on the world market for raw cotton.

bottleneck to the growth of green seed, medium-staple cotton in the American South. As cotton cultivation spread westward, planters experimented with cotton varieties and managed to double picking rates (Olmstead and Rhode 2008). The use of steamships on western rivers and of powerful presses to compress bales reduced the costs of shipping cotton to European markets. These innovations, along with abundant land and slave labour, permitted not only the rapid expansion of cotton supplies from the American South, but a large fall in the price of cotton relative to other textile fibres in Europe.

Only two developments in the cotton trade might plausibly be seen as consequences of the wars. One was the increase in supplies of short-staple cotton from India. In the 1780s (and well before) India was by far the world's leading cotton producer, and cotton in India was far cheaper than in Europe. Cotton manufacturers pressed the English East India Company to import Indian cotton, but little was ever shipped. Yet in the 1820s India was supplying 10 per cent of British imports even though the price of cotton in Europe had fallen drastically. To some extent the rise in the use of Indian cotton was due to the ability of manufacturers to adapt their machinery to its very short staple, which had been a problem in the 1780s. But it had also become much cheaper to ship cotton from India to Europe, partly as the result of technological changes in shipping unrelated to the wars and partly because the end of the East India Company monopoly and the rise of British naval hegemony permitted the use of ships that were less expensive to build and to operate.

The other wartime developments were on the demand side. During the wars military procurement was oriented more toward woolen and linen textiles, and higher taxes and higher food prices should have restrained demand for textiles from consumers in the private sector. But any such restraints on the consumption were overwhelmed by the falling absolute and relative prices of cottons.

3.2.4 Timber

The large increase in timber exports from Canada to Britain owed a great deal to the wars (Marr and Paterson 1980, 61–73). Although wood from Canada had reached Britain before the wars in the form of ships, in the eighteenth century rough and fine cut timber had come overwhelmingly from the Baltic, where labour was cheaper and more skilled and from where transport costs were lower. During the wars, the uncertainties of Baltic supplies, particularly for the navy, led the British government to encourage Canadian producers, initially through subsidized contracts for timber, then from 1804 through a tariff on Baltic timber, subsequently raised in 1810 and again in 1815. This encouragement was continued after the wars, with the result that the Canadian share of

U.K. timber imports rose from less than one per cent in 1800 to over 81 per cent in 1820.

British tariffs diverted and probably diminished Baltic timber exports (Aström 1988, 99–107). The British share of masts and rough timber exported from Riga fell during the later years of the war and even more so after their end. During the first half of the nineteenth century Riga's exports of masts never recovered pre-war levels and it took until the mid-1830s for rough timber exports to reach the level attained in the 1780s. Baltic producers did manage to increase exports of sawn timber, retaining their share of the British market for this product.

3.2.5 Indigo

Before the wars most of the indigo used in the European textile industry was imported from the West Indies and South Carolina. After the wars indigo from these sources had been replaced by supplies from India. This shift may owe something to the wars, but it was initiated in 1789 when high British tariffs on Indian indigo were reduced (Aldous 2015, 62). Exports from South Carolina were maintained into the early 1790s, particularly after the revolution in Haiti, which had been France's largest supplier, but they fell off to almost nothing during the late 1790s as Indian indigo came on stream (Edelson 1994, 4, 181). Indian exports were given a further stimulus when transport costs fell from £20 per ton in 1813 to about £5 per ton in 1835 (Aldous 2015, 61). Much of this fall was, like that for shipping Indian cotton, the consequence of the end of the East India Company's trade monopoly.

3.3 *Commodity Trade: Some General Considerations*

Examination of trade in these major commodities confirms that U.K.'s share of European intercontinental trade rose from the prewar to the postwar periods. But was this a consequence of the wars? In the cases of timber and indigo rising shares were due at least in part to commercial policy, but some more general explanations for the rise in Britain's share are also important. The British economy grew more rapidly over these years than did continental economies, perhaps itself a consequence of the wars (see the chapters on individual European countries). Recent estimates show that British GDP per capita grew by 25 per cent between 1750 and 1820. Spanish output per head grew by around 20 per cent, Dutch grew by four per cent, and Italian fell by 2 per cent (Broadberry, Guan and Li 2018, 988). It is unlikely that either France or the German territories matched British growth. But more importantly, Britain's population was growing much more rapidly, at about one per cent per annum from 1750 to 1820. The highest population growth rates elsewhere in western Europe (with the exception of Ireland) barely exceeded half a per cent, and the French and Dutch rates were 0.36 and 0.29 per cent per annum, respectively (Solar 2015).

Not only was aggregate growth thus more rapid in Britain, its industrial sector was growing more rapidly. Given Britain's booming cotton textile industry, it is hardly surprising that Britain's share of the cotton and indigo trades rose. Similarly, rapid growth in both shipbuilding and construction would have heightened British demand for timber.

The costs of the wars also had implications for much of Europe's intercontinental trade. The war and the peace settlement left the belligerent countries with large debts – France was further burdened by reparations – that had to be serviced out of postwar taxation, and government revenues at this time depended heavily on customs and excise duties (Oosterlinck, Ureche-Rangau and Vaslin 2014). Tax rates on imports had already risen during the wars and after the wars they often rose further. British customs and excise duties on sugar more than doubled between the 1780s and the 1820s, and those on tea increased seven-fold. Cotton and indigo had entered free before the wars, but were taxed at 5–6 per cent in the 1820s. In Britain sugar alone accounted for 29 per cent of customs revenue in the early 1820s. In France duties on sugar, coffee and cotton brought in almost half of customs revenue in the same period. For non-European countries such increased taxation on their exports to Europe would have had the effect of impeding the growth of trade and of turning the terms of trade against them.

3.4 *Entrepot Trade*

The rising share of Britain in Europe's intercontinental imports of sugar, tea and other commodities also owed something to the re-export of these goods, though some of the growth of this trade may been at the expense of France, Spain and the Netherlands. As the chapters on France and Spain show, these countries' re-exports of colonial produce were quite large in the 1780s, about 30 per cent of all French exports in the late 1780s, but had essentially disappeared by 1820. The French takeover of the Netherlands from the 1790s made this conflict effectively the fifth Anglo-Dutch War, the last and decisive battle for the entrepot trade in colonial and Baltic goods. During the wars Amsterdam also lost part of its trade in colonial products to Hamburg and recovered little of it after the wars.

The value of British re-exports of colonial goods to European markets increased quite substantially from the 1780s to the 1820s (Table 9.7). Only reexports of tobacco declined. The British captured more of the trade in colonial goods, but the significance of this entrepot trade should perhaps not be exaggerated. Even after the wars the size of the re-export trades in sugar, coffee,

TABLE 9.7 U.K. Re-exports

	Northern Europe		Northwestern Europe		Southern Europe	
	1784–6	1824–6	1784–6	1824–6	1784–6	1824–6
Sugar	2	209	4	217	0	101
Refined sugar	35	42	224	326	7	210
Coffee	25	131	105	451	2	53
Tea	0	0	0	30	1	3
Tobacco	27	10	450	88	8	38
TOTAL	89	492	783	1112	18	405

SOURCE: DAVIS, *INDUSTRIAL REVOLUTION*, 102–107

tea and tobacco remained small relative to British domestic consumption of these goods. Yet both re-exports and goods shipped directly from Asia and the Americas to third markets did bolster Britain's shipping, insurance and finance industries.

4 Prices

4.1 *Effects on Relative Prices in Europe*

As O'Rourke (2006) has shown, the wars, and particularly the blockades and embargoes around 1810, had very large effects on relative prices in European countries during the wars. In Britain the prices of wheat, timber and sugar relative to textiles rose markedly during most of the wartime years. The continental countries, by contrast, showed much sharper peaks in these relative prices during the Continental blockade. Much as might be expected from wartime disruptions to trade, the prices of imports rose relative to those of exports. However, O'Rourke's evidence also indicates that these wartime changes had limited long-run impact. Where his series extend back before the wars, the general impression is that after the wars relative prices reverted to prewar levels. The great exception was raw cotton, the price of which fell markedly relative to other textile fibres and to other goods more generally between the 1780s and the 1830s. But, as explained above, this change owed little to the wars.

4.2 *Effects on Prices in Europe Relative to Asia*

Between the 1780s and the 1820s the cost of shipping between Europe and Asia fell by about two-thirds (Solar 2013). Roughly half of the fall can be attributed to the early and widespread adoption of copper sheathing by shipowners in the Asian trade. Coppering prolonged ship lives and reduced maintenance leading to more and more frequent voyages and making for a large reduction in capital costs. It also significantly reduced voyage durations, as ships with cleaner bottoms sailed faster and this increase in speed allowed them to avoid stopping at the Cape. However, shorter voyage durations were only a minor element in the reduction in costs. East Indiamen were almost all coppered by the mid-1780s, so this technological change had nothing to do with the French wars.

The other half of the reduction in shipping costs had everything to do with the end of the East India Company's monopoly and the advent of British naval hegemony. As noted above, East Indiamen were large, heavily armed and heavily manned vessels because they had naval as well as commercial use. They were expensive to build and expensive to operate, and would never have been viable as trading vessels during peacetime periods, hence the need for national monopolies. With the demise of the continental companies and British control of the seas, the British and everyone else in the Asia trade went over to smaller ships, saving on both capital and labour.

This fall in transport costs between the 1780s and the 1820s was huge. The later effects of steamships and the Suez Canal acted only on the remaining third, hence were necessarily far smaller. The result should have been a narrowing of price gaps between European and Asian markets. O'Rourke and Williamson (2002) show striking falls in the margins for cloves and pepper and to a lesser extent for coffee, but wrongly attribute these changes to transport innovations, such as steamships and railways, that had not yet occurred. Neither of the two major studies of price convergence done subsequently spans the wars. De Zwart's (2016) study of prices in the seventeenth and eighteenth centuries stops in the early 1790s when his principal source, the records of the Dutch East India Company, dries up. Chilosi and Federico's (2015) work on the nineteenth century begins only in 1796 at the earliest. Although de Zwart does not discuss the war's effects, he does summarize information on mark-ups from his own work and from that of Chilosi and Federico that allows us to do so. These "mark-ups", which are actually the ratios of prices in Europe to those in Asia and are shown in Table 9.8, fell, often considerably, from before to after the wars. To this comparison we might add information on another important commodity, raw cotton. Whilst cotton prices in India remained in the range of 3–5 pence per pound from the late eighteenth century into the

TABLE 9.8 Ratios of European to Asian prices

	18th Century	1820s/1830s
Coffee	5.55	1.60
Pepper	4.89	1.92
Sugar	4.45	1.50
Saltpeter	3.23	1.90
Indigo	3.15	1.78
Tea	2.92	1.83
Silk	1.74	1.47

SOURCES: DE ZWART 2016, 526–7, 531

early nineteenth century, the price in London fell from 20–22 pence in the 1780s to 7–8 pence in the 1820s, suggesting a fall in the mark-up from around 5 to around 2.

Although Chilosi and Federico (2021) describe the nineteenth century as the "first globalization", as far as trade between Europe and Asia is concerned, most of the action took place over the wars.[6] Of the products shown above, markups had been relatively stable during the eighteenth century, with the exceptions of that for indigo, which rose, and those for tea and saltpeter, which fell. In the nineteenth century markups did fall, but they could not fall below one as long as trade in these commodities flowed from Asia to Europe. Hence the fall in the markups over the wars was, with the exception of tea, larger, usually much larger, than any conceivable reduction that could have taken place during the rest of the nineteenth century. This is not to say that the fall in markups occurred during the wars, when the dangers of seafaring drove up the costs of labour and insurance. The effects of the reduction in shipping costs only manifested themselves fully after 1815.

6 Note that their evidence does not stretch back before the wars, so their conclusions about the effect of ending the East India Company's monopoly in 1813 are based on price markups in wartime.

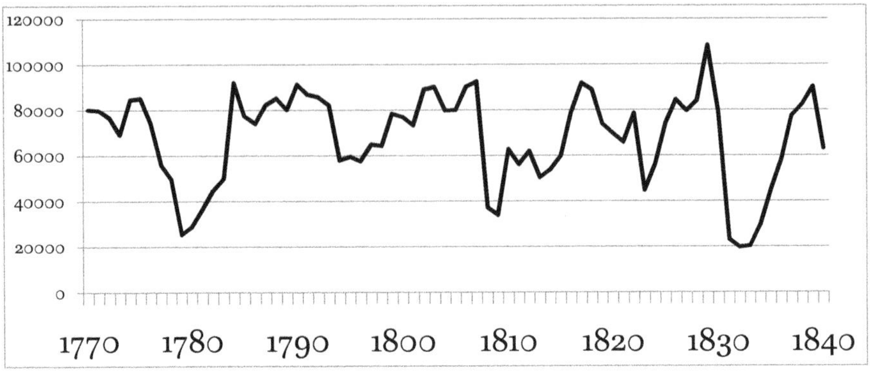

FIGURE 9.3 Transatlantic slave trade (slaves per annum)
SOURCE: SLAVE VOYAGES

5 Intercontinental Movements of Labour

During the eighteenth century the trade in slaves constituted the major intercontinental movement of labour. As shown in Figure 9.3, war certainly disrupted the trade, though it is striking that the American Revolutionary War seems to have had a larger effect than did the French Revolutionary and Napoleonic Wars. The fall in the early 1790s is much less than that in the late 1770s. Although the numbers of slaves shipped fell off markedly after Britain abolished the trade in 1807, the trade proved to be remarkably resilient well into the postwar period as destinations shifted from British and French colonies in the Caribbean to Brazil and Cuba.

What effects could the wars have had on the slave trade? The revolutionary period certainly contributed both to the Haitian revolution and to the freeing of slaves in other French colonies in 1794, though Napoleon reintroduced colonial slavery in 1804. In Britain the abolitionist movement was well underway in the 1780s, but getting Parliament to stop the trade in slaves may well have been delayed by fears of revolution in France and the colonies.

A major development after the wars was the rise of free labour migration (Table 9.9). Flows of emigrants to the Americas were quite small in the eighteenth century, and some of the emigrants were not free, being either indentured servants or convicts. There was considerable continuity in the origins of migrants before and after the wars. Most came from northeast Ireland and southwest Germany, both densely populated areas with limited opportunities for seasonal migration.

The wars impeded emigration in two major ways. First, it significantly raised the both the costs and the risks of the transatlantic passage. Even in the

TABLE 9.9 Intercontinental labour movements (1000s per year)

	Slaves	Free (USA)
1776–1800	80	7
1826–1850	71	59

SOURCES: SLAVE: SLAVE VOYAGES; FREE (USA): COHN, *MASS MIGRATION*, 15

late 1810s fares were £6–12 without provisions. Second, military recruitment absorbed large number of young men, who were the most likely emigrants. In the chapter on Britain it is conjectured that 20 per cent of all prime age males were involved, directly or indirectly, in the war effort. In addition, those that the military did not get would have faced better prospects for agricultural and industrial employment in Britain and Ireland.

A problem with the argument that the wars slowed down free migration to the Americas is that mass emigration did not take off when the wars ended, but only from around 1830. Cohn (2009) argues that the takeoff at this time owed much to the coincidence of poor agrarian conditions in Europe and improvements in the American economy. But he also argues that a number of institutional changes were important. Rather than passengers being incidental to freight, a distinct passenger business emerged with specialized ships, ticket offices and emigration agents. This helped lower fares to £3–5, still quite steep but more affordable. Even so, these costs were often paid by previous emigrants through remittances, with prepaid tickets becoming common. Had the wars not impeded emigration for more than two decades, it seems likely that these institutional developments might have occurred earlier.

6 Intercontinental Movements of Capital

Flows of capital from Europe to other continents took many forms, but were generally small in the eighteenth century. One of the more important was credit extended to planters and local merchants in the Americas, which facilitated the growth in transatlantic trade and remained important after the wars (Egnal 1998, 12–20). As for emigrants, most took little with them across the Atlantic, though some had the resources with which to set up farms, plantations and other businesses. Formal, large-scale international loans were rare since there were few public or private borrowers of substance. The incipient United States did borrow from the French and the Dutch during its Revolutionary War and, despite a poor record of repayment, the newly independent country secured further loans from the Dutch in 1787 and 1788. Colonial governments in Latin America only borrowed locally, but when nineteen newly independent states appeared after the wars, they became customers for loans on the London and other European bond markets (Flandreau and Flores 2009).

Perhaps the largest intercontinental capital movements during the eighteenth century were the flows of silver in the other direction, from Latin America across the Atlantic to Europe as well as across the Pacific on the Manila galleons and on United State merchant ships to Asia. Properly speaking, only the parts of these flows that were not payment for imports should count as capital movements, but these could still be substantial sums, providing significant revenues to the Iberian governments and sustaining the Spanish colonial enterprise in the Philippines. In addition to tax revenue, the Spanish government was also able to raise loans in New Spain in the 1780s (Marichal 2007). After the wars and with the rise of sovereign states in Latin America, not only did transfers to Spain and among its former colonies cease, silver production fell off by more than a third, partly due to chronic lack of investment and partly to destruction during the wars of independence, and only recovered its late eighteenth-century level in the 1840s (Vassoler 1998).

The flows of silver, including those paying for imports, mattered not only for their size, but for the form in which they took (Irigoin 2009). Most of the silver mined in Spanish America was minted into Spanish American pesos, which circulated widely not only in Latin America, but also in the United States, China and other parts of the world. In these areas the peso carried a premium in international transactions, which demonstrates its importance as a reliable and accepted means of payment. Since Latin America produced 90 per cent of the world's silver in the early nineteenth century, the fall in production after 1808 had a major impact on the amount of silver coin (Merrill 1930). In addition, and perhaps of greater importance, the standard of quality of the peso was eroded as the Spanish empire broke up. In China old pesos were at a premium over pesos minted by republican governments and, as a result, they were often hoarded. The demise of this silver standard may have paved the way for the rise of the gold standard in the nineteenth century (Irigoin 2020).

7 Concluding Remarks

This survey of intercontinental movements of goods, labour and capital illustrates the difficulty of distinguishing the effects of the wars from other political, economic and technological developments. The wars may have slowed the flow of free labour across the Atlantic, but their effects on slave labour remain ambiguous or unproven. They clearly interrupted and reoriented trade in many goods, but the evidence is not sufficient to say whether in the long-run they had an independent effect on the growth of intercontinental trade, particularly since the costs of paying for the wars fell heavily on imports from outside Europe. The wars and the rise of British naval hegemony hastened the demise of the East India companies, contributing to the reduction in shipping costs between Europe and Asia, but technological changes unrelated to the wars were equally important.

One unambiguous conclusion to be drawn is that the wars saw the rise of both Britain and the United States at the expense of the continental powers. Two decades of unchallenged access to markets in Asia, Africa and the Americas put both countries in a position to profit fully from the long period of peace and freer trade to come. But even here, other factors played important roles. Britain and the United States had faster rates of growth of both population and per capita income in the late eighteenth and early nineteenth centuries. Whilst these advantages may have also owed something to wartime developments, they were already present before the wars.

We might summarize some of the more prominent changes in the global economy outside Europe by indulging in some counterfactual speculation. In the absence of the wars, the eighteenth-century European empires might have persisted well into the nineteenth century. Their contours may well have changed since during the eighteenth-century the British had already slowly been increasing their share of colonial territory. Britain's growing industrial and naval power would likely have increased pressure to open up trade in other countries' empires, even if it did produce shifts in their boundaries. There would still have been frictions, which might have meant that the European powers would have remained in a naval arms race and that the East India Companies may have remained their proxies in Asian waters, limiting, through their power in Asian and European markets and their inefficiently large ships, the growth of trade within Asia and between Europe and Asia.

The Spanish empire in the Americas, had it persisted, might have continued to bring the benefits to its inhabitants of peaceful trade and some redistribution of tax revenues across the empire. The costly wars of independence and subsequent strife among the newly independent nations might have been avoided. The mines of Spanish America would not have been devastated and might have continued to produce enough standard silver pesos to facilitate trade in China and other parts of the world.

In such a world what place might the newly independent United States have found? Its abundance of land would surely have attracted immigrants from Europe, with larger numbers arriving in the 1790s and 1800s perhaps triggering an earlier start to mass emigration. In the absence of the effective protection to industry provided by high wartime transport costs and restrictions during the Embargo and the War of 1812 and of the injection of profits from lucrative wartime trade, would its industrial development have been much more limited, creating less of a constituency for protective tariffs? If free (or freer) trade became the norm, the United States might have remained, like Canada, predominantly an exporter of raw materials, foodstuffs and timber, either unsawn or made into ships. At some point might this expanding agrarian democracy have run up against a huge territory ruled from Paris and settled by French-speakers, some of them perhaps slaves of African origin? Would both this territory and the rest of the Americas have continued to be supplied by a thriving slave trade?

References

Aldous, Michael. 2015. "Avoiding 'negligence and profusion': the ownership and organisation of Anglo-Indian trading firms, 1818 to 1870." PhD diss., London School of Economics and Political Science.

Allen, Robert C. 2018. "The Hand-Loom weaver and the Power Loom: a Schumpeterian Perspective." *European Review of Economic History* 22 (4): 381–402.

Aström, Sven-Erik. 1988. *From Tar to Timber: Studies in Northeast European Forest Exploitation and Foreign Trade, 1660–1860*. Helsinki: Societas Scientiarium Fennica.

Bairoch, Paul, and Bouda Etemad. 1985. *Structure par produits des exportations du Tiers-Monde, 1830–1937*. Geneva: Droz.

Baugh, Daniel. 2004. "Naval Power: What gave the British Naval Superiority?" In Leandro, Prados de la Escosura, ed., *Exceptionalism and Industrialisation: Britian and its European Rivals, 1688–1815*, ed. Leandro Prados de la Escosura, pp. 235–257. Cambridge: Cambridge University Press.

Broadberry, Stephen, Hanhui Guan and David Daokui Li. 2018. "China, Europe, and the Great Divergence: A Study in Historical National Accounting, 980–1850." *Journal of Economic History* 78 (4) 955–1000.

Carter, Susan B., et al. 2006. *Historical Statistics of the United States: Millenium Edition*. https://hsus.cambridge.org/HSUSWeb/HSUSEntryServlet.

Chilosi, David, and Giovanni Federico. 2015. "Early Globalizations: The Integration of Asia in the World Economy, 1800–1938." *Explorations in Economic History* 57: 1–18.

Chilosi, David, and Giovanni Federico. 2021. "The Effects of Market Integration during the First Globalization: a Multi-Market Approach," *European Review of Economic History*, forthcoming.

Coatsworth, John H., and Jeffrey G. Williamson. 2004. "Always Protectionist? Latin American Tariffs from Independence to the Great Depression." *Journal of Latin American Studies* 36 (2): 205–232.

Cohn, Raymond L. 2009. *Mass Migration under Sail.* Cambridge: Cambridge University Press.

Cuenca Estaban, Javier. 2008. "Statistics of Spain's Colonial Trade, 1747–1820: New Estimates and Comparisons with Great Britain." *Revista de Historia Economica* 26 (3): 323–365.

Davis, Ralph. 1979. *The Industrial Revolution and British Overseas Trade.* Leicester: Leicester University Press.

de Vries, Jan. 2010. "The Limits of Globalization in the Early Modern World." *Economic History Review* 63 (3): 710–733.

de Zwart, Pim. 2016. "Globalization in the Early Modern Era: New Evidence from the Dutch-Asiatic Trade, c.1600–1800." *Journal of Economic History* 76 (2): 520–558.

Deerr, Noël. 1949. *The History of Sugar*. 2 vols, London: Chapman & Hall.

Denzel, Markus. 2017. "The Price of Minimalizing the Risks at Sea: The Hamburg Marine Insurance Rates in the 18th and Early 19th Century." In *The Price of Things in Pre-Industrial Times*, 365–383. Florence: Firenze University Press.

Edelson, Scott David. 1994. "Colour and Enterprise: South Carolina Indigo and the Atlantic Economy, 1745–1795." M.Litt. diss., University of Oxford.

Edling, Max M. 2015. *A Hercules in the Cradle: War, Money, and the American State, 1783–1867*. Chicago: University of Chicago Press.

Egnal, Marc. *New World Economies: The Growth of the Thirteen Colonies and Early Canada.* Oxford: Oxford University Press, 1998.

Ellison, Thomas. 1886. *The Cotton Trade of Great Britain*. London: E. Wilson.

Engerman, Stanley, and Kenneth L. Sokoloff. 2011. *Economic Development in the Americas since 1500: Endowments and Institutions*. Cambridge: Cambridge University Press.

Etemad, Boude. 2007. *Possessing the World.* Oxford: Berghahn.

Federico, Giovanni and Antonio Tena Junguito. 2018. "Federico-Tena World Trade Historical Database: World Trade." Doino:21950/HPW2AK, e-cienciaDatos, V1.

Fichter, James R. 2010. *So Great a Proffit: How the East Indies Trade Transformed Anglo-American Capitalism*. Cambridge, Mass: Harvard University Press.

Findlay, Ronald, and Kevin H. O'Rourke. 2007. *Power and Plenty: Trade, War and the World Economy in the Second Millennium*. Princeton: Princeton University, Press.

Flandreau, Marc, and Juan H. Flores. 2009. "Bonds and Brands: Foundations of the Sovereign Debt Market, 1820–1830." *Journal of Economic History* 69 (3): 646–684.

Glete, Jan. 1993. *Navies and Nations: Warships, Navies and State Building in Europe and America, 1500–1860*. Stockholm: Almqvist & Wiksell.

Haines, Michael R., and Richard H. Steckel. 2000. *A Population History of North America*. Cambridge: Cambridge University Press.

Headrick, Daniel R. 1981. *The Tools of Empire: Technology and European Imperialism in the Nineteenth Century*. Oxford: Oxford University Press.

Hejeebu, Santhi. 2016. "The Colonial Transition and the Decline of the East India Company, c.1746–1784." In *A New Economic History of Colonial India*, edited by Latika Chaudhary, Bishnupriya Gupta, Tirthankar Roy and Anand V. Swamy, pp. 33–51. London: Routledge.

Hoffman, Philip. 2015. *Why Did Europe Conquer the World?* Princeton: Princeton University Press.

Irigoin, Alejandra. 2009. "The End of a Silver Era: The Consequences of the Breakdown of the Spanish Peso Standard in China and the United States, 1780s-1850s." *Journal of World History* 20 (2): 207–243.

Irigoin, Alejandra. 2020. "The Rise and Demise of the Global Silver Standard." In *Handbook of the History of Money and Currency*, edited by S. Battilossi, Y. Cassis and K. Yago, pp. 383–410. Singapore: Springer Singapore (also as LSE Economic History Working Papers, No. 285 (2018)).

Lambert, Andrew. 1984. *Battleships in Transition: The Creation of the Steam Battlefleet, 1815–1860*. London: Conway Maritime Press.

Marichal, Carlos. 2007. *Bankruptcy of Empire : Mexican Silver and the Wars between Spain, Britain and France, 1760–1810*. Cambridge: Cambridge University Press.

Marr, William L., and Donald G. Paterson. 1980. *Canada: An Economic History*. Toronto: Gage.

Maw, Peter, Peter M. Solar, John S. Lyons and Aidan Kane. 2021. "After the Great Inventions: Technological Change in U.K. Cotton Spinning, 1780–1835." *Economic History Review*, forthcoming.

Merrill, Charles White. 1930. *Summarized Data of Silver Production*. Washington: Government Printing Office.

Mitchell, Brian R. 1992. *International Historical Statistics Europe 1750–1988*. 3rd ed., London: Palgrave Macmillan.

Morse, Hosea Ballou. 1926–1929. *The Chronicles of the East India Company, Trading to China, 1635–1834*. 5 vols, Oxford: Clarendon Press.

O'Brien, Patrick Karl, and Xavier Duran. 2011. "Total Factor Productivity for the Royal Navy from Victory at Texel (1653) to Triumph at Trafalgar (1805)." In Richard W. Unger, ed., *Shipping and Economic Growth, 1350–1850*, edited by Richard W. Unger, pp. 277–307. Leiden: Brill.

O'Rourke, Kevin H. 2006. "The Worldwide Economic Impact of the French Revolutionary and Napoleonic Wars, 1793–1815." *Journal of Global History* 1 (1): 123–149.

O'Rourke, Kevin H., and Jeffrey G. Williamson. 2002. "When did Globalization Begin?" *European Review of Economic History* 6 (1): 23–50.

Olmstead, Alan, and Paul Rhode. 2008. "Biological Innovation and Productivity Growth in the Antebellum Cotton Economy." *Journal of Economic History* 68 (4): 1123–1171.

Oosterlinck, Kim, Loredana Ureche-Rangau and Jacques-Marie Vaslin. 2004. "Baring, Wellington and the Resurrection of French Public Finances following Waterloo." *Journal of Economic History* 74 (4): 1072–1102.

Romano, Ruggiero. 1962. "Per una valutazione della flotta mercantile europea alla fine del secolo XVIII." In *Studi in onore di Amintore Fanfani*, vol. 5, pp. 575–591. Five volumes, Milan: Giuffré.

Satia, Priya. 2018. *Empire of Guns: The Violent Making of the Industrial Revolution*. London: Duckworth Overlook.

Solar, Peter M. 2015. "Why Ireland Starved and the Big Issues in Pre-Famine Irish Economic History." *Irish Economic and Social History* 42: 62–75.

Solar, Peter M. 2013. "Opening to the East: Shipping between Europe and Asia, 1770–1830." *Journal of Economic History* 73 (3): 625–661.

Sugihara, Kaoru, and Tomotaka Kawamura. 2013. "Introduction: Reconstructing Intra-Southeast Asian Trade, c.1781–1870: Evidence of Regional Integration under the Regime of Colonial Free Trade." *Southeast Asian Studies* 2 (3): 437–441.

Sugihara, Kaoru. 2009. "The Resurgence of Intra-Asian Trade, 1800–1850." In *How India Clothed the World*, edited by Giorgio Riello and Tirthankar Roy, pp. 139–170. Leiden: Brill.

Slave Voyages. https://www.slavevoyages.org.

van Zanden, Jan Luiten. 2010. "Colonial State Formation and Patterns of Economic Development in Java, 1800–1913." *Economic History of Developing Regions* 25 (2): 155–176.

Vassoler, Ivani. 1998. "The Mexican Mining Bubble That Burst", in *Alexander von Humboldt: From the Americas to the Cosmos*, edited by Raymond Erickson, Mauricio A. Font and Brian Schwartz. Online publication, Bildner Center for Western Hemisphere Studies, City University of New York, pp. 427–435.

Webster, Anthony. 2009. *The Twilight of the East India Company: The Evolution of Anglo-Asian Commerce and Politics, 1790–1860*. Woodbridge: The Boydell Press.

Index

Accumulation of military and naval capital 28–32
Act of Mainz (1831) 133
Administrative organisation of space 14
Agglomeration 101, 104, 105
Agrarian reform 97, 99, 100, 101, 102
Agricultural losses 223
Agricultural modernization
extensive margin 32
golden age 1846–73 32
intersectoral terms of trade 31, 33
prices and wages 32
supplies of manpower, food, horses and timber 30–33
the integration of Ireland 32
Agricultural Output 2, 5, 6, 13, 18, 20, 24, 223
Agriculture 2–26, 115–6, 124, 126, 129, 135
productivity 15
Aix-en-Provence 7
Albacete 3, 4, 33
Alcobaça 224
Alentejo 220, 221
Algarve 220, 221
Alsace 22
American War of Independence 7, 8, 37
Amsterdam 21, 116, 118–124, 129–133
Ancien Régime 2, 5, 6, 14, 17, 24
Andalusia 18
Anglo-Dutch War, Fourth (1780–1784) 121, 123
Anholt 92
Animal husbandry 124, 135
Annexation, of the Netherlands by France (1810) 117, 121, 123, 127, 134, 136
Antwerp 121–2, 124, 131, 133
Archangelsk 122
Armament industry 88, 89, 92
Army 141, 145, 146, 156, 164, 208, 213, 237, 238
aid 209, 210, 213, 214, 231, 240
allied armies 227
Anglo-Portuguese army 208
artillery 206
Guerrillas 206, 207n7, 240
militiamen (milícias) 206
officers 208, 235, 236, 239
royal navy 205, 256
soldiers 205, 207, 208, 211n6, 217, 221
troops 125, 127, 205, 206, 207, 208, 210, 224, 227
Astudillo 7, 8
Asturias 3
Atlantic 3, 4, 17, 20, 26
Auerstedt (battle) 99, 84, 86
Austerlitz (Battle of, 1805) 141, 207
Austria 10, 82, 83
Hapsburg land and dynasty 5, 6
economic growth 7, 8
empire 7
Italian Independence 8
Metternich 8
Versus Prussia 8
Ávila 3, 33

Badajoz 3
Baden 7, 83, 84, 87, 98, 103, 104
Balance of payments
income account 36
invisibles 36
Balassa, Béla 19
Baltic 37 121–2, 124, 135, 266–267, 268
Bank of England and suspension of cash payments 30
Banking 123, 131
Bankruptcy 88 (see also financial crisis 126, 128–9, 131)
Barbary States 37
Barcelona 8
Batavian Revolution (1795) 116, 136
Bavaria 7, 82, 83, 84, 87, 92, 99, 102, 103
Bayonne 208
Beer 125, 134
Beira 217, 220, 224
Belgium 23, 27, 29, 37, 117, 119, 129–30
Berg (grand duchy; Napoleonic satellite state) 84, 98, 103
Berlin 84, 96, 103, 104
Bills of exchange (regulation of payment systems) 98
Bloch, Marc 3
Bohemia 2

Bonaparte, Joseph 6
Bonaparte, Napoleon 2
Bordeaux 6, 26
Bouches-du-Rhône 7
Bourgogne 14
Brazil 15, 204, 205, 206, 226, 228, 229, 230, 231, 252, 260, 265, 272
Bremen 6, 122, 133
Britain 9, 20, 115–6, 119, 122, 124, 130–1, 134, 136, 204, 205, 208, 209, 212, 216, 223, 226, 230, 230, 231, 239
British East India Company 4
British empire 17
British Guiana 251, 261, 263
Brittany 21, 23
Brokers, financial 129, 131–2
Bureaucracy (state bureaucracy) 100, 102

Cádiz 21
Campo Formio (treaty of) 83
Campoformio (Treaty of, 1797) 141
Campomanes, Pedro Rodriguez de 21
Canada 17, 266, 276
Canals 129, 131, 133
Cape Colony (South Africa) 253
Capital (physical) 88, 95
Capital formation
  crowding in and crowding out 28
Capital market 87
Capital movements
  Intercontinental 273–274
Capital stock 6
Capitalism 3
Caribbean 117, 119
Carlist War 15, 18, 20, 21
Castlereagh, Lord 119
Catalonia 5, 6, 8, 19
Cavour, Camillo 164
Central Commission for Navigation on the Rhine (first IGO) 85
Centralisation 129, 136
Ceylon (Sri Lanka) 117, 119, 253
China
  canton 264
  silver coins 274
  tea 264–265
Chappe, Claude 6
Charles IV of Spain 2, 21
Church 3, 9, 10, 12, 13, 14
Cisalpina Republic (later Italian Republic) 141
Ciudad Rodrigo 3, 206
Civil law 99
Civil service 128–9
Climate 92, 94, 96
Coal 125
Code de commerce (I also use "business law") 98
Code Napoléon 158, 159, 163
Coffee 125
Coimbra 217, 227
Colonial Gains and Losses 4
Colonial goods 122, 125, 132
Colonies
  Dutch 115–117, 120
  decolonization 251–252
  Common land (commons) 97, 100
  Comparative advantages 37
  Confiscations 2, 5, 13
  Congress of Vienna 7
Congress of Vienna
  German economic growth 5, 6, 7
  post-war peace 2
  reformed international economic order 1, 15
  restoration of frontiers 3
  UK economic gains 15
Conjuncture 1
Conscription 118
Consumption 29
Continental Blockade/system 7, 94, 96, 97, 116, 121, 128
Corvée labour (probably: see serfdom) 100
Cost of government 128
Cost of living 118
Costs and Benefits 2, 5
Cotton (industry) 22, 94, 96, 97, 104, 124–5, 134–5
Covilhã 224
Cuba 20, 252, 260, 261, 263, 272
Customs (see also tariffs, tolls 121, 123, 127–8, 130, 134)

Daudin, Guillaume 27
Death rate 118–20
Debt (public debt, state debt, perhaps see fiscal policy) 86, 87, 88, 120, 127–32
Democratisation 116, 129

Denmark 122
Desamortización (disentailment) 6, 16
Development of fiscal and financial institutions 30
Disease 88
Divergence 3
Douai 7
Douro 217, 221
Dresden 104
Dye 125

East Frisia 117, 119
East India companies 254, 270
East Indies, Dutch 117, 119–121, 131, 137
Economic conjunctures and warfare 1
Economic growth 17, 20, 21, 22, 23, 26, 27, 28, 29, 39, 115, 136–7
Economic integration 4, 5, 6
Eden, William 23
Education 8
Egypt 141
Elbe (river) 85, 101
Elisa (Sister of Napoleon) 141
Emilia-Romagna 146
Empire (Holy Roman Empire) 82, 83, 102, 102, 106
Empire and warfare 30
Engineering (industry) 104
England 25, 26, 27, 29
England's republican regime 23
Enlightened absolutism 99
Enlightenment 38
Entre-Douro-e-Minho 220
Erzgebirge 95
Essen 89
Esslingen 104
Estate (in premodern political system) 82, 99, 102, 103
Estremadura 19, 27
Europe 10, 11, 17, 20, 23, 25, 26, 30, 203, 204, 207, 208, 210, 213, 215, 227, 230, 230, 232, 233, 235, 238, 240, 242
 Central 29
 East 29
 North 26
 West 26
 Western 20, 21
Évora 217, 227
Excises 127, 130
Expenditures under French rule; after Restoration 146, 156, 158
Export 115, 120–6, 130
Exports of commodities and services 33
Extremadura 217, 224
Eylau 207

Factor mobility 6
Farm animals (incl. Horses) 88, 92, 95
Farmers 5, 6, 13
Fertility 4
Finance 11, 12, 21
 Bank of England and the City of London 30
 bullionist predictions 30
 gold standard 30
 London and rival european financial cities 30
 metropolitan and country banks 30
 and public debt 2, 9, 10
Financial crisis 88 (see also bankruptcy 127)
Financial market 123, 126, 130
Financial sector, see also banking, service sector 115, 123–4, 129–30
Fiscal capacity 115, 129–30
Fiscal policy 85–87, 99, 103, 104 (see also Fiscal reforms)
Fiscal reforms 1783–92 24
Fiscal systems 6
Fisheries 115–6, 119, 125–6, 133, 136
Flax 124, 135
Flour 134
Foreign investments 123
Fox, Edward 4, 29
France 2–20, 22, 23–30, 115, 117, 119, 122, 124, 130, 136, 204–207, 212, 215, 217, 230–240
 adaptability of the ancien regime 9
 army 204–210, 213, 236
 as an economic hegemony 12
 bourbon regime in 1780s 9
 colonies, loss of 264
 costs of civil war 2
 costs and benefits 5
 East 23
 economic growth 267
 French peasantry 10
 long-term effects of the revolution and warfare 9
 manpower and demographic change 12

France (*cont.*)
navy 255–256
population growth 268
power and influence 5
prediction on European manpower and resources 11
redistribution of wealth and income 10
slavery 263
smaller towns 10
sovereignty 5
the revolution as an economic transformation 9
national debt in 1815 11
North-East 8
legacy of the revolution 6, 11, 12
soldiers 205, 207, 208, 211, 216, 221
sovereign debt 9, 10
South-West 21
taxation 268
troops 205–210, 224, 227
North 22, 23
West 23, 24, 38
Frankfurt (grand duchy; Napoleonic satellite state) 84
Frankfurt am Main (town) 87
Franz of Austria (Habsburg monarch, last Emperor of the Holy Roman Empire) 83
Freedom of trade 97, 100, 106
French army 2, 3, 4, 5, 6, 9
French conquest of Italy 153
French Empire 4, 7
French invasions and the Industrial Revolution 24, 25, 28, 31, 37, 38
French perceptions of British fiscal and financial institutions 31
Frontier economy 20
Funding warfare
taxes versus loans 28

Galicia 221
Garancine 134
GDP 14, 20, 22, 23, 24, 32, 34, 35, 114, 120, 131, 143, 156, 160, 164, 232, 233
Genoa, Republic of 147, 151, 162, 163
Gentlemanly capitalism, 1815–1941 38
Geopolitics and economic history 3, 4, 23, 35–38
German Federation 82
Germany/German States 18, 29, 37
Germany 232, 238 (see also Prussia 122–4)
costs and benefits 5
customs union 5
economic growth 267
economic integration 5
emigration 272
Frontiers 6
German polities and state formation 6
holy German Roman Empire 5
rise of Prussia 6, 8
Gibraltar 9
Gin and brandy 125
Gogel, Alexander 127
Gold 129
Gómina, Erasmo de 8
Grain 7, 121–2, 135
Great Britain 2, 18, 23, 209, 212, 216
Guilds (merchant guilds, craft guilds) 3, 94, 97, 100, 123, 129, 133, 135, 137
Guinea, West Africa 117
Guyana 119

Habsburg Empire 83, 84
Haiti 28
Hamburg 122–4, 131–3
Hamburg 6, 256, 268
Hanover 6, 104
Harvest (failure) 92, 104
Harz 89
Hessen 84
Historical memory and international relations 14
Historiography 3
Holland 37, 114–37
Human capital 92
Human capital formation derived from service in the army and navy
Deference 26–28
Discipline 26, 27
Skills 26
Hungary 2

Iberia 205
Imperial city 83
Income per head 20, 22, 23, 24, 32, 34, 35
India 17, 253, 254–255, 258, 264, 266, 267
Indonesia 253–254
Industrial developments 1783–1815 33–36

Industrialisation 100, 114, 134, 136
Industry 2–24, 115, 119–20, 124–5, 130–1, 133–5
factories 223–227, 229
products 226
Inequality 7, 21, 23, 33, 35
Infant industry (protection) 96
Inflation 87, 88, 89
Inheritance laws 7, 8
Innovation, see also technological improvement 115, 123, 125–6
Institution (institutional change, institutional reforms) 84, 85, 94, 97, 98, 101, 103, 104, 104
Institutional reforms under the French; reversal of after Restoration 158–160
Institutions 2–6, 14, 17
and cultures 1
Insurance 133
Integration of Italian market 160
Interest payments 127–31
Internal demand 23, 26, 29
International economic order 3, 11
International trade 88, 92, 94, 96, 103
Ireland 268, 272–273
Irish Parliament 4
Rebellion 1798 4
Iron 125, 134
industry 19
Italy/Italian peninsula 10, 27, 37
Italy 230, 232, 237, 238
Austrian occupation of Lombardy, Venice and Veneto 8
economic growth 267
House of Savoy and Austria 8
Napoleonic conquests and Unification 8
Kingdom of (Regno d'Italia) 141, 146, 147, 152, 153, 156, 159

Japan 117
Jena (battle) 84, 86, 99
Jena 207
Joint stock companies 98
Joseph Bonaparte 206
Jovellanos, Gaspar Melchor de 21
Junot 205, 207

Karlsruhe 104
Kassel 104

Labour 5, 130, 134
Lafay, Gérard 19
Land markets 6, 7, 13, 15, 16, 18, 20, 33, 35
Land ownership 7, 13
Land rent (see also"rent") 7, 9, 13, 20, 21, 22, 23, 32, 33, 35, 89, 90, 95
Land sales 156n12
Languedoc 22
Lazio 141, 146, 147n7
Le Havre 133
Lebrun, Charles-François, Governor General of Holland 117, 123
Leghorn (Livorno) 151
Leipzig (battle) 85, 104
Leipzig 7
Leopold I, King of Belgium 130
Liberal international economic order 37
Liberal revolution 14
Liguria 141, 142, 163
Linen 88
Literacy 8
Lombardy 141, 142, 146, 147
Lombardy-Veneto, Kingdom of 142, 147
London 21, 115, 123–4, 203n1, 216, 240
Long-term evolution of fiscal and financial institutions 30
Losses of human capital 27, 28
Louis Napoleon, King of Holland 116, 120, 127–8
Louis XIV 23
Lucca 141, 153
Luneville (Treaty of, 1801) 141
Luxemburg 82
Luxury 21, 22

Madder 124, 134–5
Madrid 5, 8, 9, 15, 21, 203n1, 206
Malthusian (economy, growth regime; post-Malthusian) 82, 92, 97–103, 104
Malthusianism 20
Manor ("manorial" in my text) 97, 100
Manpower and Labour
share of workforce mobilized 26
skilled and unskilled labour 27
underemployment 27
wages for military and naval personnel 27
Marche 141, 147
Marengo (Battle of, 1800) 141

Marine insurance 37
Market integration 9, 21, 34, 98, 101, 103, 104
Market 9, 11, 15, 16, 18, 19, 20, 34
Marriages 4, 33
Marseille 25
Massena 205, 207, 208, 224
Mauritius 261, 263
Mayorazgo 15, 16
Mechanisation 125, 134, 136
Mercantilism 131
  and warfare 3
  warfare and economic growth 22, 23, 25, 38
Merchant, marine and naval power 26
Mesta 16
Metal processing industries ("metallurgy" in my text) 88, 89
Metallurgy 131
Metric system 127
Metropolis 206, 230
Middelburg 118–9
Migration 119, 136
  Intercontinental 272–273
Milan, Duchy of 141, 147, 156
Military Keynesianism 27
Military personnel (size of; armed forces, military force, etc.) 84, 85, 86, 104
Military technology 252
Modena and Reggio, Duchy of 141
Molfetta (Puglia) 143
Monetary system 13, 30, 127, 129
Monetization (see "monetiz") 85, 87, 105
Money 3
Morrisson, Christian 27
Mortality 3, 4, 5, 33, 218 (see also War)
Mughal Empire 4
Munich 104
Murcia 8

Nantes 26
Naples, Kingdom of (later Kingdom of the Two Sicilies) 141, 153, 159
Napoleon 116–7, 121, 128, 205, 207, 208, 212, 227, 238
  invasion of Russia 31
  Voir Bonaparte, Napoleon, *Voir* Bonaparte, Napoleon, *Voir* Bonaparte, Napoleon, *Voir* Bonaparte, Napoleon
National income 16
Naval hegemony 30, 35
Navy 119
  fleet sizes 255
  Indian Ocean 256
  organization 255
  France 256
  shipyards 128
  United Kingdom 255–256
Near East 18
Nederlandse Handel-Maatschappij (NHM) 131–2, 134
Netherlands 2, 27, 114–137, 215
  Anglo-Dutch commercial treat 253
  as a buffer state 8, 12
  colonies 252–253
  congress of Vienna 8
  culture system 254
  division of 1830 8
  economic growth 267
  East India company 254, 260
  Entrepot trade 268
  French control and predation 12
  international lending 273
  navy 255
  population growth 268
  shipping 257
  United Netherlands 12
Neutrality 3
Newfoundland 17
Nobility, noble prerogatives 83, 99
Nord (French department) 7
North Africa 18
Norway 122

Oils 125
Old Castile 7, 18
Open field system 100, 101
Ottoman Empire 5, 37

Papal States 141, 147, 161
Paper 125
Paris 4, 6, 21, 23
Parma and Piacenza, Duchy of 141
Patriot Revolution, the (1784–7) 116, 136
Pax Britannica 37
Peace
  and historical memory 1815–1914 6, 14
  and rearmament 1783–92 37
  of Westphalia 5
Peninsula 205, 207, 208

Piedmont (also see Kingdom of Sardinia) 141, 147, 162, 163
Poor relief 119
Pope 141–142
Population 3, 4, 5, 9, 13, 17, 18, 20, 23, 26, 34, 35, 38, 39, 33, 82, 85, 86, 87, 92, 101, 104, 105
  growth (see also death rate, migration 116–9, 136)
Porto 206, 215, 217, 227
Portugal 9, 10, 27, 38, 122, 203–241
  and Brazil 12
  colonies, loss of 252
Post-war reconstruction 94, 95, 96
Potatoes 124, 135
Pressburg (treaty of) 83
Price (of food, of grain) 12, 13, 16, 87, 91, 92, 95, 96, 98, 101, 103, 104
  Europe relative to Asia 269
  inflation 215
  Portuguese price data 230
  relative prices, Europe 269
  PWR-Portugal data base 226
  Wheat 227
Prince Regent of Portugal 205
Printing 124
Property rights 5–7, 14, 15, 16, 17, 18, 24, 94, 97, 99, 100, 101
Protectionism 124
Proto-industries ("(regional) export industries") 88, 92, 98, 104
Provence 25
Prussia (kingdom) 10, 82–88, 97–104, 106, 116–7, 123, 133, 136, 215
  customs union 7
  Konnigratz 1866 8
  Military defeats and regeneration 8
  Posen 7
  Premier German power 8
  Silesia 7
Public finances (see also fiscal capacity, public loans 129, 136)
  extraordinary defence contribution 214
  income tax (décima) 214
  military expenditure (see War) 209, 210, 214, 231
  Portuguese treasury's accounts 210
  public debt 215, 237, 240, 241, 242, 243
  royal treasury (Erário Régio) 209, 214
Public Goods 6
Public loans 123, 127–31
Public procurements 153
Puerto Rico 252

Railways 132, 134–5
Rates of interest 29
Rayneval, Mathias Joseph Gérard de 23
Real wages 7, 12, 18, 20, 23, 32, 33, 35, 164
Redemption (of feudal obligations) 100, 101
Reichsdeputationshauptschluss 83, 103
Religion 117, 130
Rent 12, 13
  seeking 6, 94, 97
Reparations (French) 87
Réunion 261, 263
Rhine (river) 83, 85, 98, 103 (see also river trade 123, 133)
Rhine Federation (*Rheinbund*, Federation of German states under French hegemony) 83–85, 103, 106
Rhineland, Rhine province 83, 89, 92, 97, 98
Ridolfi, Leonardo 27
Riga 267
Rio de Janeiro 206
River trade, see also Rhine 124–5, 131–2, 137
Roads (paved roads) 100, 101, 104
Rome 141
Rotterdam 122–4, 132, 135–6
Roussillon 204
Royal factories 8
Russia 25, 26, 37, 122, 205, 215, 230

Saint Domingue (Haiti) 3, 17, 21, 251, 260, 262–263
San Sebastián 3
Santarém 224
Sardinia, Kingdom of (also see Piedmont) 142
Saxony 84, 92, 95, 97, 101, 104, 105
Scandinavia 37
Schimmelpenninck, Rutger Jan 116
Schnerb, Robert 14
Scotland 133
Seaborne commerce and warfare 37
Secularization 83, 97
Seigneurial system 3, 5, 10, 12, 14
Serfdom 97, 100
Service sector 115, 120
Services 2, 9, 10, 12, 14

Silver
  coins 274
  production 274
Shipbuilding 37 (see also navy shipyards 125, 131, 134)
Shippers 133
Shipping 37, 117, 119–23, 125–6, 130–7
  costs 258
  fleet sizes 256–257
  and shipbuilding 14
  technology 270–271
Sicily 142, 147, 163
Silk exports 153
Silver 129
Sinking Fund 28
Slavery 3
  abolition 262–263
  trade 272
Smithian growth, see also economic growth 136
Smuggling 9, 34
Soap 125
Sonderweg 14
South 141, 143–156, 159, 161–163, 205, 207
South Africa 117, 119
South America 205, 230
South Carolina 267
Southern Europe 207
Southern Netherlands 116, 119
Sovereign debt levels, perpetual, fixed and floating 29
Sovereignty, sovereign status (of territory) 83, 85, 101, 103, 106
Spain 27, 122, 135, 204, 205, 206, 207, 208, 216, 217, 221, 230, 232, 235, 237, 239
  colonies, loss of 252
  economic growth 267
  empire 274, 275
  Francophile claims for the invasion of Spain 11
  French occupation and end of ancien regime 11
  Iberian war and end of South American empire 12
  loans, colonial 274
  trades 253, 259
Spanish America 2, 10, 11, 14, 24
St. Petersburg 122
Staple market (Amsterdam) 130–2, 135, 137
State revenue (see fiscal policy) 86, 87
State revenues 12, 14, 16, 24, 34
State 5, 9, 10, 11, 12, 38
Steam machinery see mechanisation
Steam shipping 133
Steam transport 135
Stuttgart 104
Subsidies (British) 87
Subsidies, government 131–4
Subsistence crises 4, 5, 7, 14
Sugar 125, 134
Surinam 119, 253
Swabia 83
Sweden 122, 215, 232, 237
Switzerland 27, 29, 37

Tagus 206
Tannery and leather industry 125
Tariffs
  customs, tolls 124, 128, 130, 133–4
  and protection 34
  tolls 101–106
Tax (see fiscal policy) 85, 87, 88, 99, 105
Tax revenues under French rule; after Restoration 161, 162
Taxation 6–16 (see also customs, excises, fiscal capacity 127–9, 131, 134, 137)
  foreign policy 23
  income tax 23, 24
  levels and burdens 24
  postwar 268
Tea 121, 125, 131
Technological improvements, see also innovation 134–5
Technological innovation 33
  iron and coal 34
  Newcomen engines 34
  shipbuilding 34
  shipping 34
Technological progress 15, 22
Technology 115, 125
  cotton 265–266
  military 252
  shipping 270–271
  sugar 262–264
Terms of trade 11, 20, 34
Textile 21, 22 (see also cotton, woolens 131, 134)
  industry 8, 11, 19

The French Wars and international trade 36, 37
Thirty Years War 6
Tilsit (treaty of) 84, 86
Tilsit 205
Tithe 6, 13, 15
Tobacco 125, 134
Tocqueville, Alexis de 7
Tolls 123, 127, 133, 137
Total factor productivity 18, 34
Toulouse 14
Toutain, Jean-Claude 15, 28
Trade 3, 88, 92, 94, 96, 98, 101, 103, 116–37
- 1810 Anglo-Portuguese treaties 230
- balance of 39
- colonial 9–12, 17, 18, 21, 24, 37
- commodities 258–259
  - coffee 262, 268–269, 271
  - cotton 265–266
  - Indigo 267
  - pepper 270–271
  - saltpeter 271
  - silk 261–262, 272
  - sugar 260–264
  - tea 264–265
  - timber 266–267
  - tobacco 261–262, 268–269
- composition 258–260
- dependence 35
- domestic 2, 9
- entrepot 268–269
- European ports 230
- exports 223, 226, 228–231
- growth 258–260
- imports 224, 226, 228, 229
- international 9, 14, 17, 19, 20, 21, 34, 37, 38, 39
- national 6, 7, 20
- policy 226
- Portuguese ports 204, 230
- re-exports 229–231
- specialisation 19, 20
- tariffs
  - Indigo 267
  - timber 266–267
  - South America, post war 252
- trends 147–153

Trade policy under French rule; after Restoration 147, 151, 160
Trafalgar 1805 37
Trafalgar 7
Transport 6
Trás-os-Montes 221
Treaty of Amiens (1802) 119
Treaty of Vienna (1815) 116, 119, 129, 133
Trinidad 261, 263
Troops, see also army 116–7, 119, 126–8
Trust, of creditors 129, 131
Tuscany 141, 146, 156, 158, 160–162

Ulm 83
Umbria 141, 146
Unemployment 119, 130, 134, 136
United Kingdom 18, 37
- Abolition of slavery 272
- Anglo-Dutch commercial treat 253
- colonies 253
- comparative advantages and European balance of power 5
- investment in warfare 4
- East India company 254
- economic growth 267–268
- emigration 272–273
- entrepot trade 268–269
- Jay treaty 257
- navy 255–257
- prices 269
- shipping 256–257
- population growth 267
- tariffs 261, 266–267, 268
- taxation 268
- trade 258–260, 265, 266
- naval bases 4
- naval hegemony 1, 5

United States of America 18, 38
United States of America, South 29
Upper Douro Valley 221
Urbanisation 3, 12, 16, 17, 26, 34, 115, 118–20, 125
- urban hierarchy 98, 104

Unites States 121, 131
- cotton production 265–266
- economic growth 259, 267
- immigration 272–273
- Jay Treaty 257–258
- Loans 273
- Louisiana purchase 251, 259
- Shipping 256–257

Unites States (*cont.*)
tax rebellion 23
trade 258, 259, 265

Valdeorras 3
Valencia 19
Van Hoboken, Anthony 135
Vendée 22
Venetia 156
Venice, Republic of 141, 147
Vercelli (Piedmont) 143
Vienna (Congress of Vienna, Vienna settlement) 82, 85, 91, 101, 106
Vienna (Congress of, 1815) 142, 162
Vittorio Emanuele I (King of Sardinia, 1802–1821) 162
Vittorio Emanuele II (King of Sardinia, 1848–1861) 164
Vogtländer Kreis 95
Von Bülow, Hans (finance minister, kingdom of Westphalen und Prussia) 103

Wages 12, 86, 87, 89, 90, 91
real wages 212
War 2, 4
civil war 239
continental blockade 204, 229, 230
cost of war 208, 209, 210, 211, 212, 213, 216
economic Impact 216, 227, 229
of the First Coalition, of the Second Coalition, of the Fourth Coalition, of the Fifth Coalition (1809), of the Sixth Coalition ("Final phase", "1812–1814"), of the Seventh Coalition ("Waterloo") 83–87
emigration 272–273
invasions 203, 204, 205, 220, 221, 223 226, 228, 240
Lines of Torres Vedras 206
Military Expenditure (see Public Finance) 209, 210, 214, 231
mortality (see Population) 218
Napoleonic wars 203, 208
maval blockades 230n48
meutrality 204, 227
seven years' war 206
Spanish invasion 204
Transport costs 272
Vienna congress 230
Warfare and the growth of GDP 30
Waterloo 7, 118
Weber, Max 3, 12
Wellington 207, 210, 211, 217
West Indies 253, 258–259, 262, 265, 267
Westphalen (kingdom; Napoleonic satellite state) 84, 87, 103
Westphalia (province of the kingdom of Prussia) 84, 89, 90, 104
Wheat prices 146, 153, 160
William I of Orange, King of the Netherlands 116, 129–135
Windmills 125
Wittelsbacher (dynasty) 103
Woolens 125
Württemberg 83, 84, 103
Wuttenberg 6, 7

Zaragoza 3
Zollverein 96, 103, 104

www.ingramcontent.com/pod-product-compliance
Lightning Source LLC
Chambersburg PA
CBHW071325230926
51849CB00002B/318
* 9 7 8 9 0 0 4 4 7 2 7 3 0 *